"Theater's primary asset is immediacy, the sensuous energy that passes from the stage to the audience and back to the stage. . . . The surprise and excitement is in witnessing the actor's transformations before our eyes. The stage makes an audience conscious of the visceral facts of its life and its language as the other media technology cannot do. Stage play—because it engages the psyche on such an intimate level—has the power of renewal, liberating the imagination from the ordinary and forcing a sedentary, desensitized modern man to play **actively** with situations. . . . The stage can range to outrageous extremes and, in this state of glorious excess, achieve both its finest moments of fun and high seriousness."

—John Lahr

BANTAM MODERN DRAMA

THE GREAT AMERICAN LIFE SHOW

9 Plays from the Avant-Garde Theater

edited by *John Lahr and Jonathan Price*

RLI: $\dfrac{\text{VLM 7 (VLR 6–7)}}{\text{IL 10-adult}}$

THE GREAT AMERICAN LIFE SHOW:
9 PLAYS FROM THE AVANT-GARDE THEATER

A Bantam Book / published January 1974

COPYRIGHTS AND ACKNOWLEDGMENTS

The copyright notices are listed below and on the pages following, which constitute an extension of this copyright page.

"*In the Wine Time*," by Ed Bullins. From Five Plays by Ed Bullins. Copyright © 1968 by Ed Bullins. Reprinted by permission of the publisher, The Bobbs-Merrill Co., Inc.

"*The Serpent*," a Ceremony written by Jean-Claude van Itallie in collaboration with the Open Theatre under the direction of Joseph Chaikin. Copyright © 1969 by Jean-Claude van Itallie. Reprinted by permission of the author and Atheneum Publishers. CAUTION: Professionals and amateurs are hereby warned that "The Serpent," being fully protected under the copyright laws of the United States of America, the British Empire, including the Dominion of Canada, and all other countries of the Berne and Universal Copyright Conventions, is subject to royalty. All rights, including professional, amateur, motion picture, recitation, lecturing, public reading, radio and television broadcasting, and the rights of translation into foreign languages, are strictly reserved. Particular emphasis is laid on the question of readings, permission for which must be secured from the author's agent in writing. All inquiries should be addressed to International Famous Agency, 1301 Avenue of the Americas, New York, N.Y. 10019.

"*Operation Sidewinder*," play and songs by Sam Shepard. Copyright © 1970 by Sam Shepard. Reprinted by permission of the publishers, The Bobbs-Merrill Co., Inc.

"*Slaveship*," by Imamu Amiri Baraka (LeRoi Jones). Text Copyright © 1970 by LeRoi Jones. Published in Negro Digest. Forthcoming publication, Angela Terzani's Collection of Plays (Random House, 1972). Reprinted by permission of the author and the Ronald Hobbs Literary Agency.

"*The Kid*," by Robert Coover. Copyright © 1970 by Robert Coover. Reprinted by permission of Georges Borchardt Literary Agency. CAUTION: All performing rights in this play are strictly reserved and application for performance of it should be made to Georges Borchardt, Inc., 145 East 52nd St., New York, N.Y. 10022. No performance of this play may be given unless a license has been obtained prior to rehearsal.

"*Cop-Out*," by John Guare. From his Muzeeka. Copyright © 1969 by John Guare. Reprinted by permission of Grove Press, Inc.

"*Injun*," by Claes Oldenburg. From Happenings, written and edited by Michael Kirby. "Injun," Copyright © 1965 by Claes Oldenburg. Material from Happenings, Copyright © 1965 by Michael Kirby. Dutton paperback edition. Reprinted by permission of E. P. Dutton & Co., Inc.

"*Mysteries*," by Julian Beck in collaboration with The Living

Contents

A Life-Show introduction occurs before each piece.

THE GREAT AMERICAN LIFE SHOW

9 Plays from the Avant-Garde Theater

IN THE WINE TIME

by Ed Bullins

to Janice

Introduction by John Lahr

Ed Bullins makes street life into art. Because his plays are written for a black audience, they do not need to scream a rhetoric of defiance to make their point. The characters who clown, fight, argue are all familiar; they share a common denominator of suffering, poverty, and small pleasures snatched from the desolation of their barren cement landscape. The frantic, funny, mean moments of living emerge in Bullins' plays with both an affection and a sense of horror. His people float, dazed and defeated, through a universe of pain, a bag of woe jazzed up and momentarily conquered by drugs, drink, sex, and violence. *In the Wine Time* is a fine understated evocation of the ghetto's living death, a world of survivors where the only accomplishment is a street rep. As Cliff, the angry and boozy husband, admits: "I got a tombstone mind an' a graveyard disposition . . . I'm a bad mothafukker an' I don't mind . . . dyin'."

The atmosphere of suffocation is as carefully observed as the characters in the play. The rows of houses "forming a low, two-storied canyon" are a visual and symbolic cage. The people who inhabit this terrain may not articulate this idea, but they feel themselves trapped, and Bullins organizes their patterns of movement and response to show to a black audience how they react to being cramped and forgotten on the backsteps of society. "Four-letter words, arrow-pierced hearts, and slangy street-talk. [. . .] Tattered posters of political candidates wearing scribbled, smudged mustaches." Intuitively, the people transform their real-life set to mirror the sense of revenge and rage that overwhelms them. They try to write over their world or to deface it. Here, in this vacuum where the characters sit and sip muscatel, where music filters through the hot night, is the weight of a heavy silence kept at bay by chatter. The disc jockeys, the checker games, the fights coming out of open windows become events, perhaps even devices, which hold back the oppressive blankness surrounding them.

Faced with omnipresent death, the characters have no reverence for life or for living. Everything exists to be squandered. Cliff Dawson, a man who has given up on society, takes the rap for his wife's sixteen-year-old nephew, Ray, who drunkenly stabs to death a boy who stole his girl. "It won't be for long," Cliff says at the finale. "I was protectin' my family . . . our family." The implication of this speech has been clear from the play's opening beat: time in the ghetto is all waste; whether in prison or on the street, there is still no fulfilling purpose or dignity, nothing to do but wait. Cliff says to Ray: "It's your world, Ray . . . It's yours, boy . . . Go on out there and claim it." This may sound melodramatic, but within the context of the play the words are sharp with irony. Cliff has nothing but his life to give. His dignity is in sacrifice, but Ray is no more equipped than Cliff to triumph.

With the bleakness so concretely defined, Bullins is able to create plays which hint at the meaning *behind* the brio of street talk. Cliff's tone—his ridicule—broadcasts his real message. Educated but unemployed, the glitter of his talk is itself a revenge and a victory. He rants at God.

". . . with all of God's white stars shinin' above your black heads. Ain't that right, Lord? You old shyster. You pour white heat on these niggers, these Derby Street Donkeys, in the daytime and roast and fry them while they shovel shit for hex' to nothin', and steam them at night like big black lobsters . . . ha ha . . . the Krumps are little red lobsters of Yourn . . . and they just drink, an' screw in the dark, and listen to jive talk an' jive music an' jive *holy* music . . . but they still think they have to face You in the mornin'. That's right, face You, You jive-ass sucker! [. . .] They only got to look my god in the face once and forget about You, You jive-time sucker . . ."

The tone is narcotic; the explosion of anger itself is a way of forgetting the pain. The mockery in Cliff's voice confirms, but also emotionally denies, the death around him. He is numb with drink, but Bullins shows us how language mirrors a spiritual numbing for which mockery is an accurate barometer. As psychiatrist Robert J. Lifton, who coined the term "psychic numbing," has observed, "It is a protection against overwhelming and unacceptable stimuli, and it is associated with an inner imagery that goes something like this: 'If I feel nothing then death is not taking place'; or, 'If I feel nothing then I cannot be threatened by death all around me'; or 'If I feel nothing, then I am not responsible for you and your death.' "

"Where's your pride?" says Lou to her husband. Cliff has no source of dignity but anger. There are no images which give him back any sense of himself. "A dollar an hour don't buy that much pride, Lou. There's a big rich world out there . . . I'm goin'a get me part of it or not at all." Bullins' plays are the first to genuinely marshal so much of the black experience onto the stage. The black audience can examine—without condescension—the facts and frustrations of ghetto life. The naturalism of Bullins' best plays fits the emotional needs of his community, recognizing itself in art and seeing these impoverished lives as still *valuable.* This is no approximation of black life or suffering, and a black audience takes delight in watching an undiluted image of its quiet daily struggle to survive.

In the Wine Time, with its richness of language, its quiet lyricism and full characterizations, epitomizes the best and most accomplished direction of Black Theater. Like all the plays in Bullins' Twentieth Century Cycle, it is dedicated to making an audience acknowledge its past and its essential integrity. Bullins' art is inconspicuously radical; but if his audience can see its predicament, it can also change it. This is what Robert Macbeth, the head of the New Lafayette Theatre in Harlem, where Bullins is playwright in residence, means when he says: "Our job has always been to show Black people who they are, where they are and what condition they are in." Bullins' best plays are not manifestoes but experiences. Yet, like all of black art, theater is distinctly different in its aesthetic and its intention from much of white theater. Macbeth has written:

> While the American theatre becomes more and more of a museum for replaying the 18th, 19th and early 20th century "greats," and the "underground sex shows" are surfacing and becoming the "new art," we have become more and more aware that since Black theatre has no history of plays to revive, we must create not only new plays, but new theatre, new concepts of what "plays" are. And, in our social/political/historic/aesthetic condition, sexual frivolity and adolescent eroticism are meaningless. We must be of high purpose, of meaning, if Black theatre and Black people are to remain on the earth, and not "fly off" into some fantasy of avant-garde americana.

To take a hard look at the society, to show the black man realistically in his own life, is what the historical/political needs of the black community demand. And Ed Bullins' precise, shrewd, observing eyes serve that goal with aplomb.

In the Wine Time was first produced at the New Lafayette Theatre on December 10, 1968. The production was directed by Robert Macbeth. Sets were designed by Roberta Raysor, lighting by Ernest Baxter and Richard Macbeth. The cast was as follows:

CLIFF DAWSON	Sonny Jim
LOU DAWSON, Cliff's wife	Bette Jean Howard
RAY, Lou's nephew	Gary Bolling
MISS MINNY GARRISON	Rosanna Carter
BUNNY GILLETTE	Helen Ellis
MRS. KRUMP	Voice of V. Rachman Cyrille
EDDIE KRUMP	Voice of Leopoldo Mandeville
BEATRICE	Roberta Raysor
TINY	Yvette Hawkins
SILLY WILLY CLARK	Whitman Mayo
RED	Kris Keiser
BAMA	George Miles
DORIS	Peggy A. Kirkpatrick
A POLICEMAN	Bill Lathan

In this production the characters of MR. KRUMP, THE GIRL, and some Derby Street Residents were omitted.

THE PROLOGUE

She passed the corner every evening during my last wine time, wearing a light summer dress with big pockets, in small ballerina slippers, swinging her head back and to the side all special-like, hearing a private melody singing in her head. I waited for her each dusk, and for this she granted me a smile, but on some days her selfish tune would drift out to me in a hum; we shared the smile and sad tune and met for a moment each day but one of that long-ago summer.

The times I would be late she lingered, in the sweating twilight, at the corner in the barbershop doorway, ignoring the leers and coughs from within, until she saw me hurrying along the tenement fronts. On these days her yellows and pinks and whites would flash out from the smoked walls, beckoning me to hurry hurry to see the lights in her eyes before they fleeted away above the single smile, which would turn about and then down the street, hidden by the little pretty head. Then, afterwards, I would stand before the shop refusing to believe the slander from within.

"Ray . . . why do you act so stupid?" Lou asked each day I arose to await the rendezvous.

"I don't know . . . just do, that's all," I always explained.

"Well, if you know you're bein' a fool, why do you go on moonin' out there in the streets for *that*? . . ."

"She's a friend of mine, Lou . . . she's a friend."

August dragged in the wake of July in steaming sequence of sun and then hell and finally sweltering night. The nights found me awake with Cliff and Lou and our bottles of port, all waiting for the sun to rise again and then to sleep in dozes during the miserable hours. And then for me to wake hustling my liquor money and then to wait on the corner for my friend to pass.

"What'd the hell you say to her, Ray?" Cliff asked.

"Nothin'."

"Nothing?"

"Nawh . . . nothin'."

"Do you ever try?"

"Nawh," I said.

"Why? She's probably just waiting for you to . . ."

"Nawh, she's not. We don't need to say anything to each other. We know all we want to find out."

And we would go on like that until we were so loaded our voices would crack and break as fragile as eggs and the subject would escape us, flapping off over the roofs like a fat pigeon.

Summer and Cliff and Lou and me together—all poured from the same brew, all hating each other and loving, and consuming and never forgiving—but not letting go of the circle until the earth swung again into winter, bringing me closer to manhood and the freedom to do all the things that I had done for the past three summers.

We were the group, the gang. Cliff and Lou entangled within their union, soon to have Baby Man, and Henrietta, and Stinky, and Debra, and maybe who knows who by now. Summer and me wrapped in our embrace like lovers, accepting each as an inferior, continually finding faults and my weaknesses, pretending to forgive though never forgetting, always at each other's vitals . . . My coterie and my friend . . .

She with the swinging head and flat-footed stance and the single smile and private song for me. She was missing for a day in the last week of summer.

I waited on the corner until the night boiled up from the pavements and the wine time approached too uncomfortably.

Cliff didn't laugh when learning of my loss; Lou stole a half a glass more than I should have received. The night stewed us as we blocked the stoop fighting for air and more than our shares of the port, while the bandit patrol cruised by as sinister as gods.

She was there waiting next day, not smiling nor humming but waving me near. I approached and saw my very own smile.

"I love you, little boy," she said.

I nodded, trying to comprehend.

"You're my little boy, aren't you?" She took my hand. "I have to go away but I wanted to tell you this before I left." She looked into my eyes and over my shaggy uncut hair. "I must be years older than you, but you look so much older than I. In two more years you won't be able to stop with only wine," she said. "Do you have to do it?"

"I don't know . . . just do, that's all," I explained.

"I'm sorry, my dear," she said. "I must go now."

"Why?"

"I just must."

"Can I go with you?"

She let go of my hand and smiled for the last time. "No, not now, but you can come find me when you're ready."

"But where?" I asked.

"Out in the world, little boy, out in the world. Remember, when you're ready, all you have to do is leave this place and come to me, I'll be waiting. All you'll need to do is search!"

Her eyes lighted for the last time before hiding behind the pretty head, swinging then away from me, carrying our sorrowful, secret tune.

I stood listening to the barbershop taunts follow her into the darkness, watching her until the wicked city night captured her; then I turned back to meet autumn and Cliff and Lou in our last wine time, meeting the years which had to hurry hurry so I could begin the search that I have not completed.

ACT ONE

The people in this play are black except for the KRUMPS and the POLICEMAN.

Scene: Derby Street. A small side street of a large northern American industrial city, in the early 1950s.

At left, the houses stand together on one side of the street in unbroken relief, except for a tunnel-like alley which opens between the KRUMPS' and the GARRISONS' houses, forming a low, two-storied canyon, the smoke-stained chimneys the pinnacles of the ridges. Four-letter words, arrow-pierced hearts and slangy street-talk, scrawled in haste, smear a wooden fence, painted green, across the narrow street. Tattered posters of political candidates wearing scribbled, smudged mustaches, circuses of seasons passed and fading, golden and orange snuff containers decorate the enclosure. Each building's front is dull red, not brick colored, but a gray- and violet-tinged red, the shade the paint becomes after successive seasons of assault by the city's smoke- and grit-laden atmosphere. Precise white lines, the older ones yellowing, outline each brick of the walls, and every house has a squat stoop of five white stone steps.

A raised level, upstage right, between the fence and the houses, represents "The Avenue."

From within the DAWSONS' house black music of the period—called rhythm 'n blues by disc jockeys at that time—is heard not too loudly, and continues throughout the play, interrupted only seldom by amusing, jive-talking commercials for used cars, televisions, appliances, hair straighteners and skin lighteners. Some of the recording stars of this season are King Pleasure, Johnnie Otis, Fats Domino, Little Esther, Ray Charles and "The Queen," Miss Dinah Washington. When

MISS MINNY GARRISON raises her window gospel
music can be heard.

At Rise: It is a sultry evening in late August.
All the steps are occupied by members of the
various Derby Street households.

At the end of the street, downstage, is a corner
lighted by a streetlamp, the gas-burning variety
found still then in some sections of Philadelphia,
Baltimore, New York and Boston.

All lights are down but the corner streetlamp,
though dim shadows of the people on the stoops
can be seen carrying on their evening activities:
talking, gossiping, playing checkers and cards,
drinking sodas, wine and beer.

MR. KRUMP enters and stands at the streetlamp. He is very drunk.

Lights on the Krumps' doorstoop, the nearer
to the corner.

The Krumps' front door opens and MRS.
KRUMP leans out.

THE RADIO: And here we are folks . . . on a black
juicy, jammin' 'n' groovin' hot August night . . .
yeah . . . one of them nights fo' bein' wit' tha one ya
loves . . .

MRS. KRUMP (*strident, over the radio*): *Krumpy!* What
cha doin' on da corner? Hey, Krumpy! Hey, Krumpy!
. . . *Krumpy . . . Get the hell on over here!*

Light on third doorstoop.

CLIFF: Heee . . . heee . . . look a' ole man Krump
work out.

BUNNY GILLETTE and DORIS enter Derby Street
at the corner and see MR. KRUMP.

LOU: Hush up, Cliff.

CLIFF: Sheeet.

BUNNY GILLETTE: Look 'a there, Doris!

LOU: Be quiet, Cliff. Will ya, huh?

DORIS: Awwww, shit, girl. That's nothin' . . . it just that
god-damn Mr. Krump again . . . drunk out of his
fucken' mind.

THE RADIO: It's eighty-two degrees . . . maaan, that's hot-oh-rooney . . . yeah, burnin' up this evenin' . . . red hot! . . . Ouch! . . . But we're cool on the Hep Harrison red-hot, up-tight, out-a-sight weather lookout indicator. That's eighty-two degrees . . . that's eight two out there . . . And here's a cool number that will hit you right where you're at . . . for your listenin' pleasure . . .

> MRS. KRUMP has stepped to the center of Derby Street and calls up to her second-floor window as the music begins.

MRS. KRUMP (*raspy, urban voice*): Hey, Edward . . . Hey, Edward . . . ! Hey, Edward . . . come on down here and get your fa'tha! Hey, Edward . . .
DORIS: Hey, lissen ta that cow yell.
BUNNY: Ain't it a shame, girl?

> BUNNY starts off.

CLIFF (*disgust*): God dammit . . . Lou. You always tellin' me to be quiet . . . I don't even make half the noise that some of our *good* neighbors do.
DORIS (*to* BUNNY): Where ya goin', broad?
LOU (*sitting beside* CLIFF): Awww . . . she should leave Mr. Krump alone. All he's doin' is peein' aside the pole . . . and then he's goin' in and go ta bed.
BUNNY: Up on "The Avenue."
DORIS: Where?

> EDDIE KRUMP sticks his head from his upstairs window. He has dirty blond hair and a sharp, red nose. He is about eleven.

EDDIE: Ohhh, Christ, Ma . . . what'cha want?
BUNNY: "The Avenue," Doris.
MRS. KRUMP (*furious*): Don't you Christ me, Edward . . . Come down here right away, young man!
CLIFF (*to* LOU): I bet he ain't gonna do it.
DORIS: Ain't you gonna see Ray? That's what you come down this way for.
LOU: He might, Cliff. Besides . . . you the one that's always sayin' everybody here on Derby Street only does what they want to do most of the time, anyway.

BUNNY: He's up there on the step . . . he could see me
if he wanted . . . C'mon, girl . . . let's split.

> They exit.

CLIFF: 'Specially mindin' other people's business.

> RAY sits between CLIFF and LOU, one step below
> them.

LOU: Wasn't that Bunny, Ray?
RAY: Think I should go and help Mr. Krump out, Cliff?
CLIFF: Nawh.

> Pause.

LOU: Why, Cliff?
CLIFF: You stay yo' ass here where ya belong, Ray.
LOU: Don't you talk like that, Cliff.
MRS. KRUMP (*to* EDDIE *in window*): *Eddie* . . . are you
comin' down here?
EDDIE: Nawh.
CLIFF (*incredulous*): Did you hear that?
LOU: Remember . . . we mind our own business.

> From the upstairs window of the Garrisons'
> house, MISS MINNY GARRISON pushes her head;
> she has a bandanna tied about her head, and
> she is a huge black woman.

MRS. KRUMP (*starting for her door*): I'm going to come
up there and beat the hell out of you, Edward.

> EDDIE ducks his head in the window as his
> mother enters the door below.
>   Sounds of MRS. KRUMP's screams, the shouts
> of EDDIE KRUMP and of running feet.
>   Silence.
>   Rhythm 'n blues and gospel music mingle
> softly.
>   RED and BAMA enter at the corner. They see
> MR. KRUMP and nod to each other, then slowly,
> stiff-leggedly, stalk about the streetlamp, tight-
> ening the circle about MR. KRUMP on each full
> swing around.

MISS MINNY: Ray . . . wha don't you help Mr. Krump
git home?

RAY stands and looks up at her.

RAY: Yas'sum.

CLIFF (*to* RAY): Wha' . . . you gonna go down there and help? . . .

RAY hesitates.

LOU: Awww, Cliff . . . there ain't no harm in it.

CLIFF: No harm?

LOU: Ray always does it.

CLIFF: Well, it's about time he stopped.

MISS MINNY: Go on, Ray. Go on and git Mr. Krump.

RAY: Yas'sum.

He trots to the corner.

CLIFF (*mimics* RAY *in high falsetto*): Yas'sum.

LOU (*angry*): Stop that, Cliff!

CLIFF: Sheeet!

RED: Hey . . . Ray . . . is this lump ah shit a friend of yours? . . .

RAY: Nawh.

LOU: Why don't you stop that stuff, Cliff? Ain't nothin' bein' hurt because Ray's helpin' out Mr. Krump.

BAMA: Maybe they're related.

RED (*chuckling*): Hey, man, cool it. I know Ray don't play that. Do you, Ray?

RAY (*trying to support* MR. KRUMP): Nawh, Red. Nawh.

RED (*to* BAMA): See, Bama, Ray don't play the dozens. You better be careful.

BAMA: Shit.

RAY and BAMA exchange stares. BAMA is several years older than RAY.

RED: You seen Bunny and Doris, Ray?

RAY: Yeah . . . they headed for "The Avenue."

CLIFF: Nothin' bein' hurt? Just look at that. Look at that, Lou!

RAY has slung MR. KRUMP across his shoulder. He is husky and carries his load well.

Standing, shouting.

Hey, Ray! Make sure his pants fly is zipped up or you'll be a victim of a horrible calamity!

LOU: You think you so smart, Cliff.

BAMA (*to* RAY): Tote dat bar', boy . . . lift dat bale.

RED (*booting* RAY *in the seat of the pants*): Git along, little doggie.

> CLIFF is pleased with himself but starts as RED kicks RAY and stands, but LOU tugs at his trouser leg and he sits back down, chuckling over his wit, though scowling at RED and BAMA who turn laughing and exit.
>
> RAY carries his load to the Krumps' door. CLIFF lights a cigarette and takes a drink. LOU tries to ignore him.
>
> MRS. KRUMP, wearing a perpetual worried expression, at her door.

MRS. KRUMP: Why, thank you, Ray. Just bring him in here and put him on the couch. Thank you, Ray. That Edward is just . . .

> They go in, MRS. KRUMP at the rear, peering at MR. KRUMP's head that dangles down RAY's back.

CLIFF: That goddamn Miss Minny's always startin' some shit!

LOU: Shusss . . . Cliff. She'll hear you.

CLIFF (*bitter*): I don't care if the big sow does. Always pretendin' her ears are filled with nothin' but holy holy *gospel* music . . . when they're nothin' but brimmin' with Derby Street dirt.

> Mutters.

Ole bitch!

LOU (*uneasy*): Cliff!

CLIFF (*looks up at* MISS MINNY): Always startin' some trouble.

> MISS MINNY closes her window. Her light goes off.

LOU: See, she did hear you!

CLIFF: I don't give a damn . . . who she thinks she is anyway?

LOU: Cliff, you just tryin' to start some trouble with

Mr. Garrison. You wouldn't say those things if Homer were home.

CLIFF (*challenging*): Wouldn't I?

LOU: No, you wouldn't!

CLIFF: I would do anything I do now if ole four-eyed Homer was sittin' right over there on that step pickin' his big nose.

LOU: He don't pick his nose no more.

CLIFF: How do you know? Is that what Miss Minny told you?

LOU: No, Miss Minny didn't tell me a thing. His sister, Marigold, showed me a picture of him in his sergeant's uniform . . . and I know nobody in the United States Army who makes sergeant still picks their nose.

CLIFF: Sheeet!

Silence.

LOU: Cliff?

CLIFF (*angry*): Look what you've done to that boy, Lou. Look what you and his mother . . .

LOU (*angry*): Now don't you start in talkin' 'bout my dead sister!

CLIFF (*angrier*): Shut up!

Pause and stare.

Don't you see what all of you are tryin' to do . . . Miss Minny . . .

LOU: Who's tryin' to do what, Cliff?

CLIFF (*continues*): Miss Minny . . . you . . . all the so-called high-falutin' pussy on this block . . .

LOU (*indignant*): Now you watch your mouth . . .

CLIFF: Pussy! Cunt! Bitches! Always startin' some trouble.

LOU (*apologetic*): That was no trouble, Cliff.

CLIFF: It was so . . . Who the hell Miss Minny thinks she is anyway tellin' Ray to go down there an' get ole man Krump? And gettin' kicked by that punk Red . . . Ray's nearly a man . . . he shouldn't . . .

LOU (*cutting*): She didn't mean nothin' by it.

CLIFF: Just like she didn't mean nothin' the time she passed around that petition to have us run off 'a Derby Street when we first moved here.

LOU: She didn't know us, then . . . we was strangers. Why don't you forget it?

CLIFF (*raising voice*): What's so strange about us, huh? What was so strange about us back then when we moved in? What was so strange? Was we strange because I was goin' ta school on the G.I. Bill and not totin' a lunch pail like all these other asses? . . .

LOU: Shusss . . . Cliff.

CLIFF: I will not shusss . . . that's what they are, aren't they? Asses! Mules! Donkeys!

LOU: I'm goin' in if you keep that up, Cliff.

THE RADIO: . . . and Fat Abe . . . your local honest used car dealer is now offering a custom bargain fo' one of you real swingers out there . . .

> CLIFF reaches up and pulls the door shut with a slam, muffling the radio.

CLIFF: You ain't goin' nowhere just because you don't want to hear the truth.

> Silence. LOU sulks.

Well, they are asses . . .

> Ridicule.

Derby Street Donkeys!

LOU (*apologetic*): Well, I was workin', Cliff. And . . .

CLIFF (*cutting*): And they made a hell of a noise about that, too. Always whisperin' how you work so hard all day in a laundry for no count me who goes around carryin' books. And gets home in the middle of the afternoon and jest lays around like a playboy . . .

LOU: They did see you with them girls all the time, Cliff.

CLIFF: I ain't been with no bitches.

LOU: Cliff . . .

CLIFF: They're lies! That's all . . . every one a lie . . . and don't you let me hear you tell me them lies again.

> Silence.

LOU: Never?

CLIFF: Never!

LOU: What should I say when I find lipstick on your shirt . . . shades I don't use?

> Silence.

What should I say when I see you flirtin' with the young girls on the street and with my friends?

>   Silence.

CLIFF (*tired*): Light me a cigarette, will ya?

>   She does.

LOU: This street ain't so bad now.

CLIFF: Was we so strange because your nephew Ray stays with us . . . and don't have to work

>   Bitter.

like an ass or mule or fool . . . like a Derby Street Donkey!

LOU: Cliff!

CLIFF: Why was we so strange?

LOU: Nawh, we wasn't . . .

CLIFF: Who wasn't?

LOU: We wasn't!

CLIFF: Yes, we was!

LOU: Nawh . . . we seemed strange because we always drinkin' this . . .

>   Raising her glass.

CLIFF: Everybody else drinks somethin' around here . . . ole man Garrison puts at least a pint of white lightnin' away a night . . . pure'dee cooked corn whisky!

LOU: But their ignorant oil don't make them yell and holler half the night like this wine makes us.

CLIFF (*yells*): Who yells!

LOU (*amused*): . . . and we sing and laugh and you cuss like a sailor.

CLIFF: Who sings and laughs? . . .

LOU: We do!

CLIFF: You a liar!

LOU: Nawh, I'm not, Cliff.

>   He grabs her arm and twists it behind her back.

CLIFF: Say you a liar.

LOU: Nawh, Cliff . . . don't do that.

CLIFF (*twists it more*): Who's a liar?

LOU: I am, Cliff.

CLIFF (*a slight jerk*): Who?
LOU: *I am, Cliff. I am!*

He releases her.

CLIFF: That's right . . . sing out when I want you to. Ha ha ha . . .

He tries to caress her.

LOU (*rubs arm and shoves him*): Leave me alone.
CLIFF (*kisses her*): I'm glad you finally confessed . . . It'll do your soul some good.
LOU (*sulking*): You shouldn't do that, Cliff.
CLIFF: Do what?
LOU: You know what.
CLIFF: Give you spiritual comfort? . . . Apply some soul ointment?
LOU (*disgusted*): Awwww . . .
CLIFF: I don't know if you never tell me, hon.
LOU: You know all right.
CLIFF: That I cuss like a sailor?
LOU (*remembering*): That's right . . . and . . .
CLIFF (*cutting*): Well, you didn't say that.
LOU: I didn't?

Pause.

I did too, Cliff.
CLIFF: What?
LOU: Say that we yell and holler and sing and laugh and cuss like sailors half the night.
CLIFF (*toasts her*): Ohhh, Lou. To Lou Lou, my Hottentot queen.
LOU: I'm not!
CLIFF: My queen?
LOU: Hottentot! . . . My features are more northern . . . more Ethiopian.
CLIFF (*ridicule*): Haaaah!

Pause.

Haaaaah! More northern . . . more Ethiopian! That beak nose of yours comes from that shanty Irishman who screwed your grandmammy down on the plantation.
LOU: Watch your mouth, Cliff.

CLIFF: Watch my mouth?

LOU: Yeah, watch your mouth. Some things I just won't allow you to say.

CLIFF (*mocking*): "Some things I just won't allow you to say."

> Offended.

Watch my mouth? Well, take a look at yours. Yours comes from that Ubangi great granddaddy on your father's side . . . your "northern" nose, well, we've gone through its . . .

LOU (*warning*): Stop it, Cliff!

CLIFF: . . . but your build is pure Hottentot, darling . . . and that's why I shall forever love you . . . however the Derby Street Donkeys bray about me being with other girls . . . younger, prettier girls, mind you . . . But Lou, baby, you are married to an "A" number one ass man . . . and *yours* is one of the Hottentot greats of northern America.

LOU (*indignant*): Fuck you!

CLIFF (*fake dialect*): Wahl, hon-nee chile . . . I just wanted ta tell yawhal dat yo' husband is one ob dem connoisseurs of dem fleshy Hottentot parts which'n yous is so wonderfully invested wit'.

LOU: Fuck you, Cliff! . . . Ohhh, just listen to that. You make me say bad things, man. You think you so smart and know all them big words since you been goin' to school. You still ain't nothin' but a lowdown bastard at heart as far as I'm concerned.

> Silence.
> CLIFF takes a drink. LOU is wary but defiant.

CLIFF (*smiles*): We do cuss too much, don't we?

LOU (*smiles*): And we drink too much.

> He pulls her over and fondles her; she kisses him but pushes him away.

CLIFF: Like sailors?

LOU: Yes!

CLIFF (*amused*): I thought we cussed like sailors.

LOU: We do.

CLIFF (*raises voice*): Make up yo' mind, broad. Now what is it . . . do we cuss and drink like sailors or

cuss like sailors and drink like . . . like . . . like
. . . what?

LOU: Like niggers.

> At the last word lights go up on other stoops,
> revealing the occupants looking at CLIFF and
> LOU.
>
> Then lights dim and come up on "The Ave-
> nue." The figures of RED, BAMA, DORIS and BUNNY
> GILLETTE are seen.

BUNNY GILLETTE: Go on now, Red . . . stop messin'
with me.

RED: Awww . . . woman . . . stop all your bullshit.
You know you like me to feel your little ass . . .
c'mere.

DORIS: Stop fucken with that girl, Red.

RED: What's wrong, Doris? You jealous or somethin'?

DORIS: Man . . . if you melted and turned to water
and ran down the gutter I wouldn't even step over
you.

RED: Why . . . scared I'd look up your dress and see
your tonsils?

BUNNY GILLETTE (giggling): Ohhh . . . girl, ain't he
bad.

BAMA: C'mere, Doris. I wanna talk to you.

DORIS: You ain't never wanted to talk to me before,
Bama.

> RED has his arm about BUNNY GILLETTE's waist.
> BAMA takes DORIS's hand.

RED: C'mon, Bunny . . . I'll buy you a fish sandwich.

> To BAMA.

Hey, Bam ah lam . . . do you think these broads
deserve a fish sandwich?

BAMA: Nawh, man, they don't deserve shit.

DORIS: Hey, Bunny, we really hooked us some sports
. . . you better make it back to Ray, girl.

> Lights down on "The Avenue."
> Lights up on Derby Street. CLIFF and LOU
> laugh as RAY comes out of the Krumps'. The
> radio is muffled in the background.

MRS. KRUMP (*off*): You sure you don't want another slice of cake and a glass of milk, Raymond?

RAY: Nawh, thank you, Mrs. Krump.

EDDIE KRUMP sticks his head out of his window.

EDDIE: Thanks ah lot, Ray.

RAY: That's okay; why don't you come on down for a while?

EDDIE: Nawh . . . I can't . . . I gotta headache.

CLIFF (*to* RAY): Little white Eddie don't want to come down after you carry his pissy pukey drunk daddy in for him, huh?

LOU: Cliff!

RAY (*embarrassed*): Nawh.

LOU: Cliff . . . no wonder they sent around that petition. Just look how you act.

CLIFF (*angry*): Yeah, just look how I act . . . fuck how I act!

LOU: You got the dirtiest mouth, Cliff.

CLIFF (*angrier*): Fuck how I act . . . fuck it!

CLIFF stands and glares about at his neighbors. They turn their heads and resume their activities.

LOU: Just like a sailor.

CLIFF (*satisfied*): Yup . . . just like I always said . . . folks on Derby Street sure know how to mind their own business.

LOU: Just like the no-'count sailor I met and married.

CLIFF: Well, I am a mathafukken shit-ass sailor. The same you met and married, Lou.

LOU: Not any more.

CLIFF: Still! I still am. Once a sailor . . . always a sailor.

LOU: Not any more. Besides . . . you stayed most of your time in the guardhouse.

CLIFF (*to* RAY): Listen to that . . . listen to that, Ray. Guardhouse.

LOU: That was the reason I married you. Felt sorry for you and knew your commanding officer would go light on you if he knew you had been married when you deserted and not put you in the guardhouse for so long.

CLIFF: Yeah?

LOU: Yeah!

CLIFF: Don't think you did me any favors, baby.

LOU: Well, who else did? I went to your ship and testi-
fied . . . I kept you from gettin' a bad discharge. In
fact, I'm the one who made a man out of you even
though your mother and the whole entire United
States Navy failed.

CLIFF (*mutters*): Bitch!

LOU: Do you hear that? Failed . . . to make a man
or a sailor of ya.

CLIFF (*ridicule*): Ray. This broad, pardon the expression, this woman named Lou . . . Lou Ellen Mar-
garita Crawford Dawson . . . who calls herself your
aunt, by the way . . .

LOU: I am his aunt!

CLIFF: This bitch don't know what a sailor is.

LOU: I don't? . . . I don't? Then I guess you know
even though you spent most of your navy time in
the guardhouse.

RAY: Brig, Lou . . .

CLIFF: Thank you, son. Thank you.

LOU: What? . . .

RAY: Brig, Lou . . . not guardhouse.

CLIFF: That's right . . . that's fucken "A" right . . .

LOU (*mutters and takes a drink*): Dirtiest mouth I ever
heard.

CLIFF: That's a lie . . . your sister has the dirtiest
mouth in north, south, west and all of this town.

> To RAY.

That's your play-aunt Doris I'm talkin' about, Ray,
not your dear dead mother . . . may she rest in
peace . . .

LOU: You two-faced bastard. Listen to you soundin' like
one of them white missionaries . . . "May she rest in
peace . . ." Dirty-mouthed liar!

CLIFF: Liar? About what? My not being in the guardhouse?

RAY: Brig.

LOU: You know that's not what I mean.

CLIFF: Pour yourself a drink, Ray. Put some hair on
your . . . ding-a-ling.

> Begins humming.

LOU: I pity the day you talked me into allowing Ray to take a drink.

CLIFF: Whatta ya mean? He was a lush when he came here. His mother and him both almost drank themselves to death.

LOU: Cliff!

CLIFF (*defensive*): Ain't that right, Ray?

RAY: Sort'a. I did kinda drink along with Mamma for a while until they put her away.

CLIFF: Sort'a? Stop jivin' . . . for a youngblood you can really hide some port.

RAY (*flatttered*): Yeah . . . I do my share.

LOU: Now, Ray, I want you to . . .

CLIFF (*loud*): Quiet! You heard him . . . he does his share. Here's a toast to you, youngblood.

Lifts his glass.

To Ray who does his share.

They drink, except for LOU.

RAY: Thanks, Cliff.

CLIFF: Don't mention it, Ray. Just don't mention it at all. It's your world, son. It's really your world.

To LOU.

Well, isn't it?

Silence.

You don't feel like toasting Ray?

Silence.

Ray . . . you know, Lou is a lot like your mother used to be. Quiet, except that your mother usually had a glass up to her mouth instead of her mouth clamped tight.

LOU: You shouldn't of said that, Cliff. You're goin'a pay for that.

CLIFF: Pay? Ray, it's your world . . . does your ole Uncle Cliff have to pay?

RAY: Well, I don't . . .

LOU (*cutting*): Stop it, Cliff. Ray, I'm sorry. Cliff gets too much to drink in him . . .

CLIFF (*loud, cutting*): Nice night we havin' out here on our white well-scrubbed steps . . .

Both together.

LOU: . . . and he runs off at the mouth somethin' terrible. I know you wasn't much past twelve when I came an' got you and kept them from puttin' you in a home. And you had already started in drinkin' 'n smokin' and foolin' around with girls . . . and I knew you drank too much for a growin' boy, much less a man. But I couldn't see you in a home—it would have messed you up . . . or sent down South to Cousin Frank's. I don't mean you so young you don't know what you want to do, Ray. I'm only six years older than you . . . but Cliff still shouldn't be givin' you so much wine and teachin' you bad habits. It ain't good for none of us, not even me. I hardly know where I'm at some of the times when I start in drinkin' after I come from work . . . but it sho' do relaxes me. And your mother is gonna call me to account for it when we meet up in heaven . . . I really know that.

CLIFF: . . . with all of God's white stars shinin' above your black heads. Ain't that right, Lord? You old shyster. You pour white heat on these niggers, these Derby Street Donkeys, in the daytime and roast and fry them while they shovel shit for nex' to nothin', and steam them at night like big black lobsters . . . ha ha . . . the Krumps are little red lobsters of Yourn . . . and they just drink, an' screw in the dark, and listen to jive talk an' jive music an' jive *holy* music . . . but they still think they have to face You in the mornin'. That's right, face You, You jive-ass sucker! They don't know they got to face Your jive-hot, blazin' face . . . simple niggers . . . but they do 'cause they believe in You and Your lies. Stupid donkeys! They only got to look my god in the face once and forget about You, You jive-time sucker . . .

Remembering an old joke.

The devil's in Cliff, I know that, to do what he's doin' to us . . . and I ain't helpin' things much. Listen to what I say, Ray, and not to the devil. Listen to me, Ray.

. . . ha ha . . . she's black as night and as cool and slick as a king snake . . .

Singing.

. . . Yes, Lord, yes, Lord, yes, Lord, yes, Lord . . .

LOU: *Stop it, Cliff! You're drunk 'n' crazy 'n' drivin' me out of my head!*

Silence. CLIFF stares at her.

RAY (*to both*): It's all right. It's all right.

LOU: Ray, when I get to heaven your mother's gonna have a lot to say to me.

CLIFF (*laughs*): Heaven?

LOU: Yeah, heaven. And you better get some of the fear of the Lord in you, Cliff.

CLIFF (*disgust*): Every night. Every goddamn night when you start feelin' your juice.

LOU: 'Cause I know better, that's why.

CLIFF: Is that why when I get you in bed every night you holler:

Whining falsetto.

"Yes, Lord. Yes, Lord. Ohhh . . . Jesus . . . one more time."

RAY giggles.

LOU: You're bad, Cliff. You're bad. Bad!

CLIFF: Sho' I'm bad, hon-nee chile.

Singing.

I'm forty hands across mah chest . . . don't fear nothin' . . . not God nor death . . . I got a tombstone mind an' a graveyard disposition . . . I'm a bad mathafukker an' I don't mind . . . dyin'.

LOU (*cutting*): You're just a dirty-mouthed . . .

CLIFF (*cutting*): Yeah, I know . . . and I'll have you know that just because I spent one third of my navy time in various brigs, not just one, understand, baby

girl, but at least an even dozen between here and
Istanbul, that I was still one of the saltiest salt water
sailors in the fleet . . . on dry land, in the fleet or in
some fucken marine brig!

LOU: You wasn't shit, Cliff . . . You know that, don't
you?

CLIFF: Sticks 'n' stones, Lou . . . sticks 'n' stones.

LOU: Pour me a drink, Ray . . . and give your no-'count
step-uncle one too.

RAY pours drinks for the three of them.

CLIFF: Step-uncle? Now how in Jesus' name did I get
demoted from uncle to step?

LOU: You just did . . . suddenly you just stepped down.

RAY: Do you think I can get into the navy, Cliff?

CLIFF (grabs LOU's arm): Sometimes, Lou . . .

RAY: Huh, Cliff?

CLIFF (recovering): Navy? . . . Why sure . . . sure,
Ray. When you come of age I'll sign the papers myself.

LOU: Steps can't, Cliff. But I can.

CLIFF: I can, Lou . . . I should know.

Proudly.

I joined on my sixteenth birthday.

LOU: Steps can't.

CLIFF (pinches her shoulder): Bitch!

LOU (feigning): Owww, Cliff. Owww.

RAY: If I'm of age then you won't have to sign, will ya?

CLIFF: No, I won't. Not if you're of age, Ray.

LOU: He can't sign anyway.

CLIFF: I can too, Ray. You just watch me when the time
comes.

RAY: I'll be sixteen next week, Cliff.

CLIFF: You will?

RAY: Yeah.

CLIFF: Already?

RAY: Yeah.

CLIFF (to LOU): He will?

LOU: If that's what he says.

CLIFF: Damn . . . so soon.

LOU: Sixteen ain't old enough. You have to be seventeen before they'll even let me sign for you, Ray.

CLIFF: I went when I was sixteen . . . my sixteenth birthday.

LOU (*peeved*): That's because you were down in Virginia in the woods . . . fool! They don't even have birth certificates down there . . . you could of went when you were thirteen if your mother had'a sworn you was old enough.

CLIFF: I was too old enough!

LOU: No, you wasn't. And Ray ain't either. He's got to wait until he's seventeen. And then I might sign for him.

RAY: I got to wait? But Uncle Cliff said I could go.

CLIFF: Yeah, you can go, Ray. I'll sign the papers myself. You're goin' to the navy and see how real men live.

LOU (*angry*): He's not goin' . . . he's not old enough . . . and you ain't signin' no papers for him, Cliff. His mother wouldn't . . .

CLIFF: I'll sign anything I want fo' him. I'm his guardian . . .

LOU (*ridicule*): Guardian? How? With what? You ain't never had a job in your life over six months. What you raise him with . . . the few lousy bucks you don't drink up from your government check? You somebody's guardian . . . I . . .

CLIFF slaps her violently.

CLIFF (*low, menacing*): You talk too much, Lou.

LOU (*defiant*): It's my responsibility, Cliff. Mine. Mine. My responsibility. I'm not going to sign or let you sign. His mother . . .

CLIFF: Damn that! Damn it! I don't care what his dead mother wants. Who the hell cares what the dead want? It's what Ray wants that counts. He's got to get out of here . . . don't you, Ray? . . . Off'a Derby Street and away from here so he can grow up to be his own man.

LOU (*crying*): Like you?

CLIFF: No, not like me . . . not tied down to a half-grown, scared, childish bitch!

LOU: You don't have to be.

CLIFF: But I love you.

Lights down, up on "The Avenue."

RED slaps BUNNY GILLETTE.

DORIS: *Red . . . you mathafukker . . . Stop that!*

BUNNY GILLETTE (*crying*): Go on now, Red. Leave me alone . . .

RED: Bitch! Who you think you tellin' to kiss your ass? You want me to kiss your nasty ass?

BAMA (*reaching for him*): Hey, lighten up, Red.

DORIS: Leave her alone!

RED (*being held by* BAMA): You want me to kiss your . . .

BUNNY GILLETTE: Nawh, Red. Nawh.

DORIS (*a short knife in her hand*): You better not touch her again . . . you better not. You goin'a be sorry for this.

> Lights down on "The Avenue" and up on Derby Street.

RAY: I'm sorry, Lou.

LOU: It's all right, Ray. We've fought before . . . I'm just sorry you have to see us act like this.

CLIFF: Awww, honey . . . I'll forget it if you do.

LOU: You beat on me and I'm supposed to forget it? In my condition.

CLIFF: You got nearly six months before the baby. He can't get hurt by just a little . . .

LOU: You know the doctor told you not to be hittin' on me no mo'. You did it on purpose 'cause you don't want it.

CLIFF: I'm sorry, Lou.

LOU: It's a wonder you didn't hit me in the stomach.

CLIFF: Well, it's a wonder I didn't.

LOU: See there. You don't want it.

CLIFF: Nawh, I don't want a baby I can't take care of . . . do you?

LOU: You can get a job.

CLIFF: At a dollar an hour? Dollar-an-hour Dawson, that's me. Nawh, I don't want any kids until I can afford them. That's why I'm goin' ta school.

LOU: You studying business so you can take care of me an' your kids? What kind of job can you get in business? You got money to open you a business?

CLIFF: Lou, we've gone over this before. I'll manage.

LOU: Like you have gettin' a job?

CLIFF: Well, you want me to get a job in the laundry? Like all your cousins?

LOU: And me!

CLIFF: Startin' at a buck an hour. Hell no, I won't work!

LOU (*scared*): But what are we goin'a do when your checks run out, Cliff?

CLIFF: Me? I'll do the best I can. Maybe ship out again.

LOU: No, Cliff!

CLIFF: If I can't turn up anything . . . well, you and the kid can get on relief.

Silence.

LOU: Where's your pride? A big strong man like . . .

CLIFF: A dollar an hour don't buy that much pride, Lou. There's a big rich world out there . . . I'm goin'a get me part of it or not at all.

Both together.

LOU: You ain't no man. My daddy he worked twenty years with his hands . . . his poor hands are hard and rough with corns and callouses. He was a man . . . he worked and brought us up to take pride in ourselves and to fear God. What did I marry? I thought you was a man, Cliff. I thought because you was loud and was always fightin' and drinkin' and was so big and strong that you was a man . . . but you ain't nothin' but a low-down and less than nothin'!

CLIFF: I'm goin' ta get me part of that world or stare your God in the eye and scream *why*. I am not a beast . . . an animal to be used for the plows of the world. But if am then I'll act like one, I'll be one and turn this fucken world of dreams and lies and fairy tales into a jungle or a desert. And I don't give much of a happy fuck which. There's a world out there, woman. Just beyond that lamp-post . . . just across "The Avenue" and it'll be mine and Ray's.

LOU (*screams*): *You're nothin'!*

CLIFF: In the navy Ray can travel and see things and learn and meet lots of different . . .

LOU: *No ! ! !*

CLIFF: . . . girls and make somethin' . . .

LOU: *Is that what it did for you?*

CLIFF: Yeah, that's what it did for me!

LOU: Well, I don't want him to be like you.

CLIFF: How would you want him to be like . . . one of the Derby Street Donkeys? Or one of the ditty boppers or an avenue hype . . . or . . . a drug addict . . . or what?

LOU (*standing*): He ain't turned out so bad so far.

> Determined.

He's not goin', Cliff.

> Pause.

Ray, just get it out of your mind. I'm not signin' no navy papers . . . you're too young.

> She enters the house as the lights fade to blackness.

CURTAIN

ACT TWO

Mythic blues plays. Lights up on "The Avenue." The couples are in embrace.

BUNNY GILLETTE (*to* RED): I like you a lot . . . really I do . . . but what will Ray say?

RED: Fuck that little punk!

DORIS (*to* RED): What you say 'bout my nephew?

BAMA: He wasn't talkin' to you, Doris.

BUNNY GILLETTE: You ain't gonna fight me anymo' . . . are ya, Red?

DORIS: I'd cut that nigger's nut off if he had'a hit me like that, Bunny!

BAMA: You wouldn'a do nothin', Doris . . . you just . . .

DORIS: Yeah, I would . . . and that goes double for any jive nigger who lays a finger on me or mine!

RED (*places his hands on* BUNNY's *rear*): Why don't all you mathafukkers shut up! Can't you see I'm concentratin'?

> Lights down, up on Derby Street.
>   CLIFF and RAY sit upon their stoop. The remainder of the street is in shadow.
>   Silence.
>   From the last stoop up the street BEATRICE detaches herself from the shadows and walks toward the corner.
>   She is a buxom, brown girl and carries herself proudly. She speaks as she passes each shadowy group of forms upon the stoops.

THE RADIO: It's seventy-eight degrees . . . that's seven . . . eight . . .

BEATRICE (*passing*): Hello, Mr. Cooper. Miz Cooper.

SHADOWS: Hello, Beatrice. How you doin' tonight?

BEATRICE (*passing*): Hello, Miss Francis.

SHADOWS: Why hello, Bea. How ya doin', girl?

BEATRICE (*passing*): Hello, Mr. Roy.

SHADOWS: Howdy, Beatrice. How's your folks?

BEATRICE: Just fine.

She passes on.

MISS MINNY puts her head out her window. BEATRICE passes CLIFF and RAY without speaking, her pug nose up, her head sighting on something upon the Derby Street fence, on the far side of the street.

BEATRICE comes abreast the Garrisons' house and looks up.

Hello, Miss Minny.

MISS MINNY: Hello, Beatrice . . . how y'all?

BEATRICE (stops): Just fine, Miss Minny. How's Marigold and Ruth?

MISS MINNY: Awww . . . they're fine, Beatrice. They off visitin' mah sister this week.

BEATRICE: That's nice, Miss Minny. Tell them I asked about them, will ya?

MISS MINNY: All right, dear. Did you know that Homer asked about you in his last letter?

BEATRICE: No, I didn't. Is he still in Korea?

MISS MINNY: Yeah, he's still over there. They done made him a sergeant.

BEATRICE: Yes, I know. Marigold told me. He's doing okay, isn't he?

MISS MINNY: Oh, yes, he's just doin' fine and everything. Says he likes it over there.

BEATRICE: Tell him I asked about him, will you?

MISS MINNY: All right, Beatrice.

BEATRICE continues, and reaching the corner, she exits. MISS MINNY withdraws and shuts her window.

THE RADIO: . . . And now the genius of the great . . .

Music plays, softly.

CLIFF: Sheeet.

RAY: What'cha say, Cliff?

Silence.
Both together.

CLIFF: I said that . . .   RAY: I wonder if . . .

Silence.

Both together.

(*annoyed*): Go on!   (*embarrassed*): Excuse
                                        me.

Lengthy silence. Both take drinks and drag upon
their cigarettes.

CLIFF (*hurriedly*): How old's that broad?
RAY: How old? . . .
CLIFF: Yeah.
RAY: Oh, Bea? . . . About my age, I guess.
CLIFF: She's certainly a snotty little stuckup heifer, ain't
she?
RAY: Yeah, I guess so.

Silence.
Both together.

CLIFF (*almost leering*): I   RAY (*explaining*): She's
wonder what . . .   always . . .

Both halt. CLIFF stubs out his cigarette.

CLIFF (*yells over his shoulder*): Hey, Lou!

No answer.

To RAY.

Guess she's out back in the kitchen or the john.
RAY: Yeah.
CLIFF: Ray?
RAY: Huh?
CLIFF: Did you ever get any ah that?
RAY: Beatrice?
CLIFF: Yeah.
RAY: Nawh.
CLIFF: What she doin', savin' it for Homer?
RAY: Homer?

Laughing.

She can't stand Homer. Calls him "Ole Country."
CLIFF: What'cha waitin' on, boy?
RAY: Nothin'.
CLIFF: When I was yo' age I'd ah had every little pussy
on Derby Street all to myself.

RAY: You'd have them all sewed up, huh?

CLIFF (*not perceiving* RAY's *humor*): Yeah, sho' would.

RAY: Ahhhuh.

CLIFF: How 'bout Marigold and Ruth?

RAY: What about them?

CLIFF: You ain't gettin' none of that either?

RAY: Nawh.

CLIFF: Why not, boy? What's the matter with you?

RAY: Nothin'.

CLIFF: Nothing?

RAY: Nawh, nothin'.

CLIFF: With all this good stuff runnin' 'round here you lettin' the chance of a lifetime slip by . . .

RAY: Yeah, I guess I am.

CLIFF: . . . always over there on Thirteenth Street messin' round with li'l Bunny when you should be takin' care of business back home.

RAY: I don't like any of the girls 'round here.

CLIFF: What's wrong with them? A girl's a girl . . . well, most of them are anyway.

RAY (*embarrassed*): Well, I like Bunny. Me and her's in love.

CLIFF: In love? In love?

Cracking the door and over the music.

Hey, Lou Ellen . . . Your nephew's in love!

No answer.
Muttering.

Must'a fell in.

Looking at RAY.

Boy . . . you got a lot to learn.

RAY: I can't help it, Cliff. And she loves me too.

CLIFF: Ohhh, yeah . . . you really got a lot to learn.

RAY: Cliff . . . I . . .

CLIFF: Just because she comes down here with you on the nights that me and Lou are out don't make you be in love. You didn't think I knew, huh? Well, who the hell you think been turnin' those pillows on the couch over an' wipin' them off? Not your Aunt Lou . . . nawh nawh, she'd damn near die if she knew you were doin' what comes naturally.

RAY: I'm sorry, Cliff.

CLIFF: Forget it. Oh yeah, now that reminds me. Clean up your own mess from now on. You're big enough.

RAY: Okay.

CLIFF: Bunny's the first girl you've had?

RAY: Nawh.

CLIFF: How many?

RAY: 'Bout half a dozen.

    Silence.

CLIFF: Well . . . you ain't exactly backward . . . but still when I was your age . . . but let's forget about that.

RAY: Okay.

CLIFF: Now what about Marigold and Ruth, don't they like you?

RAY: All the girls on the street like me, I guess . . . 'cept'n Beatrice n' she used to let me kiss her . . .

CLIFF: She did, huh? Well, what happened?

RAY: I don't know.

CLIFF: Well, why don't you get one of the girls next door? Screw one of Homer's sisters.

    Chuckling.

Get some of his stuff while he's away.

RAY: Yeah . . . yeah, Marigold likes me a lot. Homer even wants me to get Marigold so I might have to marry her and he'd have a brother-in-law he'd like, but she don't want it, not like that, and I don't see the sense of goin' with a girl if I can't do it to her.

CLIFF: You showin' some sense there, Ray. An' forget about that marriage stuff too.

RAY: Yeah, and Ruth wants to get married too bad. I'm scared as hell of her.

    Silence.

CLIFF: Yeah, you better stick with fast little Bunny. Gettin' you in the service is gonna be hard enough . . . If your aunt knew that anyone was thinkin' about you and marriage . . . we'd really have a case on our hands. She'd probably lock you up in the cellar.

RAY (*contemplating*): And Beatrice thinks she's better than anybody else.

CLIFF: Yeah. I guess you do know what you're doin'
stickin' with Bunny. But you'll be gone in a month
anyway.

RAY: In a week.

CLIFF: Yeah, that's right . . . in a week . . . And
things will be different then for you.

Pause.

Hey, do you know what, Ray?

RAY (*slowly*): I met a girl the other day.

CLIFF: Do you know what, Ray?

RAY: I met a girl the other day, Cliff.

CLIFF: You did?

RAY (*more sure*): Yeah, I met her the other day . . .
she's almost a woman.

CLIFF: She is?

RAY: A pretty girl.

CLIFF: You met her where, Ray?

Lights down, and up on "The Avenue."
    The GIRL appears and stands under soft light.
She has huge eyes and her skin is a soft black.
    The couples are fixed in tableau but RED and
BAMA pull away from BUNNY GILLETTE and DORIS
and dance about the GIRL in a seduction dance,
until the two girls break their position and dance
against the attraction of the girl in a symbolic
castration of the boys.
    Lights down to fantasy hues on "The Avenue"
and up on CLIFF and RAY.

RAY: I met her over on "The Avenue."

CLIFF: Yeah, and she was pretty?

RAY: Yeah.

CLIFF: That's good. But you better not get stuck on her.

RAY: Why? Why, Cliff?

CLIFF: 'Cause you goin' away in a month. You goin' to
the navy, remember?

RAY: But she can wait for me.

CLIFF: Well . . . most women are funny. They don't
wait around too long. They get anxious . . . you
know, nervous that they won't get something that they
think belongs to them. Never could understand what
that somethin' was, but most of them are on the

lookout for it, whinin' for it all the time, demandin' it.
And I guess some of them even get it.

RAY: She'll wait.

CLIFF: Don't be too sure, son. Most of them don't.

RAY: Lou waited for you, didn't she?

Silence.

Didn't she?

Silence.

CLIFF: Yeah . . . but that was a little different.

RAY: How?

CLIFF: It was just different . . . that's all.

RAY: But how would it be different for you and Lou and
not for me and my girl?

CLIFF: Well, for one, I don't know your girl so I can't
say positively just how she'd act . . . And, two, and
you better not breathe a word of this to your aunt
. . . you hear?

Pause.

Well, Lou Ellen is different because . . . well, because she's got character.

RAY: My girl . . .

CLIFF (*cutting*): And your aunt's got principle and conviction and you have to be awfully special for that.

RAY: But, Cliff . . .

CLIFF (*continuing*): . . . Now don't tell her, your aunt,
I said these things, but she's special in that way.

RAY: I won't tell her.

CLIFF: For someone to have all them qualities in these
times is close to bein' insane. She's either got to be
hopelessly ignorant or have the faith of an angel
. . . and she's neither.

RAY: Nawh, I don't guess she is.

CLIFF: I don't deserve her, I know.

RAY: You two pretty happy together, aren't you?

CLIFF: Ray?

RAY: Yeah.

CLIFF: Don't think about her too much.

RAY: Lou?

CLIFF: Nawh . . . you know. Your girl.

RAY: Oh.

CLIFF: Yeah.

RAY (*distant*): Yeah, I guess so.

CLIFF: Why do you say it like that?

RAY: Awww, I was just thinkin'. Lou says I can't go . . . and . . . and this girl . . . she . . . well, I see her every day now and . . .

CLIFF: Have you . . .

RAY (*upset, cutting*): Nawh! We don't . . . we don't need to do anything. We just look at each other and smile . . . that's all.

CLIFF: Smile?

RAY: Yeah.

CLIFF: What else?

RAY: That's all. I just wait on the corner for her every afternoon and she comes dancing along with her little funny walk and sometimes she hums or sings to me a while . . . then smiles some more and goes away . . .

Lights down on "The Avenue" and the dancers.

CLIFF: Boy, you better git yourself another drink.

RAY: I won't see her no more if I go to the navy, Cliff.

CLIFF: There's other things to see. Get her out of your head, Ray. There's a lot more fish in the ocean . . . ha ha . . . and a lot more girls where she came from. Girls all sizes and shapes . . .

RAY (*protesting*): You don't know where she came from!

CLIFF: Why don't I? I just need to take one look at any girl and I know all about her. And with yours . . . well, your just tellin' me about her makes me know. I know all about her, Ray. And let me give you some advice . . . now you trust me, don't you?

Pause.

Good. I want you to stay away from her. There's all kinds of girls on this stinkin' planet . . . speakin' all kinds of tongues you never would think of, comin' in all kinds of shades and colors and everything. When you become a swabby, the world will open up to you.

Say, maybe you'll go to France . . . to Nice or Marseilles . . . the Riviera. Lie out in the hot sun . . . you won't need a suntan but you can lie out there anyway so those tourists and Frenchmen can see you

and envy you. And you'll see all those sexy French
broads in their handkerchief bathin' suits. Yeah, I can
see you now, Ray, out there in your bright red trunks
with sunglasses on peekin' at those girls. Or maybe
you'll go to Italy and git you some of that dago stuff.
Ha ha ha . . . best damn poon tang in the world, boy.

He ruffles RAY's woolly head and takes a good-
sized drink.

Ha ha ha . . . put hair on your tonsils.

Pause. Laughing.

Yeah, there's nothin' like walkin' down a street in
your navy blues. You know . . . you know . . . you
should get tailor-made, skin tights, Ray, with buttons
up both sides, and have your wallet slung around
back of your pants . . . I can see you now. Your
wallet will be fat as a Bible. And . . . and the pretty
little broads will be callin' out to you. "Hey, Yankee!
Hey, sailor! Hey, Joe! Fucky fucky . . . two American dollah!" Ha ha ha ha . . . yeah!
　　Yeah, that's livin', Ray. That's livin'.
RAY (*enthused*): Is it, Cliff? Is it?
CLIFF: In some ports you can get a quart of the best
imported whisky for two bucks and in some ports you
can get the best brandy for only a buck or so.
　　And the nights . . . ahhh . . . the nights at sea,
boy. Ain't nothin' like it. To be on watch on a summer
night in the South Atlantic or the Mediterranean
when the moon is full enough to give a year of your
life for, Ray. The moon comes from away off and is all
silvery, slidin' across the rollin' ocean like a path of
cold, wet white fire, straight into your eye. Nothin'
like it. Nothin' like it to be at sea . . . unless it's to
be in port with a good broad and some mellow booze.
RAY: Do you think I can get in, Cliff?
CLIFF: Sure you can. Sure. Don't worry none about
what your Aunt Lou says . . . I've got her number.
I'll fix it up.
RAY: I sure hope you can.
CLIFF: Sure I can. As long as I tell your aunt I'm fixin'
to ship out she'll sell you, herself, and probably her
soul to keep me with her.

RAY (*frowning*): You goin'a ship out, Cliff?

CLIFF: Nawh . . . nawh . . . I had my crack at the world . . . and I've made it worse, if anything . . . you youngbloods own the future . . . remember that . . . I had my chance. All I can do now is sit back and raise fat babies. It's your world now, boy.

> TINY rounds the corner.

Well, here comes Tiny.

> Knocks on door behind him with his elbow.

Lou. Lou. Here comes little Tiny.

> It has gotten darker and the shadowy figures have disappeared from the other stoops, into the doors of the houses, one after another.

LOU (*off*): What'cha want, Cliff? I just washed my hair.

CLIFF: It's Tiny . . . she's comin' down the street.

> TINY is a small, attractive girl in her late teens. As she comes abreast of the alley a large man in wide-brimmed hat jumps out at her and shouts.

CLARK: *Boo!*

TINY: *Aaaaaiieeeeee ! ! !*

> After the scream there is recognition between the two and CLARK laughs, nearly hysterically, and begins trotting first in a circle about TINY, who looks furious enough to cry, then across the street to the fence where he leans and laughs, pounding the boards with his fists.
> Windows go up.

MRS. KRUMP: Is anything wrong?

MISS MINNY: What's all dat noise out dere?

LOU (*at door, her hair disheveled*): *Clark, you shouldn't go 'round scarin' people like that!*

> The POLICEMAN passes the corner and stops and looks over the scene.

TINY (*regains breath*): You ole stupid mathafukker!

MRS. KRUMP: Is anyone hurt?

CLIFF (*stands, his arm around* TINY's *shoulder*): Nawh,

Krumpy . . . the goddamn natives are restless, that's
all.

MRS. KRUMP: Ohhhh . . . I'm sorry . . . I just wanted
to help.

> Her window closes.

MISS MINNY: You and your friends shouldn't all the
time be usin' that kinda language, Cliff . . . gives
the street a bad name. We got enough bad streets and
boys around here without you makin' it worse.

CLIFF: If you kept your head in where it belongs you
wouldn't hear so much, Miss Minny. Now would you?

MISS MINNY: I'm gonna talk to somebody 'bout you,
Cliff. Somethin' should be done about you.

> Her window closes.

THE POLICEMAN: Is everything okay, Cliff?

CLIFF: Yeah, Officer Murphy. Everything's great.

THE POLICEMAN: Well keep it that way. I want it quiet
around here, Cliff.

> The POLICEMAN turns the corner.

RAY: His name's not Murphy, Cliff.

CLIFF: To me it is . . . If he doesn't know to call my
right name I don't know his.

RAY: He said Cliff.

CLIFF: Yeah, he said Cliff like he was sayin' boy. He
didn't say Mr. Dawson.

LOU (*ridicule*): Mr. Dawson . . . and his mob.

TINY: I'm sorry, Cliff. I didn't mean to make all that
noise . . . but that stupid ole Clarkie over there . . .

CLIFF: That's okay, Tiny. It's not your fault. Old nose
for news up there has been after us as long as I can
remember.

> To CLARK.

Hey, Silly Willy . . . come the hell on over here and
stop tryin' to tear down those people's fence . . . besides, it wasn't that funny anyway.

RAY: You sho' can holler, Tiny.

TINY: I was afraid, man. Some big old stupid thing like
that jumps out at you. Damn, man . . . I'm just a
little thing . . . he makes two of me.

LOU: From the way you holler, sister, I know they'll have to want you really bad to get you.

TINY: Fucken "A," baby. If they want mah little ass they gonna have to bring ass.

CLIFF: With Clark's big bad feet he couldn't catch a cold.

TINY: I should'a known better than to be walkin' along beside some alley, anyway. If I hadn't seen you folks up here on the steps I would'a been out in the middle of the street with runnin' 'n' hollerin' room all around.

RAY: You still didn't do so bad.

> CLARK comes over, snuffling and wheezing. He has a large moon face and is in his early thirties.

CLARK (*giggles*): I'm sorry, Tiny . . . ha ha ha . . . but I couldn't help myself when I saw you over on Ninth Street turn the corner.

TINY (*peeved*): You been following me that long, man?

CLARK (*nearly convulsed*): Heee heee . . . yeah, I ran through the alley and waited . . . and . . . heee heee . . . and when . . . heee heee . . . I heard your walk I jumped out.

LOU (*angry*): Somebody's goin'a shoot you, you old dumb nut.

RAY: Wow, Tiny, you almost scared me. You sure can holler.

TINY: Yeah, man, I really can when somethin's after me.

LOU: C'mon, girl. C'mon in while I fix my hair.

> LOU's hair is long and bushy, just having been washed. It covers her head like a gigantic crown.

TINY (*steps across* RAY): Okay, girl. Hey, Ray, don't cha look up my dress.

RAY (*jest*): Why not, Tiny?

TINY: You must think you're gettin' big, boy.

RAY (*drawl*): I is.

LOU: Not that big, boy.

CLIFF: Why do you keep pesterin' the boy, Lou? If he didn't try and look I'd be wonderin' what's wrong with him.

LOU: Is that what you do, look?

CLIFF: What do you think?

> Silence.
> CLARK begins snuffling.

LOU: The only thing that's wrong with Ray is you, Cliff. I know some of those nasty things you been tellin' him.

Silence. LOU and CLIFF stare at each other.

TINY: I saw Doris and Bunny, Lou.

Pause.

They said they'd be over. Said they had some business to take care of.

Pause.

CLARK: Doris comin' over?

TINY (*to* CLARK): Yeah . . . yeah, stupid ass. She said she'd be down. And Ray, Bunny said you'd better keep yo' ass home too. She wants to ask you some questions about that girl you been seein' out on "The Avenue."

RAY: What did she say?

CLIFF (*grinning*): So it's finally got back home.

LOU (*hostile*): Yeah, it's gotten back. You don't like it?

TINY: She said you'd beter keep yo' black ass home, Ray. That's what she said.

CLIFF (*weary*): Awww . . . Lou . . . please.

LOU: Followin' after you the way he does it's a wonder he ain't always in some trouble.

CLIFF (*caressing her leg*): But, baby . . .

She pulls her leg back.

RAY (*angry*): What she mean I better keep mah black ass home? I'll go where I want . . . with who I want. She better watch it . . . or I won't be lettin' her come down here.

CLARK: Hey, listen to Tiger.

LOU: I ain't gonna let you start anything with little Bunny, you hear, Ray? Don't be hittin' on that little girl.

RAY: Awwww . . . sheeet.

LOU: What'd you say?

CLIFF: What'd it sound like he said?

LOU: Now you keep out of this, Cliff.

CLARK: You women folks are sho somethin' else.

TINY: You shut your mouth and mind your business, Clark.

LOU: Now listen here, Ray. Don't you talk to me like that, frownin' up your face an' rollin' yo' eyes. You gittin' too mannish 'round here. You hear?

RAY doesn't answer, but gives a deep sigh.

Don't you bother that girl.

CLIFF: Ray?

RAY: Yeah?

CLIFF: If Bunny fucks with you . . . you knock her on her ass, ya hear?

RAY: Yeah, that's what I'm aimin' ta do, Cliff. Right on her ass.

LOU and TINY go in.

CLARK: Hey, how 'bout pourin' me some of that wine you hidin' down there?

RAY: We ain't hidin' no wine.

CLIFF: Pour your own troubles, garbage gut.

CLARK: Why, hell, you ain't got nothin' here 'cept enough for maybe Ray here.

CLIFF: Ray, here? What do you mean "Ray here?" Why this youngblood nephew of mine will drink you underneath the table and into the middle of nex' week, ole Silly Willy Clark.

CLARK: Sheeet.

CLIFF: Can't you, Ray?

RAY (proudly): Sure as hell can.

CLARK: Well, we'll see . . . come on, let's go on up to the store and get us a big man.

RAY: A big man?

CLARK: That's right . . . a whole gallon.

CLIFF stands and beckons RAY.

CLIFF: Never stand in the way of a man who wants to part with some coins . . . and buy ya a drink at the same time, I say.

CLARK: Yeah, c'mon . . .

As an afterthought.

. . . I'm buyin'.

CLIFF (humming): Hummmm hummm hummm . . . don't mind if I do get a little refreshing night air . . . c'mon, Ray, let's take a stroll.

CLARK: Well, which liquor store we goin' to? The one up on "The Avenue" or the one down by the bridge?
CLIFF: Let's go up on "The Avenue."

Pause.

That's okay with you, Ray?
RAY: Yeah, fine with me.
CLARK: Boy, we gonna get pissy pukey fallin' down drunk tonight.
CLIFF: If you see your girl up on "The Avenue" you'll point her out to me, Ray, wont'cha?
RAY: Yeah, Cliff. Yeah.

They exit. The street is clear. Music plays, then a commercial begins.
And lights down.

CURTAIN

ACT THREE

Time: Forty-five minutes later.
Scene: Derby Street. LOU, TINY, DORIS, BUNNY
GILLETTE, RED, and BAMA sit upon the Dawson's
stoop.

A gallon jug of red wine is on the pavement
beside the steps, and everyone except RED and
LOU has a paper cup in hand.

DORIS is a small girl, not as small as TINY,
and has a full figure. RED looks like a hungry
wolf and BAMA seems to be mostly elbows and
knees.

LOU: I don't see how you folks drink that nasty ole mus-
catel wine.
DORIS (*demonstrating*): There's nothin' to it, baby sis.
RED: That's about the only goddamn thing we got in
common, Lou. I don't drink that fucken hawg wash
neither.
LOU (*primly*): If you must sit on my steps this late at
night, Red, I wish you'd respect me and the other
girls here by not bein' so foul mouthed.
RED (*indignant*): Shit, woman, talk to your ole man,
Cliff . . . I'm usin' Mr. Dawson's rule book.
LOU: Don't blame Cliff!
BAMA (*to* RED): Forget it, huh?
RED: You sometimes forget who your husband is, don't
you, woman?
TINY: Yeah . . . knock it off, you guys.
RED (*to* TINY): Fuck you, bitch!
LOU (*to* RED): I got a good memory, little red nigger.
RED: So use it . . . and don't bug me.
BUNNY GILLETTE: If you fools gonna keep this up all
night I'm goin'a go home!
BAMA: Bye!
LOU: But I got to live with Cliff, Red . . . not you . . .
hear?
DORIS (*in high voice, nearly drunk*): Do y'all want a hot
dog? Do y'all want a hot dog?

TINY: Why don't we all stop arguing? I knew this would happen if you bought more wine, Bama.

BUNNY: You been drinkin' much as anybody.

BAMA: Ahhh, don't blame me. If I didn't get it somebody else would.

BUNNY: They up on "The Avenue" gettin' some more now.

LOU: Cliff and Ray's probably out lookin' for some ole funky bitches.

TINY: That's the way those punk-ass men are, girl.

BUNNY: Sho' is!

LOU: Who you callin' punk-ass?

TINY: Not anybody . . . well, I don't mean punk . . . it's just that all men are messed up.

BAMA: What chou talkin' 'bout, broad?

RED: Hey, Bama, you better straighten your ole lady out before I have to do it.

DORIS: Do y'all want a hot dog?

BUNNY: Yeah, who's this girl Ray's been seein', Lou?

LOU: Don't ask me, chile. Don't even let him know I said anything.

RED: Tell Ray I want to meet her, Bunny.

BUNNY threatens to pour her wine on him.

TINY: When will Cliff be back?

DORIS: I said do y'all want a hot dog?

LOU: You waitin' for Cliff now, Tiny?

TINY: Yeah . . . Doris, I want one . . . but give them time to cook, will . . .

LOU: I asked you a question, Tiny.

TINY: Nawh . . . nawh . . . can't you see I'm with Bama. Ain't I, Bama?

RED (*mutters*): Goddamn . . . what a collection of cop-outs.

BAMA: Hey, get me a hot dog too.

DORIS: The mathafukkers should be done by now.

TINY (*nervous laugh*): Woman, stop usin' all that bad language. You know Lou don't like it.

DORIS: Shit on you and Lou both, it's my mouth.

LOU: Now I ain't gonna warn none of you no longer . . . Next one says one bad word has got to go home.

BAMA: Will you listen to this now?

RED: Hey, Doris, get me one of those fucken hot dogs, will ya?

LOU: That did it, Red . . . Go home!

RED: Okay.

TINY: Doris, you can't say two words without cussin'. Don't you know any better?

RED (*stands*): But before I go, Lou, tell me what did I say that was so bad?

LOU: I don't have to repeat it.

DORIS: I wouldn't be talkin' 'bout people so fucken much if I was you, Tiny. Remember I know somethin' . . . now don't I?

LOU: That goes for you too, Doris.

TINY (*frightened*): Whatta ya mean, Doris?

BUNNY: Uuuhhh uhhh . . . y'all sure do act funny when you start in drinkin' this mess.

BAMA: Yeah . . . whatta ya mean, Doris?

DORIS: I ain't talkin' ta you, Bama.

BAMA: I'm talkin' ta you.

> To TINY.

What she got on you, Mamma?

TINY: Whatta ya mean?

DORIS (*drunk*): Whatta ya think I mean?

BAMA: That's what I'm tryin' to find out . . . what ya mean.

RED: Shall we go . . . children?

TINY: That's what I'm askin' ya . . . whatta ya mean?

LOU: Now look. You broads can take that business back where you got it.

BAMA (*amused*): That's tellin' them, Lou.

TINY: Don't you be callin' me a broad!

BUNNY (*to* RED): Red . . . don't you think . . .

RED: Shut up, woman!

LOU (*amazed*): Wha' . . . I didn't . . .

BAMA (*joking*): Yeah, you did. I hear you.

DORIS (*jest*): Don't be talkin' to mah baby sister like that.

TINY (*scared and belligerent*): What you gonna do 'bout it, bitch! You gonna tell her 'bout Cliff and me?

BAMA: Hey, cool it, baby.

LOU: What did you say?

BUNNY: Now Lou . . . don't get mad . . .

LOU (*disgust*): Okay, let's forget about it. You guys don't have to go home . . . I want you to wait on Cliff.

RED (*sitting*): Wasn't plannin' on goin', anyway.

LOU: Now looka here, Red.

RED (*angry*): Goddammit! Make up your mind!

DORIS (*to* TINY): You tryin' to be bad, ain't you, you li'l sawed-off heifer?

TINY (*rising*): Little heifer!

> CLIFF, RAY and SILLY WILLY CLARK turn the corner. They have a gallon jug of wine, half-emptied, which they pass between themselves and take large draughts.
> They visibly feel their drinks and stop under the streetlamp and drink and talk.

CLIFF: Ray . . . just learn this one thing in life . . . When the time comes . . . be a man . . . however you've lived up till then . . . throw it out of your mind . . . Just do what you have to do as a man.

RAY (*not sober*): Sure, Cliff . . . sure.

CLARK (*still drunker*): That sho is right, Dawson . . . that's right . . . but why can't we be men all the time, Dawson?

CLIFF (*annoyed*): You don't know what I'm talkin' 'bout, silly ass, do you . . . do you now?

BUNNY: Here comes Cliff, Ray, and Silly Willy Clark.

DORIS (*moving toward* TINY): I'm tired of your little ass jumpin' bad around here, Tiny.

TINY (*scared but standing her ground*): You are?

BAMA (*between them*): Hey, knock off the bullshit . . . ya hear?

RED: Nawh, Bama . . . let them get it on and see who's the best.

TINY (*crying*): Bama, why you always takin' somebody's side against me?

LOU: Shut up, all of you!

BAMA: I'm not takin' nobody's side against you, baby.

DORIS: You ain't takin' my side, Bama? And what you callin' her baby fo'?

TINY (*to* BAMA): Y'are!

BAMA: I ain't. We all just out to have a good time . . . that's all . . . a good time, huh?

He pulls DORIS down beside him and puts his arm about her.

TINY (*scratching at his face*): You bastard . . . I thought you was comin' down here to see me.

DORIS pulls her small knife.

LOU: *Doris, stop!*

DORIS: What the fuck's wrong with you, bitch!

CLIFF comes up and sees DORIS's knife but doesn't appear to notice; she puts it away.

I'm goin' in an' get a hot dog.

Same high voice.

Y'all want a hot dog?

No answer. She enters the house.
BAMA, TINY, and LOU glare at each other. RED and BUNNY sit together.

RED: Well, if it ain't Mr. Dawson and nephew . . . the Derby Street killjoys. And hello, Mr. Silly Willy Clark . . . you simple mathafukker.

CLARK: Hey, everybody . . .

Passing them the bottle.

. . . knock yourselves out.

BAMA: We got ours.

LOU silently stands, looks at CLIFF and the drunken RAY and enters the house.

RED (*hugs BUNNY, looks at RAY*): Hey, what'cha mathafukkers doin'? Why don't you all have a sit down?

CLARK: Don't mind if I do, Red . . . Hey, Cliff, is it okay if I sit down on your steps?

CLIFF: Be my guest . . . you know me, don't you?

BUNNY (*pulls away from RED*): C'mon now, Red . . . stop all that stuff, man.

RED: You like it.

He feels her breasts as the two people pull apart.

LOU (*looking out the door*): I don't want to hear any

more of that nasty shit from your mouth tonight,
Red. And watch how you act!

RED: Watch how I act?

CLIFF: Yeah, that's what she said . . . watch how you
act.

LOU: Yeah, you keep your hands to yourself. I saw that.

RED: Hey, what's wrong with you goddamn people
tonight? Is there a full moon or somethin'?

BAMA: Hey, Red, let's split.

RED: Mr. and Mrs. Dawson . . . and nephew . . . I'm
sorry. Forgive me. Will you please accept my humble-
ass apology, huh? Will you Dawsons do that?

> RED places his hand upon LOU's leg; she pulls
> away.

Now what have I done?

BUNNY: What's wrong with you, Ray?

DORIS (*sticks head out of door*): Do y'all want a hot dog?

TINY: Ray's gone off somewhere behind that wine . . .
look at him slobber spit . . . probably with his . . .

BUNNY: With his what?

TINY: Nothin', hon . . . I was just kiddin' . . .

> Shakes RAY.

. . . Wasn't I, Ray?

RAY: Yeah . . . yeah.

BAMA (*mimics* DORIS): "Do yawhl wants a hot dawg?"

TINY: Don't be so mean, Bama.

DORIS: Y'all can kiss mah ass.

LOU (*caricature*): Don't be so mean, Bama.

BAMA (*furious*): *Who you tellin' to kiss your ass,
woman? I thought you saw what Bunny got tonight
up on "The Avenue" for* . . .

> MISS MINNY's window goes up.

TINY: Don't be so noisy, baby.

RED: I thought you was gonna get me one ah those
mathafukkin' hot dogs, woman.

MISS MINNY: Cliff . . . Cliff . . . I see you out there
. . . I'm callin' the police right now about all this
disturbance!

> Her window goes down.

DORIS: You better watch your little self, Tiny.

LOU: I told you about your mouth, Red.

TINY: Watch myself?

RED: My mouth . . . awww . . . Lou. You can't be serious.

CLIFF: Well, children, it's time that Daddy got to bed . . . I suggest that everyone goes home to bed or just home. Good night, all.

LOU: Ain't you gonna stay out here and wait for the cops, Cliff?

CLIFF: Good night, my love. Don't be too long . . . I think your hair's sexy.

> LOU has her hair in curlers.
> He goes in, followed by DORIS.

DORIS (off): Do y'all wants a hot dog, Cliff?

RED: If I hadn't seen Cliff beat so many bad niggers' asses I would think he's a chicken-hearted punk.

LOU: There's more than one way to be a coward.

BAMA: You better not let him hear you say that, lady.

CLARK: It's been a hard night, heh, Bunny?

BUNNY: Honey, these wine times is somethin' else.

RAY (mumbling): Sho is, baby. Sho is.

DORIS (back again, peering bleary-eyed at each one): Do y'all want a hot dog? Do y'all want a hot dog? If y'all don't, speak up . . . dese here hot dogs gonna be all gone 'cause I'm eatin' them fast as I can.

RED: Shove 'em up your ass . . . you silly bitch.

LOU: Okay, you all have to go now!

> RED rises and is followed by the rest, except RAY, who snores on the step. LOU goes back into the house and her fussing with CLIFF about RAY's condition, his friends, and TINY can be more sensed than heard.

BUNNY: Ray . . . Ray?

RAY: Yeah?

BUNNY: I gotta tell you somethin' . . . Ray? . . . Ray? . . . I got somethin' to tell ya

BAMA: Leave him alone, Bunny.

TINY: Yeah, let him sleep. He'll find out.

RAY: Yeah . . . what is it?

BUNNY: I'm Red's girl now.

SILLY WILLY CLARK gets up and enters the house.

Did you hear me, Ray? Did you hear me?

RED faces the building, and urinates in one of the wine bottles.

RAY (*groggy*): Yeah . . . I heard you, Bunny. You're Red's girl now.

BAMA (*giggling*): I guess Ray's really got himself a new girl, Bunny.

RED hands RAY the wine bottle he has just finished with.

RED: Let's toast to that, Ray.

Blindly, RAY lifts the jug to his lips, as BAMA and TINY gasp.

BUNNY: *No! . . . No, Raayyy ! ! !*

She knocks the jug out of his grasp, smashing it upon the pavement. RAY wakes instantly, perceives her action, and lashes out at her face. He lands a solid punch that knocks her sprawling in the street.

RED rushes RAY and hits him with a haymaker aside the head. RAY grabs him for support and the two fall to the pavement, grappling.

TINY screams. And MISS MINNY's window goes up.

There are shouts and noise of running feet. The fighters roll about the pavement and BAMA reaches down and pulls RAY off RED and holds him as the older boy smashes him in the face.

SILLY WILLY CLARK rushes from the house and grabs BAMA from behind. Upon his release from BAMA, RAY butts RED in the midriff and staggers him to the entrance of the alley. RED pulls a bone-handled switch-blade; RAY grabs his arm and they fight their way into the alley.

DORIS comes out of the house holding her small knife.

DORIS (*to* BUNNY): *Where's Ray . . . Where's Ray!*

BUNNY, dazed, points to the alley. DORIS enters the alley as CLIFF runs out of the door in only pants in time to see her disappear in the tunnel.

The street is lit; the Krumps' upper windows are open.

EDDIE: *Kill 'em . . . Kill 'em!*

MRS. KRUMP: Keep back, Edward . . . there may be stray bullets!

SILLY WILLY CLARK has choked BAMA into surrender.

RED (*from the alley, muffled*): All right . . . all right . . .

As CLIFF runs into the alley there is a sharp sigh, then noise of more struggle and a groan.

LOU, TINY, BUNNY, and Derby Street residents crowd around the alley entrance.

MISS MINNY: Oh Lord . . . what's happened . . . what's happened?

MRS. KRUMP: Close the window, Edward . . . Close the window!

The Krumps' window closes.

The POLICEMAN turns the corner at a run.

RESIDENT (*to another resident*): Did you see what happen, Mr. Roy?

MR. ROY: Nawh, Miz Cooper . . . but I knew somethin' had to happen with all this goin' on down here.

RAY emerges from the alley, blood on his shirt. DORIS follows him, her dress splotched with blood.

THE POLICEMAN (*running up with hand on pistol*): What's happened here?

CLIFF steps out of the alley, holding RED's knife.

CLIFF (*hands knife to POLICEMAN and points in alley*): I killed him.

LOU (*incredulous*): You killed him . . .

CLIFF nods.

RESIDENT: Did you hear that?

MISS MINNY: What happened? What happened, Miss Francis?

RESIDENT: Cliff Dawson's done killed a boy.

MISS MINNY: Ohhh . . . my Lord.

TINY (*disbelief*): You killed him?

THE POLICEMAN (*leads* CLIFF *to stoop*): Okay, everybody . . . get back and don't nobody leave. By the looks of most of you . . . we'll want to talk to you. Get back . . . Will somebody call an ambulance and wagon?

MISS MINNY: I already did.

> BAMA has revived; he looks sick and sits beside the alley entrance. BUNNY, CLARK and DORIS support RAY, who looks to be in shock.

LOU: Cliff . . . Cliff . . . don't do it . . . don't leave me! Tell the truth.

> CLIFF caresses her.

CLIFF: It won't be for long . . . I was protectin' my family . . . our family.

> LOU cries, joining TINY, BUNNY and one of the neighbors.
> DORIS appears resigned to the situation.

RAY: She's gone . . . she's gone . . .

> A siren is heard.

DORIS: Who's gone, Ray? Who?

RAY: She is . . . my girl . . . my girl on "The Avenue."

DORIS: She'll be back.

RAY: No, she's not. She won't be back.

THE POLICEMAN: I have to warn you, Mr. Dawson, that anything you say can be used against you.

CLIFF (*genuine*): Yes, sir.

> BEATRICE turns the corner.

RAY: Never . . . she'll never be back.

CLIFF: Lou . . . Lou, I want one thing from you . . .

> LOU looks at him, then at RAY.

LOU: He's all I got left, Cliff . . . He's all the family I got left.

> He looks at her until she places her head upon his chest and sobs uncontrollably.

BEATRICE (*walking up, to* MISS MINNY *in her window*): What's the trouble, Miss Minny?

MISS MINNY: Ohhh, somethin' terrible, girl . . . I can't tell you now.

CLIFF (*handcuffed to the* POLICEMAN): It's your world, Ray . . . It's yours, boy . . . Go on out there and claim it.

> Sirens nearer. Lights down and music rises.

MISS MINNY: Come down tomorrow for tea, Beatrice, dear, and I'll tell you all about it.

BEATRICE: All right, Miss Minny. The Lord bless you tonight.

MISS MINNY: He will, dear . . . 'cause he works in mysterious ways.

BEATRICE (*starting off*): Amen!

> Lights down to blackness and a commercial begins.

CURTAIN

THE SERPENT

A ceremony written by
Jean-Claude van Itallie
In collaboration with
The Open Theater
Under the direction of
Joseph Chaikin

To the memory of Roger H. Klein

Introduction by John Lahr

The theater's competition with other media refines and transforms it. The avant-garde experiments are an attempt at *reevolution* of the stage art, redefining what theater can do that other forms of public expression cannot. Film gives us a scrupulously precise naturalistic image; the detail is far greater than any realistic play can provide. Television feeds us with melodrama and situation comedy. Plays which reproduce forms already exploited by other media (musicals adapted from movies, "thrillers," domestic comedy) find themselves without sufficient audience and discourage a vital theatrical tradition.

Theater's primary asset is immediacy, the sensuous energy that passes from the stage to the audience and back to the stage. In theater we see man in his own dimension, neither swollen nor shrunk by celluloid. The surprise and excitement is in witnessing the actor's trans-formations before our eyes. The stage makes an audience conscious of the visceral facts of its life and its language as the other media technology cannot do. Stage play —because it engages the psyche on such an intimate level —has the power of renewal, liberating the imagination from the ordinary and forcing a sedentary, desensitized modern man to play *actively* with situations. In theater, for instance, we feel space. When space is manipulated or we are manipulated in the space, the change affects us as well as the content of the play. Textures, groupings, the silent and varied movements of the performers become symbolic signals of consciousness. The stage forces us to read the signs by which man communicates his needs and confusions that we may miss in the less focused arena of daily life. On stage, our energy is necessary to sustain the event and to help the actors accomplish their task. This interchange reveals our imagination to ourselves. Since experimental theater is not show *business,* it is freed from the commercial compromises that come with pleasing mass taste. The stage can range to outrageous extremes and, in this state of glorious excess, achieve both its finest moments of fun and high seriousness.

The most ruthlessly experimental of the American theaters has been Joe Chaikin's Open Theater. The whole nature of stage art has been reconsidered. Texts are not simply written but are evolved with actors, director, and playwright. Performance is not simply the impersonation of a role whose ideas and relevance are far from the concerns of the actor. The actor is not saddled with an alien "character," a mere puppet in someone else's game. The process is a long and arduous evolution, one of trial and error and editing. Fragments of Chaikin's thoughts on acting and the stage are the best means of illustrating the inner landscape which he wants his theater to physicalize. It is the dreams and fantasies where our deepest truth is hidden; and this is the area of both shock and delight which theater must isolate in order to renew its deep cultural roots in the society.

The Serpent, a ceremony created by the Open Theater under the direction of Joseph Chaikin, assisted by Roberta Sklar, words and structure by Jean-Claude van Itallie, opened in Rome at the Teatro del Arte on May 2, 1968.

The Open Theater company of actors:

JOYCE AARON	JAYNE HAYNES
JAMES BARBOSA	RALPH LEE
RAYMOND BARRY	DOROTHY LYMAN
JENN BEN-YAKOV	PETER MALONEY
SHAMI CHAIKIN	ELLEN SCHINDLER
BRENDA DIXON	TINA SHEPARD
RON FABER	BARBARA VANN
CYNTHIA HARRIS	LEE WORLEY
PHILIP HARRIS	PAUL ZIMET

The arrangers of sounds: STANLEY WALDEN *and* RICH-
   ARD PEASLEE
Associate: PATRICIA COOPER
The stage manager: KEN GLICKFELD
The administrative director: RICHARD SNYDER
Costumes by: GWEN FABRICANT

FROM THE PLAYWRIGHT

by Jean-Claude van Itallie

Theater is not electronic. Unlike movies and unlike television, it does require the live presence of both audience and actors in a single space. This is the theater's uniquely important advantage and function, its original religious function of bringing people together in a community ceremony where the actors are in some sense priests or celebrants, and the audience is drawn to participate with the actors in a kind of eucharist.

Where this is the admitted function of theater, the playwright's work is not so much to "write a play" as to "construct a ceremony" which can be used by the actors to come together with their audience. Words are a part of this ceremony, but not necessarily the dominant part, as they are not the dominant part either in a formal religious ceremony. The important thing is what is happening between the audience and the action. At each point in constructing the ceremony the playwright must say to himself: "What is the audience experiencing now? At what point are they on their journey and where are they to be brought to next?" The "trip" for the audience must be as carefully structured as any ancient mystery or initiation. But the form must reflect contemporary thought processes. And we don't think much in a linear fashion. Ideas overlap, themes recur, archetypal figures and events transform from shape to shape as they dominate our minds.

The creation of this piece was an exploration of certain ideas and images that seem to dominate our minds and lives. The only criterion, finally, of whether or not to follow an impulse in the piece was: Did it work for us or not, in our lives, in our thoughts, and in the playing on the stage.

A large part in the creation of the ceremony was "letting go." For my part, I let go a great many words, characters, and scenes. And most painfully I let go certain rigid structural concepts I had invented to replace the linear ones of a conventional play. But whatever was good of these—a funeral, a Catholic mass, an LSD trip, an inquisition, a modern mystery play—remains within the structure of the present ceremony. And so too, lengthy discussions, improvisations, and even unstated common feelings within the company remain somewhere within the final piece—in fact more, probably, than even we can remember.

When other acting groups want to perform *The Serpent,* I hope that they will use the words and movements only as a skeleton on which they will put their own flesh. Because *The Serpent* is a ceremony reflecting the minds and lives of the people performing it. What I would like to think is that we have gone deep enough into ourselves to find and express some notions, some images, some feelings which will bring the actors together with the audience, and that these images, these ideas, these feelings, will be found to be held in common.

FROM THE DIRECTOR

by Joseph Chaikin

All entertainment is instructive. It instructs the sensibility. It needn't give information in order to instruct. In fact, information can more easily be rejected than the ambiance of the entertainment.

Within the theater it is often believed that except for the concerns of the particular character he is playing, the less an actor knows about the implications of a work, the better. In a work like *The Serpent* the actor must understand as much as can be understood. Here the ideas in the piece are as important to the actor's understanding as are his individual character motivations. Since the strength of the production rests on the power of the ensemble of actors, the ensemble must address itself to the questions and images which make up *The Serpent*. The most hazardous and rewarding problem in a group effort such as this one is to find communal points of reference.

Because the main part of the piece is taken from a narrative, the story of Genesis in the Bible, it is important that the group of actors first look for images which come close to their own early pictures of these stories. The more faithful their images are to their own garden-in-the-mind, to Adam and Eve, etc., the more Jean-Claude van Itallie's text will emerge. *The text follows the narrative of Genesis, and is at the same time a repudiation of its assumptions, thus forming a dialectic.* What is deeply engaging in the biblical mythology is the discovery that its assumptions are even now the hidden bases of a lot of our making of choices.

The text gives a structure for the playing out of the story, and includes places for the company to improvise. Performing an improvisation is seldom successful without a framework to contain the kinetic happening—that which is going on in the room in a non-verbal, non-literal way. The springboard of the improvisation is within the narrative, such as in the ecstasy of Adam and Eve after the apple has been bitten. But once the actors are in the house playing out the exploration of the ecstasy, there is the other reality of people-players and audience—and here is where the delicate and mysterious encounter takes place. That encounter is not "made," but "permitted." It is not performed at that moment, but let be. It is caused neither by the actor nor by the audience, but by the silence between them.

The actors consciously confront the full bewilderment of people together in a room. Some of the audience are pleased at the shift of focus from the stage to the whole room as a larger stage. Some of the audience have been disgusted with the whole proceedings from the start, and here may express it. And others in the audience are also aware of their own bewilderment. Within the narrative are guideposts which are springboards for the actors to give form to this otherwise formless encounter. The aim in the improvised parts is not simply to assess the players' or the audience's attitudes. The confrontation is with that delicate but powerful pulse of people assembled in the same room. For this reason it is the rhythm and dynamic responses, rather than the confrontation of attitudes between the actor and the audience, which are important. This special task is possible in the particular context of the *anonymous intimacy* between players and audience, and through it the main theme which is the confrontation of our mortality.

The role of the four women who make up the chorus is multiple. They are, to the audience, hostesses. They are narrator and chorus. They are contemporary widows mourning "the good life." They introduce ideas which are thematic perspectives. They bring everything into question by juxtaposing the worldly with the other-worldly. They "de-mystify" by making common, and yet untenable, statements. They answer questions implied in the rest of the text by further questions, continually intruding on answers to bring into focus the unanswerable.

It would be difficult to overstress the importance of

the group effort. In usual theater situations the text is there, and the director follows out his own plan. But in *The Serpent* the text invites all those working on it to create what will happen on stage. The director is the agent through whom the work finds its final plan, but he does not fix anything in his mind before the work begins. The actors collaborate fully, introducing images and possibilities, some of which they will themselves eventually embody on the stage. The collaboration requires that each person address to himself the major questions posited in the material: what are my own early pictures of Adam and Eve and the serpent, of the Garden of Eden, of Cain and Abel? These questions deal with a personal remembered "first time." They are the questions we stopped asking after childhood. We stopped asking them because they were unanswerable (even though we gave or guessed at answers), and later we substituted "adult" answerable questions for them. The group must also go into these deeply dramatic questions of the "first man," "first woman," "first discovery of sex," and also into the character of God in the Old Testament. I would state that the premise of the piece is that Man made God in his own image, and held up this God to determine his own, Man's, limits.

When these questions are alive to the company of actors, there is in any of them a dangerous point when discussion must stop and the questions must be brought to the stage in terms of improvisatory actions. There are two main values in working on a piece in this way, collaboratively. One is the affirming discovery of finding deep common references. It takes time to reach these; the cliché references all need to come out first. And the second value is the astonishing power there is in the performance of an actor who is actually playing out an image which he himself introduced.

The first steps of collaborative work, then, are to open up and develop a vocabulary of image and action. Later the director becomes more important. He must find ways to select the most cogent from among possible images; he must enlarge any particular image through more specific demands of voice and movement; he must redefine the actors' intentions when they become lost;

and he must discover ways to sustain the freshness of successive performances. That part of the work which is a combination of both fixed and improvised-for-the-night must be set up with a carefully thought-out balance, so as to make possible its existence anew each time in the particular room in which it is played. Also, the single action which has been finally chosen for each part of each scene must be a formal articulation of the one choice selected from among many, the one phrase-of-action which represents the essential impulse of the scene.

Why is *The Serpent* a ceremony? What kind of ceremony is it? It is one in which the actors and audience confront the question: where are we at in relation to where we've been? The four women of the chorus go back again and again to references about "the beginning" and "the middle." Anything may have been possible in the beginning, but now we've made the choice, and that choice excludes other possibilities. It makes those choices which are still possible fewer. The ceremony celebrates this point in time: now. We can't remake the past. *The Serpent* insists on our responsibility of acknowledging that we have already gone in a particular direction. It says: where are we at? What are the boundaries we adhere to, and how have they become fixed?

In *The Serpent* the point of crossing a boundary, such as when Eve eats the apple, is a point of transformation, and the whole company crosses a boundary. Because when even one person crosses a forbidden line, nothing is the same for anyone after that.

A LETTER

Since it was first performed by the Open Theater a couple of years ago, I have had the chance to see *The Serpent* performed by three other groups. A couple of these productions were good. One I thought was abysmal. All three tried to make the piece their own, to make the images in it personal to themselves. Also all of them worked on the piece for at least six weeks together, as a company, which I think is the minimum necessary time to spend on it.

I would like to quote a few paragraphs from the angry letter I wrote to the director of the company whose production I so disliked, in the hopes that these will provide some indication to a new director approaching the piece of how I feel it should *not* be done.

Actors are not poets, at least not while they're on their feet in front of an audience. Their concentration had better not be on the invention of words while they are performing. If it is then the words are at very best trite, and the performances suffer. There are certain precise and taxing techniques necessary to acting a play like *The Serpent*. The actor needs to be keenly aware and open to himself, to other members of the ensemble, and to the audience—inventing words à la Second City of ten years ago has nothing to do with these techniques at all, and only distracts and detracts from the piece.

What of "improvisation" you say. Aren't ensemble companies supposed to improvise? The word "improvisation" is an overused one and means a lot of different things to different people. What it does *not* mean for a play like *The Serpent* is verbal improvisation in performance . . . Which moments of freedom within the text the actor does have you can best find in Joseph Chaikin's "director's notes." Just about the only moment of total freedom to follow *any* impulse of the moment comes in the "apple eating," but even here there are restrictions—there has to be a time limit, a ban on the spoken word, and an agreed-upon intent by the company beforehand. Otherwise you will lose your audience in terms of the tension of the piece.

I have found that improvisation (and mostly non-verbal at that) works best in inverse proportion to the amount of time left in a rehearsal period before performance. Of course the beginning of rehearsals by the ensemble should be exercises toward the material, and an opening of the actors to it, a personalization—but performance itself must be tight, i.e. the logic of the play, its thrust, has to be clear. This involves an awareness on the part of the director as to how he is using duration, time, and he must above all be economical and even sparing, in order to completely attract the audience's attention and tension where he wants it.

It is necessary that *The Serpent* be tightly performed, because it is such an abstract piece; it attempts to break some kind of barriers in theatrical form, and if you want to be innovative you have a particular responsibility to be *clear*. . . .

The two ensemble companies that I know and most respect—The Polish Lab and the Open Theater—never "improvise" during a performance of a play (except in the sense that every good actor and every good company is always improvising). In fact contrary to what is sometimes believed about them by some who haven't seen them, the success of their performances is due in large part to an extreme discipline, albeit one of their own devising.

Finally, another word about the text. . . . Words, as you're aware, have become terribly misused, in life also —we use them to lie and to put up barriers rather than bridges. Contemporaneously a long speech is suspect because speeches are the vehicle by which politicians and other power people deliver us their hypocrisy. "General conversation" most often conforms to the modes and intent of a repressive middle-class atmosphere, and often words curdle in our mouths as we speak them— words feel like traps set by the societal powers that be, physical and metaphysical, and often like a betrayal of where you sense the reality is actually at. To simply transfer such words onto the stage (even to mock them) is very unsatisfactory to me.

What the Open Theater and I tried to do in creating

The Serpent was to find theatrical expression (non-verbal) of certain questions. In *The Serpent* these questions have to do with guilt and disquiet. . . . The process, from the first workshop to the first definitive performance, took a year and some months. . . . The words are intended to be few and clear, as poetry—they attempt to be the "top of the iceberg" to the rest of the theatrical experience for the audience, capping off images that have already been sensed. . . .

There is, I admit, a trap in the subtitle (A Ceremony). I didn't intend it to be a trap. I used the word "ceremony" to try to break the audience's usual notion of what a play is. But for a company coming to the text in order to perform it, even *as* a ceremony, it is a play in the very usual sense that if you vary the text you do so at your own peril . . . and mine apparently. . . .

> Sincerely,
> Jean-Claude van Itallie
>> February 20, 1970
>> Los Angeles, California

THE SERPENT

WARM-UP AND PROCESSION

In all parts of the theater, including the aisle, the stage and the balcony, the actors warm up. Each does what physical exercises best prepare him for playing. The lights dim slowly and not completely. Each actor wears a costume that seems natural on him particularly, of colorful and easily falling materials that flatter the movement of his body. The total effect, when the company moves together, is kaleidoscopic. The actress who will play Eve wears a simply cut short white dress, and Adam old khaki pants and a shirt with no collar. None of the others is costumed for a particular role. As no one wears any shoes but tights or ballet slippers, a dropcloth for the stage is desirable.

After a few minutes the actors begin to move around the theater in a procession led by an actor who taps out a simple marching rhythm on a bongo drum. The players don't use their voices, but they explore every other sound that can be made by the human body—slapping oneself, pounding one's chest, etc. The actors also use simple and primitive musical instruments during the procession. During some later scenes an actor may accompany the stage action with the repeated sound of a single note on one of these instruments. The procession appears to be one of medieval mummers and sounds like skeletons on the move. All at once all stop in a freeze. This happens three times during the procession. During a freeze each actor portrays one of various possible motifs from the play such as: the sheep, the serpent, the president's wife's reaching gesture, Adam's movement, Cain's waiting movement, Eve's movement, the heron, and the old people. In countries outside the United States where it is thought that not everyone will immediately recognize all events in the piece, at these motif moments actors shout out the names King and Kennedy.

Transitions from a scene to the next will be done rhythmically, in the character of one scene or of the following, as a slow transformation or "dissolve," or completely out of character with the audience merely watching the actor go to his next place. Each transition is slightly different, but predetermined.

THE DOCTOR

When the procession is nearly over, the doctor detaches himself from it. A victim, a woman, from among the actors is carried over by two actors and placed on a table formed by three other actors. The doctor stands behind the table. He speaks in a kind of chant. His movements are slow and ritualistic. The rest of the actors, watching, will provide stylized sounds for the operation. A gunshot will be heard once in a while. We will already have heard the gunshot a couple of times during the end of the procession.

DOCTOR: Autopsy:
With a single stroke of the cleaver
The corpse is split open.

Actors make cutting sound from the backs of their throats.

The fatty tissues
Fall away
In two yellow folds.

In a corpse
The blood is black

And does not flow.
In a living person
The blood is black
And flows
From the liver
To the spine, and from
There to the heart
And the brain.
To penetrate the skull
We shave the head,
And cut out a disk of flesh
The shape of a half moon.

Actors make the sound of the saw.

We inject the exposed bone
With a steel needle
And push air into the skull
To look into the brain.
Then with a diamond drill
We enter the bone.

Actors make the sound of teeth nibbling.

And nibble at the opening
With a hammer, chisel and knife.
The brain is cream-colored.
It is a balance of chemicals.
Thought is effected
By traveling electrons.

Gunshot.

During a brain operation
Pressing at this point
With a knife
Causes live patients
To exclaim at sudden memories.
If we press here
We get fear.

Gunshot.
The patient, who so far has been lying fairly
still, climbs off the table and comes slowly toward
the audience in a state of extreme bodily tension,
making a soundless appeal.

72 VAN ITALLIE

DOCTOR: In gunshot wounds
Infection ensues
Unless an operation
Is undertaken immediately.
We excise the wound,
And suck out bits of bone
And diffluent brain matter.
If the patient survives
He may live for weeks
Or months
Or years.

> The four women of the chorus make the same small long scream at the backs of their throats that they will make when we later see Abel's ghost.

He functions barely.
He is unconscious.
Or semi-conscious.
We don't know.
We clean him,
And feed him.
But there is no measure
To what degree
The mind imagines, receives, or dreams.

KENNEDY-KING ASSASSINATION

A cheering crowd forms in a semi-circle at the back of the stage. Using four chairs, or sitting on the floor if the stage is raked enough, four actors, two men and two women, sit in the car as the central characters in the assassination of President John F. Kennedy. The governor and his wife are in front. The President and his wife are in the back seat exactly as in all the newspaper pictures. They are waving. The crowd, moving from one side of the stage to the other behind them, gives the same impression of movement as in a film when the scenery is moved behind what is supposed to be a "moving" car. When the crowd moves the first time, one figure is left to the side: the assassin. Another figure stands behind the crowd, and does not move with it. Again, everyone but the people in the car is facing the audience. The people in the car look at the audience, smile at them as if they were the crowd. The events which are the actual assassination are broken down into a count of twelve, as if seen on a slowed-down silent film. Within this count all the things which we are told factually happened, happen:

1: All four wave.
2: President is shot in the neck.
3: Governor is shot in the shoulder.
4: President is shot in the head. Governor's wife pulls her husband down and covers him with her body.
5: President falls against his wife.
6: President's wife begins to register something is wrong. She looks at her husband.
7: She puts her hands on his head.
8: She lifts her knee to put his head on it.
9: She looks into the front seat.
10: She begins to realize horror.
11: She starts to get up.
12: She begins to crawl out the back of the open car, and to reach out her hand.

Immediately after that, the numbers are started again. The numbers have been actually shouted aloud by guards who come down toward the front of the stage and kneel, their backs to the audience. Then the count is made a third time, backward this time. The crowd reactions are also backward, as if a film of these events were being run backward. Then the guards call out numbers from one to twelve at random, and the people in the crowd, as well as the characters in the car, assume the positions they had at the time of the particular number being called. The blank-faced assassin has simply mimed shooting a rifle at the count of two. He faces the audience, too. The action in the car continues, as if the count from one to twelve were going on perpetually, but we no longer hear the guards shouting. The crowd, aside from the assassin, forms a tight group at the rear of the right side of the stage. They face the audience. The four women of the chorus are in the front. The crowd shouts and marches very slowly toward the front.

At first, however, we have not understood what they are shouting. The shout is broken down into first vowels, second vowels, center consonants and end consonants. Each of four sections of the crowd has been assigned one part. The shout is repeated four times, each time through adding one of the four parts.

CROWD SHOUT: I was not involved.
I am a small person.
I hold no opinion.
I stay alive.

Then everyone on stage freezes, and the figure at the back quietly speaks words like the actual ones of Dr. Martin Luther King:

KING: Though we stand in life at midnight,
I have a dream.
He's allowed me
To go to the mountaintop,
And I've looked over.
I've seen the promised land.
I have a dream
That we are, as always,
On the threshold of a new dawn,
And that we shall all see it together.

The crowd continues its shout, building up the other stanzas as it did the previous one, but the words are still not completely clear. The characters in the car continue their slow-motion actions.

CROWD SHOUT: I mind my own affairs.
I am a little man.
I lead a private life.
I stay alive.

I'm no assassin.
I'm no president.
I don't know who did the killing.
I stay alive.

I keep out of big affairs.
I am not a violent man.
I am very sorry, still
I stay alive.

> At times we have been able to make out the words of the President's wife which she has been speaking on count twelve as she reaches out.

PRESIDENT'S WIFE: I've got his brains in my—

> The last time through the whole shout, we hear each section of the crowd emphasizing its own part, while the assassin, who has been standing on one side, facing the audience and going through, silently, the agonies of having been himself shot, speaks the words with the others, clearly.

CROWD AND ASSASSIN: I was not involved.
I am a small person.
I hold no opinions.
I stay alive.

I mind my own affairs.
I am a little man.
I lead a private life.
I stay alive.

I'm no assassin.
I'm no president.
I don't know who did the killing.
I stay alive.

I keep out of big affairs.
I am not a violent man.
I am very sorry, still
I stay alive.

THE GARDEN

Everyone's breath comes short and heavy and rhythmically, as if in surprise. The four chorus women dressed in black detach themselves from the rest of the group and in short spurts of movement and speech go to the downstage right area, facing the audience.

FIRST WOMAN OF THE CHORUS: I no longer live in the beginning.

SECOND WOMAN OF THE CHORUS: I've lost the beginning.

THIRD WOMAN OF THE CHORUS: I'm in the middle, Knowing.

THIRD AND FOURTH WOMEN OF THE CHORUS: Neither the end

Nor the beginning.

FIRST WOMAN: I'm in the middle.

SECOND WOMAN: Coming from the beginning.

THIRD AND FOURTH WOMEN: And going toward the end.

In the meantime, others are forming the creatures in the garden of Eden. They, too, emanate from the same communal "first breath." Many of the creatures are personal, previously selected by each actor as expressing an otherwise inexpressible part of himself. For the audience, perhaps the heron has the most identifiable reality. He moves about gently, tall, proud, in slow spurts; he stands on one foot, moves his wings slightly, occasionally, and makes a soft "brrring" noise. Other creatures become distinguishable. The serpent is formed by five (male) actors all writhing together in a group, their arms, legs, hands, tongues, all moving.

The chorus women have repeated their "in the beginning" lines from above. They speak these lines as a secret to the audience.

There is a sense of awe about the whole creation of the garden. The two human creatures also become discernible. As Eve sits up and sees the world, she screams in amazement. The sound of her scream is actually made by one of the four chorus women. They are also Eve. They think of themselves as one person, and any one of them at this moment might reflect Eve.

Adam falls asleep. The heron and the serpent are now more clearly discernible from the other creatures. The creatures play with themselves and each other quietly, in awe. The serpent is feeling out the environment with hands and mouths and fingers. There is nothing orgiastic about the garden—on the contrary, there is the restraint of curious animals in a strange environment.

EVE AND THE SERPENT

SERPENT 1: Is it true?
SERPENT 2: Is it true
SERPENT 3: That you and he,
SERPENT 4: You and he
SERPENT 4 AND 5: May do anything?
SERPENT 2: Anything in the garden you want to do?
SERPENT 1: Is that true?

EVE: We may do anything
   Except one thing.

FIRST WOMAN OF THE CHORUS: We may do anything
   Except one thing.

In the dialogue between Eve and the serpent the first of the chorus women echoes Eve's lines, but with the emphasis placed on different words. The four chorus women look at the audience as if it were the serpent in front of them. The serpent speaks and hisses to Eve with all his five mouths. Care must be taken by the actors playing the serpent that all the words are heard distinctly, despite overlap in speaking. Eve is almost in a state of tremor at being alive. The serpent is seducing her with his even greater aliveness, as well as with the intellectual argument. As Eve comes closer to being in the state the serpent is in, her movements begin to imitate the serpent's, and she, finally, is seducing him, too. Some of the other actors are now seated on a bench facing the audience, at the back of the stage where they sit, and rest, and pay attention to the action. This is where those who are not playing a particular scene will always go—none of the actors will ever actually leave the stage. During Eve's dialogue with the serpent, only the heron and one or two other animals in the garden are upright, but they do not distract our attention. The serpent is not only the serpent, he is also the tree, and he holds apples.

SERPENT 2: What one thing?
EVE: We are not allowed to eat from the tree.
FIRST WOMAN: We are not allowed
   To eat from the tree.
SERPENT 3: Not allowed to eat?
EVE: We may not even touch it.
WOMAN: We may not even touch it.

SERPENT 1: Not even touch?
SERPENT 4 AND 5: Not touch?
SERPENT 5: Why not even touch?

EVE: Adam said I would die.
WOMAN: Adam said I would die.

   The serpent is gently surrounding her until she has touched him without her realizing it.

SERPENT 3: If you—
SERPENT 4: If you touch—
SERPENT 4 AND 5: If you touch the tree
SERPENT 1: Adam said
SERPENT 2: If you touch the tree
SERPENT 4 AND 5: If you even touch the tree
   You will die—

SERPENT 1: But—
SERPENT 2: But—
SERPENT 3: But—

Eve realizes her back is against the tree.

SERPENT 5: Have you died?
SERPENT 4 (*whispering*): Have you died?

EVE: I don't know.
WOMAN: I don't know.

SERPENT 2: You touched the tree.
SERPENT 2 AND 3: And you haven't died.
SERPENT 4: You haven't died.

EVE: But Adam said—
WOMAN: But Adam said—

SERPENT 1: Oh, Adam said
SERPENT 2: Adam said, Adam said . . .

SERPENT 1 AND 2: Listen.
SERPENT 2 AND 3: Answer me this.
SERPENT 5 (*overlapping the others*): This.
SERPENT 4: Could it?
SERPENT 3: Could it hurt more
  To eat than to touch?
SERPENT 5: To eat than to touch?
SERPENT 1: Could it?

EVE: It is forbidden.
WOMAN: It is forbidden.

SERPENT 2: Who has forbidden it?
SERPENT 1: Who?

EVE: God.
WOMAN: God.

SERPENT 4: And why?
SERPENT 5: Why has he forbidden it?
SERPENT 4: Why?
SERPENT 3: Why does he set limits

SERPENT 2 AND 3: Against you and Adam?
SERPENT 1: Think.
SERPENT 2: Is the fruit God's property?
SERPENT 3: Is it?
SERPENT 1: He says Adam and Eve may not eat.
But are Adam and Eve
Guests in this garden?
SERPENT 2: Are they guests?
SERPENT 1: Don't they live here?
SERPENT 3: May they not eat where they want?

EVE (*turning away*): I don't know.
WOMAN: I don't know.

SERPENT 5: Also, also haven't you
SERPENT 4 AND 5: Haven't you noticed
SERPENT 4: That the younger always have rule
Over the elder creation?
SERPENT 2: Haven't you noticed,
and aren't you afraid?
SERPENT 1: Aren't you afraid
And hadn't you better hurry
SERPENT 1 AND 2: And eat the fruit now
Before the next comes to rule
Over you?

EVE: I'm not afraid.
WOMAN: I'm not afraid.

SERPENT 1 (*to itselves*): She's not afraid.
SERPENT 2: Why should she be?
SERPENT 3: How could she be?
SERPENT 4: How?
SERPENT 5: She couldn't be,
She doesn't know.
SERPENT 4: Doesn't know what?
SERPENT 3: Doesn't know she exists.
SERPENT 4: Why doesn't she know it?
SERPENT 3: Because she hasn't eaten.
SERPENT 2: If she'd eaten, she'd know.
SERPENT 1: Know what?
SERPENT 4: What worlds she would know
If she ate.

SERPENT 5: What worlds?
SERPENT 1: If she ate she would know
SERPENT 1 AND 2: And if she knew
SERPENT 1 AND 2 AND 3: She could——

EVE: What?
WOMAN: What?

SERPENT 4: You don't know
SERPENT 5: Because you haven't eaten.

EVE: Do you know?
WOMAN: Do you know?

SERPENT 2: I don't know.
SERPENT 1: I don't.
SERPENT 3: But I can imagine.
SERPENT 4: Imagine.
SERPENT 5: Imagine.

EVE: But, is what you can imagine
    What will be?
WOMAN: But, is what you can imagine
    What will be?

SERPENT 1 AND 2: How can you know
    Until you eat?
SERPENT 5: How can I know?
SERPENT 4: How can I know until you eat?
SERPENT 1: This garden
SERPENT 2: All these animals and these plants
SERPENT 2 AND 3: Were once only imagined.

EVE: Shall I risk losing all these?
WOMAN: Shall I risk losing all these?

SERPENT 1: It may be.
SERPENT 2: It may be that no garden
SERPENT 4: Is better than this one.
SERPENT 5: This garden.
SERPENT 4: It may be.
SERPENT 2: But you won't know,

serpent 1: You can't know
    Until you eat.
serpent 2: How could you know?

eve: If I eat
    And if I die
    Will you die too?
woman: If I eat
    And if I die
    Will you die too?

serpent 1: If you die
    I will die too.

eve: Why do you want me to eat?
woman: Why do you want me to eat?

serpent 5: Because I want
serpent 4: I want to
serpent 3: I want to know.

eve: Know what?
woman: Know what?

serpent 2: Know what you will know.
serpent 1: Know what will happen.

eve: I might.
    I might do it.
    I might do it if God didn't know.
woman: I might.
    I might do it.
    I might do it if God didn't know.

serpent 3: You might
serpent 4: Might do it if God didn't know?
serpent 2: But you want to,
serpent 1: And he knows you want to.
serpent 5: Is a crime
serpent 4: Only a crime
serpent 5: When you're caught?

EVE: Shall I do what I want to then?
WOMAN: Shall I do what I want to then?

SERPENT 1 AND 2 AND 3 AND 4 AND 5: Yes!

EVE: Even if what I want is to listen
   To God and not to you?
WOMAN: Even if what I want is to listen
   To God and not to you?

SERPENT 1: Yes.
SERPENT 2: If you want.
SERPENT 3 AND 4: If you want.
SERPENT 5: Yes.

EVE: Then I will eat.
WOMAN: Then I will eat.

   She bites into one of the apples held by the many
   hands of the serpent.

EVE: Because I want to.
WOMAN: Because I want to.

EATING THE APPLE

   When Eve finally eats, she is seated in the middle
   of the serpent. After a couple of frantic bites,
   there is a pause as Eve begins to savor the experience. The first woman of the chorus, who
   echoed Eve's words to the serpent, now describes
   Eve's experience.

FIRST WOMAN OF THE CHORUS: And Eve looked
   At the creatures in the garden,
   And at the ground
   And at the wind and the water,
   And she said: I am not the same as these.
   And she began to examine
   Her skin and her eyes

And her ears and her nose and her mouth.
And she began to examine her own mind.
And Eve went to Adam
To persuade him to eat.
But Adam said:
"You have eaten of that which was forbidden, and you
  shall die.
Do you want me to eat and die too?"

> Eve in a kind of frenzy has gone over to Adam,
> woken him up, and is trying to have him eat. He,
> at first, refuses but then is caught up in her
> frenzy and he eats too. After his first bite nothing
> seems to happen. The serpent freezes during
> Adam and Eve's argument, but he has shared
> Eve's ecstasy. The three other women of the
> chorus "daven" while the first woman describes
> the action. This davening is a rhythmic murmur
> like that of old women in churches and syna-
> gogues as they repeat and repeat familiar prayers
> and laments.

FIRST WOMAN OF THE CHORUS: But Adam ate.
And Adam looked
At the creatures in the garden,
And at the ground
And at the wind and the water,
And he said: I am not the same as these.
And he began to examine
His skin and his eyes
And his ears and his nose and his mouth.
And he began to examine his own mind.
And he could neither spit out the fruit
Nor could he swallow it.

> Adam takes a second bite. All the actors, in a
> kind of ecstasy, form the serpent, moving in the
> same manner as we saw the serpent move with
> fewer actors earlier. The serpent, as played by all
> the actors, is still a display of the tree of life. It is
> seductive and inviting. Then the serpent sepa-
> rates.
>   A bag of apples is found on one side of the
> stage. An actor empties it out on the stage. The

actors play with the apples, eat them, and carry them out to the audience to share their pleasure with them.

THE CURSES

Adam begins to cough a little. It is clear that he can indeed neither swallow the fruit nor spit it out. Suddenly, an actor who has been playing one of the creatures in the garden pulls Adam up from under the arms. Adam himself speaks for God when God is speaking to Adam. When speaking for God, Adam uses a voice which is larger and more resonant than his usual one, and the actor who lifts him mouths the same words. Adam's own attitude, as he speaks for God, is one of surprise and dismay. Whenever God will speak, all the actors on stage will whisper his words too.

GOD (*speaking through Adam*): Where are you?

The actor who had lifted Adam up now drops him and goes back to playing a creature in the garden. Adam tries to hide, and he tries to cough up the fruit to be able to speak clearly to God. But the fruit remains stuck in his throat. The same actor picks him up again.

GOD (*speaking through Adam*): Where are you? Why do you not answer me?

The actor lets Adam drop and becomes a creature in the garden again.

ADAM (*answering God*): I hear your voice in the garden And I am afraid.

Adam is picked up again. Whenever he is picked up to speak, his body goes limp.

GOD (*speaking through Adam*): Before When you heard my voice

You were not afraid,
Yet, now you are afraid.

    Adam is dropped again.

ADAM (*answering God*): I am afraid
Because I am naked
And I have hidden myself.

    Adam is picked up again from under the arms.

GOD (*speaking through Adam*): Who told you
You were naked?
Have you eaten of the tree
From which
I commanded you not to eat?

    Adam is dropped.

ADAM (*answering*): Lord, so long as I was alone
I did not fall into sin.
But as soon as this woman came
She tempted me.

    *Another actor now lifts up Eve in the same way
    Adam was lifted, and Eve is limp and speaks for
    God in a voice that is larger and more resonant
    than her usual one. The actor who lifts her, and
    the others, whisper the same words she is speak-
    ing.*

GOD (*speaking through Eve*): Woman, have you eaten
of the tree
Whereof I commanded you not to eat?

    *Eve is let drop, and the actor who had lifted her
    goes back to playing a creature in the garden.*

EVE (*answering God*): It was the serpent, Lord.
He tempted me, and I ate.

SERPENT 1: You gave them a command,
    and I contradicted it.
SERPENT 2: Why did they obey me
    And not you?

    *From now on the voice of God is heard similarly
    through the different actors on the stage. All,*

except the four women of the chorus, lift each other in turn and speak with a voice that is larger than their usual ones. After lifting or being lifted, the actors return to being creatures in the garden. As the curses continue, there is a shorter space of time between them, and greater agitation in the garden. And as the curses are spoken each by one actor, the other actors simultaneously whisper them to the audience.

GOD (*speaking through one actor who is lifted from under his arms by another actor*): Because you have done this
You are cursed over all animals.
Upon your belly shall you go
And dust shall you eat.

GOD (*speaking through another actor*): Because you have eaten
Of the tree of which I commanded you,
Saying: You shall not eat of it,
Cursed is the earth for your sake.

GOD (*speaking through another actor*): You shall use your mind
Not to understand but to doubt.
And even if you understand,
Still shall you doubt.

GOD (*speaking through another actor*): When your children shall be found to murder,
You shall make laws.
But these laws shall not bind.

GOD (*speaking through another actor*): You shall be made to think,
And although few of your thoughts shall exalt you,
Many of your thoughts shall bring you sorrow,
And cause you to forget your exaltation.

GOD (*speaking through another actor*): Now shall come a separation
Between the dreams inside your head
And those things which you believe
To be outside your head
And the two shall war within you.

GOD (*speaking through another actor*): Accursed, you shall be alone.

For whatever you think,
And whatever you see or hear,
You shall think it and see it and hear it, alone.
Henceforth shall you thirst after me.

GOD (*speaking through another actor*): In the day shall
you endure
The same longing as in the night,
And in the night shall you endure
The same longing as in the day.
Henceforth shall you thirst after me.

GOD (*speaking through another actor*): And your chil-
dren shall live in fear of me.
And your children shall live in fear of you,
And your children shall live in fear of each other.

GOD (*speaking through another actor*): Accursed, you
shall glimpse Eden
All the days of your life.
But you shall not come again.
And if you should come,
You would not know it.

GOD (*speaking through another actor*): And in the end
The earth shall wax old like a garment
And be cast off by me.

GOD (*speaking through another actor*): For that you
were not able to observe the command
Laid upon you, for more than one hour,
Accursed be your days.
Henceforth shall you thirst after me.

> With the volume increasing, the curses begin to
> overlap. They are repeated and fragmented,
> spoken and whispered louder by an increasing
> number of actors. Many actors are regularly
> picked up and dropped. It becomes increasingly
> impossible to distinguish whole phrases. All the
> voices build into a frenzy and a din of sound.

VOICES: And in the day
Shall you endure the same longing
As in the night.

Henceforth shall you thirst after me.

And in the night

Shall you endure the same longing
As in the day.

Henceforth shall you thirst after me.

And now shall come a separation.

Accursed.

Between the dreams inside your head.

Accursed.

And those things which you believe to be outside your
    head
And the two shall war within you.

And your children shall live in fear of me.

And in the end the earth shall wax old like a garment
And be cast off by me.

And your children shall live in fear of you.

You shall not come again to Eden.

And your children shall live in fear of each other.

And if you should come, you would not know it.

Accursed, you shall be made to think.

Accursed, you shall be alone.

And even when you understand,
Still shall you doubt.

Accursed.

Accursed.

Accursed.

Suddenly, there is silence. All the actors remain
frozen a few seconds. Then Adam and Eve repeat, and contine to repeat throughout the next
scene, their "locked" action of, respectively, accusing, and of reaching and subsiding.

STATEMENTS I

The four women are still kneeling.

FIRST WOMAN OF THE CHORUS: In the beginning any-
thing is possible.
SECOND WOMAN OF THE CHORUS: I've lost the beginning.
THIRD WOMAN OF THE CHORUS: I'm in the middle.
FOURTH WOMAN OF THE CHORUS: Knowing neither the
end nor the beginning.

Now they stand. They sway slightly from side to
side.

FIRST WOMAN: One lemming.
SECOND WOMAN: One lemming.
THIRD WOMAN: One lemming.
FOURTH WOMAN: One lemming.

When they are not speaking their own statements, each of the women continues to say softly
"one lemming" as an accompaniment to what the
others are saying.

FIRST WOMAN: I try sometimes to imagine what it's like
to be somebody else.
But it's always me pretending.
It has to be me.
Who else is there?
SECOND WOMAN: I hugged my child
And sent him off to school
With his lunch in a paper bag.
And I wished he would never come home.
THIRD WOMAN: I'm concerned
Because what you reject

Can still run your life.

FOURTH WOMAN: I passed my friend on the street.

SECOND WOMAN: I passed quite near.

FOURTH WOMAN: I don't think she saw me.
If she did, I don't think

SECOND WOMAN: She saw me see her.

FOURTH WOMAN: I think she thought

SECOND WOMAN: If she saw me

FOURTH WOMAN: That I didn't see her.

THIRD WOMAN: If God exists
It is through me.
And He will protect me
Because He owes His existence to me.

FIRST WOMAN: Old stories
Have a secret.

SECOND WOMAN: They are a prison.

THIRD WOMAN: Someone is locked inside them.

FOURTH WOMAN: Sometimes, when it's very quiet,
I can hear him breathing.

SECOND WOMAN: Sometimes I feel there's nothing to do
But help other people.
But as soon as I join a committee or a party
I know that has nothing to do with it at all.

FOURTH WOMAN: Whatever I know

SECOND WOMAN: I know it without words.

FOURTH WOMAN: I am here as a witness.

SECOND WOMAN: To what?

FOURTH WOMAN: I don't know.

THIRD WOMAN: It was different when I was a child.
I don't see any more bright colors.
There are no solid blocks
Or familiar rooms.

FIRST WOMAN: I went to a dinner.
The guests were pleasant.
We were poised,
Smiling over our plates,
Asking and answering the usual questions.
I wanted to throw the food,
Ax the table,
Scratch the women's faces,
And grab the men's balls.

SECOND WOMAN: When asked, I blamed it on the other
person.

It wasn't me, I said.
It must have been her.
I could have said it was me,
But I said it was her.

THIRD WOMAN: My home was Cleveland.
Then I came to New York
And I didn't have to account to anybody.
I smoked: pot, hashish, opium.
I slept with a man.
I slept with a woman.
I slept with a man and a woman at the same time.
But I'm a gentle person, and I collapsed.

FOURTH WOMAN: I'm still a child.

SECOND WOMAN: So am I.

FOURTH WOMAN: Sometimes people nod at you,
And smile,
And you know they haven't heard.

FIRST WOMAN: On a certain day

SECOND WOMAN: Of a certain year

THIRD WOMAN: One lemming

FOURTH WOMAN: Starts to run.

FIRST WOMAN: Another lemming, seeing the first,

SECOND WOMAN: Drops everything,

THIRD WOMAN: And starts to run too.

FOURTH WOMAN: Little by little

FIRST WOMAN: All the lemmings

SECOND WOMAN: From all over the country

THIRD WOMAN: Run together

FOURTH WOMAN: For tens

FIRST WOMAN: And hundreds of miles

SECOND WOMAN: Until,

EOURTH WOMAN: Exhausted,

FIRST WOMAN: They reach the cliff

SECOND WOMAN: And throw themselves

THIRD WOMAN: Into the sea.

CAIN AND ABEL

The four women continue to daven, but now
without words, except when indicated. Davening-
without-words is like a rhythmic humming, and
it continues under the voices of the individual
women who are speaking. Cain chops wood. Abel
tends two sheep. The scene begins slowly to un-
fold between them. It will continue beyond the
recital of the action by the chorus.

FOURTH WOMAN: And when they were cast out
Eve and Adam remembered me.
And Eve conceived
And bore Cain,
And she said:
FOURTH AND SECOND WOMEN: "Lo, I have gotten
A man from the Lord."
FOURTH WOMAN: And again Adam and Eve remembered
me.
And Eve bore Abel.
And again she said:
FOURTH AND SECOND WOMEN: "Lo, I have gotten
A man from the Lord."
FOURTH WOMAN: Then Eve had a dream,
And she ran and told it to Adam.
And Eve said:
"Lo, I saw Adam's blood flow from Cain's mouth."
And wishing to divert any evil that might come,
Adam separated Cain from Abel.
And Cain became a tiller of the ground,
And Abel a keeper of sheep.
And in time Cain offered unto the Lord
A sacrifice of first fruits,
While his brother Abel offered a firstborn lamb.
And the Lord had love for Abel and for his offering.
But for Cain and for his offering
The Lord had no respect.
And Cain said:
FOURTH AND FIRST WOMEN: "Why did He accept your
offering

And not mine?"

FOURTH WOMAN: And Cain's face grew dark,
And his words were not pleasing to the Lord,
And Cain said:

FOURTH AND FIRST WOMEN: "Why did He accept your
    offering
And not mine?"

FOURTH WOMAN: "There is no law
And there is no judge."
And the Lord spoke within him,
And He said:
"If you will amend your ways
I will forgive your anger.
Yet even now the power of evil
Crouches at the door."
But it occurred to Cain
That the world was created through goodness,
Yet he saw that good deeds bear no fruit.
And God said:
"It depends on you
Whether you shall be master over evil,
Or evil over you."
And Cain said:

FOURTH AND FIRST WOMEN: "Why did He accept your
    offering
And not mine?"

FOURTH WOMAN: And it occurred to Cain
That the world
Is ruled with an arbitrary power.
And Cain said:
"There is no law and there is no judge."

FOURTH AND FIRST WOMEN: "Else
Why did He not accept my offering,
Yet He accepted yours?"

FOURTH WOMAN: And it occurred to Cain
To kill his brother.
But it did not occur to Cain
That killing his brother
Would cause his brother's death.
For Cain did not know how to kill
And he struck at his brother.
And broke each of his bones in turn
And this was the first murder.

And Cain said:
"If I were to spill your blood on the ground
As you do the sheep's,
Who is there to demand it of me?"
And Abel said:
"The Lord will demand it. The Lord will judge."
And Cain said:
"There is no judge. There is no law."
FOURTH AND FIRST WOMEN: "Else
Why did He accept your offering
And not accept mine?"
FOURTH WOMAN: "Why yours?
Why not mine?"
And it occurred to Cain
To kill his brother.
But it did not occur to Cain
That killing his brother
Would cause his brother's death.
For Cain did not know how to kill.
And he struck at his brother
And broke each of his bones in turn.
And Abel said: "The Lord will judge."
And Cain said:
"There is no judge. There is no law."
FOURTH AND FIRST WOMEN: "Else
Why did He accept your offering
And not accept mine?"
FOURTH WOMAN: "Why yours?
Why not mine?"
And this was the first murder.
For it occurred to Cain
To kill his brother.
But it did not occur to Cain
That killing his brother
Would cause his brother's death.

> Cain has come over to Abel. He feeds Abel's
> sheep, to get them out of his way. He looks at
> Abel, and Abel looks back at Cain. The rest of
> the actors, not including the chorus, breathe
> together regularly and quietly—they are breath-
> ing Abel's breath. Cain tries different ways of
> killing Abel. After trying each different way, he

looks at Abel to see the result of what he has
done, and to try to decide what to do next. The
rest of the company watches, and the sheep remain quietly by. Some of the things that Cain
does to Abel are to pull at his limbs, to hold him
in the air and think of dashing him on the
ground. Finally, he lays Abel down on the ground,
and seeing that there is still movement in the
respiratory area, Cain uses his hands to chop at
Abel's throat. Abel's breathing stops. All the
sounds for hurting Abel and for the chopping at
him with his hands have come from the actor
playing Cain, rather than from the actor playing
Abel. Now Cain listens for Abel's breathing,
which he misses hearing. He tries to breathe
breath back into Abel from his own mouth. Then
he tries to stand Abel up. He puts grass into his
lifeless hand to try to have Abel feed the sheep.
Finally, he lays Abel down on the backs of his
two sheep, standing behind him, swaying slightly
from side to side, waiting, waiting for life to start
up again in Abel. The heron from the garden is
back, and it wanders near, making its gentle
noise and standing on one leg and then the other.
Cain continues to wait. The four women of the
chorus make a small, long screeching sound
from the backs of their throats. Abel, as a ghost,
now crawls on his knees toward the front of the
stage. He confronts the audience. The actor playing Abel is, at this moment, experiencing extreme tension throughout his body, and reseeing
in his mind's eye what just happened to him.
Cain, still watching the place where he put Abel's
body on the sheep, continues to wait.

BLIND MEN'S HELL

The two actors who played the sheep, and one
other actor, are on their backs on the floor. All
the others, with the exception of the chorus,

walk around and through them. All are blind and
as if experiencing tremendous fatigue. They are
like people who have lived too long. None of those
who are walking may stop or fall—if they do,
they must immediately get up and go on. Those
on the floor grope upward, grabbing at parts of
the moving people. This continues during Statements II.

STATEMENTS II

FIRST WOMAN OF THE CHORUS: In the beginning
  Anything is possible.
  From the center
  I can choose to go anywhere.
SECOND WOMAN OF THE CHORUS: But now the point
  Toward which I have chosen to go
  Has a line drawn
  Between itself
  And the beginning.
FOURTH WOMAN OF THE CHORUS: I no longer know the
    beginning.
  I am in the middle.
  On a line
  Between the beginning
  And a point toward which I chose to go.
THIRD WOMAN OF THE CHORUS: I have fewer choices
    now.
  Because when I change my direction
  The change can only start
  From a line already drawn.

    Now the four women smile. They keep smiling
    unless they are speaking. They sway slightly
    from side to side.

SECOND WOMAN: I'm collecting things.
  Beads.
  I'm buying plants,
  Curtains—

With which to make a home.
I'm buying things
To make a good life.

THIRD WOMAN: When I was thirteen
I wanted a house of my own.
The girl I was then
Would say to me now:
"What have you done with your advantages?"
You could have married a rich man,
And had a big house.
Instead, you're a freak."

FIRST WOMAN (*as the other women and herself open
and close one fist*): Open.
Close.
Open.
Close.
No effort
Makes these two movements
One.

SECOND WOMAN: My husband is in that coffin.
In the day he goes to work.
In the evening we discuss household matters,
And at night
He climbs back into the coffin.

THIRD WOMAN: Even if you sit and do nothing,
Even so,
Your back is strapped to a wheel,
And the wheel turns.

FOURTH WOMAN: While we were in bed I asked a boy,
SECOND WOMAN: I asked him if he should be around
FIRST WOMAN: If he should be around when I die,
Would he hold and rock me in his arms
For half an hour afterwards.

THIRD WOMAN: Because they can't tell.
FOURTH WOMAN: They can only approximate.
SECOND WOMAN: They can't tell when you're really dead.
FIRST WOMAN: Not exactly.
THIRD WOMAN: Not the exact moment.
SECOND WOMAN: When I was a child
This story was told to me in secret by a friend:
"A little boy came into his mother's room
And saw her naked.
'What's that?' he asked.

'It's a wound,' she said.

'What happened to your penis?' he asked.

'Oh,' she said,

'God chopped it off with an ax.' "

THIRD WOMAN (*with other women speaking and emphasizing the words "he," "his," and "him"*): It's my
husband.

He keeps me from it.

It's *his* fault.

He keeps me down, holds me at *his* level.

I could be happy

If it weren't for *him*.

FOURTH WOMAN: The doctors lie.

My mother died screaming with pain.

Did you know you could go into eternity

Screaming with pain?

FIRST WOMAN (*as the other women and herself open
and close one fist*): Open.

Close.

Separate movements.

Stretched-out fingers.

Nails into skin.

One to open.

One to close.

Separate

Motions.

No matter how I try,

These movements

Are not one.

There is a stop between open

And close, and between close

And open.

No effort

Makes these two movements

One.

Close.

Open.

Close.

SECOND WOMAN: You can see them having lunch,

FIRST WOMAN: Their faces pale,

THIRD WOMAN: Laughing.

They are corpses laughing.

FOURTH WOMAN: You can see them on the streets,

SECOND WOMAN: Combed and brushed.

FIRST WOMAN: They are colored pictures.

FIRST AND THIRD WOMEN: The men have killed each
  other.

SECOND AND FOURTH WOMEN: The king is dead.

FOURTH WOMAN: He was shot in the head.

FIRST WOMAN: By an unknown assassin.

SECOND WOMAN: The men are dead.

THIRD WOMAN: And no man can say
  Of work or land:
  "This is mine."

FIRST AND SECOND WOMEN: The men are dead.

SECOND WOMAN: We mourn them.

THIRD AND FOURTH WOMEN: We are dead.

THIRD WOMAN: We mourn ourselves.

FOURTH WOMAN: If a bulldog ant
  Is cut in two,
  A battle starts
  Between the head and the tail.
  The head bites the tail.
  The tail stings the head.
  They fight
  Until both halves are dead.

THIRD WOMAN: So Man created God.
  What for?
  To set limits on himself.

FIRST WOMAN: Would my dreams recognize me?
  Would they come to me and say
  "She's the one who imagined us"?

THIRD WOMAN: I was queen over a country
  Where the air was sweet.
  We ate honey and fruit.
  And at night
  It was quiet.

SECOND WOMAN: Suddenly—
  This moment.
  Here, now.
  I am here,
  And you.
  In this place, now
  We are together.

FIRST WOMAN (as the other three women, and finally

she, begin to make the body sounds of the entering
procession): At the very end.
Even after the end,
Even when the body is on its own,
The human being can make such a variety
Of sounds that it's amazing.
A field of dead men is loud.
Teeth clack, bones crack,
Limbs twist and drop,
And the last sound of all
Is a loud trumpet
Of escaping wind.

BEGATTING

Now all together the four women begin davening
again, for a moment without words. The Blind
Men's Hell has dissolved. Two actors, a man and
a woman, begin very slowly approaching each
other from either side of the stage. The four
women are kneeling and rocking back and
forth. All the others begin gently to explore each
other's bodies.

THIRD WOMAN (*as the other three daven under her*
words): And Adam knew Eve and Eve knew Adam
And this was the first time.
And Adam knew Eve and Eve knew Adam
And this was the first time.

The actors are exploring each other's bodies as if
for the first time. The women now open a book
and read the "begats" from the Old Testament
of the Bible. Each woman reads some part and
then passes the book to another. But all are continually davening and, frequently, the exact
words of the begatting are lost in favor of the
rhythmic davening and the rocking back and
forth toward the audience.

THIRD WOMAN (*reading*): And Adam lived a hundred and thirty years and he begat a son in his own likeness and he called his name Seth.

And the days of Adam after he had begotten Seth were eight hundred years, and he begat sons and daughters.

And Seth lived a hundred and five years and he begat Enos.

And Seth lived after he begat Enos eight hundred and seven years, and he begat sons and daughters.

And Enos lived ninety years and he begat Cainan.

And Enos lived after he begat Cainan eight hundred and fifteen years, and he begat sons and daughters.

And Cainan lived seventy years and begat Mahalaleel.

The man and woman come closer and closer to touching. The others have paired off, too, and are still exploring bodies.

FOURTH WOMAN (*reading*): And Cainan lived, after he begat Mahalaleel, eight hundred and forty years, and he begat sons and daughters.

And Mahalaleel lived sixty and five years, and he begat Jared.

And Mahalaleel lived, after he begat Jared, eight hundred and thirty years, and he begat sons and daughters.

And Jared lived a hundred and sixty and two years, and he begat Enoch.

And Jared lived after he begat Enoch eight hundred years, and he begat sons and daughters.

And Enoch lived sixty and five years and he begat Methuselah.

And Enoch walked with God after he begat Methuselah three hundred years, and he begat sons and daughters.

And Enoch walked with God and he was not, for God took him.

And Methuselah lived a hundred and eighty and seven years, and he begat Lamech.

And Methuselah lived after he begat Lamech seven hundred and eighty and two years, and he begat sons and daughters.

And Lamech lived a hundred eighty and two years

and he begat a son, and he called his name Noah.
And Lamech lived after he begat Noah five hundred
and ninety years, and he begat sons and daughters.
And Noah was five hundred years old, and Noah begat
Shem and Ham and Japheth.

> By now, the two people have met in the center
> of the stage and embraced. All the couples are
> now exploring each other more gymnastically.
> They are trying to find how to make the con-
> nection between the male and the female body.
> They try various difficult positions. Eventually all
> make the connection and they copulate in in-
> creasingly faster rhythm.

FIRST WOMAN (*reading*): And these are the generations
of the sons of Noah and Shem and Ham and
Japheth and the sons that were born to them after
the flood:
The sons of Japheth were Gomer and Magog and
Madai and Javan and Tubal and Meshech and
Tiras.
And the sons of Gomer were Ashkenaz and Riphath
and Togarmah.
And the sons of Javan were Elishah and Tarshish
and Kittim and Dodanim.
And the sons of Ham were Cush and Mizraim and
Phut and Canaan.
And the sons of Cush were Seba and Havilah and
Sabtah and Raamah and Sabtechah.
And the sons of Raamah were Sheba and Dedan.
And Cush begat Nimrod, and he began to be a mighty
one on earth.
And Canaan begat Sidon, his firstborn, and Heth.
And unto Shem were born Elam and Ashur and
Arphaxad and Lud and Aram.
And the children of Aram were Uz and Hul and Gether
and Mash.
And Arphaxad begat Salah, and Salah begat Eber.
And unto Eber were born two sons, and one was called
Peleg, and his brother's name was Joktan.
And Joktan begat Almodad and Shelaph and Hazar-
maveth and Jerah.
And Hadoram and Uzal and Diklah.

All the couples reach their climax at approximately the same time. Immediately afterward, the women go into labor, and they then give birth. Their sons are played by the actors who played their lovers. After the birth, the mothers teach their children how to talk, walk, play games, etc.

SECOND WOMAN (*reading*): And Obal and Abimael and Sheba,
and Ophir and Havilah and Johab.
All these were the sons of Joktan.
And these were the generations of Shem.
Shem was a hundred years old and begat Arphaxad two years after the flood.
And Shem lived after he begat Arphaxad five hundred years, and he begat sons and daughters.
And Arphaxad lived five and thirty years and he begat Salah.
And Arphaxad lived after he begat Salah four hundred and three years, and he begat sons and daughters.
And Salah lived thirty years and he begat Eber.
And Salah lived after he begat Eber four hundred and three years, and he begat sons and daughters.
And Eber lived four hundred and thirty years and he begat Peleg.
And Eber lived after he begat Peleg four hundred and thirty years, and he begat sons and daughters.
And Peleg lived thirty years and he begat Reu.
And Peleg lived after he begat Reu two hundred and nine years, and he begat sons and daughters.
And Reu lived thirty and two years, and he begat Serug.
And Reu lived after he begat Serug two hundred and seven years, and he begat sons and daughters.
And Serug lived thirty years and he begat Nahor.
And Serug lived after he begat Nahor two hundred years, and he begat sons and daughters.
And Nahor lived twenty and nine years, and he begat Terah.
And Nahor lived after he begat Terah a hundred and nineteen years, and he begat sons and daughters.

And Terah lived seventy years, and he begat Abram
and Nahor and Haran.
And these are the generations of Terah.

> From being small children, the men of the com-
> pany have become very old people. They are
> brought forward, helped slowly, to the front of
> the stage by their mothers, who have remained
> young. One or two of the actresses play old
> women and also stay at the front of the stage.

THIRD WOMAN (*reading*): Terah begat Isaac, and Isaac
begat Jacob and Jacob begat Judah and his
brethren.
And Judah begat Phares and Zarah, of Thamar.
And Phares begat Esrom.
And Esrom begat Aram.
And Aram begat Aminadab.
And Aminadab begat Naasson.
And Naasson begat Salmon.
And Salmon begat Booz, of Rachab.
And Booz begat Obed, of Ruth.
And Obed begat Jesse.
And Jesse begat David the king.
And David the king begat Solomon, of her that had
been the wife of Urias.
And Solomon begat Rehoboam.
And Rehoboam begat Abia.
And Abia begat Asa.
And Asa begat Josaphat.
And Josaphat begat Joram.
And Joram begat Ozias.
And Ozias begat Joatham.
And Joatham begat Achaz.
And Achaz begat Ezekias.
And Ezekias begat Manasses.
And Manasses begat Amon.
And Amon begat Josias.
And Josias begat Jechonias and his brethren about
the time they were carried away to Babylon.
And after they were brought to Babylon, Jechonias
begat Salathiel.
And Salathiel begat Zorobabel.

And Zorobabel begat Abiud.
And Abiud begat Eliakim.
And Eliakim begat Azor.
And Azor begat Sadoc.
And Sadoc begat Achim.
And Achim begat Eliud.
And Eliud begat Eleazur.
And Eleazur begat Mathan.
And Mathan begat Jacob.
And Jacob begat Joseph.

OLD PEOPLE

There is now a line of old people facing the audience at the front of the stage. They speak out a name or two, or mumble, from the many names of the "begatting." The four women of the chorus are davening without words. The other actresses, the ones who have just played the mothers, are at the back of the stage, and they daven, too, softly.

THE SONG

The actors move about freely on the stage. Each is overtaken by a slow kind of dying, not so much a physical one as a kind of "emptying out," a living death, which soon slows them to a complete stop. Each actor has a final small physical tremor. Then, as if ghosts, the actors begin to sing a sentimental popular song from twenty or thirty years ago. No longer as ghosts but as themselves they continue singing the song as they leave the theater, walking out through the audience.

OPERATION SIDEWINDER

A Play in Two Acts

by Sam Shepard

Introduction by John Lahr

Sam Shepard is fascinated by America—its archetypal characters, its music, its slang, its sickness. *Operation Sidewinder* is an epic fable about the nation's rootlessness, a society of aliens—cut off from history, from themselves, from any unifying and creative life force. As one of the country-rock songs which counterpoint the odyssey puts it:

> And this is the place I was born, bred and raised
> And it doesn't seem like I was ever here.

Operation Sidewinder begins with an image of strangulation. The lights come up on an arid desert. A mammoth snake, its eyes blinking like red beacons, is poised as if to strike. Two tourists—Honey and her husband Dukie—stop to photograph the curiosity. While Dukie sets up his tripod, Honey gets too close to the snake. The snake leaps; she is caught in its powerful coil. Dukie photographs the event while barking orders to her, and then he runs for help. The image sets the tone of the play: grotesque, horrific, and darkly comic. Things are out of joint, and people, surrounded by images of disintegration and death, are as numb to them as is Dukie, who photographs the outrageous embrace. Each scene is like a panel in a medieval triptych (a small mystery which is clarified only after immersion in the entire event). The theatrical experience is deepened by the musical one, which like print in medieval illuminations, is for a modern audience an explicit but less familiar language than that of the stage image. In its sounds, its fantastical plot, *Operation Sidewinder* has a visionary thoroughness. It leads us through a grotesque spectacle of our psychic death to a final image of the possibility of rebirth.

Shepard's stage world is a dream landscape where the sights and sounds are at once logical and familiar, outrageous and threatening. A six-foot sidewinder, which is really an escaped military computer; black, white, and Indian renegades plotting to capture Air Force planes by putting dope in a military reservoir; a Hopi snake dance whose ritual transforms the sidewinder computer from military property to religious icon. The play has the frantic pace of farce, and it conveys the obsessive groping of the young to survive the suffocation of the modern world. Everyone—including the snake—is trying to survive the society. Everyone has been eroded by it, victims as well as victimizers. "Men are most apt to kill or wish to kill when they feel themselves symbolically dying—that is, overcome by images of stasis, meaninglessness, and separation"; psychiatrist Robert J. Lifton's observation in *History and Human Survival* is the drama Shepard is fleshing out. When the snake is threatened, it attacks; when the freaked-out fall guy for the crackpot radical scheme—the Young Man—cannot get a mechanic to fix his car, he shoots him; when the Young Man discovers he has no belt to use as a tourniquet to shoot up, he uses the sidewinder's body. Stage exaggeration, like the extremes of bombing and beating, is a barometer of need and of despair. The Young Man is trapped, drugs can take him out of the culture but not beyond it. "'I am whipped. I am chained. I am prisoner to all your oppression. I am depressed, deranged, decapitated, dehumanized, defoliated, demented and damned! I can't get out."

Operation Sidewinder is the product and also an example of the contemporary quest for new images of action. Shepard's Young Man longs to get outside his flesh, to shed the crustaceous American experience the way a snake sheds its skin. His compulsive need for change is a yearning for rebirth. The play weaves an

elaborate tapestry of America's sense of death with its
groping for a new history and clear direction through
drugs, sex, revolution, even scientific invention: all means
of being symbolically born again.

Shepard stuns his audience with the vivid surprise of
his images. The props of *Operation Sidewinder*—a car
rack, a '57 Chevy, a seven-foot snake—have a concrete-
ness which counterpoints the spiritual inquiry he is dramatizing. *Operation Sidewinder* is a religious play. Shepard's fascination with Hopi ritual—like the Young Man's
—comes out of a demand for a new sacredness in life
and new symbols to bring it about.

It doesn't matter what you try it's all about take and give
It doesn't matter how you die but only how you live

The song "Catch Me" has a sense of commitment which
is physicalized in the play's final image where the world of
spirit (the Indians) is challenged by the material world (the
military). Paratroopers, claiming the sidewinder as their
property, interrupt the Hopi snake dance just as the
snake's head is united with its body, fulfilling the prophecy
of the Indians' transcendence. Honey and the Young Man
have allied themselves with the Indians, discovering an
identity and a sense of spiritual continuity. The radical
scheme and the drugs are abandoned for mystical "grace."
To the Indians, Honey and the Young Man are saviors; but
they are also saved. Chanting while the soldiers fire into
their crowd, the Indians cling to the snake. No one falls.
Finally, a soldier wrestles the snake away. He rips off its
head. His victory is the destruction of the world. The
Indians, untouched, move toward their salvation; the
soldiers twitch in a violent death. Smoke fills the theater.
This final poetic image brings together the destinies of two
cultures: the apocalypse and the salvation.

Operation Sidewinder is a vision. It casts its net wide,
touching on the sights and sounds of the American
moment. To understand it, you must look as much to the
society as to the literature which has preceded it. This is
what *Life-Show* teaches and what *Operation Sidewinder*
epitomizes. Plays are not only pastimes but also prophe-
sies; and the audience must be seduced and shocked by
new energy, awakened from its life-sleep, that numbing

complacency it uses to survive the nation's spiritual decay by pretending it doesn't exist.

*Dedicated to the following
for their keen inspiration:*

MICHELANGELO ANTONIONI
DAPPER TOMMY THOMPSON
CRAZY HORSE
THE STONES
THE HOLY MODAL ROUNDERS
THE HOPI
NANCY
GABBY HAYES
OLD ORAIBI
MICKEY FREE
1968
O-LAN

Operation Sidewinder was first produced on March 12, 1970, at the Repertory Theater of Lincoln Center/Vivian Beaumont Theater, New York City, with the following cast in order of appearance:

DUKIE	Robert Phalen
HONEY	Barbara eda-Young
MECHANIC	Michael Miller
YOUNG MAN	Andy Robinson
FOREST RANGER	Robert Riggs
BILLY	Roberts Blossom
COLONEL WARNER	Joseph Mascolo
CAPTAIN	Robert Phalen
CADET	Gus Fleming
MICKEY FREE	Don Plumley
1ST COHORT TO MICKEY FREE	Ralph Drischell
2ND COHORT TO MICKEY FREE	Arthur Sellers
CARHOP	Catherine Burns
BLOOD	Garrett Morris
BLADE	Paul Benjamin
DUDE	Charles Pegues
GENERAL BROWSER	Paul Sparer

DOCTOR VECTOR	Ray Fry
SPIDER LADY	Michael Levin
EDITH	Joan Pringle
CAPTAIN BOVINE	Philip Bosco

INDIANS

José Barrera, Paul Benjamin, Gregory Borst, Gus Fleming, Robert Keesler, Michael Levin, Clark Luis, Richard Mason, Muriel Miguel, Louis Mofsie, Santos Morales, Garrett Morris, Jean-Daniel Noland, Joan Pringle, Barbara Spiegel

1ST DESERT TACTICAL TROOP	Robert Priggs
2ND DESERT TACTICAL TROOP	Robert Phalen
3RD DESERT TACTICAL TROOP	Michael Miller

Directed by MICHAEL A. SCHULTZ
Settings designed by DOUGLAS W. SCHMIDT
Lighting designed by JOHN GLEASON
Music by HOLY MODAL ROUNDERS

ACT ONE

SCENE 1

The houselights come down. The stage is black.
The sound of a rattlesnake rattling. A coyote in
the distance. The rattle grows louder. A soft blue
light fills the ceiling of the stage then flashes off.
A bright flash of yellow light from the center of
the stage floor then black again. The blue light
comes on and goes out. Again the yellow light
flashes, then comes on again slowly and glows
brightly, with the rest of the stage dark. It forms
almost a perfect circle. In the center of the circle
can be seen a very large sidewinder rattlesnake,
coiled and ready to strike. The light seems to be
coming from the snake itself. When stretched
to its full length the sidewinder measures over
six feet and looks like it weighs over thirty
pounds. The eyes are ruby red and blink on and
off. The tongue spits. The rattle rattles. The
snake's skin is bright yellow with black diamonds.
It undulates in a mechanical rhythm. Its hissing
grows louder and the rattle too. The head sways
from side to side. Sound of a jet going across the
sky very loudly, then into silence, then a sonic
boom. Silence. Sound of a car passing on a highway. A MAN'S VOICE is heard.

MAN'S VOICE: Look, Honey!

Sound of car screeching to stop, then backing
up, then stopping again. Sound of car door
slamming. Bright yellow desert light comes up
and fills the stage, making it hard to see the
snake except for the black diamonds and the ruby
eyes. The snake keeps up its rhythmic rattle,
sway, blink, hiss as the MAN enters from stage

> left with a fancy-looking movie camera, straw
> cowboy hat, open shirt, hairy chest, Bermuda
> shorts and Hush Puppies. He yells back off left.

MAN: Bring the tripod, Honey! Hurry up!

> He starts focusing his camera on the sidewinder
> and inching in on it, taking his eye away from
> the view finder every once in a while to make
> sure he's not getting too close. HONEY, a very
> sexy chick with long blond hair and tight pants,
> high heels, etc., comes running on from left
> with a tripod.

Take it easy! Not so fast! We don't want to get him
aggravated.

HONEY: Boy, what a monster! I've never seen one so
huge.

> She hands him the tripod. The MAN sets up the
> camera on the tripod and moves in for a close
> shot.

Be careful, Dukie. They're deadly poisonous. I read
it in one of those desert manuals. They're the only
thing to really be afraid of out here.

MAN: Don't worry. I didn't spend the best part of my
years in the Philippines for nothing you know.

> HONEY makes a wide circle around the side-
> winder as she talks and the sound of the camera
> whirring is heard as the MAN shoots. The side-
> winder just keeps up his tense rhythm.

HONEY: He's actually kind of beautiful when you look
at him close. I was always taught to be afraid of
snakes but actually they're not so bad. I mean he's
just out here trying to get a suntan or something.
There's nothing awful about that. He looks kind
of tense but I'll bet he'd loosen up in no time at all if
he got the right kind of attention. You know what I
mean, Dukie? Little mice and stuff. I'll bet he'd make
a nice pet.

> The MAN straightens up from his camera.

MAN: Maybe we oughta aggravate him a little, Honey.
He blends right into the background when he's not

moving. I don't want to waste any more film than I have to.

HONEY: O.K.

> She stomps her foot and hisses at the sidewinder.

MAN: Now wait a minute! For crying out loud! Not like that.

HONEY: Well how then?

MAN: Well I don't know. Aren't there some stones around we could throw at him?

HONEY: Nope. Just sand.

MAN: Well how about a stick then?

HONEY: I don't see any.

> Suddenly the sidewinder leaps out and grabs HONEY around the neck and pulls her to the ground. She screams. The MAN jumps and crashes into his camera; it smashes to pieces. He falls on the ground and frantically scrambles away as the snake coils around HONEY's body. She screams and kicks but the sidewinder coils tighter so that it's completely wrapped around her from her neck to her feet. The MAN watches on his hands and knees as the eyes of the sidewinder blink, the tongue spits and hisses, and the rattle rattles.

MAN: Now, Honey, take it easy! Don't fight it. You'll just make him madder than he already is. Just relax and I'll go try to find a Forest Ranger.

HONEY: Oh fuck! He's really got me. Don't leave! Dukie!

MAN: I'll be right back. Try to relax, Honey. Don't make a move until I get back.

> He runs off right.

BLACKOUT

> The song "Do It Girl" comes on in the blackout. The red eyes of the sidewinder blink in the dark.

Do It Girl

Everytime I see you wanna do it girl
Right out in the street I wanna do it girl

In front of everybody wanna do it girl
I'm losing my control I feel it in my soul

I wanna do it I wanna do it
I wanna do it, do it, do it, do it,
do it, do it, do it, do it, do it

Like a reindeer in the tundra
Wanna do it girl
Like a reptile on a mesa
Wanna do it girl
Like a tiger in the jungle
Wanna do it girl
So lay it on the line
I need you all the time

I wanna do it I wanna do it
I wanna do it, do it, do it, do it,
do it, do it, do it, do it, do it

I know you're going to love the way
I do it girl
I know you're going to bless the day
I do it girl
There really isn't much to say
But do it girl
The time is going fast, so let the
Good times last

I wanna do it I wanna do it
I wanna do it, do it, do it, do it,
do it, do it, do it, do it, do it

by PETER STAMPFEL & ANTONIA

SCENE 2

The song fades out. The blinking red eyes turn to yellow lights and slowly rise about ten feet off the ground.

Voices are heard in the dark as the lights fade up and reveal a small Volkswagen in the air on a hydraulic lift with the tail end facing the audience, its yellow tail lights blinking on and off. Below the car is a MECHANIC dressed in greasy coveralls holding a wrench, rag and oil can. Next to him is a YOUNG MAN with long blond hair down to his shoulders, a bright purple T shirt, tight leather pants and bare feet. They are both looking up underneath the car with their backs turned toward the audience as they talk.

MECHANIC: So for no reason at all they just all of a sudden started blinkin' on and off?

YOUNG MAN: Well it seemed like the whole car shook for a second and then they started to blink. All the lights.

MECHANIC: Well, it could be your voltage regulator or the generator. I'll just check out yer wiring here to make sure.

YOUNG MAN: Thanks.

MECHANIC: Could've picked yerself a better time to make a movie ya' know. Days get pretty hot and long this time a' year.

YOUNG MAN: Yeah. I know.

MECHANIC: Even the all year arounders usually leave 'round about now. They migrate around May or June at the latest, then come back toward the tail end of September.

YOUNG MAN: Where do they go?

MECHANIC: Oh, some move into the San Berdoo Valley, some even go to Hollywood, L.A., around in there.

YOUNG MAN: No kidding.

MECHANIC: Yeah. You come here from there and they go there from here. Crazy.

YOUNG MAN: Crazy.

MECHANIC: I suppose what with all the earthquake scares and riots and all, there's gonna be a lot more folks movin' out here in the desert.

YOUNG MAN: Yeah. I suppose.

The MECHANIC fiddles around with some wires under the car. The YOUNG MAN is getting impatient.

MECHANIC: Well, you're gettin' paid good for your work so why should you care. How much do you get for a movie anyway?

YOUNG MAN: It depends.

MECHANIC: At least a thousand, right?

YOUNG MAN: At least.

MECHANIC: Where'd you go to college?

YOUNG MAN: I didn't.

MECHANIC: Me neither. I'm in the wrong racket though. You know how many months I gotta work to clear a thousand? Take a guess.

YOUNG MAN: A million months. Look, what about my car? Can I get going pretty soon?

MECHANIC: Sure, sure. . . .

> A pistol falls from under the car onto the ground. The MECHANIC looks at it then at the YOUNG MAN. The YOUNG MAN bends down and picks it up.

Say, you better hadn't let the Ranger catch you with that thing, son. No firearms allowed in the National Monument.

YOUNG MAN: Oh, it's all right. It's not mine. I'm taking it to a friend of mine who lives on the desert. It's his. I had it cleaned for him and put a new chamber in. He's a prospector so he never gets a chance to come into town much. So I told him I'd do it for him.

MECHANIC: Well I never heard of no prospector using a weapon like that.

> Sound of a car coming up fast and screeching to a stop. The YOUNG MAN tries to hide the gun in his pants but it won't fit so he just sticks his hand inside his shirt with the pistol bulging out. The MAN from the first scene rushes on from stage right.

MAN: Oh——oh——help——I need some help. Anyone. You've got to come quick. Help——

MECHANIC: Take her easy there, mister. Catch your breath. I'll get you something to set on.

> The MECHANIC goes off right and comes back with a wooden crate. The MAN is panting and

looking at the YOUNG MAN who is getting up-
tight. The MECHANIC sets down the crate and sits
the MAN down.

Here now. Here. Sit down for a second and get your
breath back.

MAN: Oh——you've got to send help.

MECHANIC: What's the problem now?

MAN: My wife, Honey. My wife. She——

YOUNG MAN: What about my car!

MECHANIC: What *about* your wife?

MAN: She's——she's been attacked.

MECHANIC: Attacked?

YOUNG MAN: Come off it.

MAN: By a snake.

MECHANIC: You mean she got bit? Was it a rattler?

MAN: A huge snake.

MECHANIC: Now calm down and try to tell me where
she was bit. It's important.

MAN: In the neck. Then——all over. All over.

The YOUNG MAN whips out the pistol and holds
it on the MECHANIC.

YOUNG MAN: Now stop fucking around and fix my car,
you dumb grease monkey!

MECHANIC: Now just a second, kid.

MAN: You've got to help me. My wife's going to die!

The MAN becomes hysterical and jumps up from
the crate, rushing toward the YOUNG MAN who
fires the pistol hitting the MAN in the stomach
and sending him backwards. He lies in a heap,
dead. The MECHANIC moves toward him. The
YOUNG MAN stops him with the gun.

YOUNG MAN: Hold it! Get my car down off the rack!
Hurry up! Get it down!

MECHANIC: You're in some pickle now, son.

YOUNG MAN: Don't say anything. Just get my car down!

MECHANIC: And what if I don't?

YOUNG MAN: Then *I'll* get it down!

He fires again, hitting the MECHANIC in the
stomach. The MECHANIC falls back on top of the
MAN's body. The YOUNG MAN rushes to a lever

under the lift and pulls it. Nothing happens. He yanks it to the right and left. Nothing happens. He kicks the lever. Still nothing.

YOUNG MAN: Come on, come on! Work, mother fucker! Work! Why won't you work! Work! Please work! Please! Pretty please! Work. Oh work! Please work! Work! Work! Work! Work! Work!

Sound of bell in gas station and car pulling up and stopping off left. The YOUNG MAN runs off right leaving the car up on the rack. Sound of jet passing overhead. Silence. A man is heard whistling off left.

VOICE: Shorty! Anybody home?

A FOREST RANGER comes on from left, dressed in uniform and sipping a Coke. He just wanders onstage without seeing the bodies and glancing up at the car.

BLACKOUT

"Pipeline" by the HOLY MODAL ROUNDERS comes on in the dark.

Float Me Down Your Pipeline

Float me down your pipeline sometime
I came here with my guidebook
With my license in hand
But the landing field keeps slipping out of line
And this ain't what they told me I'd find
The biggest laugh around here
Is the changing ground here
Down in the alley
When the game gets fast
There ain't no piece of paper
Gonna save your ass
So float me down your pipeline sometime

I need to find a guideline sometime
These old concentric circles
Are spinning me out
And everything I do goes down in doubt

So won't you show me which way is out
I guess this is the moment
When I might need a friend
Backwater waiting for my mind to break
Guess you're the only chance that's left to take
So float me down your pipeline sometime.

by ANTONIA

SCENE 3

The song fades into the sound of the sidewinder's rattle. The blinking red eyes are seen in the dark.

The lights come up on BILLY, an old prospector with a long gray beard, floppy hat, yellow shirt, red bandana, overalls with suspenders, long boots, pots and pans attached to his waist so they clang when he walks, and a pack on the floor beside him. He is sitting on his haunches directly behind HONEY who is lying frozen in the same position with the snake coiled around her body. BILLY talks to her in a calm soothing voice. The snake continues its rhythms.

BILLY: Well, that was just about nineteen-o-six when they was a' gettin' all het up about the area. Yep. If you'd a told any one a' them ten thousand folks back then that their boom town weren't a gonna have nothin' left but a shanty and some wild burros come nineteen-seventy-one, why there wouldn't a' been a one of 'em would a paid ya' no never mind. No sir. They smelled that gold pumpin' through the rhyolite and there weren't no one gonna stop that town from boomin'. 'Course there's still a few old tough ones like myself and Death Valley Smiley and Wheelburro Tex and Dapper Tommy Thompson and some a the others. Still loco enough to believe them old yarns.

HONEY makes a low groaning sound and starts to undulate with the sidewinder. She seems to get more and more turned on as BILLY tries to calm her.

BILLY: Now, ya' don't want to move around much there, Miss. I've seen these here critters strike so fast it'd make yer head swim. 'Course now this one's a bit extra sized. Can't say fer certain when I ever did see such a big one. If it weren't the middle of the American desert here I'd even be prone to say she was a boa constrictor. Like they have in Africa and such. 'Course that's a tad far fetched. Never can tell though. Them Air Force boys pull some mighty funny stunts out here. There's a bunch of 'em stationed just close by here ya' know. Over at Fort George. Maybe you seen 'em roarin' by. Roarin' by. Testin' the sky fer holes or somethin'. Nothin' else to do. Could be one a them fellas dropped this big feller right out a' the sky. Aint likely. I mean, first off they'd have to fly off to Africa to get the damned thing in the first place. Then fly it back out here. Ain't likely. Could just be though. They get so gall-darned bored I'll betcha'. Testin' all the time. Sure. Nothin' else to do but fly around makin' explosions. Droppin' snakes. Probably think it's funny. Get a big charge outa' trappin' young ladies. I'll betcha'.

> HONEY has an orgasm as the YOUNG MAN comes running on from right. BILLY smiles and stands up, his arms outstretched. The YOUNG MAN crosses down left paying no attention to HONEY or the sidewinder.

BILLY: Jimmy boy! Right on time. Just like clockwork. Look at what I found here, Danny. Just lyin' here while I was a waitin'. Come by to wait and here she was, all bound up and chokin' to death. So I tried to tell her a thing or two about the desert and snakes and such.

YOUNG MAN: Come here, Billy.

BILLY: What ya' got there, Johnny? I been a' waitin' like ya' told me. I don't ferget.

> BILLY crosses down to the YOUNG MAN who takes out the gun and runs his hands over it. The YOUNG MAN turns to BILLY and holds out the gun for him to see. BILLY takes it.

BILLY: Oh, now Jimmy, ya' shore got a nice one. Ya' needn't a' got such a nice rod fer that half breed. He don't know the difference 'tween a B.B. gun and a thirty-odd-six.

YOUNG MAN: I want him to have this one. You'll see that he gets it, Billy?

BILLY: Shore. I'll hand it right over. No trouble 'tall.

YOUNG MAN: Now listen carefully. I've run into some trouble so I'm going to have to do some doubling back. Now tell Mickey Free to meet me right here tomorrow at sunrise. You got that?

BILLY: Sunrise tomorrow.

YOUNG MAN: Right. Now tell him to come alone and not to bring the gun. I'll explain the rest when he gets here.

BILLY: Alone and no iron. I savvy, Johnny.

YOUNG MAN: O.K. Now get going.

BILLY: What about the lady?

YOUNG MAN: What lady?

> BILLY motions to HONEY who again has become rigid as the sidewinder blinks and spits and rattles.

She's got nothing to do with me. Now get going and remember what I just told you.

BILLY: O.K., Danny. Adios!

> The YOUNG MAN hurries off right. BILLY walks up to HONEY and around behind her. He picks up his pack and slings it over his shoulder. He bends over and looks into HONEY's face. Her eyes are into a blank stare. BILLY shakes his head and goes off left twirling the pistol and singing softly.

"A beautiful bird in a gilded cage.
A beautiful sight to see.
You may think she's happy and free from fear.
She ain't though she seems to be."

> The lights fade to

BLACKOUT

as BILLY exits.
"Generalonely" is heard in the blackout.

Generalonely

Sad news has come to town, the blues it came in
Right up through my front door, looked like it was
   staying
My aide de camp replied, "What's that it's saying"
The blues has come to town looks like it's staying

A General am I and a General only
Generally I'm generally lonely
A General am I and a General only
Generally I'm generally lonely

Generally I'm generally lonely
Generally but a General only
Then my aide de camp replied, "The legal tenderly
And now we are all registered blues members"

by STEVE WEBER

SCENE 4

The song fades out as the lights come up on an
Air Force COLONEL seated behind his desk with a
glass of brandy and a cigar, his foot up on the
desk. Across from him is a CAPTAIN, also sipping
brandy but slightly drunker than the COLONEL.
Behind them is a huge colorful map of the U.S.
An American eagle. Photographs of jets in flight.
Trophies on the desk.

COLONEL: Trouble with that bitch was, you just didn't
get her out in the world enough, Henry. A young
bitch like that's gotta come in contact with a whole
lotta people and noise. Otherwise you'll never get
her cured. There's a world of difference between your
dog and your bitch. A lot of breeders forget that. Just
like people. Now a woman's just naturally gonna be
more sensitive than a man. No two ways about it.
Same with a dog.

CAPTAIN: I don't know about that, Warner. I've seen some pretty spookey males in my day.

COLONEL: Sure! You're gonna get your share of gun-shy males too. No way around it. That's that old argument. That heredity and environment thing. I wouldn't be the one to take sides for either. They both got their strong points. But I'll tell you this much. You can't expect a young pup, male or female, to grow up into a healthy bird dog if he's had a bad surrounding when he was little. Like a pup who's been around a lot of little brats pestering him all the time and making loud noises right in his ear. He's not gonna grow up as brave as the pup who had a quiet peaceful home. Have some more brandy, Henry.

CAPTAIN: No. No thanks.

COLONEL: Aw, go on. Don't cost me nothin'.

CAPTAIN: All right.

The COLONEL pours him another drink.

Say, Warner, you know that big stud dog you got? The one with the speckled chest?

COLONEL: Bruce. Sure. Oh no. I'm reading your mind right now, Captain.

CAPTAIN: What?

COLONEL: I suppose you want to breed that gun-shy bitch of yours to my male.

CAPTAIN: Well her conformation makes up for her temperament. You gotta admit that much. She's got one of the best heads you'll see in a long time.

COLONEL: A pretty head don't mean she can smell birds. Some of the best hunting dogs I've seen have been ugly as sin. Now come on, Henry. You don't want my Bruce to go getting a trauma right off the bat. He's only sired two litters so far, and if she gives him a bad bite he might never get over it. I mean I gotta think of his future too.

CAPTAIN: She's not gonna go biting your male, Warner. Besides, we could muzzle her.

COLONEL: Oh no. Absolutely not! I never muzzled a dog in my life and I never will. I don't care if it's the meanest dog around. That's something you just don't do to an animal. I saw a dog almost suffocate on its own saliva once. Just from that very same thing.

CAPTAIN: Well we wouldn't go off and leave them alone.
I'd stand right there and hold her.

COLONEL: I'm sorry, Henry. It's just not the way I like
to breed my dogs. It's a very touchy game. You're
dealing with living animals, not machines.

A loud knock on the door.

Come in!

A CADET enters and salutes stiffly.

At ease.

CADET: Colonel, sir. Your presence is requested immediately at the laboratory, sir. It seems the sidewinder
computer has escaped.

The COLONEL stands abruptly, knocking over his
brandy glass. The CAPTAIN tries to get out of his
seat but he's too drunk.

COLONEL: Escaped! What do you mean escaped! It's
under strict surveillance!

CADET: I'm not sure, sir. That was the message from
General Browser, sir.

COLONEL: How could a computer escape? Answer me
that!

CADET: I have no idea, sir. That was the whole message,
sir. General Browser and Dr. Vector are waiting in the
lab, sir.

COLONEL: Tell them I'm on my way. Go on!

CADET: Yes sir!

The CADET salutes and exits.

COLONEL: Of all the goddamned nerve! Escaped!

BLACKOUT

"Catch Me" comes on in the dark.

Catch Me

Catch me if you can while I last 'cause there's nothin' to
keep me around

Touch me with a ten foot pole and I'll make both your
feet leave the ground

Watch me if you can't come along 'cause I got enough
  here for us both
It's eating me inside out but I know that it won't stunt
  my growth

It doesn't matter what you try it's all about take and give
It doesn't matter how you die but only how you live

I'm burning up ninety-nine pounds of rubber up here in
  the sky
I don't know just how I got wheels or why it's so easy to
  fly
I can't see for millions of miles it looks like a fog up
  ahead
Catch me if I crash to the ground and make sure I don't
  land on my head

It doesn't matter what you try it's all about take and give
It doesn't matter how you die but only how you live

by SAM SHEPARD

SCENE 5

The song fades into the rattle of the sidewinder.
The blinking red eyes. Hissing. The lights come
up on HONEY, still entangled by the sidewinder.
  Three men are standing behind her, watching
the sidewinder intently. MICKEY FREE is in the
middle with two Apache INDIANS standing slightly
behind him, one on either side. All three have
long flowing black hair which falls down over
their shoulders.
  The two INDIANS are very dark skinned and
dressed in the renegade Apache costume of the
late eighteen hundreds, but unique from each
other. Knee length moccasin boots, rawhide
pants, long loin cloths with Mexican type designs,
heavy shirts, suit jackets captured from way-

ward whites, tooth and bone necklaces, straight brimmed black hats with Mexican silver coin headbands, two wide belts of ammunition crisscrossing from shoulder to waist, knives sticking out of the tops of their moccasins and 30.30 rifles from the cavalry times.

MICKEY FREE is a half breed: Mexican, Irish, Apache; his skin is lighter but he looks Indian. He's half blind in his right eye so he squints it constantly and moves his head in strange ways. He is dressed like the Apaches but flashier in spots and more heavily armed. His prize weapon is a huge Bowie knife with a turquoise and silver handle which he keeps in a beaded deerskin sheath which hangs down over his crotch, like a cock piece.

All three of them watch HONEY and the sidewinder in silence as she goes through throes of agony-ecstasy with the sidewinder continuing his relentless moves and rhythms. Finally her eyes open and she looks up at MICKEY FREE.

HONEY: Help me.

The INDIANS are silent. MICKEY FREE stares at her with his one good eye.

Please. Help me.

MICKEY turns to the INDIANS. The INDIANS speak to him in Apache. The language should sound like a mixture of Spanish and Oriental.

1ST INDIAN: Natcha la oot. Gracha om laate.
2ND INDIAN: No me ta santo. Este un gran mal muerta.

MICKEY FREE is silent. He turns back to HONEY and looks down at her.

HONEY: Please, help me. Please. Help me.

MICKEY takes out his huge Bowie knife and kneels down beside HONEY. He strokes the head of the sidewinder with his left hand very gently and makes a soothing sound in his throat. Suddenly his left hand seizes the neck of the sidewinder and squeezes it. The jaws pop open revealing huge fangs.

He makes one sudden slash with the knife and the head comes off, leaving the body writhing and squirming on HONEY, who screams and goes into hysteria. She flings the body downstage and collapses. The body writhes as MICKEY slowly stands up still holding the head with the eyes still blinking.

The INDIANS make sounds of approval and touch the snake's head. MICKEY smiles and wipes the knife off on his pants, then puts it back in the sheath. He drops the head into a beaded pouch which he wears on his waist. The body stops writhing. The VOICE of the YOUNG MAN is heard off right.

YOUNG MAN'S VOICE: Mickey? That you, Mickey?

MICKEY and the INDIANS look off right. HONEY is in delirium daze.

HONEY: Dukie?

The YOUNG MAN comes on from right.

YOUNG MAN: Mickey! You made it!

He looks at HONEY.

I see you're free now. Why don't you split?

HONEY looks bewildered. The YOUNG MAN moves center downstage, MICKEY follows with the INDIANS close behind. The YOUNG MAN takes two plasticene bags filled with white powder out of his crotch and sets them on the ground. He sits down cross-legged. MICKEY sits beside him with the bags between them. The INDIANS stand behind.

YOUNG MAN: Did Billy give you the gun?
MICKEY: Yes.
YOUNG MAN: Is it all right?
MICKEY: Yes.
YOUNG MAN: Good. Now——

MICKEY: I'll need more than one gun.

YOUNG MAN: O.K. I'll see what I can do. How many do you want?

MICKEY: Two more.

YOUNG MAN: O.K. I'll get them by next week. How's that?

MICKEY: Good. Give them to Billy. He give them to me.

YOUNG MAN: Yeah. Now. . . .

MICKEY: You have a ready roll?

YOUNG MAN: Sure.

> He takes out a cigarette and hands it to MICKEY.

MICKEY: You have two more?

> The YOUNG MAN offers the pack to the two INDIANS.

YOUNG MAN: Here. Keep the pack.

> The INDIANS take the pack and take out ciga-
> rettes. MICKEY puts out his hand to the INDIANS.
> They give the pack to MICKEY who puts it in the
> top of his moccasin. MICKEY takes out a butane
> lighter from his other moccasin and lights his
> cigarette, then he lights the INDIANS'.

YOUNG MAN: Now, this is the stuff. It's more than enough to do the trick.

MICKEY: Trick?

YOUNG MAN: Yeah. Trick, job.

MICKEY: Job.

YOUNG MAN: Now your job is very easy but you have to pull it off without fail. There's a lot of people count-ing on you. People you've never seen before. You're going to mean a lot to them if everything works the way we have it run down. Now the reason we've come to you is because you know the layout of Fort George probably better than anyone in the desert, mainly because you helped them get it started.

MICKEY: Yes. I find them low ground.

YOUNG MAN: Right. And that's valuable to us because now you can take these bags directly to their reservoir and dump them without anyone getting suspicious. Now here's the plan: tomorrow, you and your friends ride into the fort at high noon. You go straight to the commanding officer's headquarters and ask to speak to General Browser. They'll ask you what you want to see him about and you tell them that you're looking for work.

MICKEY: Work!

YOUNG MAN: Yeah. Work, job. You need a job. And then they'll tell you they're very sorry but they have no work, come back some other time, and you say all right and start to leave. Then you ask them if it's all right if you water your horses out at the reservoir because you've been riding all day and they're really wiped out. Then they'll probably give you a pass to enter the reservoir area. If they don't, then ask them for one. Then you take the pass, get back on your horses, with the dope in your saddle bags.

MICKEY: Dope?

YOUNG MAN: Yeah, the stuff! And ride into the reservoir area. I doubt if they'll have a guard on duty there but if they do I'm sure you can handle him. Just show him the pass and play dumb. When you get to the reservoir, dismount and water your horses. Then just take the dope out of the saddle bags and cut the bags open and let all the powder fall into the water. Be sure to put the empty plastic bags back in your saddle bags. Don't leave them at the reservoir. Then just get back on your horse and ride away. You got it?

MICKEY: Yes.

YOUNG MAN: Good.

MICKEY: I have more friends who wish to help too. They say anything that will make the silver birds leave the skies will be pleasing to the Spider Woman.

YOUNG MAN: Tell them to wait. Anything can happen. We'll let them know.

MICKEY gives an order to the INDIANS.

MICKEY: Nanza nienta paz. Para los caballos.

The INDIANS go to the plasticene bags. One of them has a leather saddlebag which he opens while the other one puts the bags inside. MICKEY stands up with the YOUNG MAN. They shake hands by clasping each other's wrists.

YOUNG MAN: I'll come to your place next week and let you know how things went.

MICKEY: Good.
YOUNG MAN: Good luck.
MICKEY: Hasta luego.

> The three of them go offstage left. The YOUNG
> MAN looks at HONEY who is staring at him with
> a blank gaze.

YOUNG MAN: What're you looking at?

> He reaches into his pocket and pulls out a small
> leather pouch with a zipper. He sits down and
> zips it open. He takes out a needle, an eye-dropper
> syringe and a small vial of liquid. He lifts up his
> T shirt and feels for his belt. He notices he's not
> wearing one.

Hey! Do you have a belt on you? Or a tie?
HONEY: Belt? No.

> He looks around the stage angrily. He sees the
> sidewinder's body. He reaches for it and grabs
> the rattle end, pulling it close to him. He fixes
> up the needle, opens the vial and draws the liquid
> up into the syringe.

Do you have any water?
YOUNG MAN: Yeah. It's in the canteen.

> HONEY scrambles to the canteen, opens it and
> takes a long drink. The YOUNG MAN struggles
> with the snake's body, trying to tie it as a tourni-
> quet around his left arm.

HONEY: What are you doing?
YOUNG MAN: Trying to get off. What does it look like.
Fuck! Would you come here for a second.
HONEY: What?
YOUNG MAN: Just come here. I'm not going to bite you.

> HONEY crawls to him on her hands and knees.

Would you wrap this tight around my arm and just
hold it.
HONEY: Are you crazy? That thing almost strangled me
to death.
YOUNG MAN: Well now it's your turn to strangle it. Come
on. Look. He's dead.

He shakes the sidewinder's body in her face. She jumps back.

Dead! Just do it for a favor. O.K.? Please? Come on. Be a sport.

She takes the snake and wraps it around his left arm.

Pull. Now just hold on to it. Don't let go.

HONEY pulls the snake tight. The YOUNG MAN rubs his vein and jabs the needle in. HONEY makes a shriek and jumps back, letting the snake go. The YOUNG MAN lets out a yell.

Oh fuck! You stupid cunt! You almost broke my point! My last point! You almost ripped out my vein! Jesus Christ!

He rubs his arm in agony.

HONEY: I'm sorry. I didn't know you were gonna poke yourself.

YOUNG MAN: I told you not to let go. Now would you wrap it tight and hold on this time.

HONEY: All right.

She goes through the same thing again with the snake. He jabs the needle in this time and gets a hit.

YOUNG MAN: All right. Now let go slowly. Slowly. Easy. That's it.

She slowly releases her grip on the sidewinder. It falls to the floor. The YOUNG MAN relaxes and smiles at HONEY.

Now. That wasn't so bad, was it?

HONEY: Are you a diabetic?

YOUNG MAN: Yeah. I need lots of sugar.

HONEY: Could I have some?

YOUNG MAN: You think you need it?

HONEY: I can't seem to get up any energy. I mean you use it for energy, don't you? That darn snake knocked the wind out of me.

YOUNG MAN: I suppose I could spare some. Just to get

you up on your feet. Don't come asking me for more, though.

HONEY: Oh, I won't. I just need a boost. Boy, I'm really glad you came along. You know? I thought I was gonna be stuck out here forever. There's a lot of creepy people out here. You're the first decent person I've seen.

He wraps the snake around her right arm.

YOUNG MAN: All right. Now grab both ends and pull tight. Close your eyes and don't look. O.K.?

She follows his orders as the YOUNG MAN fills the syringe and HONEY talks with her eyes closed. The lights fade out to black as the YOUNG MAN shoots her up.

HONEY: It's not going to hurt, is it? I've had enough pain for one day. I just have to get up enough energy to look for Dukie. He's my husband. He just all of a sudden ran off some place to get some help and I haven't seen him since. We were on our way to Las Vegas to get a divorce. It's not that we weren't happy or anything. We were very happy. We just needed a change you know. A sort of a vacation from each other. So we decided to make it a vacation together. You know what I mean. I mean so long as we were getting divorced we might as well make it a vacation. Kill two birds with one stone. Then this snake got me and I don't even know what happened. One minute we were together and the next minute we were separated. Just like that. I guess this desert does funny things to your brain or something. It's not going to hurt me, is it?

BLACKOUT

HONEY screams. "Euphoria" is heard in the dark.

Euphoria

Ma's out here switchin' in the kitchen
And dad's in the living room grousin' and a bitchin'
And I'm out here kicking the gong for "Euphoria"

Euphoria when your mind goes wheelin' and a walkin'
Your inside voices go squealin' and a squawkin'
Floating around on a belladonna cloud
Singing Euphoria

There's a man in the corner underneath a table
He sat makin' faces at a union label
He pitched his ears and then he rolled his eyes
And whispered "Euphoria"

Euphoria when your mind goes wheelin' and a walkin'
Your inside voices go squealin' and a squawkin'
Floating around on a belladonna cloud
Singing Euphoria

I went for a walk and just got back
I saw a junkie mother boosting Similac
She had her baby on her back and her works in her hand
She hollered "Euphoria"

Euphoria when your mind goes wheelin' and a walkin'
Your inside voices go squealin' and a squawkin'
Floating around on a belladonna cloud
Singing Euphoria

Pinched Eve on the bottom, patted Adam on the back
Smiled at the serpent and it winked back
Took a bite from the apple with two bites gone
And hollered "Euphoria"

Euphoria when your mind goes wheelin' and a walkin'
Your inside voices go squealin' and a squawkin'
Floating around on a belladonna cloud
Singing Euphoria

by ROBIN REMAILY
Copyright—Windfall Music 1968

SCENE 6

The song fades out. The lights slowly come up on a '57 Chevy convertible. Three Blacks are sitting in the car. BLOOD is driving. BLADE and DUDE sit in the back. Above them hanging in midair is a huge hot dog sign. A CARHOP enters from left and walks up to the car. She is young and dressed in a stupid white mini outfit with a funny hat, a checkbook and pencil.

CARHOP: Can I help you guys?

BLOOD (*to the two in back*): What do you want?

BLADE: Let me have a cheeseburger, a chocolate malt and a order a fries.

DUDE: Yeah. Same thing for me except make it vanilla.

CARHOP: The malt?

BLADE: Right.

CARHOP: Say, are you guys with the Panthers?

DUDE: No, we're with the Rams.

BLOOD: Let me have a B.L.T. on whole wheat toast with mayo.

CARHOP: A B.L.T. on whole wheat.

BLOOD: And a large milk.

CARHOP: Sure. You know I've been wanting to talk to some of your people for a long time. I go to City College and it seems like there's this whole huge gap in dialogue between what we're trying to do and what you're trying to do. You know what I mean? Like I can really dig this whole unity thing that you guys are into but it seems like we could be doing something to help bind it all together. You know. I mean you people have such a groovy thing going.

BLOOD: Yeah, right.

CARHOP: I mean all this shit about the pigs, man. I mean fuck the pigs. Forget all those gray people. We're not going to turn on any of those zombies. We gotta find our own people. Turn ourselves on. Make something happen for us.

DUDE: For us?

CARHOP: Yeah, us. You and me. Fuck them. All that

festering bullshit is just going to collapse anyway. I mean I gotta work to pay for my school but once that's over man, I'm gone. You know? I mean I'm going to go out and help organize, help get it together. Because if we don't get it together pretty soon we're gonna be had. Am I right?

BLADE: Right.

CARHOP: And I'm not just doing a rap to make myself feel good either. Because I got nothing to lose. Least of all this shitty job. I mean I can see where things are at. With you guys it's all laid out. With me it's different. I got a lot of guessing to do. With you it's armed struggle. I'm for that. I think it's a necessary step. A revolution begins when a faction seizes power and begins to use it to change society. Armed struggle comes before the revolution. Armed struggle begins when the oppressed people pick up guns and are willing to die for the revolution. I'm willing. I know you guys are. I got a gun right in my house man and I'm ready to use it too.

BLOOD: Good. What kind is it?

CARHOP: What? The gun? I'm not sure. A thirty-eight or something. But listen, we can't afford to compromise anymore. Some people are saying all they want is a piece of the American pie. Well we can't have a piece of that pie because that pie exploits our brothers in Vietnam, in Latin America and in Africa.

BLOOD: Let me have a piece of cherry pie with that too.

CARHOP: Cherry pie?

BLOOD: Yeah. With the B.L.T.

CARHOP: Oh. O.K. All right. One cherry pie. Right. I'll be right back.

> She writes it down on her checkbook and exits right.

BLOOD: Now, down to business.

DUDE: Yeah, what's the story with this flower child in the desert? You really trust him to deliver the goods?

BLOOD: Don't worry, once that dope takes hold, the Air Force is going to be doing some mighty funny things.

BLADE: How's it supposed to work anyway?

BLOOD: Mickey Free makes the drop. Right?

BLADE: Right.

BLOOD: The pilots get a good taste of supersonic water. They start feeling funny. They hear voices. They see things in the air. They hear music. They get stoned like they never been before in their lives.

DUDE: Then what?

BLOOD: In the middle of the night they all get up in unison like Dracula and his sisters and walk straight out into the night. They climb into their sleek super duper F-one-elevens and take off. They fly straight for a little island just south of Miami whereupon they land and await further instructions.

DUDE: Sounds pretty shaky to me.

BLOOD: How come?

DUDE: I don't know, it's like James Bond or something. Why don't we just go in and take the thing over?

BLADE: Yeah, I can't see getting involved with this hippie cat, Blood. His mind's been burned out. The drug thing just isn't going to pull it off.

BLOOD: We gotta give it some time. It's just a step.

DUDE: Watch it, here comes the S.D.S.

The CARHOP enters again with their order. She walks up to them.

CARHOP: Say listen, I'm sorry I go so carried away before but I really meant what I said.

BLOOD: Right. You got the milk?

CARHOP: Milk? Oh. Yeah. Here it is. I mean we can't debate whether we want revolution or whether we don't want revolution because for our survival we're going to have to make revolution. Right? I mean I guess you guys already know that.

BLADE: Pass the french fries.

BLACKOUT

"Synergy" is heard.

Synergy

CHORUS: Superman's on the can contemplating synergy

Lone Ranger on the range and Dr. Strange got synergy

Cool heads certainly agree concerning synergy
Likewise Liberace's momma
Donald Duck and Dalai Lama
Yes sir!

Come along, sing with me sing a song of synergy
Find that peace in your soul
We're all one and heaven is our goal

CHORUS

Synergy will get us all and it's going to be a ball
Kick that gong, ring that bell, synergy will save us all
   from hell

CHORUS

Be a friend, lend a hand, try your best to understand
We are all born alone, but the light of love can lead us
   home

CHORUS

Get undressed, plant a tree, make love to machinery
Throw away all the locks, open up the jails and stop the
   clocks

CHORUS

We can have paradise right now at a bargain price
Heaven is ours to make, peace on earth is there for us
   to take

CHORUS

by PETER STAMPFEL & ANTONIA

SCENE 7

The Air Force Laboratory at Fort George. Test
tubes, vials, bunsen burners, a general clutter of
chemical and electronic gadgets. In the middle
of all this is DOCTOR VECTOR, sitting in a wheelchair, dressed in a white chemist's smock. He is
very tiny and his entire body is twisted and bent.
He wears extra thick dark glasses and elevator
shoes and speaks with a weird shifting accent.
When he wants to move his wheelchair he presses
a button on one of the arms and the chair propels
itself electronically. On either side of him are
GENERAL BROWSER, obviously pissed off but trying
to keep his cool, and COLONEL WARNER who goes
into fits of temper but snaps out of it by the
GENERAL's presence.

COLONEL: I've never in my whole career in the United
   States Air Force heard of such a half-cocked idea as
   this one! I mean freedom to experiment to my mind
   has always meant for the experimenter, I mean the
   person or persons doing the experiment, not the goddamn experiment itself! Now that's just never ever
   been done before, Doctor Vector, and I for one . . . .
GENERAL: Now settle down, Warner. I'm sure the doctor
   had his reasons for allowing this to happen. What's
   done is done. The fact is that I should have personally
   seen to it that the arrangements for Operation Sidewinder were made more clear to everyone involved.
   Including myself. I certainly had no idea you were off
   on a tangent like this, Doctor Vector.
DR. VECTOR: What tangent? No tangent. This now is
   marking the beginning of the stage I had so long
   awaited. You should both be beaming with the joy I
   now feel. The sidewinder computer has now chosen
   to go off on its own accord. It has chosen to be free and
   exist on its own. For weeks I have watched it writhing
   and squirming with its wonderful powerful body.
   Sidewinding its way around its little artificial desert.
   Searching for a way out. Searching every corner. Its

magnificent head straining toward the top of the glass then back down to the bottom. Knowing that all around, outside, out in the real world was a desert and sky so vast and so free. A captive with more cosmic secrets than a man could learn from the whole of history. Finally I saw the decision lay in my hands, gentlemen. In my hands. It was up to me to either keep this creature in its cage and continue to feed it my steady diet of limited knowledge or to set it free and have it discover its true potential. Do you realize the magnitude of this action? It means for the first time ever we can begin to study the effects of the machine's own decisions on its own survival. For the first time in history we shall see if it is possible to produce a machine with its own brain and its own synthetic form of life and have it survive on its own without our constant presence and supervision. All this and still have it retain the willingness to achieve the purpose for which it was programmed. Oh sure, you say it's already been done before. Some biochemist in New Jersey might be maybe come up with some small germ of plastic bacteria that he says is life. All year they watch it under glass and give it injections and change the light and switch around the soils but so what! That is no experiment! Not like the sidewinder! The sidewinder computer this very minute is surviving on one of the most inhospitable deserts in the world! Surviving by its own synthetic wits! And you two talk as though we have thrown away a lifetime! Bah! The Army should never have nothing to do with Science!

COLONEL: This is the Air Force, Doctor! And it's not a lifetime that you've thrown away but almost two billion dollars! How does that grab you?

GENERAL: Now wait a minute, Colonel. The Doctor seems to feel that his sidewinder computer will perform better and reveal more information to us if left on its own. That's all well and good. However, I'm left with certain uncertainties, Doctor.

DR. VECTOR: Yah, General?

GENERAL: From a purely pragmatic point of view, now that the computer has escaped, or in your words ventured off on its own, how is it possible for you to program it or even trace its existence, if in fact it is still alive. I mean . . . .

COLONEL: Alive! Judas Priest!

DR. VECTOR: Gentlemen, gentlemen! Operation Sidewinder was begun by the government in late 1964 Yah? (Yah!) in an effort to produce a tracing computer which would help to solve the questions of whether or not unidentified flying objects actually existed. Oui? (Oui!) Since that time we have discovered that they do in fact exist Dah? (Dah!) and the next step, as you both are well aware, was of course to trace their flight patterns in an effort to learn their trade routes and possibly the planet or star from where they are living.

COLONEL: Now come off it, Doc. We all know that Constellation Pegasus has . . . .

GENERAL: Please, Colonel! Let the Doctor finish.

DR. VECTOR: At this stage it became apparent to me that all man-made efforts to produce this type of information were useless and that a much more sophisticated form of intelligence was necessary. A form of intelligence which, being triggered from the mind of man, would eventually, if allowed to exist on its own, transcend the barriers of human thought and penetrate an extraterrestrial consciousness. This is when I began my studies of the Western rattlesnakes and experimenting with the possibilities of their rhythmic movements being directly connected with the movements of the planets and the flight patterns of the UFO's. These studies resulted in the initial design for my sidewinder computer. Now, whether or not the sidewinder will be able to attain this realm of extraterrestrial consciousness is something none of us will know until we are ready. One thing is for certain, the sidewinder must have complete freedom to discover this realm for itself. And gentlemen, if it succeeds we will be the first to know. Think of it, gentlemen! We will be in direct contact with these flying objects and eventually with those who operate and control them!

COLONEL: What a bunch a' horse shit!

BLACKOUT

"Dusty Fustchuns" comes on in the dark.

"Dusty Fustchuns"

Don't leave me dying in the desert
Don't leave me dangling in the dust
I don't wanna live here with these here lizards
They look at me with a cold and hungry lust
Big bird circlin' in the sky is a buzzard
Think he got his eye on me
The ever shiftin' sand is the only sound I hear
And that mirage over there is the only water near

I got a pound of sand in my navel
When night comes I turn into ice
At high noon brains melt like butter
No one to talk to but the toads and the mice

Devil take away these damn sand dunes
Devil take away this sun
Devil take away this dry dusty hole
This is all a mistake and
I'm cooked 'til overdone

(*Coyote howls for last verse.*)

by ROBIN REMAILY

SCENE 8

The song fades into the sound of crickets. A
coyote howls. A full moon glows in the dark.
Stars come out. The lights fade up slowly to
bluish moonlight.

    The YOUNG MAN and HONEY are lying on their
backs upstage staring at the night sky. The body
of the sidewinder is downstage left. HONEY moves
voluptuously around on her back, stretching and
unbuttoning her blouse. The YOUNG MAN just
stares at the sky.

HONEY: Oh, it's so gorgeous. A full moon. And the stars.
    I never felt so good in my whole life. Everything smells

so wild out here. Smell the yucca. It's so peaceful and nice. Hey, what's your name anyway? Do you have a name? My name's Honey. That's because my husband called me that. He said it was because of my honey hair. My yellow honey hair. Dukie said it even smelled like honey. You wanna' smell my hair? You can smell it if you want. Sometimes I even smell it. I used to all the time. When I was a little girl. I'd go in the closet and smell it. I never cut it because my Mama said that sometime . . . someday I'd make my living from my hair. That's what she told me. That I should come to Hollywood and the very next day, just from walking around the streets and everything, that someone would see my hair and ask me to come and get a screen test. And that before very long I'd be famous and rich and everything. I'd never have to worry about a man supporting me or anything because I'd have enough to support myself. And then I met Dukie and . . . .

> A shock of blue light goes off above the stage, like a huge flash bulb. Then a beam of white light goes across the sky behind them from left to right and disappears. HONEY sits up. The YOUNG MAN stays relaxed on his back. HONEY stares up at the sky.

HONEY: Hey! Did you see that!

YOUNG MAN: Shooting stars.

HONEY: Boy. I never saw one before. It looks like it's still there.

YOUNG MAN: Why should it go away?

HONEY: Well, don't they just fall and then . . . Look! Look at the way it's moving. Sideways. I'm scared.

YOUNG MAN: Why be scared of a star?

HONEY: What if it's not a star? What if it's one of those creepy saucer things?

YOUNG MAN: What if it is?

HONEY: Boy, you don't get very excited about anything, do you?

> She lies back down next to the YOUNG MAN, moving closer and trying to turn him on.

YOUNG MAN: Only when it counts.

HONEY: I'll bet you're really something when you get excited. How come you don't get a haircut?

YOUNG MAN: 'Cause my Pappy told me that one day I'd make my living from my hair.

HONEY: Are you making fun of me?

YOUNG MAN: No. It's true. My Pappy was way ahead of his time. He said, son, in a few years all a young man'll have to do to make a few bucks is just grow his hair long and set on a street corner and things'll just start happening to him. Like magic.

HONEY: Do you believe in magic?

YOUNG MAN: I used to. I walked through the crowd. I saw my best friends there. Real friends. I felt such a warm bond between us. Like we were all in the same place at the same time for the same reason.

HONEY: What are you talking about?

YOUNG MAN: And suddenly I felt free, my mind was lifting up, up, up in flight. Not like that thirteen year old wild, crazy, out of the house on Friday night feeling but something much deeper. Like nothing could hurt me. Nothing could touch my peace.

HONEY: Boy, you're really weird.

YOUNG MAN: It was like all that oppression from the month before had suddenly cracked open and left me in space. The election oppression: Nixon, Wallace, Humphrey. The headline oppression every morning with one of their names on it. The radio news broadcast, TV oppression. And every other advertisement with their names and faces and voices and haircuts and suits and collars and ties and lies. And I was all set to watch "Mission: Impossible" when Humphrey's flabby face shows up for another hour's alienation session. Oh please say something kind to us, something soft, something human, something different, something real, something—so we can believe again. His squirmy little voice answers me, "You can't always have everything your way." And the oppression of my fellow students becoming depressed. Depressed. Despaired. Running out of gas. "We're not going to win. There's nothing we can do to win." This is how it begins, I see. We become so depressed we don't fight

anymore. We're only losing a little, we say. It could
be so much worse. The soldiers are dying, the Blacks
are dying, the children are dying. It could be so much
worse. Everything must be considered in light of the
political situation. No getting around it. It could be
so much worse.

HONEY: Think about something nice.

YOUNG MAN: Let's wait till four years from now when
we can take over the Democratic Party. Teddy Kennedy is still alive. Let's not do anything at all. It can
only get worse. Let's give up. And then I walked
through the crowd of smiling people. They were loving
and happy, alive and free. You can't win all the time.
You can't always have everything your own way.
You'll be arrested. You'll be arrested, accosted, mo-
lested, tested and re-tested. You'll be beaten, you'll
be jailed, you'll be thrown out of school. You'll be
spanked, you'll be whipped and chained. But I am
whipped. I am chained. I am prisoner to all your
oppression. I am depressed, deranged, decapitated,
dehumanized, defoliated, demented and damned! I
can't get out. You can get out. You can smile and
laugh and kiss and cry. I am! I am! I am! I am! I am!
I am! I am! I am! I am! I am! I am! Tonight. In this
desert. In this space. I am.

> Another flash of blue light that seems more pro-
> longed this time. Again the beam of light goes
> across the sky from stage left to stage right. At
> the same time the body of the sidewinder lights
> up green and jumps. The rattle rattles and the
> end of the tail begins to twitch. HONEY screams
> and cuddles close to the YOUNG MAN who sits
> up slightly.

YOUNG MAN: What's the matter now?

HONEY: That snake! It's still alive! It moved!

YOUNG MAN: Bullshit.

HONEY: It did! It lit up green and moved. There! Look
at it! It twitched! Didn't you see it!

YOUNG MAN: You're just hallucinating. Relax.

HONEY: I swear it moved. Listen! Can't you hear it?
It's rattling. It's still alive! Sit up and look at it!

The YOUNG MAN lies on his back and stares at the sky. The sidewinder moves again. As HONEY watches it and talks, the sidewinder's body slowly inches its way across the stage.

HONEY: Well I don't want to get strangled again. Once is enough. It's moving again! Hey! Hey!

YOUNG MAN: Take it easy. It's all in your mind.

HONEY: It's not in my mind! It's right there! It's moving and rattling and I'm looking right at it! Why don't you look and see for yourself. Please look at it. You're scaring me. I know I'm not going crazy! Who are you anyway! Hey! Talk to me! I've told you everything about me and you haven't told me one thing. Hey!

> The YOUNG MAN suddenly grabs her and pulls her to the ground and then rolls over on top of her. He kisses her and feels her up. HONEY screams and squirms. Another flash of light from above. The beam of light across the sky. The sidewinder lights up red and twitches wildly. The rattle grows louder as it inches its way across the stage.

HONEY: What are you doing! Let go of me! Let me go! Stop! Stop it! Get off! Get off of me! My husband's going to get you for this! Dukie! Help! Help! Somebody!

> The YOUNG MAN rips off her blouse and starts kissing her tits and stomach. HONEY gets turned on and runs her fingers through his hair.

Oh. Oh. OOOOOOOOH. Yes. Yes. Oh. Lick me. Lick me. Yes. Oh. You're fantastic. Oh. Yes. Yes. Yes. Lick me! Lick me!

> The YOUNG MAN stops suddenly and stands up, straddling HONEY with his legs.

What's the matter? You can kiss me. It's all right. What's wrong? You're really weird, mister. I'm leaving. I want to leave!

> The YOUNG MAN looks up at the sky with his back to the audience and stares. HONEY begins to panic. From this point on there are more fre-

quent blasts of blue light. Each time the side-winder lights up alternately green and red and the rattling grows louder as he slithers and inches across the stage.

YOUNG MAN: It's all going to happen now.
HONEY: What is? I'm leaving here!

She tries to leave. The YOUNG MAN puts his foot gently on her chest and pushes her back down.

YOUNG MAN: You can't. We're caught. We're captured.
HONEY: Not me! Nobody's capturing me or kidnaping me or anything else! I'm free! I can come and go anywhere I like! You can't make me stay here!
YOUNG MAN: You're right.

He lets her up. She stands but can't move. She seems almost hypnotized.

HONEY: Wait a minute. Wait . . . What did you give me anyway? What was in that needle? You're no diabetic! I've seen diabetics before and you're not one of them! Who are you anyway? How did you get here? Where are you from?
YOUNG MAN: I am from the planet Crypton. No. I am from the Hollywood Hills. No. I am from Freak City. That's where I was raised anyway. A small town. A town like any other town. A town like Mama used to make with lace doilies and apple pie and incest and graft. No. It's not true. I am an American though. Despite what they say. In spite of the scandal. I am truly an American. I was made in America. Born, bred and raised. I have American scars on my brain. Red, white and blue. I bleed American blood. I dream American dreams. I fuck American girls. I devour the planet. I'm an earth eater. No. I'm a lover of peace. A peace maker. A flower child, burned by the times. Burned out. A speed freak. A Tootsie Roll, an Abazaba. I came to infect the continent. To spread my disease. To make my mark, to make myself known. To cut down the trees, to dig out the gold, to shoot down the deer, to capture the wind. But now I'm myself. Now I'm here. And it's all going to happen now. Right now. It's all going to happen.

HONEY collapses.

BLACKOUT

Bright flash of light. Beams of light go back and forth across the sky. Then back to blackness. A sonic boom. Above the proscenium a large neon "Intermission" sign in red blinks on and off continuously as the song "Alien Song" by the HOLY MODAL ROUNDERS comes on.

Alien Song

You don't have to do me no favors
You don't have to tell me no lies
Just tell me what happened to my neighbors
When all I can see is black flies

It wasn't so long that I wandered
It wasn't so long I was gone
But now I come back and there's no wooden shack
And the turnips I grew are all gone

You don't look to me like a native
The way that you move is so strange
I wish I was feeling creative
But maybe it's time for a change

Maybe I took the wrong highway
Maybe I made a mistake
But this is the creek where I caught pollywogs
And I know 'cause I just took a drink

Maybe we could make conversation
I see that your lips have no skin
There must be a simple explanation
But how come you're wearing a grin

I couldn't go back where I came from
'Cause that would just bring me back here
And this is the place I was born, bred and raised
And it doesn't seem like I was ever here

It looks like your forehead's on fire
But maybe I'm losing my grip

It sounds like your voice is a choir
And now both my feet seem to slip

Now I can see my whole body
Stranded way down by the creek
It looks so alone while it looks for its home
And it doesn't hear me while I shriek

by SAM SHEPARD

ACT TWO

SCENE 1

Black stage. The houselights go down. The sun
glows on stage and becomes brighter and brighter
revealing the '57 Chevy seen in Act One, center
stage. The three Blacks are seated inside. They
are on the desert. The radio in the car is blaring
Booker T. and the M.G.'s "Green Onions." The
Blacks sit motionless and listen to the tune for a
full sixty seconds. Then BLOOD turns the radio
off with a sharp snap. DUDE and BLADE slowly
open their doors on either side and get out of
the car. They slam the doors shut and walk to the
back of the car as BLOOD sits motionless behind
the wheel staring straight ahead.

DUDE: Keys, Blood!

BLOOD takes the keys out of the ignition and
without looking back, puts his arm out the window and tosses them back to DUDE who catches
them. DUDE unlocks the trunk and raises it.
Inside are the YOUNG MAN and HONEY with their
hands tied behind their backs and gags in their
mouths. DUDE and BLADE lift them out of the
trunk and pull them around to the downstage
side of the car and slam them up against it. The
YOUNG MAN and HONEY make muffled screams
and protests as DUDE and BLADE pull out guns
and level them at their heads, as though to
execute the two of them.

BLOOD: Hold it!

BLOOD opens his door and slides out. He walks
up to HONEY and the YOUNG MAN and stares at
them, then reaches up simultaneously with both

hands and grabs their gags and yanks them out
of their mouths.

YOUNG MAN: Hey Blood, what's . . .

BLOOD: Shut up!

HONEY: You guys better not hurt us. They got Forest
Rangers out here. They make the rounds every half
hour.

YOUNG MAN: What's going on, Blood? Did something
go wrong?

BLOOD: Yeah, something went wrong. Your friend
Mickey Free didn't make the drop.

YOUNG MAN: What? Why not? What happened?

BLOOD: You tell me.

YOUNG MAN: I left him with the dope. I trusted him completely.

BLOOD: Seems as though he took off into the desert with
a very valuable computer and just forgot all about
our plan.

YOUNG MAN: I don't know anything about a computer.

BLOOD: It also seems like there's a couple dead men in
a garage somewhere who can easily be traced to a
Volkswagen which can be easily traced to us.

YOUNG MAN: I had to shoot them. They were slowing
me down.

HONEY: You shot somebody? You never told me you
shot anybody.

YOUNG MAN: Shut up!

BLOOD: One thing I figured sure was that we could
shape a psychedelic head any which way once we
gave it the proper injections. Once we set it straight
on a few political scores. 'Course there might be such
a thing as an overdose of that technique. I mean I can
dig it. The revolution looks old fashioned once you
seen the universe. Ain't I right now. I mean all them
lovelies floatin' around the street lookin' for a taste
of acid pants and some insights into their karma and
the right sign to match up to theirs. I mean there ain't
much of a choice between balling all day and getting
high or becoming a responsible revolutionary. Now
ain't that the truth. I mean shoot, you didn't spend all
them years fightin' the draft just to get the same bullshit from a bunch of crazy Blackmen.

YOUNG MAN: O.K. man, look.

BLOOD: Oh, now he's calling me man! He speakin' my language! Yeah, brother! Bring on the chitlins! You gonna have to be a whole lot hipper than hip to get out of this mess, chump.

YOUNG MAN: I'm trying to talk to you!

BLOOD: Rap!

YOUNG MAN: I ran into a jam at a garage. The car was doing weird things. So I went into this garage to get it checked out. I was there for a couple hours trying to get it fixed. Then this crazy guy comes running into the gas station saying his wife got bit by a huge snake or something.

HONEY: When was that? You never told me about that.

YOUNG MAN: Just shut up!

HONEY: That was me he was talking about.

YOUNG MAN: Shut up! So this guy comes running in and gets the mechanic all hung up in his thing. So I shot him. I shot them both.

HONEY: That was Dukie! That was my Dukie! You shot him! You shot my Dukie!

> HONEY starts screaming and kicking at the YOUNG MAN. BLOOD gives a command and BLADE steps in and jams the gag back in HONEY's mouth. She goes on sobbing and kicking.

BLOOD (*to young man*): You're real stupid. You know that?

YOUNG MAN: Come on, Blood. I did everything you told me.

BLOOD: But nothing worked! Nothing worked! You fucked up! Now we're right back where we started.

YOUNG MAN: I can find Mickey. I'll go look for him and find out what happened.

BLOOD: There's bigger stakes now.

YOUNG MAN: What do you mean?

BLOOD: The Sidewinder Computer. That snake you heard that guy screaming about?

YOUNG MAN: What about it?

BLOOD: We want that snake. We want it bad. You dig?

> A FOREST RANGER enters from right. The Blacks are very cool. HONEY desperately tries to gesture to the RANGER.

RANGER: You folks having trouble?

BLOOD: Yeah. As a matter of fact we are. We've been trying to get to Ubehebe Crater for the past hour and a half now and we haven't been able to find it.

RANGER: Well you folks should have stopped in at the Ranger station before venturing off on your own. This desert's no place to play around in.

BLOOD: Yeah, we realized that but we just got so excited about seeing the sights that we couldn't wait.

RANGER: Things are especially dangerous now since there were two men killed not too far from here just last week. We still haven't found the killer.

BLOOD: Is that right. Well if we see anything we'll . . .

RANGER: Is the young lady all right?

BLOOD: Sure, she just got a little sunstroke.

RANGER: What's she got in her mouth?

BLOOD: A wet cloth. They say that's the best thing for a sunstroke.

RANGER: Well not stuffed in her mouth like that. She's liable to suffocate.

BLOOD: She'll be all right in a little while.

RANGER: Say, how come she's tied up like that? Now wait a minute. I'm no fool.

> BLOOD pulls out a gun and levels it at the RANGER.

BLOOD: You're the biggest fool around baby. Now drop your gun. Go on!

> There is a long pause as the RANGER considers what to do next. Suddenly he tries to draw his gun and BLOOD fires three shots into him. He falls dead. HONEY sobs through her gag. BLOOD points the gun at the YOUNG MAN's head.

BLOOD: Now you got one last chance to redeem yourself, Charlie. That extra-sized snake that Mickey Free's got is something we need. We need it bad. Now I want you to find it and bring it back to us. The head and all. You dig? Now if you goof once more I suggest that you and your foxy lady here head for south of the border and start yourself a pot farm or something 'cause we're gonna be after your ass.

> BLOOD turns the YOUNG MAN around and cuts his arms loose with a knife.

YOUNG MAN: I can travel better on my own. Can't you take her back with you?

BLOOD: She's gonna lead you to that snake boy. Now you cut her loose.

BLOOD hands the knife to the YOUNG MAN.

BLACKOUT

"Bad Karma" is played.

Bad Karma

I got that bad karma baby
Gonna lay it on you
Got that bad karma baby
Nothing better to do
And when that bad karma hits you
Gonna holler and moan
Got that bad karma baby
Gonna bring it all home
I try so hard
I try to behave
But that bad karma baby gonna lead me to my grave.

I'm as down as a wart hog on a summer day
I'm as down as a depth charge in my own sweet way
I'm a down bringing back biting evil thing doer
I was born in an outhouse and I live in a sewer
I try so hard
I try to behave
But that bad karma baby gonna lead me to my grave.

When I'm reincarnated I get meaner yet
You may think I'm the lowest it's a damn good bet
But if I ain't the lowest I'll find out who is
And if his karma's badder I will rip off his
I try so hard
I try to behave
But that bad karma baby gonna lead me to my grave.

by PETER STAMPFEL & ANTONIA

SCENE 2

The song fades out. Candles are lit on stage. Soft yellow light comes up revealing a small cave in the mountains. The home of the SPIDER LADY. She is a wizened old Indian shaman with long white hair, Mexican blankets hung around her shoulders and across her lap, long tooth and bone necklaces, turquoise rings, etc. She is seated cross-legged in the cave to stage left with several candles around her. Seated directly across from her is MICKEY FREE with the sidewinder's head held in his cupped hands and the red eyes blinking on and off and the tongue spitting out. Behind them, upstage in the cave, are the two INDIANS seen with MICKEY FREE in Act One. They are also seated cross-legged and pass a small bowl of steaming liquid back and forth between them from which they drink. Around them are their rifles, ammunition and more candles. Hanging from the roof of the cave are several long ribbons, red fox tails and religious artifacts. Bowls of incense are lit and placed in niches in the wall of the cave with smoke gently rising out of them.

MICKEY FREE: I am afraid, Spider Lady. I find myself holding a great power. I have not the wisdom to use it. Speak to me of its secret.

SPIDER LADY: A great war is about to begin. It will mark the end of the Fourth World and the preparation for the Emergence to the Fifth. Do not be afraid, Mickey Free. You have a part to play in this Emergence. Do not seek shelter. It is only materialistic people who seek to make shelters. Those who are at peace in their own hearts already are in the great shelter of life. There is no shelter for evil. Those who take no part in the making of world division are ready to resume life in another world. They are all one, brothers. The war will be a spiritual conflict with material things. Material matters will be destroyed by spiritual beings who will remain to create one world and one nation under one power, that of the Creator. The time is not far off. The head of this serpent has come to you as a sign. You must see it through to its rightful end.

MICKEY FREE: What does it mean? This spirit head.

SPIDER LADY: In the beginning there were the Star Gods. They descended to earth in flaming discs and created two great clans of man. One, the Snake Clan, the other the Lizard. To each were given tasks. The Lizard Clan was to harvest the crops and raise the children and the Snake Clan was to see to the spiritual needs of the people. For this purpose the Snake Clan was given a giant spirit snake to communicate with the Gods and keep peace in the hearts of the people. The Lizard Clan soon grew jealous and wanted the giant snake for its own. There came a day of the great tug of war between the two clans. The Lizard Clan pulling the head, the Snake Clan pulling the tail. Suddenly the serpent spirit split in two parts, the head going with the Lizard Clan, the tail going with the Snake. At that moment, it is said, the people lost all knowledge of their origin. The Gods vanished from the earth. The people were lost. The two tribes went separate ways and wandered endlessly and with no purpose. More and more people left the clans and wandered their separate ways, taking up homes and founding separate communities, until all over the earth there was mistrust and hatred. Then a vision occurred to a small group of chosen ones who today live on the high mesas of this desert. A blue star descended to earth in the form of a spirit from the Star Gods and told the people that their Emergence was at hand. It spoke of the severed halves of the ancient spirit snake and that they soon would be joined together again on a night of the great dance. That once the two halves were joined the people would be swept from the earth by a star, for they were to be saved from the destruction at hand. That soon after the spirit snake would again be pulled in half by the evil ones and the Fourth World would come to an end.

MICKEY FREE: What must I do?

SPIDER LADY: You must be strong. For too long now you have been used by the white man's cavalry, Mickey Free. You have cheated your red brothers to the south.

You have tracked and hunted down your own kind for
the white man's money. . . .

MICKEY FREE: And for my freedom! Better to hunt and
kill than to be trapped behind bars in their camp!
How could I choose! Geronimo was ready to surrender!
I had no choice!

SPIDER LADY: You must let this head speak to your heart,
Mickey Free. You must see the truth of this myth I
have told you. You can read it in the earth itself. In
the stars. Within your own conscience. Take this
powerful spirit and deliver it to those who await it. To
the Chosen Ones atop the high mesa.

MICKEY FREE: But what of the body? I have lost the
body.

SPIDER LADY: It will come. It is written. All things have
a plan, Mickey Free.

MICKEY FREE bows his head slowly to the SPIDER
LADY as the lights dim out.

"I Disremember Quite Well" is played.

BLACKOUT

I Disremember Quite Well

You'll pardon me if I act strange
but we've been out of touch
I know that time is on your side
but time can do so much.
Are you still making it with time?
I disremember quite well

Yes I can see as I come close
time has been good to you
Just for a moment's truth you almost
had the face I knew.
But now, of course, it's not for real
I disremember quite well

I used to know you when you turned
your water into wine.
You played the shell game with yourself
and won it every time.

But where are you going to keep your prize?
I disremember quite well

I used to walk on water too
and float above the sand.
And hang the stars like diamonds on my
outstretched greedy hands.
But I've forgotten how that games goes
I disremember quite well

And did you ever do whatever thing
It is you're for?
Or does an old idea like that have meaning
anymore?
The maybe that I loved has gone, but where?
I disremember quite well

by ANTONIA

SCENE 3

The song fades out. A woman STENOGRAPHER'S
VOICE *is heard in the dark.*

STENOGRAPHER'S VOICE: Ready, Captain Bovine!
CAPTAIN BOVINE'S VOICE: All right. Let's see 'em.

A large color slide is shown on the upstage wall
in the darkness. All the slides are of outlaws
from the 1800s. CAPTAIN BOVINE speaks in the
dark. The slides keep changing.

CAPTAIN BOVINE'S VOICE: Now these faces that you're
gonna see here, Billy, are all known criminals that,
as yet, we haven't been able to pin down. Besides the
young man in question here, if you happen to run
across any other faces that you might have seen on
the desert, it would be more than helpful if you
pointed them out.
BILLY'S VOICE: Nope. Not a one.

BOVINE'S VOICE: Well, take your time now. We got a whole stack to go through.

> The faces keep flashing on the wall upstage. They get faster and faster as they go on, creating a strobe effect.

Any identifying marks that you can remember? I mean besides the long hair and bare feet. That's pretty common amongst your outlaws anyhow. Any scars or things like that?

BILLY'S VOICE: Nope. Nary a one.

BOVINE'S VOICE: Did he have an accent? A limp? Anything at all would be helpful, Billy.

BILLY'S VOICE: Nope. Healthy as a yearling colt, that one.

BOVINE'S VOICE: What about the others? Any of the others ring a bell?

BILLY'S VOICE: Nope. Nary a one.

> The last slide is a full head shot of the YOUNG MAN with a mustache. It stops still.

BOVINE'S VOICE: Shall we go through 'em once more for you, Billy? You might have missed a couple and it's very important for our records.

BILLY'S VOICE: I think not. I mean—I think—

BOVINE'S VOICE: Yes?

BILLY'S VOICE: You folks wouldn't have a hot cup a' java layin' around the back room here, would ya'? Jest a little somethin' to wet the old whistle.

DR. VECTOR'S VOICE: Java? Java?

GENERAL'S VOICE: Lights please, Edith!

> The lights pop up revealing BILLY with his pots and pans sitting in a chair downstage with his back to the audience and his pack on the floor beside him. Next to him is the STENOGRAPHER, Edith, who is shutting off the projector and turning the lights on, etc. GENERAL BROWSER and COLONEL WARNER are sitting behind a table upstage, facing BILLY. CAPTAIN BOVINE, Chief Inspector for the CIA, paces around the middle of the stage, chain-smoking cigarettes and dressed in a gray suit. DOCTOR VECTOR is also seated at

the table with the COLONEL and GENERAL
BROWSER.

GENERAL: Edith, would you get Billy a cup of coffee,
please. Do you take cream and sugar, Billy?
BILLY: Nope. Black like midnight.

> The STENOGRAPHER goes out and closes the door.
> The room is plastered with Air Force insignia,
> the flag, photographs of planes, the desert, slo-
> gans, etc., including: "To protect and to serve"
> in large letters. The three pistols that the YOUNG
> MAN gave to BILLY are sitting on the desk in
> front of the GENERAL. CAPTAIN BOVINE walks up
> to them.

CAPTAIN BOVINE: Now, Billy, you're gonna have to
understand something here right off the bat. Unless
we come up with some evidence leading us to this
kid you say you got these guns off of then we got no
other choice than to assume that these weapons belong to you.
BILLY: Oh now don't go handin' me that malarkey,
Captain Bovine. What the hell's a prospector out in
the middle a' no man's land gonna do with three
new-fangled irons like them.
CAPTAIN BOVINE: Exactly. What is he going to do?
BILLY: Nothin'! He's gonna hand 'em over to Mickey
Free like he said he was 'cause Danny paid him to.
That's what. Nothin' else. Shucks, the way you fellas
carry on here anyone'd think there's a plot goin' on to
overturn the damn government.
CAPTAIN BOVINE: Danny? Did you say Danny? Was
that the kid's name? Answer me, Billy! There's no
point covering up for him. If we don't get him someone else will.
BILLY: Danny, Johnny, Jimmy! I don't know what his
handle was. I never paid it no never mind. We just
got to know each other so well we didn't need no
names.
BOVINE: Now listen, Billy. You may not realize it, since
you've been out of touch with society for some time,
but this country's in trouble. Big trouble. Over the

past few years there's been a general breakdown of law and order and a complete disrespect for the things we've held sacred since our ancestors founded this country. This country needs you, Billy. It needs your help to help root out these subversive, underground creeps and wipe the slate clean once and for all. You don't realize the trouble they've been giving us. Every time there's a holiday or a bunch of people want to have a good time and just peacefully celebrate some national hero or something, there's always a bunch of these creeps hanging around making faces and giving the finger and shouting obscene things around and carrying cards and doing wild dances and what not. It's become worse than a disgrace, Billy. It's not even funny anymore. There was a time when the whole thing was a joke. But not anymore. Now they've got sympathizers, inside agitators and con men in the White House. All over the country it's going on. I saw it all coming a long time ago. Ever since those bushy-haired creeps started infiltrating from England in 1964. Before that even. Playing Negro music and gyrating their bodies and stuff like that. I'm telling you, Billy, it's about time we brought this whole thing to an end. If we don't do something soon we'll be overrun with these creepy faggots and leather-jacket types. Things have stayed the same for too long now. It's time for a change!

> The STENOGRAPHER enters with the coffee and gives it to BILLY. Then she sits down behind a steno machine and starts taking down the proceedings as though it were a court trial.

STENOGRAPHER: Here you are, Billy. A nice hot cup of java.

DR. VECTOR: Java?

BILLY: Well now. That's fine. Thank ya', peaches.

STENOGRAPHER: You're welcome.

GENERAL: Captain Bovine, perhaps we could find out something more about this Mickey Free.

CAPTAIN BOVINE: Later. First I want to nail this kid. He's the source. Mickey Free was obviously a go between, just like Billy here. How does that make you feel, Billy? To know that you were used by this punk.

BILLY: No different. I knew it all along. Me and him was pals. I coulda' cared less about what his real aims were. We just struck it off real fine and let me tell ya', that's a rarity on the desert. Yessir. Why I could tell you stories—

CAPTAIN BOVINE: Good. Tell us a story right now, Billy. The story of how you met this kid and everything you can remember about him. We'll listen.

BILLY: Well I was out near the Harmony Borax Works out there trying to tap a vein that I'd had me an eye on for quite a spell. Seems like forever. Well, with me, ya' know, it's more of a way a' life than anything else. I mean, not like them weekenders what come out fer a taste a' yeller fever, all hog tied with them electric Geiger counters and metallic·metal finders and what all. Us old timers, a lot of us, don't really hanker for no heavy pay loads. Naw. Just a little chicken scratch to keep the vittles comin' is cause enough to keep us on.

CAPTAIN BOVINE: What about this kid?

BILLY: I'm a gettin' there, mister. And don't get yer hackles up on this old buzzard, sonny, 'cause I'm as likely to clam up on ya' as spew on about somethin' close to my heart when I ain't got no willin' ears to catch it.

CAPTAIN BOVINE: All right. I'm sorry.

BILLY: I come down off the shale part a' the slope and headed toward my burro when I look and see this here kid what appears to be takin' a sun bath. Yeah. Right out in the middle of the blazin' sun he's a lyin' on his backside and gazin' right into thet big yeller ball. So I walks up and right off I offer him some rashers and a hot cup a' java. Figured he could use somethin' in that belly. Looked like it ain't done nothin' but gurgle for the last fifty miles. So we set ourselves down and get right into talkin' and spinnin' yarns. And let me tell ya' he had some doozers.

CAPTAIN BOVINE: What did you talk about?

BILLY: Well, he told me some a' the galldarndest tales

I ever did hear. Dope peddlers, prostitutes, pretty girls and I don't know what all. Told me one about some street up in Frisco where he stayed and had hisself a different woman every darn night for over a week. Now don't that beat all? Enough to make an old man skiddadle off the desert like a water bug.

CAPTAIN BOVINE: Did he ask you any questions?

BILLY: Danny? Never seen nobody with so many questions. Day in and day out he'd be askin' me stuff about the desert, the Indians, the sky, the night, the sun, the stars, any damn thing he could lay his brain on.

CAPTAIN BOVINE: How much time did he spend with you then?

BILLY: Must a' been well over a fortnight.

CAPTAIN BOVINE: How long is that? Let me see. A fortnight?

BILLY: Better part of a couple weeks. I thought you coppers was supposed to know everything.

CAPTAIN BOVINE: All right. It slipped my mind. You say he asked you about the Indians. What did he ask?

BILLY: Everything. Their magic, how they cooked corn. Where the reservations were. How to get to them. The different drugs and medicine. How to tell the tribes. The symbols, the legends, the religion. How to make water out of sand. Stuff like that. So after a while I figured if he was so all het up about the red man I might as well introduce him to a real live one. Let him learn from the horse's mouth. So I took him up to meet Mickey Free. He ain't a full blood but a half breed has all the wits of a Indian plus the gumption of a white man. Mickey's one a' the few real wild ones left. I believe you boys might a' even heard tell of him. Seems like he helped ya' find yerselves some a' this Indian land yer settin' on right now.

GENERAL: Yes. The name rings a bell.

BILLY: Yup. Old Mick's been doin' dirty work for white men ever since he was knee-high to a scorpion. Most Injuns hate his guts. Say he's cold-blooded, turns in his own kind. Yup. He's the one supposed to have out foxed Geronimo. Boxed him into a canyon or somethin'.

COLONEL: Captain Bovine, do we have to sit here all day listening to this? There's important business at hand!

GENERAL: Please, Warner.

CAPTAIN BOVINE: Let me handle this, gentlemen. Now listen, Billy. You'll have to understand that what we're primarily interested in here is the young man who gave you these guns and how it's tied up with these Indian affairs. You can skip all the local color.

BILLY: Well I'll try to scrape it right down to the bone for you fellas, but there's an awful lot bouncin' around this old head a' mine. Can't rightly figure where one thing leaves off and the other begins.

CAPTAIN BOVINE: We understand. It would help if you could clear up the connection between Mickey Free and this punk for us.

BILLY: Well, like I say. I left Johnny off up there at Mickey's wickiup. They hit it off like grease hits the skillet, them two. Just a cracklin' back and forth between 'em. They stuck it out together for quite a spell, then that blond boy up and left. He come back to me and started talkin' all different from what he done before. Talkin' about a plan with a bunch a' poor folk back in the city. How I was to figure in this plan by deliverin' guns to Mickey. Then one night I'm sittin' out there in a lonely spot, moonlit and all, waitin' for Danny when I hears these low kind a' moanin' sounds and I looks down and layin' right in front a' me there is——

CAPTAIN BOVINE: Just the pertinent facts, Billy!

BILLY: Boy, I do believe you fellas wouldn't let the light a' day shine on a sidewinder in the zoo, 'less you had the keeper there beside ya'.

DR. VECTOR stands abruptly.

DR. VECTOR: Sidewinder! Did what you say was sidewinder?

GENERAL: Take it easy, Doc. Sit down.

COLONEL: He did say "sidewinder" though. I heard him say it.

CAPTAIN BOVINE: Why did you mention the word "sidewinder," Billy?

BILLY: Just came off the top of the head, gents. The Hopis say the top of the head has a door and if you keep that door open all kind a' wonders come to ya'.

CAPTAIN BOVINE: Have you ever heard that word used on the desert before?

BILLY: You must be pullin' my long johns, sonny. That's a snake. A tiny poisonous rattler what likes the shade and——

CAPTAIN BOVINE: Did you ever hear the kid use that word? Answer me!

BILLY: I think if it's all the same to you, boys, I'll just mosey on.

> BILLY starts to get up. CAPTAIN BOVINE shoves him back down in his seat. DR. VECTOR sits back down.

CAPTAIN BOVINE: You'll stay right here until you're released. Withholding information from a government official is punishable by law, in case you're not aware of it.

BILLY: Well slap my daddy. Thought I was too old to get myself into more trouble.

CAPTAIN BOVINE: Whether you like it or not, Billy, you've gotten yourself mixed up in a pretty messy situation. A very confidential government-authorized computer has escaped from this Air Force base. This computer goes under the code name of "Sidewinder." Your mention of the name has only further confirmed our suspicions that you are in some way connected with its disappearance. Unless you reveal to us more useful information in this regard then I will have no other recourse than to arrest you for possession of arms without a license.

BILLY: The only reason I was— It was just a figure o' speech. I mean—I was a' gettin' set to tell ya' about this other snake that I seen.

> DR. VECTOR rises again. The GENERAL coaxes him back in his wheelchair.

DR. VECTOR: Snake! What snake?

BILLY: Like I say, I was waitin' for my rendezvous with Danny when I hears these groanin' sounds comin' out a' the night. I looks down and there in front of me I sees this pretty young thing all tangled up in the biggest most gigantic galldanged sidewinder I ever did see. I mean I think it was a sidewinder. It had them tell-tale horns over the eye sockets. But she was so damn big!

> DR. VECTOR lets out a jubilant shout. He starts buzzing around in his wheelchair.

DR. VECTOR: That's it! My sidewinder! It's alive! My sidewinder is alive! It lives! It lives! It lives! My beautiful sidewinder lives! Beautiful, beautiful sidewinder!

GENERAL: Doctor, please! Dr. Vector! Calm yourself!

BILLY: Nope. It's dead.

> DR. VECTOR's wheelchair comes to a screeching halt.

DR. VECTOR: Dead!

BILLY: I mean I think so. It has to be.

DR. VECTOR: What does this mean! You just said it lived! It was alive!

COLONEL: What's this all about.

CAPTAIN BOVINE: Explain yourself, Billy.

BILLY: Well I seen the head up on top of the high mesa with Mickey. They were worshiping the damn thing. Minus the body. I went lookin' for Mickey up at his wickiup but he'd flew the coop. Couple a' his side kicks says he went off to the high mesa to take part in some ritual of the tribes. So I followed his trail and sure enough there he was right in the middle a' the most high-falootin' ceremony I ever did see. And I seen plenty. Lots a tribes were there. All gathered together peaceable like and gathered around the snake head like it were some kind a' god or somethin'. And there was Mickey, old "one eye" himself, just a' sittin' there pretty as ya' please, beamin' from ear to ear and holdin' that head right in his lap. So I sallies over to him and show him the guns. Figured he'd be pleased as punch. But nothin' doin'. All of a sudden the whole shootin' match comes to a dead stop and they all just stand there a' starin' right at me like I brought the devil his self. Well right off the bat I could tell I done somethin' out a' step. Then I look in Mickey's face and see that toothy grin a' his disappear fast as a swaller and he stands up and looks real serious and sad and mad all at once and tells me he don't want nothin' never more to do with guns or killin'. I mean I like to drop my silver fillin's right on the spot. Words like that comin' from the most feared Injun-killin' bronco the West ever knowed. Then he reaches in his pouch and pulls out these here little plastic bags and tells me to take the guns and these bags back to the white devil what he got 'em from.

CAPTAIN BOVINE: What bags? What do you mean?

BILLY: Right here. I got 'em right in my pack.

> BILLY reaches into his pack and pulls out the plastic bags of dope that the YOUNG MAN had given MICKEY FREE in Act One. BOVINE snatches them away. Rips them open, wets his finger and sticks it in the bag, then tastes the powder. He marches to the telephone and picks it up.

CAPTAIN BOVINE: Hello. Get me a special detail of Desert Tactical Troops over here immediately. It's an emergency!

> BOVINE hangs up the phone. BILLY stands.

DR. VECTOR: But what of my sidewinder!

BILLY: You can't send no soldiers out there, Captain Bovine. They'll interfere with the ceremony. The Indians won't hanker to it one bit. You better pick up that phone and call off them troops. I ain't kiddin', Captain. That's serious business them redskins are up to. I wouldn't mess with it to save my soul.

CAPTAIN BOVINE: Pipe down, old timer. It's just a routine checkup.

BLACKOUT

"CIA Man" comes on in the dark.

CIA Man

Who can tell if Egypt's got the bomb
Even if the atmosphere is calm

Fuckin A Man CIA Man

Who can train guerillas by the dozen
Train 'em all to kill their untrained cousins

Fuckin A Man CIA Man

Who can plant the bug on anyone
Who would never eavesdrop just for fun

Fuckin A Man CIA Man

Who will do just what he has to do
All the way from Dallas to Peru

Fuckin A Man CIA Man

Why is Mao scared to start a hassle
Mao isn't man enough to rassle

Fuckin A Man CIA Man

Who is diplomatically immune
Who else but the hero of this tune

Fuckin A Man CIA Man

by PETER STAMPEL, TULI KUPFERBURG & ANTONIA

Copyright—United International 1966

SCENE 4

> The song fades out. Total silence. Black stage.
> Thundering sound of many feet pounding on the
> floor. Silence. Low moaning sound of many
> voices chanting in unison.

Hopi Chants

The lights come up slowly as the chanting goes on. Center stage is MICKEY FREE's wickiup, a small oval-shaped structure made out of bent twigs, old sheets of metal, mud, strips of cloth and a dark blanket covering the door. A thin column of smoke comes from the top. Stage left of the wickiup is a group of eight INDIANS seated in a semi-circle around an open pit. These are the SNAKE PRIESTS. They are chanting and preparing themselves for a ceremony. In front of them are three large pottery jars, the tops covered with antelope skins. Behind them is the snake altar: a large screen of antelope skin stretched on four long sticks. Three large Hopi Kachina dolls are painted on the skin with other symbols, semi-circles and figures. Large snake bodies and heads protrude from the skin in bright colors; these operate like hand puppets from behind the screen, so at a certain point in the ceremony they will come alive and wriggle to the dance.

In front of the screen are several stalks of corn and tall poles with feather and ribbon streamers dangling from their tops. Encircling the entire group and the altar is a line of sacred yellow cornmeal. All the INDIANS are very dark skinned, have long black hair with eagle feathers at the back of the neck, are naked except for loin cloths and moccasins. A large white oval is painted over each of their breasts and shoulder blades, their foreheads and the fronts of their throats are painted white, the rest of their faces are painted black, the forearms and legs below the knees are painted white. They each wear turquoise and shell necklaces; their loin cloths are blue with a black snake design in front and back. They wear belts with long fringe around the waist, and a fox skin and tail fastened to the belt in the rear. Tied to each right knee is a tortoise shell rattle. Their moccasins are reddish brown buckskin with fringe and shell designs. They wear white armlets around the bicep and anklets just above the moccasins. The CHIEF SNAKE PRIEST, who sits more or less in the center, holds a bow standard decorated with feathers and horsehair.

They chant in a low moaning unison for a

while and sway from side to side. The CHIEF
SNAKE PRIEST slowly places both his hands on
one of the jars, the others follow and place their
hands on the other two jars. The CHIEF removes
the skin from the top of the jar and tips the jar
toward the pit. The other priests do the same
with their jars. The chanting mounts in volume
and intensity. Suddenly, on cue from the CHIEF,

BY WAH LAY YEAH BY-WAH-LAY BY WAH LAY YEAH BY-WAH-LAY BY-WAH-LAY
BY WAH LAY — BY-WAH-LAY   BY WAH LAY — BY-WAH-LAY

they all dip the jars down into the pit. Dozens of
snakes of all sizes and colors slither from the
jars into the pit. The chanting keeps up until all
the snakes have disappeared into the pit.

HONEY and the YOUNG MAN pop onto the stage
from left; the sidewinder's body is in the YOUNG
MAN's hand. The INDIANS are jolted into silence.
The YOUNG MAN and HONEY stare at them. The
INDIANS rise in unison and walk off left.

HONEY: Maybe we oughta' come back tomorrow.

YOUNG MAN: Shut up.

HONEY: Look, I've done my bit already. I found you
your dumb snake so why don't you let me go. You
said before that I just slowed you down.

YOUNG MAN: I need you around.

HONEY: 'Cause you're scared. You've been scared right
along and you thought I didn't know it. Right? You're
scared shitless.

YOUNG MAN: Will you cool it!

HONEY: No, I won't cool it! I'm not one of your hippie
sluts you can drag through the streets and any damn
place you feel like going! Giving her clap and hepatitis
and everything else.

YOUNG MAN: Look——

HONEY: No, you look! You killed my Dukie! I'll never

forgive you for that. Just 'cause I go to bed with you doesn't mean I forgot.

YOUNG MAN: Just hang loose a little bit longer, all right? Please? I promise as soon as we're through getting this snake put back together we'll go into town and have a really neat time. O.K.?

HONEY: Can we go to the movies?

YOUNG MAN: Sure. Anything you want. We'll get us some hot apple pie and coffee at the truck stop and then we'll go to the movies.

HONEY: There's a new Elvis Presley movie on. Did you see it?

> The low sound of chanting comes from the wickiup. The YOUNG MAN sneaks toward it with HONEY behind him.

YOUNG MAN: I saw *Jailhouse Rock*.

HONEY: No. This is a new one. He plays the part of this stock-car driver who always wins, so he gets real rich. But he's such a good guy that he gives all his money away to his friends and people who are poor. You know, he buys them cars and refrigerators and stoves and TV's and all that kind of stuff. But then he gets in trouble—I mean all his friends like him and everything and he's real popular but he gets in trouble with the Internal Revenue Service because they say he didn't pay a lot of his taxes. So he tells them he wrote off all those gifts as tax deductible charities. But the Internal Revenue doesn't go for that and they say he has to go and take back all those things that he bought for all those people and give them to the government. So he goes and takes back a few things but what happens is that all his friends start hating him because they think he's an Indian giver and everything. So——

> Suddenly the two INDIANS who were with MICKEY FREE in Act One jump out of the wickiup with knives and pin the YOUNG MAN and HONEY to the ground. HONEY screams.

YOUNG MAN: Wait a minute! Wait a minute! Paza! Paza! Tanta muy bien amigo! Amigo! Tosa entra por

Mickey Free! Nada mas! Nada mas. Para Mickey Free. Entiende? Sabe?

> MICKEY FREE comes out of the wickiup slowly. His face is painted with white zigzags. He is stripped to the waist and wears an embroidered loin cloth and high buckskin moccasins and an Apache headband around his head. The huge knife still dangles down from his crotch. He crosses slowly to the YOUNG MAN who is still pinned to the ground. He smiles and releases the INDIANS. They back off.

YOUNG MAN: Mickey.

MICKEY: Kachada. Why have you come back?

YOUNG MAN: I have to talk to you.

MICKEY: I talk no more of guns and drugs. Of plans to conquer worlds. If you come to get back your guns I have already give them to Billy.

YOUNG MAN: No. The guns don't matter. It's the snake. The snake you found on Honey. What did you do with the head?

HONEY: Remember? You saved my life. You cut off its head.

YOUNG MAN: This is the body. You have the head.

> The YOUNG MAN holds up the sidewinder's body to MICKEY, who stares at it, then smiles broadly and lets out a shrill scream. He hugs the YOUNG MAN and picks him up, dancing with him and laughing. The other INDIANS smile.

MICKEY: You are the Pahana! You have come! You have brought us our salvation!

> MICKEY grabs the sidewinder's body and holds it over his head, dancing with it wildly. The other two INDIANS join in. The YOUNG MAN tries to grab the snake back. HONEY lies dazed on the floor.

YOUNG MAN: Wait a minute! Wait a minute! That's mine! That belongs to somebody else! Mickey! Cut it out! You can't have that snake! They'll kill me if I don't bring it back! Mickey! You've got to give it back! Give it back!

MICKEY: The Spider Lady has told me the truth. She said you would come. The body would join the head of its own will. And now it is here. The ceremony can begin!

YOUNG MAN: What ceremony? That's a machine, you creep! It's not real. The Air Force cooked it up to trace flying saucers! The spades want it to trace the Air Force. I want it because it means my life if I don't get it back to them.

MICKEY: My brothers and I have followed many separate ways, sometimes killing each other. Tonight we shall all see the kingdom. Tonight the spirit snake shall become one again and with it shall join all its people. You and your bride might also come on this journey, Pahana.

HONEY: He's not my husband. He killed my husband.

YOUNG MAN: That's a machine, Mickey. A computer. Not a god.

MICKEY: You are free, Pahana. You have brought us to our Emergence. It will take us to a place we will never come back from. You are welcome to enter and follow us there or stay here on this earth and follow your will. The stars will watch you as you go.

> MICKEY turns and walks back into the wickiup with the sidewinder's body in his hand. The INDIANS follow him in.

YOUNG MAN: Let's go. Come on.

HONEY: Wait. What did he mean?

YOUNG MAN: Never mind. Let's get out of here.

> The chanting comes again from the wickiup, low and then rising.

HONEY: What's that?

YOUNG MAN: Never mind! Are you coming or not?

HONEY: I never heard that before.

YOUNG MAN: They're sacred songs. It'd take you a year to understand the first word.

HONEY: It's so soothing. Like hearing the wind.

YOUNG MAN: I know. I know. If you get hooked on it we'll never get out of here. Now come on! Look, we gotta head for Mexico right now! Blood is going to be after my ass before too long. It was you who wanted to go see the movie before! Remember? Honey! Get up, and let's go!

> She is in a kind of trace state. She rises slowly and moves toward the wickiup. The YOUNG MAN runs to her and grabs her shoulders. He shakes her. She stares at him blankly.

YOUNG MAN: Goddammit! I'm not walking back down into that desert alone! Do you hear me! It's the middle of the night! I might get shot for having long hair or smelling bad or something! Honey! Snap out of it! It's not for white people's ears! It's secret stuff! It'll make you crazy! If we go in there, they'll never see us again! Never! We'll be scooped up! Taken away! Can't you understand me! I need you! I need you with me! I can't come back here again! Why don't you listen! Honey!

> He shakes her, then lets her go. She walks like a sleepwalker straight into the wickiup. The chanting reaches a kind of chord as she enters.

Honey! You'll never see daylight again!

> A blue flash in the sky. The sound of a jet as the YOUNG MAN looks up at the sky. The chanting grows louder. The YOUNG MAN clenches his hands together and starts to say the Lord's Prayer as he walks slowly toward the wickiup.

Our Father who art in Heaven. Hallowed be thy name. Thy kingdom come, thy will be done, on earth as it is in heaven. Give us this day our daily bread and forgive us our trespasses as we forgive those who trespass against us. Lead us not into temptation but deliver us from evil. For thine is the kingdom, the power and the glory. Forever and ever. Amen.

The chanting grows to an incredible pitch as he enters the wickiup on the word "Amen." A pause as just the wickiup is seen with the chanting coming from it. Another flash of blue in the sky. Then the beam of light going across from stage left to stage right as in Act One. Then one at a time eight ANTELOPE PRIESTS come out of the wickiup in single file. They are dressed similarly to the SNAKE PRIESTS except they have painted themselves ash gray with white zigzag lines running up from their breasts to their shoulders, and down the arms to the fingers and down the front of the legs to their big toes. They each carry a large gourd-like rattle and one holds a large antelope drum which he pounds in a steady rhythm. Their chins are outlined by a white line drawn from ear to ear. Their loin cloths are white with black snake designs and embroidered sashes. They are followed closely by the eight

SNAKE PRIESTS. They all continue the chant in a low murmur and walk single file to the snake altar where they face each other in a double line, eight on either side of the snake pit. Simultaneously they stomp with their right feet on the floor. A loud boom like thunder comes forth. They all begin to sway from left to right in unison and shake the rattles in time. They form a circle, then fan out into single file again and circle the entire stage four times chanting over and over again in rhythmic pattern and stomping their right feet in unison on the beginning accent of the word. Each time they stomp, the sound should come like thunder. The rhythm is slow, deliberate and powerful. Everything about the dance is spiritual and sincere and should not be cartooned or choreographed beyond the unison of the rhythmic patterns.

After they have circled the stage four times they again go to the snake pit and line up across from each other, but close to each other this time and forming a circle of bodies. They link arms and bend over the pit. They make a chord with their voices, rising from a low pitch to extremely high and shrieking. As they do this, the CHIEF PRIEST of the snake group kneels down and puts his head into the pit. He comes up with a snake in his mouth. The others fan back and the CHIEF SNAKE PRIEST dances with the writhing snake in his mouth. The ANTELOPE PRIESTS fan off and dance to the right side of the stage and stand in a line, swaying from side to side and chanting as they stomp their right feet.

The SNAKE PRIESTS line up stage left and do the same. One of the SNAKE PRIESTS dances out from the line toward the CHIEF and waves two long eagle feathers over the snake's head as the CHIEF dances with it. The snake goes limp and the CHIEF lets it drop to the floor. A third SNAKE PRIEST dances out with a stick and waves it over the snake, then bends down, picks it up with both hands, holds it aloft and dances over to the ANTELOPE PRIESTS. He hands it to one of the

ANTELOPE PRIESTS at the end of the line. He takes it and holds it, coaxing it with one hand as he continues to chant. The CHIEF walks back to behind the snake altar where he starts to operate one of the snake puppets in short jerky movements. Another SNAKE PRIEST puts his head into the pit and comes up with another snake between his teeth. The same process goes on as with the CHIEF until each ANTELOPE PRIEST in the line has a snake in his hand and each SNAKE PRIEST has danced with a snake and returned to behind the snake altar to operate one of the puppets. Once this is finished the ANTELOPE PRIESTS are all visible, dancing and chanting with the snakes. The SNAKE PRIESTS are all unseen behind the snake altar, and the snake puppets are moving vigorously around. MICKEY FREE comes out of the wickiup. He is dressed the same way, stripped to the waist, but he wears a blue kachina mask on his head. He holds the head of the sidewinder in his left hand, the body in the right. He holds them aloft. Behind him are HONEY, the YOUNG MAN, and the two INDIANS from before. HONEY's face is painted like the SNAKE PRIESTS' and the YOUNG MAN's like the ANTELOPES'.

HONEY wears a long black dress, a blue loin cloth over it and a white and red cape. Her hair is loose, with eagle feathers attached at the back. Around her neck is a necklace of turquoise and shell. She holds an earthen jar out in front of her containing sacred oil. The YOUNG MAN has an eagle feather tied to the front of his hair, his body is painted ash gray with white zigzag lines like the ANTELOPE PRIESTS' on his body, arms and legs. He also holds a jar filled with oil. The SNAKE PRIESTS come out from behind the altar single file and line up downstage. The ANTELOPES follow suit on the stage right side. One of MICKEY's INDIAN friends leads HONEY by the arm to the line of SNAKE PRIESTS where she kneels in front of the CHIEF.

The YOUNG MAN is led to the ANTELOPES by

the other INDIAN and he kneels to their CHIEF
PRIEST. Both HONEY and the YOUNG MAN seem to
be in a totally different frame of mind now.
Calm, spiritual, totally accepting of the whole
ritual. MICKEY stands downstage center, chanting and holding the segmented sidewinder aloft,
moving the two parts toward each other, then
away. The SNAKE CHIEF and the ANTELOPE
CHIEF exchange places and walk to opposite
sides of the stage. The ANTELOPE CHIEF faces
HONEY and the SNAKE CHIEF faces the YOUNG
MAN. They each simultaneously place their
hands on HONEY's and the YOUNG MAN's heads,
then slowly push their heads down into the jars
of oil they hold in front of them, so that their
hair becomes saturated. They raise their heads
up. HONEY and the YOUNG MAN stand. They are
led by the respective CHIEFS downstage in front
of MICKEY FREE. The CHIEF PRIESTS exchange
positions again and then wash HONEY's and the
YOUNG MAN's hair in the oil. They touch their
heads together and then twist their hair together
so that it becomes tied. The chanting continues
the whole time.

MICKEY, at the moment HONEY's and the
YOUNG MAN's hair has been tied together, joins
the sidewinder's body to its head. A tremendous
bolt of blue light issues from the sidewinder,
matched by one in the sky. Thunder booms. The
sky lights up blue again. The combination of
the voices chanting reaches an incredible shrieking, like lightning. The whole scene crackles like
high voltage wires. Then suddenly everything
stops abruptly as three "DESERT TACTICAL
TROOPS" with machine guns, pistols, helmets,
uniforms, etc., enter briskly from right. The
INDIANS freeze.

1ST DESERT TACTICAL TROOP: All right! Everybody put
up your hands! Everyone! Put 'em up!
2ND DESERT TACTICAL TROOP: Let's see some identifica-
tion! That goes for everybody! Get it out!
3RD DESERT TACTICAL TROOP: You people are in big

trouble! You got any idea what you got in your hand there, buddy? That's government property! United States Government property, buster! Now let's have it!

The 3RD DESERT TACTICAL TROOP grabs for the sidewinder which MICKEY still holds over his head. A bright blue light comes from the sidewinder, then from the sky. The D.T.T.'s jump back. All the INDIANS and HONEY and the YOUNG MAN stay frozen.

3RD DESERT TACTICAL TROOP: Now look, buddy! I don't know what's going on here but that snake belongs to us! Now hand it over!

The 3RD DESERT TACTICAL TROOP makes another move toward the sidewinder and again it lights up, answered by a light in the sky.

You wanna get run in for resisting arrest too? We're not playing games here with you punks!

Suddenly MICKEY begins the chant "Wunti Hayano Diwitia" and all the INDIANS plus the YOUNG MAN and HONEY join in. They start to move slowly toward the three DESERT TACTICAL TROOPS with MICKEY leading them, still holding the sidewinder over his head. They begin to form a large circle around the D.T.T.'s as they try to get away from them.

Wunti Hayano Diwitia

2ND DESERT TACTICAL TROOP: All right! Hold it right there! Hold it!

1ST DESERT TACTICAL TROOP: Stop that singing! Stop
where you are!

3RD DESERT TACTICAL TROOP: We're going to open fire
in about three seconds if you don't stop and hand over
that snake! One! We're not kidding around! Two!
This is no joke! We mean business! This is your last
chance! Stop in the name of the law! Three!

> The DESERT TACTICAL TROOPS open fire on the
> INDIANS with their machine guns. The INDIANS
> keep coming. They form a circle with MICKEY
> at the head of it and the DESERT TACTICAL
> TROOPS in the center firing again and again. The
> INDIANS just sway back and forth to the rhythm
> of the chant. The sidewinder lights up, the sky
> lights up. The 3RD DESERT TACTICAL TROOP
> rushes straight toward MICKEY FREE, firing his
> machine gun into him. MICKEY just chants and
> sways. The 3RD DESERT TACTICAL TROOP reaches
> up and grabs the sidewinder and yanks it from
> MICKEY's hands. The body separates from the
> head again. Bright bolt of blue light from the sky.
> The D.T.T.'s scream as though being blinded.
>
> The lights go to black after the blue light, then
> back to bright blue. Each interval of light and
> dark lasts about five or six seconds. From pitch
> black to bright blue. Huge gusts of wind blow
> from upstage directly out into the audience,
> changing from hot to cold. Wind also blows across
> stage. Streams of smoke come from all around the
> proscenium arch and upstage. The chanting
> increases. A high frequency whine. The chant-
> ing becomes amplified. The bright blue light
> flashes on, the INDIANS are in ecstasy as they
> chant. The D.T.T.'s are cringing on their knees
> center stage. The lights go to black. The blue
> light again and this time all the INDIANS plus
> the YOUNG MAN and HONEY are gone. Just the
> DESERT TACTICAL TROOPS holding their ears and
> shielding their eyes. The lights stay up and be-
> come brighter. The whine and the chanting get
> louder, then everything goes black.

THE END

SLAVESHIP

The Chelsea Theater Center Production

by *Imamu Amiri Baraka*
(LeRoi Jones)

Introduction by John Lahr

> We are unfair and unfair
> We are black magicians, black art
> We make in black labs of the heart.
>
> LeRoi Jones
> *Black Dada Nihilismus*

Imamu Amiri Baraka wants to make new myths for the black American, to substitute a Black Warrior for the White Man's puppet. *Slaveship* is dangerous theater. It ignites energy: It shows the black man the common bond of his past in order to give direction to his future. Baraka creates a spectacle of the black man's origins so that his race may rediscover its racial dignity and forge a new radical consciousness. *Slaveship* is meant to arouse both unity and disgust. This is the strongest black theater a white audience has yet witnessed, because Baraka rubs our noses in history and makes us understand the sources of rage that filter down to us on stage and in life as mockery or suicidal violence.

Baraka creates an environment where humiliation cannot be escaped. He sits his audience around the sunless steerage of a slaveship. Blacks are chained to the floor, the ceiling is three feet above their bodies in a space slightly larger than the actual slaveship quarters. Whatever cultural degradation blacks have experienced, nothing is more shocking, revolting or obscene than the *fact* of the cramped violence of the space. We have not seen many pictures. History does not usually relate the black past. *Slaveship* serves as a reminder of this anguish and of the profound betrayal built into the American soil. The spectators watch a tableau of psychic castration, a people stripped of its language and its freedom. The Africans call out in Yoruba. Their language, like their relationship to the land and sun, will be drastically altered in a brutal America. For over half an hour the audience experiences the shrill, claustrophobic voyage. No English is spoken, there are only the Yoruba words and anguished cries. Bodies are thrust upon bodies, sweat holding scraps of food to numb lips. The ship becomes the fulcrum from which the play moves backward and forward in time. It is the moral backdrop from which all the black identities emerge. The lyric resilience of the new warrior contrasts with the Southern coon two-stepping for Massah with the canned laughter which reminds us of the joy we took (take) in Amos 'n Andy stereotypes. Pink mouths scream the rage of Nat Turner. Eyes—white-hot with anger—bear down on the audience. The actors crawl beneath our feet; their shackles clink as they move. Slinking to get away, howling ("Beasts. You murdered women and children. You white shit!"), they surround the audience with their madness and their despair.

Slaveship displays the grotesque caricatures of black role playing. Baraka is dramatizing the masks which allow the colonized to survive but which, paradoxically, feed their self-hatred and erode their real being. No man lives without personality (*persona* = dramatic mask), but *Slaveship* makes the distinction between a man's choosing his own role (the warrior's strength and prowess) and adopting one which will please his oppressor ("I jes stand here and I scratch my own nigger head"). Baraka is contrasting identities which liberate the black man to discover his power and life force, to see himself as a heroic (and hence tragic) figure rather than a cornpone clown, with those roles—from porter to preacher—which make the black acquiesce to his living death and diminish his sense of self. Sickness is part of any condition which keeps an individual from feeling and discovering his full potential. A slave is an object; the new warrior is an active, aggressive force. If the latter role has the power to take life, it also has the power to give it. The madness which *Slaveship* evokes is not merely the fiery rage at injustice, but also the schizophrenia that consumes any man forced to accept an untenable situation. Faced with a culture that broadcasts life, liberty, and the pursuit of happiness, that prides itself on human equality, the black man's exploitation and continued betrayals at the hands of government become an archetypal "double-bind" situation. R. D. Laing has written of the sources of this insanity in a way that clarifies the white world's amnesia toward black problems and the black man's resulting violence and confusion. "Those who deceive themselves are obliged to deceive others. It is impossible for me to maintain a false picture of myself unless I falsify your picture of yourself and of me. I must disparage you if you are genuine, accuse you of being a phoney when you comply with what I want, say you are selfish if you go your own way, ridicule you for being immature if you try to be unselfish, and so on. The person caught within such a muddle does not know whether he is coming or going. In these circumstances what we call psychosis may be a desperate effort to hold onto something. It is not surprising that the something may be what we call 'delusions.' "

Getting beyond black roles which accept the stalemate is *Slaveship*'s avowed intention. The actors weave among the audience and ask the black brothers to acknowledge each other and a new world.

> When we gonna rise up
> When we gonna show the world who we really are
> When we gonna take our own place brother
> Like the world was just begun.

Slaveship is unfair; as propaganda, it must be. The black torment, the cruelly simple facts of black exploitation give the play its roots in a fierce moral truth. In making a new history, metaphor triumphs over fact. To make a myth of the warrior, the black audience must be shown African kings as just men, although many of them dealt away the outcasts of their tribes to the slave traders. The new black warrior must see his people as totally oppressed by whites in America, although free black men often had slaves themselves. Historical subtlety is not what is demanded of the black masses whose consciousness is not yet firm or whose sense of history is not certain enough for such differentiations. *Slaveship*'s excesses are a barometer of a race's despair and confusions. At the end of the play a Negro preacher talking integration and bowing to the white world is killed and symbolically beheaded in revenge for centuries of black deaths. The head is hung with the black liberation flag. The moment is chilling, and in it lies the strength and failure of Baraka's argument. Unwittingly, the visual statement contradicts the purity and nobility of the new black nation. In killing the preacher (and acting their violence out on the deck of the very slaveship from which they have escaped), black victims turn into victimizers: the process of oppression against which they have rebelled turns back on them. Revolution is made in the name of *life*, and when it forgets a larger humanity, it loses its moral force and social promise.

Nevertheless, *Slaveship* isolates the dilemma of the colonized American black, and its rage is typical of his frustration. Baraka himself, in turning away from the white community, in assuming an African name and working in the ghettos of Newark, embodies the central energy and intellectual thrust of a revolutionary spirit trying to create a black national culture. His voice is full of hatred, but it also holds out hope. His tone has the hard edge of mockery as a tactic for sidestepping death, but it lacks humor because laughter admits human failure —an emotional fact which no revolutionary, at this time in America, can afford to admit. Frantz Fanon has observed. "The colonized man who writes for his people ought to use the past with the intention of opening the future, as an invitation to action and a basis for hope. But to ensure that hope and to give it form, he must take part in action and throw himself body and soul into the national struggle. You may speak about everything under the sun; but when you decide to speak of that unique thing in man's life that is represented by the fact of opening up new horizons, by bringing light to your own country, and by raising yourself and your people to their feet, then you must collaborate on the physical plane."

Imamu Amiri Baraka's life mirrors the commitment Fanon describes. *Slaveship* is a powerful example of revolutionary writing, which brings the black man both literally and symbolically to his feet. As a play, its conclusions may be debated, but as an emotional experience, it is undeniably profound.

PART ONE

On the ship:

DADEMI, nursing Moshake.

TAWA, crawls around ship, sick, looking
for an exit in desperation.

AKOOWA }
SALAKO } chained together, sleeping fitfully.

LALU, talking to himself.

House opens; music is playing.

Musicians play signature tune.

The music stops.

Action in hold: All in hold go into motion.

TAWA: She bumps into the shit bucket and
recoils. Loud screams

SALAKO: dragging AKOOWA goes to bucket to
relieve himself. LALU helps. As he is over
bucket . . .

AKOOWA: He and SALAKO then go back to
original position.

SAILOR: Bangs whip on ramp and brings in:

ADUFE, who resists strenuously. Dropped in
from hatch on top of cover.

IMANI, resists. When they get under spar at
center of ship, she stops and turns toward
SAILOR. She yells "Olala, Olala." The SAILOR hits
her and she falls over women's side of hold.

OLALA (*off stage*): Iya! Iya!

SAILOR grabs IMANI, opens hatch, drops her in,
closes hatch, and returns to ramp. When IMANI
is in hold, she hugs TAWA and is back under
hatch when . . .

NOLIWE is brought in. She is pregnant.

ATOWODA: Noliwe? Noliwe!? No! No!

SAILOR holds NOLIWE's wrist chains out in front
of her with one hand and pushes against the

small of her back with the other hand. She falls beside women's hatch. She is put into hold screaming. NOLIWE and TAWA are terrified of each other at first but hug when they realize who each other is.

IYALOSA: brought in in a stately manner. At woman's hatch, after he opens it, she spits at him . . . Freeze for seven seconds. Music and action in the hold stop. She then crumples (*sound:* Ughhhh.) and action starts again. SAILOR jumps in women's hold and puts her in, jumps out, closes hatch. SAILOR adjusts rope on mast on way to get . . .

OLALA, who is carried in. SAILOR stops on deck, puts him down, sees wooden knife in his belt, takes it and throws it out ramp exit.

OLALA: Iya! Iya!
IMANI: Olala? Olala?

SAILOR puts OLALA in men's hold.

SAILOR exits ramp, bangs whip on ramp, *enters with ATOWODA. AKANO jumps him from the rear, SAILOR throws ATOWODA on ramp, turns and knees AKANO in the groin, throws ATOWODA onto ship, hits him and he doubles up on deck.

ATOWODA: Atowoda! Atowoda!
DADEMI (*loud and hard*): Atowoda! Atowoda!

SAILOR puts ATOWODA in the hold.

TAWA: screams and screams and screams*

AKANO moves onto ramp. SAILOR returns on ramp; ATOWODA leaves ship and remounts ramp. The above is then repeated from * to *.

After ATOWODA is in ship second time, SAILOR jumps in hold, chains ATOWODA, jumps out, returns for AKANO, who scurries crablike in front of SAILOR down ramp before SAILOR. On ship he stands, SAILOR hits him in stomach, AKANO doubles over and falls. SAILOR drags him to hatch, puts his legs in, then dumps AKANO into hold. SAILOR hangs whip on mast, enters men's hold, starts to drag AKANO to left.

AKANO: Otiiiiiiiiiii!

> Everyone goes into slow motion. AKOOWA kicks SAILOR, who reaches over and hits AKOOWA in the groin.
>> AKOOWA: Long, loud cry of pain.
>> SAILOR resumes dragging AKANO.

AKANO: Oti!

> Everyone goes back into regular motion. SAILOR drags AKANO downstage left, in men's hold, takes one chain off wrist and chains wrists to leg chains.

ATOWODA (*by wall next to hatch*): Imani! Imani!

> Moans and cries.
>> Sound of chains being sawn on bars.

Dademi! Dademi!

> TAWA calls attention to ATOWODA's cries to DADEMI.
>> SAILOR goes to hatch, is half-way out——.

VOICE (*tape*): Okay, let's go

> SAILOR closes hatch.

A good cargo of black gold. Let's go, we head west. We head west.

> Laughter; tape and SAILOR.

Black gold in the west. We've got a full cargo!
SAILOR: Aye, aye, Cap'n, we're on our way!

> Laughs.

VOICE 2 (*tape*): Riches be ours, by God!
VOICE 1 (*tape*): Aye, riches be ours. We're on our way!
SAILOR: Americaaaaaaa . . .

> TAPE AND SAILOR: Long, loud laughter.
>> The ship lurches three times.
>> SAILOR goes to left, then to right, then to left, on the lurches.
> Takes off T-shirt during this and wipes sweat off his body. After last lurch, ship starts rocking

violently. SAILOR, laughing, finally leaves ship.
Ship stops rocking.

IYALOSA (*ringing prayer bell. She has pushed slop bucket
to area between holds*): Obatala!
IMANI: Shango!
IYALOSA: Obatala!

Ship quiets down.

DADEMI: Moshake, Moshake, be calm. Moshake, Orisha,
save us.
ATOWODA, AKOOWA, AKANO: Iyalosa? Iyalosa?

IYALOSA: Eni s'oju se mu   WOMEN (*very low*): Orisa
ni ma sin

Ada ni b'o tiri   Orisa ni ma sin

Eni ran mi wa   Orisa ni ma sin
Some men join in.
Eni s'oju se mu   Orisa ni ma sin

Ada ni b'o tiri   Orisa ni ma sin

Eni ran me wa   Orisa ni ma sin

Continues with very
low prayer.

Silence for a couple of beats. Bell stops ringing.
Music stops. The presence of God seems to
enter the room.
TAWA laughs, tentatively at first, then stronger.
Others join in laughter. It gains in confidence.
Prayer starts again. IYALOSA very low. Music
starts.
AKOOWA: Three claps.

IYALOSA: Eni s'oju se mu   ALL (*louder*): Orisa ni ma
sin
Ada ni b'o tiri

Orisa ni ma sin

Eni ran mi wa
Very low.   Orisa ni ma sin

Kabiesi a agbara
Fun wa l' agbara
Ran wa lowo
baba omo
s'ogun f'ono o
Omo o l'ogun o

AKOOWA: three
claps.
IMANI: Aaaaaaaaiiiiiiii-
eeeeeee!
ATOWODA: Quiet, woman.
Save your strength for
the child.

IMANI: Aaaaaaaaiiiiiiiieeeeeeee!
ATOWODA: Quiet, foolish woman. Be quiet!

Noise rises in ship.

OLALA: Iya! Iya!
DADEMI: Moshake, Moshake, be calm. Moshake it give
you oooooooooooooooooooooo.

Prayer continues quietly under.
Loud scream from woman.
NOLIWE: crying.

AKANO: Noliwe? Noliwe?
ATOWODA: Shango. Obatala.

Ship quiets down to low noise level.

Make your lightning, beat the inside bright with paths
for your people. Beat . . . Beat . . . BEAT

Music starts up. General chanting from all
people. "Lu . . . Lu . . . Lu . . ." Men beat in
rhythm.

"Sorrow Song"

ADUFE: Oro——oooooo
IYALOSA AND TAWA (*sing to* ADUFE): Toba ti wa logorun
ödun to lo
Oro——oooo

ALL WOMEN: K'emi na ma   AKANO: Shango
lo
K'emi na ma lo
K'emi na ma lo   Fun wa agbara
K'emi na ma lo
K'emi na ma lo
K'emi na ma lo
Oo——rr——oo   ALL MEN: O!

Toba ti wa logorun odun	
to lo	O!
Oo-rrrr——oooo	Fun wa agbara
K'emi na ma lo	O!

NOLIWE and IYA-
LOSA come together
at passage.

K'emi na ma lo	O!
K'emi na ma lo	Fun wa agbara
K'emi na ma lo	Fun wa agbara
K'emi na ma lo	O!
K'emi na ma lo	Wa agbara
Oo-rr-oo	O!
Toba ti wa logorun odun	
to lo	O!
Oo-rr-oo	Fun wa agbara
K'emi ma ma lo	O!
K'emi ma ma lo	Fun wa agbara
K'emi ma ma lo	O!
K'emi ma ma lo	Fun wa agbara
K'emi na ma lo	O!
K'emi na ma lo	Wa agbara
O-rr-oo	

AKOOWA: Fukwididila. Fukwididila. Igbe, Orisha.

Song stops.

Where are you now, Black God? Where you be now?
Help me. I be a strong warrior; I no woman. I strain
to break these chains. But you must help me, Orisha.

Pause.

Obatala!

AKANO: Quiet, you fool, you frighten the women!

ADUFE: Baba, Baba!

SAILOR enters with whip and three buckets, stick,
and funnel. Puts funnel down by men's hatch,
opens men's hatch and drops in one bucket, closes
hatch, goes to women's, puts in two buckets,
closes hatch, and goes back to men's hatch.

SAILOR opens men's hatch, looks in and sees
that AKANO and ATOWODA are not eating, enters
men's hatch with funnel and stick. Goes to AKANO,

knocks out teeth and puts funnel in his mouth, and proceeds to forcefeed him. Places food bucket in front of ATOWODA, who then eats. Returns to deck. Closes men's hatch, goes to women's hatch, looks in—IMANI is below hatch, eating—moves to downstage right corner, enters, and goes to IYALOSA in the downstage left corner.

AKOOWA: Why didn't you eat?

During the AKANO-ATOWODA action in the men's hold, the women are eating. NOLIWE gets to the food first, then ADUFE and TAWA, and finally IMANI. She takes the buckets and tries to get the last bit of food out of them. TAWA bumps into DADEMI, who backs away.

DADEMI: Get away—get away—you crush my child.

She backs into her corner.
    SAILOR drags IYALOSA to under the hatch. TAWA and IMANI bite him on his leg. He pushes IYALOSA up on the deck . . .
    She crawls on the deck to the rape area to try and escape the SAILOR. He goes over to her and takes off her leg chains, makes her spread her legs, and tortures her with his stick. Throughout this she is reaching to the audience and yelling.

IYALOSA: Help Me! Please Help Me!

The SAILOR unties her top piece and then lies on top of her . . .
    IYALOSA screams as the lights go out. The drums stop and there is quiet for a couple of beats. SAILOR helps her out of her wrist chains in the darkness.
    IYALOSA takes off her upper garment, picks up her headband and bowl from its preset place left of ramp, adjusts skirt, places bell in bowl, and starts down the ramp to the well . . .
    SAILOR lies on deck in rape area, groaning pleasurably through the following.

TAWA: Duro! Duro!

Crawls over and touches IMANI.

IMANI (*when* IYALOSA *is at well and kneeling*): Ifanami,
Ifanami, where you? Where you? Oh, please, God.
ATOWODA (*shamefully*): Obata.

> The rest of the ship quiets down.
> IYALOSA: Is kneeling at the well, puts down
> bowl and headband and bell, makes motions at
> the water, takes small bowl, and pours water
> from well into large bowl.

ATOWODA: Iyalosa! Iyalosa!
IYALOSA: K'aiye won O toro . . .

> Pause.

. . . bi omi . . .

> Pause.

. . . a f-oro-pon.

> Puts large bowl on headband on her head, rises,
> starts back to ship, ringing bell.

AKANO: Iyalosa!
TAPE: May their lives be clear and pure like water drawn
from the spring.
AKANO: Iyalosa!

> As IYALOSA starts down ramp toward ship . . .

Devils. Devils. Devils. White beasts. Shit eaters.
Beasts.

> IYALOSA gets back on floor, large bowl and head-
> band back in place. SAILOR helps gather her
> blouse and chains, which she takes and gathers
> to her breast, and then SAILOR starts to drag her
> back toward women's hatch. IYALOSA moans . . .
> When IYALOSA and SAILOR have cleared rape
> area . . .
> SAILOR drags her to women's hatch, jumps in,
> and puts her back in the women's hold. Jumps
> out, closes hatch, is on knees.

> Silence.

IYALOSA (*long, loud scream*): Aran-mi-omo.

> The men move to the wall divide in the hold.

AKANO: Pull, pull, break, break.

> IMANI, TAWA, and ADUFE go to IYALOSA and try
> to comfort her. They proceed to try and wash her.
> Screams and moans from the women.
>   SAILOR starts to laugh. When he puts his hand
> to his crotch . . .
>   At the end of laughter on tape . . .
>   Ad libs from hold: cries, moans, etc. SAILOR,
> laughing loudly, finally ends up flat on back on
> the women's hatch.

NOLIWE: Akano! Akano! Akano! Akano!

> In men's hold, men get loose from chains and
> group together and start to try and break down
> wall between them and women. AKANO is first
> and then ATOWODA, LALU, AKOOWA, SALAKO.

AKOOWA: Break it!

> They are unsuccessful, and they regroup, with
> ATOWODA at the head of the line. AKANO was
> hurt the first time. They are rhythmically chant-
> ing and try to break the wall down again. The
> chant is "Break . . . Break . . . break . . ."
> etc. The third grouping puts AKANO back in
> front, and the chant is now "E—Wa. E—Wa, E—
> Wa." When they succeed in breaking wall, and
> on AKANO's cue, all go into slow motion. The cue
> is AKANO slapping the deck.
>   Just before the men succeed in breaking
> through to the women, DADEMI strangles
> MOSHAKE with her chains. As the wall is broken
> and slow motion starts, she succeeds in stran-
> gling herself with her wrist chains.

DADEMI: Aaaaaaaaaaaaiiiiiiiiieeeeeoeeeee . . .

> She now exits hold upstage left and gets into
> the area just outside ship. This is after men
> have broken wall and have gone into slow
> motion.

NOLIWE: Aa . . . Ka . . . No . . .

> Regular motion starts again.

AKANO goes to NOLIWE, AKOOWA goes to ADUFE, returns to men's hold. LALU goes to TAWA.

IMANI: Ifanami, Ifanami! Where you?

ATOWODA: Has gone to upstage right in women's hold upon recognizing IYALOSA. Embraces her, she whispers in his ear.

ATOWODA: Dademi? Dademi? Dademi? etc.

ATOWODA crawls over to where DADEMI committed suicide. IYALOSA and TAWA follow him. He looks at the spot where she was, not where she is standing now.

IYALOSA: K'aiye . . .
ATOWODA: God, she's killed herself.

Ship quiets down. Pause.

. . . and the child.

Long pause.

Oh, God. Oh, God.
IYALOSA (*downstage left in women's hold. Low, almost keening*): She strangled herself, with the chain. Choked the child.
IMAN (*hugging Olala*): Why you leave us, Lord?
ATOWODA: Dademi . . . Dademi . . . She dead . . . she dead . . . Dademi . . . Dademi . . . Dademi . . .

Ad libs: "Dademi, where you?" etc.
IYALOSA: Crawls from women's hold into downstage left of men's hold, screaming, almost berserk, flailing arms, and others get out of her way.

IMANI: Ifanami, Ifanami. Where you?

IMANI: After IYALOSA has cleared the passageway between holds, she starts to crawl into men's hold . . .
LALU touches and grabs IMANI by the foot.

IMANI: Oh, please, please don't touch me! . . .

IMANI breaks free and goes into the men's hold.

Please . . . Ifanami,   where   you?   Akiyele . . .
please . . .

> Yoruba dialogue.

please . . . don't touch me, don't touch me . . .

> LALU goes to IMANI and mounts her.

Please, Ifanami, where you? Please help me . . .
Go . . .

> TAWA shows the action to SALAKO, who pulls
> LALU off IMANI, and they fight. TAWA takes OLALA
> away, LALU breaks down. The SAILOR reacts, on
> deck, to the rape.
> SAILOR has been listening with ear to deck
> to this last, is now laughing. Is joined by laughter
> on tape.

SALAKO: What you doing?

> Pulls LALU off.

Get away from that woman. That's not your woman.
You turn into a beast too.

> TAWA takes off IMANI's wrist chains.
> IMANI crawls away from rape area and takes
> OLALA with her. She goes to below men's hatch,
> and after she has crossed center of hold and is
> about to start into women's hold,
> SAILOR and TAPE are laughing and laughing.
> Finally laughter subsides. SAILOR ends up flat on
> back on women's hatch, exhausted from the
> laughing.
> Noise in ship subsides.

AKANO: Beasts, beasts, you murder women and children, you white walking slut. I'll kill you; I'll kill you!

> DADEMI now downstage under ramp, exits from
> the set for elastic strap for the baby.

IYALUSA (in downstage left corner; very low moan): Oh,
God, she's dead . . .

> Pause.

. . . and the child!

SAILOR laughs again, ends up fanning himself with red kerchief.

Near-silence descends on ship. Suddenly ship lurches to the left, on cue from drums.

Cries and moans from all.

NOLIWE: Long, loud scream. She starts last stages of labor.

TAWA: Noliwe, Noliwe??!!

IMANI crawls on floor through audience left to dancing platform.

Adufe! Adufe, come! (Ran-mi-wa)

Birth scene now takes place downstage right in women's hold. NOLIWE is surrounded by TAWA and ADUFE, who help in the labor. The women sympathetically make sounds to help the labor.

The birth continues for a time. On cue from TAWA, after birth takes place . . .

IYALOSA: Gives baby cries from her place downstage left in men's hold. The baby is carried by TAWA, after being wrapped in IYALOSA's headband, to AKANO, who is waiting in men's hold by hole in the wall.

Music starts.

Song plays once.

AKANO gives the baby to TAWA.

Song plays the second time.

TAWA takes the baby back to NOLIWE.

Song plays the third time.

Song plays fourth time.

END OF FIRST PART

PART TWO

Positions at start of Part Two:
    Dancing platform:
      ADUFE, right ⎫
      TAWA, center ⎬ standing
      IMANI, left, sitting on floor
    Offstage:
      OLALA
      ATOWODA
    Ramp and Dock:
      AKANO, audience level left
      SALAKO, "well"
      AKOOWA, center
    Audience:
      DADEMI
    Top Platform:
      LALU
    Deck:
      SAILOR, on ship's ladder
    Hold:
      NOLIWE
      IYALOSA

AKANO: Oyo Mabo, Oya Kalo Oya
WARRIORS: Oyo Mabo, Oya Kalo Oya
  Oyo Mabo, Oya Kalo Oya
  Oyo Mabo, Oya Kalo Oya
  Oyo Mabo, Oya Kalo Oya

> Twenty-four beats after conga drums join
> in . . .
> Women's dance. They stop, take bowl they
> have been pounding in, and pour contents into
> large flat sieve, go back to pounding pulse. 4th
> pound . . .

TOM: Yassa, boso, yassa massa Tim, yassa, boss I'se as
happy as a brand new monkey—ass, yassa, boss,
yassa, Massa Tim, Yass, massa Booboo, I'se so happy,
I'se so happy I just don't know what to do.

Sings "Swanee River"

Yass, Massa, boss, you'se so han'some and good and youse hip, too, yasss, I'se so happy . . . I'se so happy . . . I'se so happy I jus' stan' and scratch my ol' nigger haid.

Scratches groin and . . .
   SAILOR laughing on deck with tape.
   4 counts and . . .
   Warrior Dance . . . 24 beats or after 4th leg movement . . .
   Women's Dance—20 beats or after back and forth starts again . . .

TOM: Yassa, boss, yassa Massa Tim, yassa, boss, I'se happy as a brand new monkey, ah yassa, boss, yassa Massa Tim, Yass, Massa Booboo, I'se so happy, I'se so happy, I just don't know what to do.

("Swanee River.")

Yass Mass, boss, you'se so han'some and good and you'se hip too, yass, I'se so happy, I'se so happy, I'se so happy I jus' stan' and scratch my ol' nigger haid.

   SAILOR and tape laughing.
   4 counts later . . .
   SAILOR leaves ship, crosses upstage left, and changes for Reverend Turner scene.
   Warriors Dance . . . 12 counts and . . .
   Women's Dance joins . . . 8 counts and . . .

TOM (*on tape*): Yassa, boss, yassa massa Tim, yassa, boss I'se as happy as a brand new monkey, yassa boss, yassa massa Tim, Yass massa Booboo, I'se so happy, I'se so happy I just don't know what to do. (Hums Swanee River) Yass, Massa, boss, you'se so han'some and good and you'se hip too, yass, I'se so happy I jus' stan' and scratch my ol' nigger haid.

   TOM does headstand on platform, then goes into the DADEMI special area in audience. When he is in freeze position . . .
   1 beat and then . . .
   During the above speech, women dancers leave dance platform, go to Reverend Turner

platform. DADEMI takes her place on dance platform.
    AKOOWA and SALAKO cross to plantation plat-
form, change costume, and sit right and left on
platform.

DADEMI (*on dance platform*): Moshake . . . Moshake,
be calm.

    IYALOSA gives small baby cry.
    IMANI under ramp gives scream.
    IMANI then crawls toward Ifanami platform.

PLANTATION SCENE ON PLATFORM UPSTAGE

    Sitting right, AKOOWA and ADUFE standing behind
    Sitting center, SAILOR
    Sitting left, TURNER and TAWA standing behind
        AKOOWA touches hat . . .
        REVEREND TURNER moves arm . . .

AKOOWA: Reverend, what we gon' do when massa come?
TURNER: We gon' cut his damn throat!

    TOM does Swanee dance on platform. End of
    dance; hand out . . .

SAILOR: Reverend Turner, what we gon' do when the
white man come?
TURNER: We gon' cut his fucking throat!
AKANO (*in hold of ship. Low and threatening*): Devil!
Devil! White beasts! I break these chains! I crush your
face. I break your neck! I'll kill you! I'll kill you!
AKOOWA (*rises, crosses to right of Turner*): Reverend
Turner, sir, what we gonna do when the Massa come?
TURNER (*stands*): Cut his Godless throat.

    People start to leave platform. When TURNER is
    on second step . . .
        AKANO in hold saws chains through following
    action.

AKOOWA, on passing NOLIWE, touches her, motions for her to join, and she refuses.

People from platform sneak through audience toward revolt platform. As they near revolt platform . . .

Ending positions on revolt platform: From audience left, TURNER, TAWA, ADUFE, AKOOWA, SAILOR.

When SAILOR and others in position . . .

TOM (*eating porkchop on platform*): Uhh, das right, massa Tim . . . dey gon' 'volt.

TAPE: What? Vote? Are you crazy?

TAPE (*laughs*): When, boy?

TOM: Ahh, t'night, boss, t'night . . . they say they gon' . . . 'scuse de 'spressiong . . . cut your . . . uhh uhh . . . uhh . . . fockin' . . . uhh throat . . .

TAPE: And who's gonna be in charge of this 'volt?

TOM: Uhh . . . Reverend Turner . . . suh.

TAPE: What?

TOM: Uhh . . . dass right . . . Reverend Turner . . . suh . . . Now can I have dat extra p'oke chop you promises me???

IYALOSA makes baby cries under following.

NOLIWE (*leaves baby alone for a minute*): Akano? Akano?

AKANO slowly opens men's hatch, creeps out onto deck of ship. When he is in front of center mast . . .

AKANO: White Devil!

ATOWODA appears on ramp with gun, fires at AKANO, kills him.

NOLIWE screams . . .

3 count . . .

3 count . . .

IYALOSA gives louder baby cry, NOLIWE returns to her child. Revolt continues live and on tape till tape runs out.

TOM: Cringes, looks at revolt, reacts. End of revolt. He throws away porkchop bone. Prop man throw fresh chop into his hat. TOM eats and hums "Swanee River," one verse, as he does slow turn in place . . .

TURNER gets on ship in hanging position under spar.

DADEMI: Moshake . . . we be all right, now . . . Moshake, be calm . . .

TURNER (*hangs himself*): White Beasts!! . . .

ATOWODA (*on ramp*): All right. Line up there.

DADEMI leaves woman dancers' platform.

IMANI (*on floor near Ifanami platform*): Ifanami, Olala, husband, child; where you? Please help me!!

NOLIWE: Akano? Akano!?

IYALOSA: Baby cry.

AKANO (*again exits slowly from men's hatch*): White Devils!

AKANO is shot by ATOWODA. Falls upstage left men's side of ship.

DADEMI: Moshake.

AKANO: Noliwe . . . Touch my hand, woman!!

IYALOSA gives loud baby cry.

DADEMI walks around ship and exits for slave sale.

IMANI (*on Ifanami platform. To Ifanami*): Ifanami, Ifanami! No, No!!

Takes off his manacles, helps get rid of the dummy.

AUCTIONEER (*ascends plantation platform, turns*): Sam, I thought I told you to clear this platform?

SAM moves stools to right side, ad libs

You better watch out, boy, or you'll find yourself on the end of that line.

After all slaves are on the platform, AUCTIONEER leaves it and goes to ship platform. Takes out imaginary knife and cuts down REVEREND TURNER. TURNER hits deck and remains there. TOM

joins him on deck, bringing ADUFE, and the AUC-
TIONEER drops body down hole in ship.

AUCTIONEER: You better get over here. I'm not going
to do all your work for ya.

Order in which people are tied up for the Slave
Sale: OLALA, TAWA, ADUFE, AKOOWA, and SAILOR.

SLAVE SALE

1. OLALA: carried to deck by TOM; sold.

IMANI: No! John! Take me! Take me!

Carried to audience.

2. TAWA: sold. Sees SALAKO, hysterics, and
then bites TOM. Put in Audience.

3. ADUFE: haughty, walks in front of TOM
onto deck. TOM exposes her breasts and turns her
around. Sold to someone in front of the Tom platform. She is taken down the ladder, and when
TOM puts her in place, she turns and spits at
him, he hits her in the stomach, and she crumples
on the floor.

AUCTIONEER: I declare, Sam, you sure got a way with the
heifers.

4. Slow-motion fight on platform. LALU starts
slow motion from the bottom of the steps.

5. AKOOWA: sold. Crosses to behind Tom platform.

6. SAILOR: sold. Brought to audience.

7. REVEREND TURNER: lifted, TOM at head,
AUCTIONEER at feet. Sold.

8. AKANO: TOM raises his head, sold.

9. NOLIWE: dragged from hold with baby by
TOM. Runs off ramp into audience right. TOM
chases, carries her back. NOLIWE is sold and then
hit. She falls on SALAKO. Her baby is grabbed

from her arms, and the baby is sold and then
dropped in audience lap by TOM. IYALOSA gives
baby cry.

    10. TOM: hit on the head and then sold.

    ATOWODA goes into men's hold, gets IYALOSA
on deck.

ATOWODA: What the hell you waitin' for.

IYALOSA (*is lifted from the men's hold, leans against
the mast*): Obatala!

    Stands, backs away and feels AKANO's legs against
hers. She turns, sees him.

Obatala!

    Stumbles against the mast again.

Obatala!!

    Sinks under the spar during following.

NOLIWE: Save us.
TAWA: Lord.
SALAKO: Shango.
IMANI: Lord of the forest.
DADEMI: Obatala, Obatala!

    Loud—cue for the music.
       The lines build to a crescendo.
       Ends as music builds and stops.

IYALOSA: Give us back our strength!!

    Sinks to deck.

AUCTIONEER: Sold!

    IMANI starts humming "Oh, Lord Deliver Me,"
and the others join in. Take the following positions:

    AKANO: kneeling on ramp, pot and pole in
place.

    DADEMI: standing behind AKANO.

    NOLIWE: down ladder, gets baby back from
audience, exchanges it for burned baby under
plantation platform. Gets on platform.

    TOM: closes both hatches, leaves by ladder.

IYALOSA: gathers together clothes, leaves by ladder.
All clear deck of ship.
Snare drum starts very low roll . . .

AKANO (*kneeling*): Baba eje. Baba reen. Give me weapons. My spear my bone and muscle make tight with tension of combat. Baba eje. Baba reen. Give me fire and death to give to this beast. Sarava. Sarava. Baba eje.

Bends over—head to floor.
Congregation kneels, one by one—SAILOR, TOM, NOLIWE—etc., saying "Jesus." IMANI starts song:

JESUS,
JESUS,
JESUS, JESUS,
JESUS,
Ooo . . . Oooo.

Singing continues, low, under the following.

SAILOR: Oh, my lord!

AKANO: Baba eje. Baba reen. Give me weapons. My spear. My bone and muscle make tight with tension of combat. Baba eje. Baba reen . . . Give me fire and death to give to this beast.

Pole in pot . . . Flash powder.
AKANO drinks from pot, replaces it.

Sarava, Sarava, Baba eje!

Kneels, head to floor.
Congregation sings louder, clapping hands, etc. PREACHER gets bible etc. from left of plantation, goes to Tom platform, shakes hands, goes to center stair, and ascends plantation platform . . .
DADEMI comes off ramp and makes her way slowly to her special light area.
AKANO puts pole and pot back in place.

NOLIWE: May I kiss your cross?
PREACHER: By all means.

NOLIWE (*kisses cross*): Jesus!
PREACHER: Bless her Lord! Bless her.

> PREACHER ad libs with congregation, and then
> returns to center. IYALOSA gives him top hat.

Jesus, Jesus, Jesus, Jesus!

> Turns, bows to Ifanami platform, to others,
> leaves platform, ascends ship ladder . . . Re-
> lief. Fans face, one sock up, shines one shoe—
> freezes—fear. Scratches rear. Pause. Bewildered.

Yass, we understand . . . the problem.

> Confidence.

And personally, I think some agreement can be
reached.
ATOWODA: He sho' kno' what to say out of his mouth.
ALL (*ad lib*): Yass, yass.
PREACHER: We will be non-violint . . .

> Poses.

. . . to the last.

> Hums "Swanee River."

Because we understand the dignity of pruty mcbonk
and the greasy ghost.

> Opens Bible.

Of course, diddy rip de bink . . .

> Shuffles feet.

. . . of vout juice. And the penguins would do the
same. I HAVE A TRAUMA that the gold sewers won't
integrate . . . Present fink. I have an enema. . . .
a trauma, on the coaster with your wife birdshit.

> 3 beats . . .
> Explosion sounds and bright lights right over
> NOLIWE bump on.
> Cries and moans.
> LALU crosses and gets baby. TAWA goes to com-
> fort NOLIWE.

DEDEMI (*in special area*): Moshake! Moshake . . .
beeba . . . beeba . . . Wafwa ko wafwa ko fuk-
widdidilas.

IYALOSA (*to* NOLIWE): The Lord will make a way, sister,
yes he will.

> Moves down ladder two steps.
> SALAKO with burned baby and SAILOR descend
> plantation, ascend ship. SALAKO on left. SALAKO
> shows baby to PREACHER and puts it at his feet.
> PREACHER steps over it. SAILOR picks up baby,
> shows it to PREACHER and lays it at his feet. He
> steps over it again . . . SALAKO picks up baby,
> shows it again to PREACHER, lays it at his feet
> . . . This time the PREACHER steps on the
> baby . . .
> Shocked comments from the Plantation plat-
> form.

PREACHER: Uhhherrrr . . . As I was sayin' . . . Mas'
. . . un, Mister Tastyslop . . . We Kneegrows

> Slaps knee.

are ready to integrate.

> SALAKO picks up baby, and he and SAILOR leave
> by ladder.

. . . the blippy rum of stomach bat has corrinked a
lip to push the thimble.

> Plantation people take places in audience for
> song.

Yas, yas, yas, yas, yas, yas, yassssss.

> Freezes in TOM position.
> Music builds to a crescendo, stops.

AKANO (*standing on ramp*): Beasts! Beasts! Beasts!
Ogun let me kill!!

ALL: Ohmmmmmmmmmmmmmmmmmmmmmmmmm.

TAPE: Laughter, to which PREACHER reacts.

> DADEMI exits, takes off chains, takes place
> when ready.

When We Gonna Rise Up

Spoken:
AKANO: Rise
LALU: Rise
ATOWODA: Rise
SALAKO: Cut these ties, Black Men Rise
SAILOR: We gon' be the things we are
Song:
    When, we gonna rise up
    When, we gonna rise up
    When, we gonna rise up
    When, we gonna rise up

    When we gonna lift our heads and voices
    Show the world who we really are
    When we gonna rise up, brother, brother
    When we gonna rise up.

    When, we gonna rise up
    When, we gonna rise up
    When, we gonna rise up
    When, we gonna rise up

    When we gonna rise above the sun
    When we gonna take our own places, brother
    Like the world had just begun
    When we gonna rise up

AKANO: When we gonna lift our heads and voices
    When we gonna rise up
LALU: Show the world who we really are
    When we gonna rise up
SAILOR. Warrior Gods and lovers
    When we gonna rise up
ATOWODA: The first man to walk this star
    When we gonna rise up
SALAKO: Yes, yes, the first man to ever walk this star
    When we gonna rise up
LALU: Yes, yes, the first man to ever walk this star
    Doo, Doo, Doo

    When, we gonna rise up
    When, we gonna rise up

When, we gonna rise up
When, we gonna rise up

How far, how long will it be
Before the world belongs to you and me
When we gonna rise up, brother, brother
When we gonna rise up, brother, brother
When we gonna rise up, brother, brother
Spoken: When we gonna rise up

> IYALOSA: on marriage platform. Has small bowl with ashes and bandanna containing shells in front of her. Scatters ashes; kneels, makes circle.

IYALOSA: Kabiesi a agbara
Fun wa l'agbara
Ran wa lowo
Babaomo
S'ogun f'omo o

> Shakes shells, throws them on bandanna. Looks at DADEMI.

DADEMI: Moshake! Moshake!
AKANO (*quietly, threateningly*): Ogun, give me steel.
IYALOSA (*looks at* PREACHER. *Spits out very softly*): KILL.
ALL: Ooo, ooo, ooo, ooooo,
When we gonna rise up, ooo, ooo, ooo
When we gonna rise up, ooo, ooo, ooo
When we gonna rise up, ooo, ooo, ooo
When we gonna rise up, ooo, ooo, ooo

> IYALOSA crosses to downstage right of ship.

PREACHER: Please boss, these niggers goin' crazy; please boss, throw your lightnin' at 'em white, Jesus boss! RIGHT NOW!
TAPE: Fool.

> Laughter.

Fool.

> Laughter.
> All actors now go onto deck from below.

PREACHER: Throw your white lightning at 'em, white

Jesus boss. Boss man, you know I'd do anything for
you. Please, boss . . . Please, please, boss, boss!!

> On knees.
>
> Actors make a ring around the preacher. Toss
> him from person to person.
>
> On the third toss, when people hold hands up
> in "V," SAILOR and AKANO chase PREACHER onto
> ramp. They catch him and break his neck. After,
> PREACHER is on wall and head slumps. Other
> actors are kneeling in two lines on deck watch-
> ing, beating on the deck with hands. Actors rise
> and file off ship, down ramp, and onto audience
> floor. When first two are on floor:

TAPE. (*as actors converge on plantation platform*): Ha,
Ha, Ha, Ha, . . . now what . . . you, ha, ha, can't
touch me . . . you scared of me, niggers. I'm God.
You can't kill white Jesus God. I got long blond
blow-hair. I don't even need to wear a wig. You love
the way I look. You want to look like me. You love me.

> AKANO gives cue for slow motion.

You want me. Please. I'm good. I'm kind. I'll give you
anything you want. I'm white Jesus savior, right?
God . . . I'll pay you money, nigger. Me is good God
be please . . . please don't . . .

> TAPE: Long, diminishing scream.
>
> Uncle Sam head disappears into middle of
> actors. Black Power banner is raised. All raise
> hands in salute. After final gesture . . . 4
> counts . . .
>
> 3 counts . . .
>
> Actors have all risen in blackout and are star-
> ing at the audience, unmoving.
>
> Music starts, actors start to move. They leave
> the platform and dance in the audience. AKANO
> gets emblem and dances on deck of ship. ATO-
> WODA dances banner to ship and hangs it on
> mast. AKANO gives emblem to SALAKO. When
> TOM gives the orchestra the signal to stop the
> music . . .
>
> Tom head is tossed to AKANO on the deck. He

throws it to ATOWODA in the audience, right of
ship. He throws it to SAILOR in the audience, left
of ship, who throws it back to AKANO, who hangs
it on the mast . . .

ALL: Oyo Mabo, Oya Kala Oyo
    Oyo Mabo, Oya Kala Oyo
    Oyo Mabo, Oya Kala Oyo

All actors leave down backstage ramps shouting
the above cry.
    Sharp cut off of chant.
    Orchestra starts up again.

END

THE KID

by Robert Coover

Introduction by John Lahr

Theater has the ability to create myths and to destroy them. The myth-making power of the stage lies in the conviction with which dramatic situations are fleshed out to embody ideas and attitudes influencing the collective unconscious of a culture. Musicals, for instance, are the American form because their lush extravagance and up-beat optimism offer the middle-class American audience images of moderation and well-being which sustain its faith in the system. The fantasy world of musicals—from the story to the luxurious stage they are mounted on—focuses on money, which is usually a crucial ingredient of the drama. Buoyancy is the rhythm of the American musical, and the gigantic tableaux confirm what we want to believe—that everything's coming up roses. In a world so blatantly swollen by daydreams, dreaming is a very crucial experience. After all, if you don't have a dream, how you gonna have a dream come true? The storms of life are conquered by faith. Every cloud has its silver lining and can be survived by keeping your head up high. No matter what happens to the characters of musicals, the main strategy for survival is waiting. Something's coming, something good—if you can wait.

But the plays that comment on myth operate on two levels at once. They give the audience the archetypal figure of faith, and once established, they turn these figures on their heads to show how the culture posits its energy in false gods and emasculating assumptions. Robert Coover's *The Kid* explores America's mysterious will to believe, which produces a panoply of false gods. His play dramatizes the process by which the profane is transformed into the sacred. He revives the ritual duel between the Bad Man and the Sheriff. Coover offers an audience the externals of the old Western melodrama, complete with ballads and gunfire. His intention is not an easy parody of familiar forms; he wants to expose the murky need behind this yearning. The cowpokes in the saloon talk in simple sentences; no man is differentiated from another. There are also a number of girls, all called Belle [Starr], emphasizing the mythic quality of the event: the Kid is coming to town. Excitement is in the air. The Sheriff has sworn to do away with him. Yet despite the Kid's outrageous "evil," the cattle-town chorus idealizes him. The songs, coupled with the cowpokes' reaction, flesh out the process of myth making. Before the Kid arrives in town, the cowpokes sing of his glory:

> He's killt Apaches, Cayuses,
> And Potawatami papooses,
> And buggered the Chickasaw chiefs!
> Rid the country of snakes,
> And shit in the lakes. . . .
>
> He's the Savior of the West!
> He's the Savior of the West!

The true believer never asks questions, every historical betrayal becomes a victory.

If the Kid is to be mythic, he must speak in tongues, as does every great magician. He does: "Coma ti yi youpy youpy yea" are his only words. Coover sees the mythic figure defined by silence; his power does not reside so much in himself as in those who fill his silence with a sense of magical strength. Nobody else is allowed to speak his special language. When the chorus tries to echo his doggerel, the Kid's six-shooter riddles a poker game.

Cowpoke 44: Whew! I reckon he didn't like yuh shufflin them cards!

Cowpoke 45: Reckon he didn't like you breakin the silence!

Cowpoke 46: S-s-sorry, Kid!

Cowpoke 47: The Kid's big on silence!

Cowpoke 48: You said it, podnuh!

Cowpoke 49: *Very* big!

Cowpoke 50: The biggest!

In Coover's fable the Kid is gunned down by the Sheriff. While conventional melodrama would end here, Coover mystifies his audience by pursuing more profound conclusions. After applauding his fast gun, the chorus of cowhands begins to refashion the Sheriff in the image of the Kid—dressing him with the Kid's spurs and his "shootin' irons" until the Sheriff becomes the Kid. The Sheriff protests, but the cowboys see what they want to see; they kill their imitation hero when he protests that he is not the Kid. The belief in sacred mystery supersedes man's belief in himself. The ambiguity Coover poses on stage is a modern predicament: man's need for mystery and also his denial of it. Even after dispatching the Sheriff/ Kid, the cowpokes return to their nostalgia for the magical experience. The Kid's luminous aura glosses the ignorance and violence for which he stands. The need, as Coover proves, is more important to the culture than are the consequences. Disliking paradox, the mind forges an impossible picture of coherence. The cowpoke chorus, in its final song, intones a hymn to its mythical hero, mixing fantasy and anticipation with the memory of victory: "He was mean, he was magic, he was real!/ Sweet Jesus, he was somethin tuh see!"

Characters
The Kid
The Sheriff
The Deputy
A Barkeep and several
Cowpokes and Belles

Inside an Old West frontier town saloon. BAR-
KEEP and ten to twelve COWPOKES: four or five
playing poker at a big table, another five or six
drinking at the bar, others scattered, reading
papers, dozing, etc. Among the men at the bar
are THE SHERIFF and his DEPUTY. THE SHERIFF is
one of those soft-spoken goodguy worrier types
from the Western flicks, average height and
build, about forty or so, the kind who is always
rubbing his jaw thoughtfully, gazing off, wanting
and praying that the Marshall will turn up, a little
clumsy, ingenuous, modest, yet heroic and de-
pendable. His DEPUTY is skinny, amiable, a
little goofy, maybe an older gent. The rest of
the men in the town saloon are the usual run
of Western extras, generally a little swarthy,
beardy, slovenly in dull gray and brown cowboy
duds, none of them looking too trustworthy.
Lights or curtain can go up on a tableau (cards
about to be dealt, drinks about to be drunk, foot
about to be raised to the rail, etc.), set into motion by some signal (e.g., the swinging doors
suddenly slapping open, or gunfire, or the amplified crack of a playing card): noisy hubbub of
drinks being ordered, stories being told, argu-
ments being waged, drinks sliding along the bar,
betting of cardplayers, etc., interrupted almost
immediately by the breathless arrival, through
the swinging doors, of three or more dance-hall
ladies, all called BELLE. Sudden silence and all
eyes—except THE SHERIFF's—on them. (The
BELLE and COWPOKE lines, here numbered con-
secutively for convenience, should be passed out
randomly enough to make it difficult to distin-
guish the character of one BELLE or COWPOKE
from another. In fact, they may, if they wish,
trade off lines in different performances; each
line has its essential character and place, and
it shouldn't matter who delivers it. Clarity, con-

trol, and a fairly fast pace [no ad libbing!] are essential to the play.) In all that follows, the girls reveal—clicking their heels, whirling their skirts, rubbing their hips, and so on—a mounting sexual excitement, their lines delivered to the world, not the COWPOKES.

BELLE 1: He's comin! I seen him!
BELLE 2: Out on the flats!
BELLE 3: Stirrin up the dust, boys!
BELLE 4: Stirrin up the wind!
BELLE 5: Clappin mean spurs tuh his big red roan!
BELLE 6: Movin acrost the desert like a wild blue eagle!
BELLE 7: Movin acrost the grasslands like white lightnin!
BELLE 8: Splittin the breeze! Pourin it on! Ridin like all forty, boys!
BELLE 9: Like a bat outa hell, boys!
BELLE 10: Like all possessed!
BELLE 11: Good Lord! He's *beautiful!*

Since the moment the girls burst into the saloon, the COWPOKES have been motionless, apprehensive yet calm, silent, as though poised for action. Some of those seated have half risen, and the men at the bar have swung about to give full attention to the ladies—all but THE SHERIFF, whose back is turned still, and THE DEPUTY, who is watching THE SHERIFF. Now, one of the men breaks in:

COWPOKE 1: *Who,* Belle? *Who* did yuh say was comin?
BELLE 12: The *Kid,* hombre! *The Kid's comin!*

Now THE SHERIFF does turn from the bar, slowly, as though troubled, weary, yet alert, hands coming to rest lightly on the butts of his two holstered six-shooters. He seems to be mulling over what he's just heard, thinking things out, looking at the girls, yet gazing beyond them. He flexes his hands, rubs them absently on his hips and holsters. THE DEPUTY, now staring at the BELLES in open mouthed wonderment, lets his glass slip through his shaking hand and crash to the floor (slightly amplified). The other men in the saloon

turn to THE SHERIFF, most of them in dead seriousness, as though perhaps waiting for him to
make a move, issue commands, lead them forth—
but two or three COWPOKES seem about to erupt
into laughter. One of these latter, suppressing a
grin, says with great feeling:

COWPOKE 2: Oh no! Not the Kid!

DEPUTY: Gosh all willikers!

BELLE 13: Yes, the Kid, damn it! Ridin tall and easy
in the saddle through the great clean silence!

BELLE 14: Yes, strikin sharp spurs tuh his lean wire-
tough chestnut, boys, and burnin up the prairie!

BELLE 15: Wingin it over the ridges at a long swingin
lope, big hands clamped hard on the reins!

BELLE 16: Hands big on the pommel, boys!

BELLE 17: Ridin hard in the saddle!

BELLE 18: In the saddle, boys! Sweet in the saddle!

BELLE 19: Pushin that big silver stallion, hot from
wranglin dogies in the Badlands!

BELLE 20: From runnin broomtails and bustin broncs!

BELLE 21: Bustin banks, boys!

BELLE 22: Jammin hot spurs in the flanks a that Barb!

BELLE 23: Packin the mail!

BELLE 24: Oh, he's fleet as a deer, boys, and tougher'n a
mule!

BELLE 25: Yes, and purty as a pitcher!

BELLE 26: And he's nobody's fool, boys! He's nobody's
fool!

DEPUTY (*squeaking out in the silence*): No! No, he ain't!

This causes a light ripple of laughter among the
COWPOKES (THE SHERIFF is still silent, thought-
ful, preoccupied), as the BELLES step forward to
sing the ballad, "The Savior of the West," assisted
by the COWPOKES. Some of the COWPOKES play
guitars, harmonicas, banjos, fiddles, etc., or al-
ternatively, they pretend to play them while the
accompaniment is piped in electronically. Occasional "whoopee's" and "yahoo's." THE DEPUTY
joins in on the first chorus, but he is loudly
off key—one of the COWPOKES, grimacing at the
noise, swats him playfully with his hat to shut

him up. The BELLES, sharing the verses, may
pay a handmike among them. Their performance
is a cross between a dance-hall routine and country gospel singing: a hillbilly mix of sex, senti-
ment, and self-righteousness.

The Savior of the West

Come hear the Kid's story,
It's bloody and gory,
And it's shore tuh put hair on yore chest!
He kin lick any man,
And he don't give a damn!
He's the Savior of the West!
    He's the Savior of the West!

He left eighty men dyin
Down south of the line,
And robbed sixteen trains of their gold!
Shed blood by the bucket,
Told the Marshall tuh fuck it,
Before he was twelve years old!
    Before he was twelve years old!

CHORUS: Yes, a gent or a dame,
    It's all the same
    Tuh the Kid when he puts em tuh rest!
    Cuz killin's his game,
    They all know him by name,
    He's the Savior of the West!
        He's the Savior of the West!

He's killt Apaches, Cayuses,
And Potawatami papooses,
And buggered the Chickasaw chiefs!
Rid the country of snakes,
And shit in the lakes,
And hung all the schoolmarms and thiefs!
    Hung all the schoolmarms and thiefs!

When the killin's all done,
They ain't anyone
Left standin 'cept fer the Kid!

He's the number one gun,
And fer him it's jist fun,
Surveyin all the dead!
   Surveyin all the dead!

CHORUS: Yeah, the Kid is his name,
   And he's too tough tuh tame,
   He's the fastest, the meanest, the best!
   Jist blam! blam! blam!
   And he don't give a damn!
   He's the Savior of the West!
     He's the Savior of the West!

> Whooping and hollering after the song, shouts of "Amen!" "That's tellin it!" and so on, excited embraces. Then they all turn toward THE SHERIFF and THE DEPUTY. They nod suggestively toward THE SHERIFF, apparently trying to remind THE DEPUTY of something. THE SHERIFF remains as before, gazing thoughtfully off. THE DEPUTY looks puzzled, then seems suddenly to remember.

DEPUTY: Hey! Sheriff!

SHERIFF: Yeah?

DEPUTY: Sheriff, the Kid's hit town!

SHERIFF: Yeah . . . I know . . .

DEPUTY: Well, uh, whadda we gonna *do*?

SHERIFF: I dunno. (*Sighs.*) We'll do what we have tuh do, I reckon.

DEPUTY (*swaggering a little*): Yuh mean we're gonna go after that mean lowdown nogood varmint, Sheriff?

SHERIFF: I figger we ain't got no choice. He's broke the law and he's hurt a lotta people.

DEPUTY (*still swaggering*): Yup, I knowed that's what yuh'd say, and yuh know what?

SHERIFF: What?

DEPUTY (*swagger collapsing*): I'm *skeered*, Sheriff!

SHERIFF (*smiling gently, clapping a reassuring hand to his* DEPUTY's *trembling shoulders*): Aw, c'mon now, podnuh! Y'ain't gonna let these jaspers here catch yuh in no lily-livered funk, are yuh?

DEPUTY (*still quailing*): I reckon I ain't got no more choice about that than you got about chasin varmints, Sheriff!

THE SHERIFF laughs loosely, then strides manfully toward the swinging doors. There, he turns, addresses the COWPOKES in the saloon. They listen attentively, a little guiltily at first (a practiced guilt: they've been through this before), then later with some (real) surprise. The BELLES turn their back on THE SHERIFF.

SHERIFF: Men, I got somethin tuh say tuh yuh. It won't take long and it pains me some tuh talk of it, but I might never git another chance tuh speak tuh yuh like this, and I feel as how I gotta say it.

COWPOKES seem a little uneasy, though some wink at each other.

I'm shore yuh all know by now: the Kid's back in town.

Some COWPOKES react as though getting the news for the first time.

Now, I know what you're thinkin. You're thinkin, that goldurn Sheriff's gonna ask us tuh help him go after that ornery varmint. And yuh don't want tuh go. Nobody's ever outshot the Kid, and yuh don't wanna git killt. You're skeered. Well, I don't blame yuh none. I'm skeered, too. But you're wrong. I *ain't* gonna ask yuh to go with me!

Mild surprise, artificial relief, some gathering consternation. The BELLES, curious, now turn to attend him.

I ain't never told yuh this before, but, well, yuh see, this here star I'm wearin, it means a whole lot tuh me. Like a lotta you boys, I first come in tuh this here community with nuthin but the shirt on muh back and the hoss I was ridin . . . and even the damn hoss was half dead!

This was meant as a joke, and THE SHERIFF pauses, smiling. A few COWPOKES chuckle awkwardly, glancing uneasily at each other.

But this here town's been good tuh me, the folks here is decent and law-abidin, and it's a place where a man kin be his own man. And I wanna say, right here and now, I was mighty proud the day yuh all seen fit tuh make me yore Sheriff. Might seem like a mite small thing tuh some of yuh, but, men, I gotta tell yuh straight out so's yuh know how I feel: it's the greatest goldurn thing ever happened tuh me, and, well, like I say, I'm mighty damn proud.

> THE SHERIFF fingers his star thoughtfully, proudly.

And so I been thinkin: what could I do tuh live up tuh this here badge? What could I do tuh live up tuh the trust you folks've put in me? And then it come tuh me. Sheriff, I says tuh myself, Sheriff, fer them: *you gotta face the Kid alone!*

COWPOKE 3: Uh, now hold up, Sheriff——

COWPOKE 4: They ain't no need tuh——

SHERIFF: No, boys! I done made up muh mind! It's me or the Kid!

COWPOKE 5: But——!

SHERIFF (*fully worked up now*): No "buts" about it, boys! It's law and order has made this town great, and it's my job as Sheriff tuh see it's kep, that's what yuh elected me fer, that's why yuh give me this here badge, and I mean tuh do what's gotta be done!

> THE SHERIFF wheels about and slaps his way out through the swinging doors before anyone can answer. THE DEPUTY blinks once at the COWPOKES in registration of his own astonishment, then squares his shoulders bravely, shoves down on his six-shooters with determination— and pushes the gunbelt right down off his hips, tripping over it as he attempts to follow THE SHERIFF out, falling to his face on the barroom floor. He jumps up sheepishly and staggers hurriedly out, trying to pull up his gunbelt as he stumbles along. Saloon erupts in full-bellied laughter. A couple COWPOKES leap up and dance a little impromptu jig with the BELLES, slapping them playfully on their behinds.

COWPOKE 6: Hey, yuh don't think he's gonna screw it up, do yuh?

COWPOKE 7: Who, the Sheriff? Haw haw!

COWPOKE 8: I mean, he kinda got things crossed up there, like he——

COWPOKE 9: Deppity'll keep an eye on him!

COWPOKE 10: Hey, yuh got everything ready?

COWPOKE 11: Ready as she'll ever be!

> COWPOKE 11, holding one fist over his head, crossing his eyes, and lolling his tongue, does a little dance on his toes as though hanging himself, as another COWPOKE, off tune, sings a snatch of the final song:

COWPOKE 12: Oh, the West was a place a grace and glory . . . !

> General laughter.

COWPOKE 13: This is gonna be good!

> Whoopeeing and music-making is interrupted by a COWPOKE standing near the swinging doors, looking out.

COWPOKE 14: Hey! *Here he comes!*

> COWPOKES and BELLES fall rapidly into poses around tables, at the bar, etc. Total silence in the old saloon, as all wait breathlessly. In strides THE KID. He slaps the swinging doors hard as he enters, making BELLES and COWPOKES gasp and start. He is tall, blond, broad-shouldered, narrow-hipped, graceful, elegant. He might wear, for example, a white Stetson (brim flattened up cockily on the sides), white full-cuffed gloves, white gunbelt and boots, tight navy-blue shirt and pants, red kerchief around the neck. Bright silver six-shooters in white holsters, strapped low on his thighs. There might even be a special spot turned on him to give him additional radiance. He is, in short, a real impressive piece of magical meanness. He surveys the room, hands at hips. Tips back his hat with his thumb as he gazes defiantly at the COWPOKES, his expression cold and humorless. He turns his steady gaze on THE BARKEEP, sweating motionlessly behind the bar.

COWPOKE 15: Hey, uh, better pour the Kid a drink there, podnuh!

COWPOKE 16: Yeah, right! Hurry it up, Mac! The Kid's waitin!

COWPOKE 17: The Kid must be purty damn thirsty after his long ride!

COWPOKE 18: Thirsty! Right!

COWPOKE 19: Ain't that right, Kid?

> Slowly, keeping his eye warily on THE KID, THE BARKEEP is meanwhile setting a shotglass on the bar, filling it. Now, faster than the eye can see, THE KID draws and fires, blasting both shotglass and whiskey bottle with the same shot. BARKEEP grimaces, but doesn't flinch. COWPOKES and BELLES fall back, some taking cover. The gunblasts should be very loud, accompanied if possible by puffs of gunsmoke from the barrels; the sounds of shattering glass (and all other sounds that follow) should be amplified. To augment the illusion of THE KID's speed, the gunblasts should sound at virtually the same moment the guns are drawn from their holsters. Dialogue should move very fast, though each line should be played for all it is worth. No mumbling or vague crowd noises—all lines specific and clear. Some of the lines may be distributed to BELLES, if desired.

COWPOKE 20: Whatsamatter? Yuh don't like that brand, Kid?

COWPOKE 21: Reckon the Kid don't go fer that cheap kinda whiskey, Mac!

COWPOKE 22: Reckon yuh better find somethin a little better!

COWPOKE 23: Somethin a little smoother!

COWPOKE 24: Reckon yuh better make it pronto, podnuh!

COWPOKE 25: Yuh don't fool around none with the Kid!

COWPOKE 26: By God, yuh *don't!*

> THE BARKEEP, keeping his eyes on THE KID, reaches behind him for another bottle, but no sooner does he pick it up than THE KID blasts

it out of his hand. THE BARKEEP, eyes narrowing, grabs up six or seven bottles and sets them on the bar, then ducks behind it. THE KID, firing rapidly, blasts away every bottle but one. THE BARKEEP's hand appears, setting a new shotglass on the bar, but THE KID grabs up the remaining bottle, smashes its top off with a blow against the bar, and chugalugs its contents. Meanwhile, this has been going on:

COWPOKE 27: Hey! Did yuh see *that!*
COWPOKE 28: Shot up ever damn bottle but one!
COWPOKE 29: Jist blam blam, man!
COWPOKE 30: That Kid's got taste, podnuh!
COWPOKE 31: I reckon he *does!*
COWPOKE 32: Blam blam! Gawdamighty!
COWPOKE 33: Hey, I reckon he's some kinda drinker, too!
COWPOKE 34: Yuh betcha life, hombre! Lookit him go!
COWPOKE 35: Boys, they ain't nuthin the Kid cain't do better'n any ten men!

Sudden blast from THE KID's six-shooter—his free hand—though without a pause in his drinking, and this COWPOKE's hat flies off. The other COWPOKES duck.

Woops! Uh, make that *fifty* men!
COWPOKE 36: *Fifty* men okay, Kid?
COWPOKE 37: I say a *hunderd!*
COWPOKE 38: Hell, yes!
COWPOKE 39: How's a *hunderd*, Kid?
COWPOKE 40: Boy, he's *somethin!*
COWPOKE 41: Boy, *ain't* he!

THE KID has been ignoring them, finishing off the whiskey. He now heaves the empty bottle away (amplified splintering crash of the bottle), wipes his mouth with the back of one white-gloved hand, and flatly, without expression, though perhaps faintly threatening:

THE KID: Coma ti yi youpy youpy yea.
COWPOKE 42: Right! Hah! You bet, Kid! Whoopee.
COWPOKE 43: Youpy youpy yea, man!

COWPOKES and BELLES all join in happy repetitions of THE KID's line, with variations. Brief silence follows. One COWPOKE (46) absently shuffles a deck of cards (amplified flutter of the shuffle). THE KID draws, fires a single blast, and a card flies out of the deck. THE COWPOKE shakes his hand loosely from the wrist, blows on it, etc., as though it were burnt.

COWPOKE 44: Whew! I reckon he didn't like yuh shufflin them cards!

COWPOKE 45: Reckon he didn't like yuh breakin the silence!

COWPOKE 46: S-s-sorry, Kid!

COWPOKE 47: The Kid's big on silence!

COWPOKE 48: You said it, podnuh!

COWPOKE 49: *Very* big!

COWPOKE 50: The biggest!

COWPOKE 51: What card did he shoot outa there?

COWPOKE 46 (*picking up the card and examining it; in wonder*): Jack a spades!

COWPOKE 52: How bout that! Jack a spades!

COWPOKE 46 (*again*): Shot him plumb through the left eye!

COWPOKE 53: Hey! Lemme see that!

He grabs the card, looks at it, passes it around. All admire it, whistle, show it to others, etc. One BELLE finally tucks it in her bodice or garter, casting long suggestive glances toward THE KID. THE KID makes a gesture with his six-shooter toward the COWPOKE (46) with the cards.

COWPOKE 54: Hey! It looks like the Kid wants somethin!

COWPOKE 55: It looks like he's got somethin on his mind!

COWPOKE 56: Whadda yuh want, Kid?

COWPOKE 57: I git it! The Kid wants yuh tuh shuffle them cards agin!

COWPOKE 58: Yeah, that's it! Give em another riffle there, podnuh!

Watching THE KID warily, the COWPOKE (46) with the cards again sits at the table, picks up the deck, shuffles the cards loosely and loudly. Three fast gunblasts from THE KID's six-shooters, and three more cards fly from the deck. COWPOKE 46 jumps up, kissing his hand, pressing it between his thighs, grimacing, etc., as other COWPOKES and BELLES rush for the three cards. As they pick them up:

COWPOKE 59: Jack a diamonds!

BELLE 27: Jack a hearts!

COWPOKE 60: Goddamn! Jack a clubs!

COWPOKE 61: Goddamn! He shot all three jacks clean outa there!

COWPOKE 62: Goddamn! That's somethin tuh *see!*

COWPOKE 63: You kin say yuh was *there,* podnuh!

COWPOKE 64: Shot all three goddamn jacks outa there!

BELLE 28: Four, hombre! Four!

COWPOKE 64 (*again*): Four! Goddamn right, Belle! All four!

BELLE 29: And hey! Lookit here, boys! He shot all four of em in the *left eye!*

COWPOKE 65: Goddamn! Drilled em neat as a pin!

COWPOKE 66: They's somethin the Kid don't cater to about *left eyes!*

COWPOKE 67: He ain't very big on *left eyes!*

COWPOKE 68: What you got agin *left eyes,* Kid?

COWPOKE 69: He's a lot bigger on silence!

COWPOKE 70: Jist blam blam, hombre! Holy shit!

THE KID (*flatly, as before*): Youpy youpy ti yi youpy youpy yea.

COWPOKES and BELLES once more imitate THE KID, working variations on his line. Any variations will do, and they should all overlap chorally, but they should be celebrative, clear, and resonant, not mumbling or blurred. A man steps through the swinging doors—THE KID spins and fires eight or ten shots, dropping the stranger, who kicks and jerks with each shot. COWPOKES and BELLES rush excitedly over to examine the body. The BELLES, who have been throwing occasional coy glances toward THE KID, now begin to flirt more openly with him, but he pays absolutely no attention to them. He is completely self-absorbed, though his blue eyes are ever watchful.

COWPOKE 71: Whew! That fella's suddenly about as dead as he's ever gonna be!

COWPOKE 72: Right smack in the *left eye!*

COWPOKE 73: And about ever place else tuh boot!

COWPOKE 74: Ain't enough fer the Kid jist tuh kill em, he's gotta tattoo em!

COWPOKE 75: Gotta sign his name! Haw haw!

COWPOKE 76: Boys, lemme tell yuh, they ain't *nobody* like the Kid!

COWPOKE 77: Hey, but who's the poor fuckin stranger?

COWPOKE 78: Hard tuh tell. Ain't all that much left of him!

COWPOKE 79: Hey, boys! It's the Marshall!

COWPOKE 80: Be damned if it ain't! Whew! Cain't hardly reckanize him after what the Kid done to him!

COWPOKE 81: Mebbe somebody oughta go tell the Sheriff!

COWPOKE 82: Whoa, man!

COWPOKE 83: Sshh! Yuh wanna git killt?

COWPOKE 84: Hoo boy! It shore don't pay tuh be no Marshall when the Kid's around!

COWPOKE 85: It shore ain't the happiest time tuh be a goddamn lawman, now when the Kid's in town!

BELLE 30: God in heaven! that was *beautiful*, boys! I'd like tuh see that agin!

COWPOKE 86: Yeah, but we ain't got no more Marshalls, Belle!

COWPOKE 87: Marshalls is gittin hard tuh come by!

During this scene, a couple COWPOKES should drag "the Marshall's" body out through the swinging doors. "The Marshall" may in fact be played by one of the COWPOKES, who has sneaked off the set through the back, and who later sneaks back on again the same way.

COWPOKE 88: Seems as how we oughta have *somethin* fer the Kid tuh shoot at, though!

COWPOKE 89: Seems like it!

COWPOKE 90: Hey, how about them Injuns over by Doc's place?

COWPOKE 91: That's thinkin, podnuh!

COWPOKE 92: Let's git the Kid some Injuns!

COWPOKE 93 (*shouting out through the swinging doors toward the men who have been dragging "the Marshall" out*): Hey, Clem! Go brang us some Injuns fer the Kid tuh shoot!

> At the first two occasions of the word "Injun," THE KID has spun, and now with the third he fires wildly toward the swinging doors. All COWPOKES within range drop to the floor, covering their heads, or dive under tables.

COWPOKE 94: Whoa there, podnuh!

COWPOKE 95: Look out!

COWPOKE 96: Boy, jist say the word "Injun" and—!

> THE KID again spins and fires, and this COWPOKE dives for cover. For the first time, THE KID seems to have lost control. He is suddenly jittery, wild, impulsive. In the lines that follow, the COWPOKES are actually playing with THE KID like a trapped animal, alternating the lines from one side of the set to the other, keeping THE KID spinning. THE KID blasts away at every mention of "Injuns," but for all the wild shooting, none of the COWPOKES is hit. The BELLES stay out of this game, but may scurry out from behind one table to another, pop up like a jack-in-the-box from behind the bar, etc.

COWPOKE 97: Whoopee! It's shore plain he don't like Injuns—!

> Blam!

COWPOKE 98: No kindsa Injuns!

> Blam!

COWPOKE 99: Nuthin could be plainer than the Kid's policy on Injuns—!

> Blam!

COWPOKE 100: Seems like Injuns

> Blam!

make the Kid see red, man!

    Blam! Blam!

COWPOKE 101: Haw haw! That's a good un! Yuh git it, Kid?

COWPOKE 102: Injuns

    Blam!

makes the Kid see red!

    Blam!

COWPOKE 103: —Man!

    Blam!

COWPOKE 104: Haw haw! Looks kinder like even red

    Blam!

makes the Kid see red, man!

    Blam! Blam!

COWPOKE 93 (*the one who first shouted for Indians*): Hey, Clem! Fergit them Injuns!

    Blam!

We don't need em!

    Blam! Blam!

COWPOKE 105: We got all the damn Injuns

    Blam!

we need right here without usin up real ones!

DEPUTY (*bumbling in through the swinging doors*): Hey, fellas! Have yuh seen the Sheriff! I cain't——

COWPOKE 106 (*pointing at* THE DEPUTY): Hey, Kid! There's a Injun!

        THE KID opens fire, both barrels blazing, and THE DEPUTY does a fancy dance, then scrambles for cover. While ducking:

DEPUTY: I jist only come tuh ask yuh if

    Blam!

the Sheriff

> Blam! Blam!

—YOUCH!—if the Sheriff

> Blam! Blam!

—*Halp!*—if he's been by

> Blam!

YOWEE! Escuse me, fellas!

> He hightails it out of there.

COWPOKE 107: Haw haw haw! Way tuh go, Kid!
COWPOKE 108: Hey, Kid! Behind the bar! More Injuns!

> THE KID spins and blasts away. THE BARKEEP diving for cover. Amplified splintering noises again.

COWPOKE 109: Look out, Kid! Comin in the doors!

> THE KID wheels and blasts away at the swinging doors. They should leap and waggle on their hinges with the impact of the shots.

COWPOKE 110: Down from the ceilin, Kid!
COWPOKE 111: Under the tables, Kid!
COWPOKE 112: Outa the walls, Kid!
COWPOKE 113: Under the chairs! Injuns!

> THE·KID has been whirling, spinning, firing insanely in all directions. Suddenly, he runs out of ammunition. He pauses, breathing heavily. He seems confused, rattled. Slowly then, he gathers his wits, regains his former cool, and begins to reload his six-shooters. The COWPOKES and BELLES, meanwhile, get back on their feet, come out of the corners, brush themselves off, straighten their hats, etc.

COWPOKE 114: Whoopee!
COWPOKE 115: Holy shit! He's somethin *else!*
COWPOKE 116: He's the best damn Kid I ever seen!

> One of the BELLES now sidles up behind THE KID, wraps her arms around him, strokes his chest. THE KID ignores her, busy with his pistols.

BELLE 31: Now, how bout punchin a few holes in lil ole Belle, cowboy?

> No response.

I mean, I ain't been shot up like that in a coon's age!

> No response. More desperately:

I may not *look* Injun, Kid honey, but I'm all Injun down *here!*

> Strokes herself. THE KID stares at her coldly, then turns away. She withdraws, looking hurt.

COWPOKE 117: Belle hon, yuh better be thankful he ain't takin yuh on!

COWPOKE 118: Yuh know the legend, Belle!

COWPOKE 119: They say he don't carry the usual equipment down there!

COWPOKE 120: They say he's the only three-gun killer in the West, Belle!

COWPOKE 121: They say any lady sleeps with the Kid, Belle, she sleeps fer a good long spell!

BELLE 32 (*stepping forward*): Well, I heard that legend, boys, and it's nearly true. I'm a eye-witness and a little bit more!

COWPOKE 122: Tell us about it, Belle!

> BELLE 32 steps forward and sings "The Kid with Blue Eyes." Some COWPOKES perhaps accompany her on instruments as before, and interject "Yahoo's" and the like from time to time. They all sing the choral lines. THE KID remains generally aloof, though he seems at times, especially when his skills or appurtenances are being described, to be listening critically, making sure the song is accurate, showing disdain when the descriptions seem to him short of the mark. If desired, BELLE 32 may use a hand microphone, amplified accompaniment.

The Kid With Blue Eyes

Now, boys, yuh all know me, I was once purty wild,
I'd never been rode, I was easily riled!
I'd left many a cowpuncher lame or half dead

From tryin tuh break me and take me tuh bed!
They wasn't a cowboy in the whole blesséd West
That could stay in the saddle, I'd busted the best!
But, boys, lemme tell yuh, I got quite a surprise
The day I got bestrid by the Kid with Blue Eyes!

CHORUS: When she got bestrid by the Kid with Blue
Eyes!

He was tall as a jackpine and mean as a skunk!
A blond blue-eyed beauty with plennya spunk!
He trampled the vineyards and made the earth quake!
As soon as I seen him I started tuh shake!
His hands was like lightnin, he roared when he spoke!
They wasn't a fuzztail that he hadn't broke!
They was ice in his heart and fire in his glance,
And he caused a tornado when he lowered his pants!

CHORUS: He stirred a tornado when he dropped his
pants!

Well, his legs was like pillars, his cheeks was snow white!
His balls weighed a ton and packed real dynamite!
The rest yuh kin guess, but they's one thing tuh tell:
His weapon is big, but it's blacker than hell!
Yes, blacker than hell, you boys heard me right!
When I seen it it give me a turrible fright!
And they's another thing more, I'm tellin yuh true!
It is blacker than death and its eye is true blue!

CHORUS: Wow! blacker than death and an eye that's true
blue!

Well, he leaps in the saddle and screws me down tight,
And he crawls to muh middle, but I goes on the fight;
I rears and I bucks and I goes up on high,
Take a gyratin jump, I'm feelin right spry!
I goes tuh sun-fishin, I'm shore feelin grand!
He'll have tuh be good before *my* ass he'll brand!
I rolls round on my side and I'm high in the skies—
But I still ain't unsaddled that Kid with Blue Eyes!

CHORUS: She still ain't got rid a that Kid with Blue Eyes!

Well, I make one last try tuh git outa his grip,
And I take the high dive, but he's clear got me whipped!
Then we hit with a jar that shore gives me a scare,
And I'm way down below him, I don't know jist where!
I'm all busted up and I'm sore and I'm lame!
That blond buckaroo is awinnin the game!
I feel like a million years older that day
When the Kid with Blue Eyes starts blastin away!

CHORUS: Oh, that Kid with Blue Eyes, he's ablastin away!

Now, I've told yuh it's black with a little blue eye,
But it's worse than that, boys, and I'll tell yuh why:
It's also as cold as the stone on a tomb
On a dead winter's night and it froze up muh womb!
So, boys, here's the moral tuh my little story:
They's all kindsa fame and they's all kindsa glory,
But as fer my own, I tell yuh no lies:
I wisht I'd never been rode by the Kid with Blue Eyes!

CHORUS: Oh yeah, she's been had by that Kid with Blue
    Eyes!

> Loud applause and hallooing as the song ends.
> THE KID steps forward, and a hush falls.

THE KID (*flatly, as before*): Youpy youpy.
COWPOKE 123: Oh, hell yes, Kid! Ti yi youpy yea!

> Again the gleeful chorus of "youpy yea's," inter-
> rupted as THE SHERIFF steps through the swing-
> ing doors. A sudden hush descends. THE KID's
> back is to the doors, but he is taut, alert. THE
> DEPUTY creeps in abjectly on hands and knees,
> and hides behind the nearest available object.

SHERIFF: You're at the end a yore rope, Kid.

> Prolonged pause.

SHERIFF: I've . . . I've come tuh take yuh in.

> Again a pause, all tense.

COWPOKE 124 (*softly, cautiously, as though trying to
    get* THE SHERIFF *to cool it*): Uh . . . Sheriff . . .
    pssst!

SHERIFF (*shaking off the* COWPOKE *with a quick impatient gesture*): I'm askin yuh tuh go quiet, Kid . . .

> THE KID suddenly whirls and draws. THE SHERIFF draws simultaneously, and there's an explosive exchange of gunfire. THE SHERIFF, almost disbelievingly, remains standing, as THE KID, surprised at his own wound, slowly crumples. Prolonged shocked silence, as THE KID sinks to the floor and dies. The whole saloon is momentarily spellbound. THE SHERIFF breaks it giddily.

SHERIFF: Hey! I'll be durned! Hey, I—I *done* it! I got him, boys! *I got the Kid!*

> COWPOKES stare at THE SHERIFF with astonishment, disappointment, even some gathering disgust. Silence maintains until COWPOKE 125 steps forward, looks down at THE KID, then up at THE SHERIFF.

COWPOKE 125 (*genuinely upset*): Aw shucks, Sheriff! Yuh fucked it up!

DEPUTY (*creeping out from hiding*): What'd he do?

COWPOKE 125 (*again*): Hell, he killt the goddamn Kid!

DEPUTY (*standing now, moving forward to see for himself, no longer the comic foil*): Oh, *shit!*

COWPOKE 126: Christ, whadda we do *now?*

COWPOKE 127 (*disbelievingly*): He jist gunned him down!

SHERIFF (*confused by this reception, but still smiling, still a little delirious over his unexpected victory*): I . . . I don't git it, fellas! What's the matter . . . ?

> A brief moment of general indecision and frustration, while THE SHERIFF speaks, the COWPOKES and BELLES looking at each other for ways of getting on with it, THE DEPUTY gazing thoughtfully at THE SHERIFF. Then, THE DEPUTY, who has emerged suddenly as the authority present, calls the COWPOKES nearest him into a huddle— and they swing almost immediately into a sudden celebrative mood, led by the three COWPOKES who complained above. THE DEPUTY's word is quickly passed to the other COWPOKES and BELLES.

DEPUTY (*back in weak-kneed comic character*): Good golly! Wha—what happened?

COWPOKE 125 (*again*): Hey! The Sheriff got him!

COWPOKE 126 (*again*): What!!!

COWPOKE 127 (*again*): He got the Kid! The Kid is dead!

DEPUTY: Jumpin gee-willikers!

> THE SHERIFF is having trouble following all this, but he gradually gives in to the flattery, stops trying to puzzle it out.

COWPOKE 128: He outshot the Kid!

COWPOKE 129: They said it couldn't be done!

COWPOKE 130: But the Sheriff done it!

DEPUTY: Waal, I'll be horn-swoggled!

COWPOKE 131: He's gotta be *it*, boys!

COWPOKE 132: *The fastest gun in the West!*

BELLE 33: *The fastest gun in the West!*

COWPOKE 133: *The fastest goddamn gun in the West!*

SHERIFF (*chuckling awkwardly in genuine embarrassment, still somewhat confused*): Now . . . now, fellas . . .

COWPOKE 134: Hey! Let's set em up fer the Sheriff!

COWPOKE 135: Hey, bartender!

COWPOKE 136: Hey, consarn it! Git a leg on! This calls fer a goddamn celybration!

> THE BARKEEP hurries back behind the bar, lines up shotglasses on the bar, pours out drinks. He is kept bustling throughout the scene that follows, as COWPOKES and BELLES contrive to get THE SHERIFF thoroughly drunk.

COWPOKE 137: To the fastest gun!

> They cheer, drink, pour out more.

COWPOKE 138: The Sheriff has saved our goddamn town, boys!

SHERIFF (*holding back*): Lissen, boys, I . . .

BELLE 34: He's made it safe tuh walk in the streets agin!

COWPOKE 139: He's saved the West!

BELLE 35: He's number one!

COWPOKE 140: He shot the Kid!

SHERIFF: Well, now, yuh don't understand. It wasn't nuthin . . .

COWPOKE 141: That's right, Sheriff! It wasn't nuthin! Nuthin but the greatest thing that's ever happened tuh the whole goddamn West!

BELLE 36: The Sheriff's done made *histry,* boys!

COWPOKE 142: Drink up, Sheriff! Drink up, boys!

COWPOKE 143: Tuh histry!

COWPOKE 144: Tuh the West!

COWPOKE 145: Tuh the fastest gun!

BELLE 37 (*seductively, as all the* BELLES *work at getting* THE SHERIFF *loaded*): You kin make *my* lil ole histry *any* time, Sheriff hon!

COWPOKE 146: Whew! Jist lookit that coyote lyin there dead!

COWPOKE 147: All shot tuh shit, man!

> Throughout this scene, THE DEPUTY, while hopping about giddily, sloshing drinks around, etc., is at the same time passing instructions, whipping up the frenzy, maybe even providing the speakers with their lines. Now he stops midstage and declaims drunkenly:

DEPUTY: Crime don't pay, boys!

COWPOKE 148: Haw haw! Yer durn tootin, it don't!

COWPOKE 149: Haw haw! The Kid here kin tell yuh, podnuh!

COWPOKE 150: Shit, the Kid cain't tell yuh *nuthin,* man!

COWPOKE 151: Haw haw!

SHERIFF (*pleased with himself, but still wanting to make some point or other*): Right! That's right! About crime, I mean! It don't pay! And not only that——!

COWPOKE 152 (*cutting him off*): That's right, ain't it, boys? It don't!

COWPOKE 153: Not when yuh got the number one gun in the West fer Sheriff!

COWPOKE 154: Haw haw! That's tellin it, podnuh!

COWPOKE 155: Consarn it, boys, let's hear it fer the Sheriff!

ALL (*loudly, arms raised in a toast*). YOUPY TI YI YOUPY YOUPY YEA!

> THE SHERIFF tries, without effect, to protest; then uneasily drinks with the others. A BELLE, seeing his reluctance, tips the glass up for him (in pre-

tended flirtation) to make sure he drinks it all. He stands away from the bar.

SHERIFF (*with feeling*): Thank yuh, boys. Thank yuh. It's right kind of yuh, I mean that. But . . . uh . . . mebbe this ain't exackly the best time tuh—

COWPOKE 156: Ain't the best time, Sheriff? After all that's happened?

COWPOKE 157: Tuh celybrate the conquest a *evil*, Sheriff?

COWPOKE 158: Why, Sheriff! This is gonna be a national holiday!

SHERIFF (*embarrassed, not convinced, but flattered, turning to look down at his victim*): Well, mebbe, but I was thinkin mebbe first we oughta bury the Kid here . . .

COWPOKE 159: Say a few prayers, Sheriff? Is that it? Say a few prayers over the Kid?

COWPOKE 160: Prayers! Haw haw! The Sheriff wants tuh say a prayer, boys!

COWPOKE 161: Let's have a prayer, boys! A prayer fer the Kid!

The COWPOKES remove their hats, assume woeful expressions, put their heads together, and joined by the BELLES, commence to sing a kind of dirge or plainchant:

ALL: YOUPY YOUPY COMA TI YI YOUPY—

THE SHERIFF looks a little troubled. THE DEPUTY notices this.

DEPUTY (*interrupting sternly*): Now, wait a minute, boys! Wait jist a dadblame minute here! I won't have yuh makin riddycule a the efFICKacy a prayer! Why, many's the time when the Sheriff and me, we seen a prayer come through when nuthin else'd work! Ain't it so, Sheriff? Why, remember Ash Holler! And Bad Axe! Sand Crick! Mountain Meaders!

The COWPOKES and BELLES look abashed, drift apart, as before.

DEPUTY: And, Zeb, you was there when we had tuh massacree them Pueblos, what would we a done that day, ifn it hadn'ta been fer prayer?

Someone acknowledges this for "Zeb."

DEPUTY: Why, it was like that time along the Snake River back in '49! Remember that time, Sheriff?

> THE SHERIFF doesn't look like he remembers. Somebody has filled his glass again. He drinks absently.

COWPOKE 162: Along the Snake? Hey, ain't that the time them Injuns whupped up a thunderstorm or somethin, Deppity?

DEPUTY: Yup, but that weren't the end of it!

COWPOKE 163: Weren't the end of it!

COWPOKE 164: Yuh mean, it was wuss'n that, Deppity?

DEPUTY: It was wuss'n that, boys . . . and it was better!

COWPOKE 165: Huh! Sounds like the beginnins of a story, Deppity!

> The COWPOKES settle back to hear a story, THE SHERIFF among them. Throughout the story, the BELLES and COWPOKES work at their project of getting THE SHERIFF drunk, the COWPOKES slipping over one by one to have a toast with him, the BELLES cuddling him and tipping drinks down him playfully, etc. THE DEPUTY commences the tale in his natural voice, then fades out as amplified (radio) sounds and voices—indicated by (V) in the script below— fade in. Preferably, sounds and voices should be broadcast stereophonically from amplifiers situated all around the auditorium. During the amplified portions, THE DEPUTY engages in a pantomime, not so much of the different speaking parts, as of basic emotions and gestures (fear, effort, victory, confusion, self-defense, etc.). THE DEPUTY can work out his own set of movements pursuant to his vision of the material, using barroom gear, the dead body of THE KID, the COWPOKES and BELLES, as he wishes. If he designates a COWPOKE to "play" THE SHERIFF at any point, he may "borrow" THE SHERIFF's star and pin it on the COWPOKE, where it remains to the end of the play. THE DEPUTY's performance should suggest

priestly rituals, the magic gestures with validity of their own, prior to the "story" being amplified over them. Emphasis in the latter should be on sound effects, voice tones, and the implications of actions (the words themselves can well be lost at times). BELLES and COWPOKES may form shifting choral groups that respond antiphonally to the turns of the story.

DEPUTY: Well, yes, boys, so it is, and it happened like this. Me and the Sheriff had signed on as outriders with a wagon train fulla prospectors headin out west to civilize Utah, and we hadn't no more'n reached the Sangre de Cristo Pass, when suddenly we got set upon by a buncha wild Injuns, Lord, they was comin at us . . .

Fade out as radio voices and the noise of wagons rolling and squeaking, horses clip-clipping, shouts, etc., fade in . . .

DEPUTY(V) (*shouting in panic*): . . . Lord, they're comin at us from all four directions, Sheriff! Comanches! And Navahos, too! We're done for!

Simultaneously: distant galloping and wahooing of attacking Indians. Horses nearby whinny with fear. General confusion in the wagon train.

SHERIFF(V) (*shouting over the panic*): Stop blubberin, podnuh, and draw a bead! Quick, you men! Git them wagons pulled around there! C'mon, boys! Pluck up! Git a leg on! Tip em over there!

Crash of wagons being wheeled around, tipped over. Confused shouts. Galloping and wahooing augments. Rifle shots and ricocheting bullets. Thuds of arrows striking wood. Occasional screams and grunts as Indians bite the dust or settlers fall wounded. Meanwhile:

SETTLER(V): We ain't got a chance, Sheriff!

SETTLER(V): They come up on us too fast!

SETTLER(V): Look out! Comin up behind! It's—*AAR-RGHH!*

SETTLER(V): It's Apaches! They're gangin up on us!

DEPUTY(V): Goldurn it, Sheriff! It ain't fair!

SHERIFF(V): C'mon, don't give it up, boys! While they's still one of us alive and kickin, they ain't won the day!

SETTLER(V): It's no use, Sheriff!

SETTLER(V): We'll never hold out!

SETTLER(V): Hey! What's that I hear, boys?

DEPUTY(V) (*blubbering*): Ain't nuthin out thar but mad crazy red varmints, and they——

SHERIFF(V): No, wait, Deppity! Lissen! I hear it, too!

> Distantly, behind the Indian whooping and hollering: the bugle call of the U.S. Cavalry, the crack of rifle fire.

DEPUTY(V): Durn muh britches! it's the Cavalry! boys, it's the Cavalry!

> Shouts of joy as Cavalry noises augment. The Indians fall into confusion. The settlers shout encouragement, as the Cavalry put the Indians to rout. Indian noises diminish and disappear. Horses gallop up, snort and whinny, as settlers cheer, proclaim victory, etc.

DEPUTY(V): Hey, you fellers come jist in time!

COLONEL(V): Howdy, Deppity! Howdy, Sheriff!

SHERIFF(V): Howdy, Colonel! Say, it shore was great to hear you boys comin over the hill! We was in a bad state—

COLONEL(V): Well, Sheriff, yuh ain't outa hot water yet! Scouts tell us they's tribes a Pawnee and Walapai up ahead, and when these Comanches who got away have joined em—say, did yuh see who was ridin with them Comanches?

SETTLER(V): Navahos, Colonel!

SETTLER(V): And Apaches!

SHERIFF(V): Mebbe some Flatheads, too, though it was hard tuh see fer sure.

DEPUTY(V): Ain't none of em got heads yuh'd call normal!

> Off-mike laughter.

SHERIFF(V): Whadda yuh think we oughta do, Colonel?

COLONEL(V): Well, Sheriff, I reckon yuh better keep

the wagons movin, git out from under these bluffs
before sundown!

SETTLER(V): Ain't yuh comin along with us, Colonel?

COLONEL(V): Yuh got the Sheriff and his Deppity here
tuh help, we'll move on ahead, see what we kin do
about mebbe clearin the way fer yuh a nite.

SHERIFF(V): Thanks, Colonel! Thanks a lot!

> The settlers echo THE SHERIFF's sentiments. Fade
> out.
>> Fade in: sounds of the wagon train rumbling
> along. A horse gallops up.

SETTLER(V) (*shouting as he approaches*): Hey, Sheriff!
It's gonna be dark purty quick! Reckon we oughta
pull up now, or—?

SHERIFF(V): I dunno! Seems tuh me as how we mebbe
oughta wait fer the Colonel tuh—hold on! There they
come now!

> Sounds of Cavalry galloping up.

COLONEL(V) (*off mike*): Whoa, there!

> Horse whinnies and snorts. Sounds of greetings.

SHERIFF(V): Hullo, Colonel! How's it look up thar?

COLONEL(V): Bad, Sheriff! We wiped out the Walapai
okay, but they's still the Pawnee and the others, and
they's signs a Cheyenne and Blackfeet comin tuh
join em, they got a real united pow-wow goin! And
. . . somethin *wuss'n* that!

DEPUTY(V): What? Wha—what's happenin up thar,
Colonel?

COLONEL(V) *gravely*): They've started up a rain dance!

> Settlers gasp and mutter.

SETTLER(V): Mebbe it's time fer us tuh do a little prayin
of our own, boys!

> Sounds of approval and general anxiety.

SETTLER(V) (*off mike*): We could pray fer the measles
or the smallpox tuh come down on em! We've worked
that lotsa places!

SHERIFF(V): No, I don't think we wanna bother gittin
God in on it yet, men! He's done a whole heap fer

us already, what with the Colt and these new breech-loadin rifles, I think it's up tuh us tuh stand on our own two feet! Leastways, long as we kin! Whadda *you* think, Colonel?

COLONEL(V): That's right, Sheriff! We ain't run clean outa our own resources yet! Ain't I seen some dynamite in some a these wagons?

SETTLER(V): Yeah, we're fixin tuh take that tuh Virginia City, Colonel, tuh git at that silver!

COLONEL(V): Yup, well, we won't need but a coupla bundles or so. And somebody tuh trap two or three buzzards.

SETTLER(V): Buzzards!

DEPUTY(V): Whoa, Colonel! You ain't been eatin some a them Injun mushrooms, have yuh?

There is a distant rumble of thunder.

COLONEL(V): Yuh heard me! And on the double, boys! That was thunder! We ain't got much time!

General shouts of settlers rushing off to get dynamite and buzzards, widespread anxiety. More thundering.

SHERIFF(V): Hey, I git it, Colonel! Yuh reckon tuh upset that prayer-meetin a theirs a mite!

COLONEL(V): That's right, Sheriff. The buzzard, as yuh know, is the Injuns' thunder bird. They figger it avenges em agin their enemies, and part a ever rain dance cerymony is when they attract these buzzards down and smear em with the blood a white men. Only, huh! this time them Injuns is gonna git a little lesson in the futility and foolishness a their heathen superstitions!

Fade out.
   Fade in: sounds of thunder, high winds, light rain.

COLONEL(V) (*shouting over storm*): All right, shake a leg, men! Yuh got the dynamite tied tuh them buzzards?

Sounds of birds flapping and squawking, shouts of "Yup! ready tuh go!" etc., amid the storm.

COLONEL(V): All right! Let em go!

> Sounds of flapping wings, squawks and mews, disappearing into the gathering storm.

SETTLER(V): It's startin to blow purty turrible, Colonel! Ifn this don't work . . .
COLONEL(V): It'll work. What we gotta hope is it works fast enough!

> Storm sounds augment. Horses whinny and people shout, trying to hold things down, etc.

SETTLER(V) (*shouting desperately over the storm*): We ain't gonna make it, Colonel!
SETTLER(V) (*ditto*): It's too late!
SETTLER(V)(*ditto*): Hurricane!
COLONEL(V) (*shouting over the storm and panic, sound of his horse rearing about, whinnying*): Hang fast there, you jaspers!
SHERIFF(V) (*ditto*): Git a grip, men! Deppity, git over thar and help that family hold down their gear!
COLONEL(V) (*ditto*): Any man lose his head, I'm puttin a bullet through it! What'd yuh come West fer? Did yuh think it was some kinda tea party out here? C'mon, git the lead outa yore britches!

> Sudden distant but terrific explosion. Storm sounds diminish. Men cheer and whistle: "Whoopee! We done it!" etc.

SHERIFF(V) (*a little breathless from exertion*): Whew! gotta hand it to yuh, Colonel! That one was a stroke a genius!
DEPUTY(V) (*ditto*): Whoo-ee! I ain't felt so good since ole Custer went one way and we went t'other!
COLONEL(V): Yup, well, we may not be in the clear yet! Them damn heathens may not dance em up another rain fer a spell, but we probably ain't seen the last of em!
SETTLER(V) (*off mike*): All right, men, it's gittin dark! Let's make camp here tonight!

> Campmaking noises, horse whinnies, etc.

We got a long day ahead of us!

COLONEL(V) (*private to* THE SHERIFF): And I hope we see it, Sheriff! I hope we see it!

Fade out.

COWPOKE 166: Wow! That was some story, Deppity!

COWPOKE 167: Wasn't that buzzard trick somethin, though?

COWPOKE 168: Like the Sheriff said, a—what'd you say, Sheriff?

THE SHERIFF looks up blearily, half-smiling. Somebody pours him a drink. The COWPOKES shift about a bit in this interval, pouring fresh drinks, attending to THE SHERIFF, pinching BELLE bottoms, etc. THE DEPUTY, who has paused in his mime, now scrutinizes THE SHERIFF briefly.

COWPOKE 169: A stroke a genius! That's what the Sheriff said!

COWPOKE 170: Right, too! Stroke a genius!

COWPOKE 171: I bet all yuh could see a them Injuns after that was their hairy red hunkers ahumpin acrost the hills like ninety!

General laughter.

DEPUTY: No, boys, that's where you're wrong!

COWPOKE 172 (*disbelievingly*): What! Yuh mean them dumb Injuns hadn't learnt their lesson yet?

DEPUTY: That's right. In fact, they durn near put us all under sod that night! I tell yuh, it was a bad un! One oldtimer even tried tuh make out as how it was the Colonel's fault, usin firepower like that agin the Injun gods, said it was a sacrilege, and even the God of our own fathers mightn't look on it too kindly!

COWPOKE 173: Huh! Somebody shoulda shot that old-timer!

General laughter and approval.

DEPUTY: Now, boys, yuh know that ain't our way! Ever man's got a right tuh his own way a thinkin!

COWPOKE 174· Yeah, and he's got a right tuh git shot fer it, too!

Laughter and approval.

COWPOKE 175: But what happened, Deppity?

DEPUTY: Well, I was jist inta my third plate a jerk and beans and a sweet widder, when this scoutin party come back and says more Injuns has gathered, Chippewas, Arapaho, and Nez Perce among em now, and they was up tuh some peculiar religious cerymony, the likes a which they ain't never seen before! That was when this oldtimer spoke up, gripin bout that buzzard flimflam, and makin out as how the white man didn't stand a chance agin the Injun . . .

    Fade out.

OLDTIMER(V) (*fade in over* DEPUTY's *words*): . . . agin the Injun on his own huntin ground. Oh, it was different when we was fightin em back East, we wasn't all alone back there, we could always skedaddle back and git more guns and grub and help, ifn we needed to, and what we did, we did on accounta we had to, on accounta we was supposed to! But we wasn't supposed tuh cross the old Miss, no, we been pushin God's hand——

SETTLER(V): Aw, oldtimer, you're always bitchin! A few years ago, you was skeered tuh cross the Appalachias!

OLDTIMER(V): Now you lissen, I'm tellin yuh fer yer own good! Out here, the Injuns is gonna whup us! They know the land, they kin come out of it from nowhere and disappear right into it again, you see how they do it! They're fightin fer their homes and we—

SETTLER(V): Yeah, but they're *heathens*, oldtimer! They ain't much better'n animals, they're jist game meant fer shootin, and ifn we cain't——

OLDTIMER(V): That's jist it! Animals! They got a feelin fer this land, and we ain't! We cain't do nuthin but blow it up——

COLONEL (V) (*galloping up*): What's all this bullroarin about, oldtimer?

DEPUTY (V): All these spooky Injun cerymonies tonight has got the old feller shook up, Colonel. He thinks them dumb nekkid savages has got a chance agin us Christian gentlemen!

    General laughter.

OLDTIMER(V) (*irate*): All right! You jist keep alaughin! But you'll see which side a yore mouth you're laughin outa tomorry! Ifn yuh still got one and we ain't all been scalped——!

SHERIFF(V) (*interrupting*): Now, take it easy, old-timer! It's a long haul, it ain't easy, I admit, but we *know* more'n they do, and we always will and sooner or later——

OLDTIMER(V): But I'm tellin yuh, Sheriff, the kindsa things we know ain't never gonna do us no good out here! This ain't Virginny! It ain't even Illinois! We're jist gittin ourselves killt fer nuthin!

SETTLER(V): Gold ain't nuthin, oldtimer!

SETTLER(V): Land ain't nuthin! Furs and silver ain't nuthin!

SHERIFF(V): But, Colonel, what's all this about peculiar cerymonies?

COLONEL(V): I dunno exackly, Sheriff. Mebbe they're jist stallin fer time. Anyhow, I don't think tonight we're apt tuh——

Distant rumbling noise.

DEPUTY(V): Woops! What's that rumblin noise?

COLONEL(V): I dunno!

OLDTIMER(V): Yuh dunno, Colonel? Well, I ain't surprised! It's like I'm tellin yuh, you're never gonna hold this land agin the Injuns! I kin tell yuh what that is! It's bad news, that's what it is!

Rumbling augments. Anxiety again starts to sweep the wagon train.

SETTLER(V) (*anxiously*): What is it, oldtimer? What is it?

OLDTIMER(V): That's a herd a buffalo, son! Mebbe lotsa herds all at once! They're stampedin! And they're headin this way!

SETTLER(V): Here comes a scout!

SCOUT(V) (*galloping up*): Colonel! Colonel! They're comin at us from all round us!

COLONEL (V) (*alarmed*): What's comin?

SCOUT(V) (*breathless*): Buffalo. Elk. Wild horses. Longhorns. Even grizzlies and wolves! It's the damnedest thing yuh ever seen!

Rumbling steadily augments.

OLDTIMER(V): What'd I tell yuh, boys!

COLONEL(V): Shut up, oldtimer! Everybody git hitched up! Quick! We may have tuh move outa here fast! C'mon!

SHERIFF(V): I'll ride out and see what I kin see, Colonel!

He gallops off. Rumbling augments. Shouts of confusion and nighttime terror amid the preparations. Wild whinnies and shouts of struggle.

SETTLER(V): Colonel! All the horses is goin wild! We cain't control em!

SETTLER(V): Our cattle is breakin loose! It's like they gone crazy!

SETTLER(V): One of our dogs is eatin my baby!

DEPUTY(V): Whadda we gonna *do*, Colonel?

COLONEL(V): I dunno! Them goddamn Injuns! But we gotta think a somethin, Deppity, and damn quick! Lissen! Do yuh hear warwhoops?

Amid the augmenting rumble of the advancing herds: the distant warwhoops of thousands of Indians.

DEPUTY(V): Here comes the Sheriff back, Colonel!

SHERIFF (V) (*galloping up*): Injuns, Colonel! Millions of em! Follerin up the herds! It's like as how each tribe is comin with its own kinda beast!

COLONEL(V): My God! So that's it!

SHERIFF(V): I reckon the time's come, Colonel. I reckon it's time tuh pray.

Rumbling, panic augmenting.

COLONEL(V): I hate tuh admit it, Sheriff. But I think you're right!

Shouting:

All right, men! Everbody on his knees! Is there a preacher among us?

SETTLER(V) (*shouting from near distance*): The old-timer's done some preachin, Colonel!

Rumbling and warwhooping, whinnying and general turmoil, all rapidly augmenting.

COLONEL(V): All right, they're nearly on us! C'mon, oldtimer! Let's git tuh singin! let's git tuh prayin!

OLDTIMER(V) (*shouting above the turmoil with evangelical fervor*): Remember the Book, boys! Remember what it says! It says, And the Lord said, I have surely seen the affliction a my people!

ALL(V): Yes, Lord! Hear us!

OLDTIMER(V): And he says, I know their sorrows!

ALL(V): Oh, God of our fathers, help us! Help us in our sorrows! Help us in our time a need!

OLDTIMER(V): And he says, I am come down tuh deliver em outa this here land, and I'm gonna brang em up unto a good land!

ALL(V): Yes, Lord, save us, Lord!

OLDTIMER(V): Yes, a good land, and a large land! Yes, he says, I'm gonna deliver you unto a land flowin with milk and honey! Do yuh hear me, boys! Flowin with milk and honey!

ALL(V): Milk and honey, Lord! Oh, they're comin, Lord! Hurry, Lord! Hurry!

> Herds and Indians thundering down on them. They shout above the deafening noise.

OLDTIMER(V): And he says, I'm gonna stretch out muh hand and smite yore enemies with all muh wonders, says he! Go git the elders and let em see!

ALL(V): Oh yeah, God! Smite em, God! Hurry, God! Save us!

OLDTIMER(V): And I'm gonna give this people favor ——!

COLONEL(V) (*shouting above the rest*): Wait! What's that?

> Distantly, behind the thunder of hooves and howls and whinnies: a train whistle.

DEPUTY(V): I dunno, Colonel! But ifn I was back East, I'd say that was——

SHERIFF(V): It is, Deppity! It is! Look, Colonel, there tuh the East! It's a train! It's comin outa nowhere!

> Train blowing loud and clear now, but still at some distance. Slowly it augments until its thunder matches the thunder of the stampede. The settlers sing "The Battle Hymn of the Republic."

SETTLER(V): Lookit that light! *It's bearin down on us!*
DEPUTY(V): *We're all gonna git killt!*
OLDTIMER(V) (*still shouting, his voice fading in over the tumult, then out again*): . . . and he says, you shalt take water outa the river and pour it on the dry land, and that there water, took outa the river, it shall become blood on the dry land! Yes, and it shall come tuh pass . . .
SETTLER(V) (*shouting over the tumult, praying, etc.*): They're breakin! The herds is breakin!
SETTLER(V) (*ditto*): Lookit em there in the light! They're turnin tail!

> Train roar now much louder than the stampede. Sounds of frantic whooping, screaming, whinnying, etc. Train roars by, then slowly fades. As it fades, it is the only sound heard, except for a few settlers still singing strands of "The Battle Hymn of the Republic." Fade out.
> THE DEPUTY fades in, in time with the voices fading out, singing "The Battle Hymn of the Republic" alone, squeakily, out of tune.

COWPOKE 176 (*interrupting*): Wow! Yuh mean that a train jist come outa nowhere like that, and sent all them Injuns and buffalo ascatterin?!
DEPUTY: Yup, it come and went, jist like that, *whoosh!* roarin outa the East, fadin off inta the West, outa the night and inta the night, and when it had gone, they wasn't no sign a them Injuns nor all them herds they'd wizarded up like that! Weren't no rails nor tracks nor nuthin! And somethin else, boys: I seen it go by. It had "The Train a Peace" writ on it! And they weren't nobody drivin that train! *Nobody!*
COWPOKE 177: Whew! Right outa the night!
COWPOKE 178: And nobody up there!
COWPOKE 179: Makes yuh think, don't it!
COWPOKE 180: Makes yuh learn a little humility, don't it!
COWPOKE 181: Whew! That was some story, Deppity!
COWPOKE 182: Them were the days, boys! It was a great ole place then!
COWPOKE 183: That's when the West was the fuckin West!

COWPOKE 184: They had all the fun back then!

      Gazing down on THE KID:

Now all we got left is . . .

      He gives THE KID's body an irritable boot.

COWPOKE 185: How come you never told us about that, Sheriff?

> THE SHERIFF is very drunk. He stands blearily away from the bar and BELLES, but cannot see too clearly who has spoken to him.

SHERIFF: Well . . . uh . . . tuh tell the truth, I don't rightly——

DEPUTY (*interrupting*): Hey, boys! We plumb fergot! I shouldn't be tellin all these here stories! This here's the Sheriff's day!

COWPOKE 186 (*with difficulty mustering enthusiasm*): Yeah, right, right. He killt the Kid, didn't he?

COWPOKE 187 (*picking it up*): That's it! Shot him down! Last damn Kid we'll ever git, too!

BELLE 38: He's our man!

COWPOKE 188 (*raising his glass*): Here's tuh the Sheriff, boys!

COWPOKE 189: Tuh the Sheriff!

ALL: YOUPY YOUPY TI YI——

SHERIFF: *Hold on, boys!*

> He gestures with his hand, spilling some of his drink. Stares at it curiously, then drinks it off.

SHERIFF: Boys . . . boys . . . thank yuh! But . . .

> Again he gestures, and again he interrupts himself to stare at the glass. Working methodically, he pivots carefully, sets the glass firmly on the bar, nearly knocks it off trying to let go of it, then turns around, hands on his lapels, to face the BELLES and COWPOKES. Trying to look wise, he raises one hand as though to ask for silence, though in fact no one is speaking.

SHERIFF: Yuh ask . . . about the story . . .

      He belches.

COWPOKE 190 (*hastily interrupting*): Hold it, Sheriff! Belle here's got somethin tuh say tuh yuh!

Hoarse urgent whisper:

The six-shooters, Belle!

> He shoves BELLE 39 forward, as THE BARKEEP hurriedly refills THE SHERIFF's glass. One of the COWPOKES shoves the glass into THE SHERIFF's hand.

BELLE 39 (*hurried and uncertain at first, but with increasing seductiveness*): Uh, Sheriff, seein as yuh . . . Sheriff, why, seein as how you're now the fastest gun in the West, seems like, seems tuh me like yuh oughta put . . . yuh oughta be wearin them fancy silver shootin irons, Sheriff . . .

> She casts a suggestive glance down at THE KID.

SHERIFF (*still in a drunken declamatory stance*): Hunh? . . . Well . . . well, Belle, that's jist it, I was jist gonna . . . yuh mean the Kid's—? Aw . . . well, thanks, Belle . . . but I don't reckon——

COWPOKE 191 (*interrupting*): Hey! Yuh got a point there, Belle!

COWPOKE 192: The Kid's shootin irons!

COWPOKE 193: He earned em!

COWPOKE 194: Damn if he didn't!

SHERIFF: Aw, thanks, fellas . . . but no, I——

COWPOKE 195: Sheriff, git that ugly old gunbelt off!

> The BELLES and COWPOKES hastily strip a mildly protesting SHERIFF of his gunbelt, while others remove the belt from THE KID's body. They handle THE KID's weapons gingerly, as though carelessness might trigger them off. This is just the first step in the transformation of THE SHERIFF into a kind of makeshift ragtag KID. In what follows, the BELLES should take a major role in dressing THE SHERIFF, keeping him distracted with little caresses, kisses, etc. He mumbles in incoherent protest, the only person present, in fact, free to mutter or ad-lib conversationally. As the girls strip THE KID, they might occasionally look with

undisguised longing on his body, maybe even get a quick kick in the rump from one of the COWPOKES for not moving fast enough.

COWPOKE 196: And lookit them fancy white gloves! Our Sheriff should oughta have him a pair a gloves like them!

COWPOKE 197: And boots! Hombre! Them white boots is plumb outa sight!

COWPOKE 198: You said it, podnuh!

BELLE 40: Take a mighty big man tuh step inta *them* boots!

COWPOKE 199: And, Belle, we *got* the *man!*

DEPUTY: Boys, I ain't never seen a Stetson purty as this un!

Puts THE KID's hat on his own head, and it falls down around his ears.

COWPOKE 200 (*grabbing* THE KID's *hat off* THE DEPUTY's *head angrily*): Whoa there! Whaddaya doin?

COWPOKE 201: Who do yuh think yuh are, cowboy?

COWPOKE 202: Did *you* outgun the Kid, podnuh?

DEPUTY (*shamefacedly*): Well . . . uh . . . no, but—

COWPOKE 200 (*again*): Only one man in town got a right tuh *that* hat, hombre! And you ain't him!

Clamps the hat grandly on THE SHERIFF's head.

COWPOKE 203 (*admiring* THE SHERIFF *in his new duds*): Hey now! Take a lookit *that*, boys!

COWPOKE 204: Hah! he's gittin there!

SHERIFF: Now, jist hold on one minute——!

BELLE 41: Jumpin gee-willikers, ain't he a pitcher!

COWPOKE 205: Here, lemme see him!

COWPOKE 206: No, turn him thisaway—hey now!

They spin him about, getting him dizzy and confused.

COWPOKE 207: What about the pants and shirt?

COWPOKE 208: Yuh reckon he needs em?

SHERIFF: Now, doggone it, fellas——!

BELLE 42: Hey, boys, I seen some right purty critters in my day, but I ain't never seen nuthin tuh match this un!

BELLE 43: Ain't he somethin, though!

The BELLES caress him, turn him about, while the COWPOKES continue to strip THE KID. THE SHERIFF breaks free. He is flustered, excited, troubled, breathing irregularly.

SHERIFF: NOW, KNOCK IT OFF, I SAID!!

The COWPOKES, taken aback, leave THE KID lie, turn to attend THE SHERIFF, effective at last. He calms, but watches them warily. They are alert, intent, sober. THE SHERIFF is struggling to be clear-headed about it, but is ultimately too befuddled.

SHERIFF: Okay. Okay. I know yuh mean well. I know. Appreciation. I understand. You're thinkin, what kin we do fer the Sheriff, after all . . . you know, after what he's done fer us. Killt the Kid and all. Hell, boys, I'd feel the same way, any decent man would.

COWPOKE 209: Aw, lissen, fergit it, Sheriff! Drink up!

They all press forward again, picking up in the game where they left off.

COWPOKE 210: Tuh the Sheriff, boys!
COWPOKE 211: Tuh the fastest——
SHERIFF (*authoritatively*): NO, DAMMIT, HOLD ON!

They stop short.

I ain't said muh piece, boys!

They shrug, glance impatiently at one another.

So jist take a grip on yore feelins there and hear me out, cuz it's somethin yuh gotta know!

He pauses, as though thinking it all out, swaying some, belching.

What I wanted tuh say was this. Somethin like this. Well, okay. It was me or the Kid. That's easy tuh folla. And the Kid got it. But . . . but it coulda jist as easy been me, see?

He pauses, frowning.

No . . . no, that ain't it. That ain't exackly right. Whoo! Ifn I didn't know you boys better, I'd say yuh was tryin tuh git me drunk!

He chuckles loosely, but laughs alone.

See, what I'm tryin tuh tell yuh, boys, is they ain't no such thing as the fastest gun in the West. Yes! *That's* what I'm tryin tuh say! Me and the Kid there, see, it jist happened like. It don't mean a thing. It . . . it's purty hard explainin it tuh yuh, boys, but it's important. It's very important . . .

> He hesitates, losing it again, rubs his face in an effort to clear his head. He gazes down on the six-shooters on his hips, cups his hands as though to draw. COWPOKES and BELLES shrink away as though getting ready to duck for cover. But THE SHERIFF doesn't draw; he looks up blearily and proceeds with his revelations.

SHERIFF: Right. The fastest gun. Tellin yuh about that. The fastest gun, well, we jist make all that up. See, yuh gotta learn that. I seen it soon as I seen the Kid go down. If somebody'd only told the Kid, why, mighta saved his life. Now . . . now, I know how bad you wanna believe it. I ain't no different, boys, I wanna believe it, too. I mean, I understand about why you're fixin me up in the Kid's duds, cuz it's somethin important tuh yuh, and yuh don't wanna lose it, I know. And I like these duds. I like how yuh think a me now. Shucks, Belle, you never even looked at me before, and . . . I mean, it'd be easy for me tuh pretend, tuh take yuh all in, make yuh think I'm somethin I ain't, and all the easier cuz it's what you *want* me tuh do! Yuh think yuh *need* it. But you're wrong, boys! Yuh gotta face up to it! I don't wanna hurt yuh, but I love this town, and sometimes, why, sometimes love hurts, don't it? Sometimes love makes yuh—

DEPUTY (*interrupting coldly*): Shut up, Sheriff.

SHERIFF: Hunh?

DEPUTY (*stepping forward to confront* THE SHERIFF): I said, shut yer fuckin mouth!

SHERIFF (*confused, hurt*): Lissen, it ain't I ain't grateful——

DEPUTY: Sheriff, gimme them side irons.

SHERIFF: Hunh? Yuh mean the Kid's—?

Smiling hopefully:

Sure, sure! That was jist what I was wantin tuh——

> As soon as THE SHERIFF reaches for the guns, they blast away and THE DEPUTY spins and crashes to the floor. THE SHERIFF lets go the six-shooters, still in their holsters, stares in shock at the dying DEPUTY, then in wonderment at his own hands.

COWPOKE 212: Good gawdamighty! Did yuh see that!

COWPOKE 213: His own Deppity!

COWPOKE 214: Right between the fuckin eyes!

COWPOKE 215: Greased lightnin, man!

SHERIFF (*still in awe at his own hands*): That . . . that's not what I——

COWPOKE 216 (*loud and commanding, as though suddenly taken aback*): Whoa there! Hey! Stand back, you jaspers!

COWPOKE 217: Hunh?

COWPOKE 218: What the——!

COWPOKE 216 (*again*): You see what *I* see?

COWPOKE 219 (*in overdrawn astonishment*): Well, I'll be horn-swoggled! It ain't the Sheriff at all!

COWPOKE 220: The Kid!

COWPOKE 221: It's the Kid hisself!

COWPOKE 222: THE KID'S COME BACK!!

> A BELLE screams. The COWPOKES fall back, leaving THE SHERIFF alone and perplexed, gazing down on the dead DEPUTY. He looks up, deeply pained.

SHERIFF: This . . . this ain't it at all, fellas! I . . . I don't——

COWPOKE 223: J-just t-take it easy now, K-K-Kid!

COWPOKE 224: We're jist plain folks . . .

COWPOKE 225: Decent and law-abidin, Kid!

COWPOKE 226: Cain't shoot worth a damn!

COWPOKE 227: We ain't aimin tuh cause yuh no t-trouble, Kid!

COWPOKE 228: Jist take anything yuh want, Kid, only d-don't shoot!

COWPOKE 229: Don't sh-shoot——!

SHERIFF: Now, wait a damn minute——!

COWPOKE 230: Ain't nobody gonna t-try yuh, Kid!

COWPOKE 231: We know you're the f-fastest gun in the W-W-West!

SHERIFF: No!

> Flings away THE KID's hat.

Goldurn it! Yuh gotta LISSEN tuh me, men!

> Flings away THE KID's gloves.

Don't yuh reckanize me? Cain't yuh see I'm the man yuh elected——

> THE SHERIFF draws the pistols to fling them away, but as soon as they're out of their holsters, they start blasting away. COWPOKES and BELLES dive for cover, some of them jerking and crumpling as though gunned down. Glass shatters, bullets whine, bells ring, women scream, horses whinny, hooves clatter, Indians yowl, barrels crash and rumble, etc., as the silver six-shooters blast away. As suddenly, they are silent. THE SHERIFF drops them to the floor.

SHERIFF (*in anguish*): Yuh wouldn't lissen! Yuh wouldn't LISSEN tuh me!

> The remaining COWPOKES and BELLES creep out of hiding, slip forward, encircle THE SHERIFF, restrain him.

COWPOKE 232: Easy now, Kid!

COWPOKE 233: Yore killin days is over, Kid!

COWPOKE 234: Brang the rope, Belle!

SHERIFF: Yuh wouldn't lissen . . . !

COWPOKE 235: We heard what yuh got tuh say, Kid. We cain't wait no longer.

COWPOKE 236: Some of us is dead, Kid, from waitin too long already.

COWPOKE 237: We cain't take no chances, Kid. You understand.

SHERIFF: I thought, if I could jist git the Kid, everything'd be okay . . .

COWPOKE 238: It's the end of the road, Kid.

COWPOKE 239: The end of the rope.

A BELLE comes forward with a rope, and they prepare to string THE SHERIFF up from a rafter in the saloon. With the noose around his neck, he blurts out:

SHERIFF: But wait! Why . . . why ME?
COWPOKE 240: Why?

Pause.

I'll tell yuh why. Because you're *dumb*, Sheriff. Because you're *dumb*.
SHERIFF: *But I don't wanna die! I been a good man, boys! I loved this town! I don't wanna—ACKK!*

As THE SHERIFF *jerks and dances at the end of* the rope, the BELLES and COWPOKES step forward to sing "The Day They Strung Up The Kid." This is hillbilly gospel singing, full of pathos and energy and triumph. It is sung mainly in full chorus, with four solo verses, preferably sung by four different persons, including at least one of the BELLES and THE DEPUTY—who, along with the other COWPOKES and BELLES who have fallen (but not THE KID), now rise and join in. One of the COWPOKES pulls his gun while the guitars are warming up and shoots THE SHERIFF in the belly to stop him jerking around.

The Day That They Strung Up the Kid

Let us study the Kid's wondrous story!
Ain't nobody ever done what he did!
The West was a place a grace and glory
Till the day that they strung up the Kid!

SOLO: He was mean, he was magic, he was real!
Sweet Jesus, he was somethin tuh see!
He was white as the lilies a the field,
And as pure and as wild and as free!

SOLO: He taught us that a man must live fer beauty!
You ain't worth shit if you're only second best!
The law ain't nuthin but the guy who's fastest shootin!
If millions croak, well, that's the legend a the West!

So jist reflect upon the Kid's wondrous story!
Ain't no cowpoke ever done what he did!
The West was a place a grace and glory
Till the day that they strung up the Kid!

SOLO: He gunned down moralists and misfits and mer-
      chants!
  Egalitarians he ground up fer manure!
  He cleansed the country a philosophers and virgins,
  And robbed the rich, and jist fer fun shot up the poor!

SOLO: But though they hung him up and blew his balls
      tuh heaven,
  His story, they say, may not be done!
  They say the world will be his tuh fuck forever!
  For the Spirit a the West goes marchin on!

So bethink yuh of the Kid's wondrous story!
Ain't no cowboy ever done what he did!
The West will EVER be a place a grace and glory,
Since the day that they strung up the Kid!

COP-OUT

by John Guare

For Ron and Linda

Introduction by John Lahr

John Guare's *Cop-Out* picks up where Robert Coover leaves off. If *The Kid* shows us how myth takes shape, Guare satirizes the spiritual confusion when fantasy overwhelms our sense of the real world. Guare's fabulous theatrical invention is mixed with a very strong sense of the madness in the social fabric of our lives, where every medium turns into a dream machine to steer us farther from ourselves and from the violence we perpetrate on the world. In its comic vaudeville structure, one set-piece of crime folklore gives way to another, pitting a policeman's fantasy self, Brett Arrow, against a universe of crime and debauchery.

Arrow is prepared to purify the world.

Arrow: I know you're out there, Mr. Big. I'm not going to rest till you're a bloody pulp, till I destroy your
Dago
Woppo
Kike-O
Dyke-O
Niggo
Spicko

Faggo
Micko
Mafia.
Your days are numbered, Mister Big.

In America, where government yells conspiracy after
every pratfall, it is important to confront the attitude and
the madness. In all the masquerades, Guare evokes the
central sadness of modern America—a culture groping for
a destiny it betrayed: violent and ruthless in its old age.

Cop-Out was given its first New York performance at the Cort Theatre, on April 7, 1969. It was directed by Melvin Bernhardt. The scenery and costumes were by Fred Voelpel, the lighting by John Gleason, and the environmental sound by James Reichert. It was produced by Norman Twain in association with Albert I. Fill. The cast was as follows:

ALL MALE PARTS   Ron Leibman
ALL FEMALE PARTS   Linda Lavin

Prior to the New York production, the play was first performed at the Eugene O'Neill Memorial Theatre Foundation in Waterford, Connecticut.

Characters
POLICEMAN
ARROW
OLD LADY
GIRL
LARUE
PANHANDLER
WHEELS
GIB
GARDENIA GERTIE

Note on cast of characters:
One actor plays all the male parts. One actress plays all the female parts.

The only scenery in the scenes between the POLICE-MAN and the GIRL is a very realistic police barricade. The signs she carries will always be blank.

In the detective scenes, the scenery is, any props are, lushly stylized as in a Universal/MGM film.

The link between the two worlds of the play is the movie screen at the rear of the stage.

The POLICEMAN/GIRL scenes are acted as if in a super-real documentary.

The ARROW scenes are MGM dynamic, as if every character has been nominated for best performance in a supporting role. ARROW, of course, is the world's toughest super-star.

As the audience comes into the theater, they hear a Billie Holiday sultry voice singing:

Whodunit, my love
Youdunit, my love
With a love so completely new
If I gun it, my love
Would you shun it, my love
But why shoot it or boot or try to toot it
Do you want to know why?

Our love is a crime
A criminal I'm

To be always testing
A love so arresting
Is surely a crime.

If you beat me to death with your gun
I wouldn't blame you
And at your trial, would I name you?
No
No
No
Whodunit, my love?
Youdunit, my love
And I do.

> As the house lights come down, the song is repeated, but this time sung in a very jazzy, Astrud Gilberto, breathy, Bossa Nova style. At the end of the song, the lights are out. In the darkness, we hear a thonking noise. Ten counts. Lights up on an astonished brightness focused down on a POLICEMAN in full uniform. The rest of the stage is dark. He slaps his night stick against the palm of his hand, making the thonking noise. Slow steady rhythm. He glares at us as if looking for an offender, daring some offense. His brass buttons shine. His cap is pulled down to the bridge of his nose. Ten counts.
> Blackout.
> Lights up immediately and his whole manner has changed and the stage lighting is bright and warm and jolly. His cap is pushed to the back of his head. He unbuttons his collar and smiles the broad smile of a very shy person. He's relaxed and as warm and as bright as the lights.

THE POLICEMAN (*to us*): When I was a kid, my father—my *pop* played a fabulous joke on me. We walked and walked one Maytime Sunday looking for fires to go to. Up streets. Down streets. Sniffing for smoke. Ears cocked for sirens. He held my hand and we walked and walked which was really nice as I had only learned how to a few weeks before and the sense of one step, two step was still very new. He held my hand. A very crisp, pleasant, uninflammable Sunday, all in all. All quiet. All nice. Streets of empty apartment houses because the whole world had gone off to church. My father—my *pop* suddenly picked me up and whispered in my ear—this ear—a truly strange request. Would I please yell out loud as my new pink vocal chords would, would I yell out the word Lease-Po? That I was going on two and I should start speaking if I was going to walk and it would mean a lot to him, he said, if my first words were—well, he said, I hate to put words in your mouth, but it would mean an awful lot to me if your first words were—and he said it again—if your first word was Lease-Po. I looked him in the eye, simultaneously learning the brand new emotion of bewilderment. I hated not understanding. Not understanding. That's the worst thing there is. Say it, he said. I said it. No, louder, he said, jiggling me in the crook of his arm. Lease-Po. I want to see the blue veins pop out in your pink throat. The fireworks on your first Fourth of July— remember? I shrieked out the word so loud. My first word. Lease-Po. And the breath rushed through my mouth. And he kept jiggling me, yessing me on, right there on the quiet streets. Lease-Po. Lease-Po-Lease-PolicePOLICEPOLICEPOLICE—PO—Po—po—Policemen dropped out of fire escapes. Squad cars screeched to halts. Policemen ran up out of what I thought were deserted subway stations, and policeladies appeared and pulled talcumed guns out of their navy blue garters. We were circled. My father—my *pop* blossomed bright red with embarrassment that flowered into laughter and he waved his fingers like a gun at the temple of his head. Kid's crazy, my dad said. And his laughter filled up the quiet streets. The wife took Thalidomide, my dad says. The wife took Thalidomide and drank hard liquor and went to night school while she was pregnant so the kid as a consequence got born without any brain. No, I shrieked for my second word. No nono. He told me to, I said to the circle of guns. My father pinched me tight and whispered a brand new word; Squealer. He clapped his hand over my mouth and waved his fingers crazily and policeladies started to cry and weeping policemen patted my father on the shoulder and my father held me up

and we tsktsktsked our way through all the blue uniforms and, over my father's bobbing shoulder, I
watched all the blue capped hands waving goodbye
and the sun polished their buttons and these

> Indicates billy club.

and talcumed guns vanished back into the policeladies' garters.

Now that my arms are as strong as the crook of the
arms of my pop, and now that my father is dead, on
odd occasions when the streets are empty and the sun
fingers these numbers on my chest, I throw back my
head on the empty Sunday streets and scream out:
LEASEPO!!!!! And *I* come running . . .

> He pulls his cap down onto the bridge of his nose
> and buttons his collar. His manner is stern and
> tough. He resumes beating the billy club against
> his palm.

I'll teach my father to make jokes.

> Count five. Blackout. The movie screen at the rear
> of the stage suddenly comes to life. A lobster-
> scope, a strobe light behind the screen, flashes at
> the audience. Music plays: pow-pow-pow music
> like the music that would play at the credits of a
> detective film. The actor who plays the policeman
> has stripped off his policeman's coat. A jaunty
> fedora replaces the policeman's cap. He appears
> behind the screen and in silhouette with the
> music blaring begins firing the two pistols he car-
> ries. Pow pow pow. What a fabulous shot! Lights
> up on stage. The strobe stops flashing. He comes
> down to us. Tough, cocky, cool, super-cool. His
> guns are drawn. He searches the audience. His
> name is ARROW.

ARROW: I know you're out there, Mister Big. I'm not going
to rest till you're a bloody pulp, till I destroy your
Dago
Woppo
Kike-O
Dyke-O
Niggo

Spicko
Faggo
Micko
Mafia.
Your days are numbered, Mister Big.
Or my name isn't Arrow.

>   Flashes his badge.

Brett Arrow.

>   He sits in a permanently tilted desk chair. He
>   puts his feet up on an imaginary desk. He takes a
>   swig of whisky from a flask in his pocket. He
>   returns his guns to the holsters under each arm.

I love being a plain-clothes man. Even in the shower,
you feel you got your uniform on. And the dames you
meet. I mean, they don't call us dicks for nothing.

>   He winks at us.
>   A knock at the door.
>   Then another knock.
>   He stiffens. He whips into action! His guns
>   flash out of his holsters. He leaps out of his chair.

Not to mention the eternal danger.

>   A very old lady enters. She is covered with blood.
>   She stumbles blindly forward. She has arm
>   crutches that she uses with great power. She
>   clomp clomps blindly downstage with great pain
>   and difficulty.

OLD LADY (*gasping in a Mittel Europa accent*): Arrow?
Arrow?
ARROW (*to us*): Those crutches aren't crutches. Those
crutches are rifles. She's been sent here to do dirt. To
do Arrow dirt.
OLD LADY (*gasping*): Arrow?
ARROW (*coming up behind*): Old lady, my ass!

>   And in the deftest of karate-styles, kicks the
>   crutches out from her. She screams and falls and
>   struggles and gropes in terror. He examines the
>   crutch.

You don't do dirt to Arrow.

OLD LADY (*her arms flailing*): Help? Help!

ARROW: This is strange. This is a crutch.

OLD LADY: HELLLLLLLLPPPPPP!!!!!!!!

> ARROW leaps behind her and grabs her arm in a half-nelson.

ARROW: Okay, old lady, start talking and start talking fast. Who are you? Or else my buddy in my holster will start talking for me.

> The OLD LADY reaches behind to feel Arrow's face.

OLD LADY: Arrow, is that you—

> The OLD LADY screams. Her hand has pressed up against the cigarette hanging from Arrow's mouth. She cries.

ARROW (*tightening his grip*): A lot of people have said that and then tried to put a bullet in my heart.

OLD LADY: Arrow, I'm the old lady who sells newspapers on the corner, who sells flowers in the bar—

ARROW (*looking at her*): Gardenia Gertie?

OLD LADY (*clutching*): Help me find the murderer?

ARROW: Murder?

> Music stings the moment. ARROW picks up the crippled OLD LADY and plants her in his chair, which is permanently tilted back in that position. She gets herself adjusted in the chair. Her legs dangle. But she now proceeds into the speech she trusts will win her the Oscar for the best supporting actress of the year.

OLD LADY: Stockton is dead. Dead. I come home from the used-gardenia warehouse and the cabbie walks me to the door like usual and I open the door and there's Stock Stock Stock Stock—

ARROW: Calm. Calm. Arrow's here.

OLD LADY (*gulps*): I'm all right now. Blood—blood—Stockton in a pile. His hands outstretched by the fireplace. Eyes looking up. Broken glass. Broken furniture. My entire life gone. Love letters ripped. My shepherd's lady in bits. Everything a stew and over it, the awful gravy of Stockton's blood. I pick up Stock Stock—

ARROW: Easy. Easy.

OLD LADY: . . . I'm okay now. I pick up Stockton. Is there life? I put my mouth against his. Breathe. Breathe. No steam on the mirror I hold under his nose. I—I—I—I take his tongue and place it in my mouth and bite, Arrow. Bite hard, hoping the sudden pain would bring an Easter morning, that he'd sit up and smile and everything would be the same. But the pain only forced more blood out of the slash in his throat. And the blood gushed onto my face like a lip-sticked mouth saying Dead Dead and saying that one of three people did it.

> She pulls a ripped, bloody sheet of paper out of her shopping bag.

My nephew, Gib. My niece, Larue.

> She spits at the mention of LARUE.

My lover, William. Here are the addresses. Written in blood.

ARROW (taking the paper): I think I can guess whose blood it is.

OLD LADY: Those unloved hate owners of love. Stockton owned all my love and they hated him because of all this money that at my death would go to Stockton.

> From her shopping bag, she takes out an enormous pile of cash.

Take the money. Take it all.

ARROW (aghast at the sum): . . . Policemen don't take money.

OLD LADY: Take the money. Time can't be lost.

ARROW (touching the money): We're paid for out of your tax dollar.

OLD LADY: A hundred thousand clams. Take it. There's more.

ARROW: No!

> But he takes it and gapes at it.

OLD LADY: I'd rather have a fool get it than one of those killers.

ARROW: Now wait—

OLD LADY (struggling out of the chair): You're a good

man. You bought gardenias from me for your lady
friends and you were never too tough to have a friendly
word. I'll be home watching Stockton's body. Keening
over it. He won't be buried till justice is done. Help
me, Arrow. You're a tough man, but a good man. I'll
be home trying to glue my shepherd's lady back together.

> She starts to exit with great dignity and difficulty.

But all the king's horses and all the king's men . . .

> She is at the door.

Could you lend me three bucks for the cab ride home?

> Her arms are filled with crutches and shopping
> bags. ARROW puts the money between her teeth.
> She looks at him appealingly. She goes out the
> door. He turns jubilantly to us, waving the shop-
> ping bag full of money at us.

ARROW: You see this, Mr. Big. I'm going to fight you on
your own ground. This money will go to the Police
Athletic League to find young boys and raise them
to be cops. My dream: a police force of five-year-olds,
six-year-olds, so you grow into your job with a whole
sense of life-force and purpose. And some of the
money will stay with me, so I'll never be tempted by
any of your Mafia bribes, Mr. Big-Soon-To-Be-Mr.-Tiny.
There's a lot of temptations being a cop, and I'm
proud to say I've only fallen fourteen times. I love
money. It's what this country's built on.

> He starts counting it.

Virtue is rewarded. There is a God and his badge
number is A-One.

> The strobe behind the movie screen begins flash-
> ing. The lights go down on ARROW. Blackout. The
> sounds of a demonstration. Lights up: the bright
> clear intense warmth of reality. A young teeny-
> bopper, very bright, very cute, carries a picket
> sign and walks in a circle that covers most of the
> stage. The POLICEMAN comes on and stands in

place down right. He tries to give his billy club a professional swing, but it gets caught up, the leather thong of it gets caught in his thumb. She keeps walking, not particularly involved. She gives her sign a few shakes upward. He begins thonking his club as at the beginning. When she passes by him, the second time she's passed him, she looks at him. She stops but there are other people in the circle, and she must keep up the pace. Her eyes are never off him. He keeps thonking. When she passes him, she smiles.

GIRL: I love your rhythm.

No response. She makes one full circle. Then:

I love the radio.

No response. She makes one full circle. Then:

You like the radio?

He stops his thonking for just a split second. She makes one full circle. Then:

You know why I like the radio? The surprise.

She steps out of line in front of him.

On records, you always know——

She catches up to her place in line and makes one full circle, then steps out of line again. Breathless:

You always know what you're going to hear because they're your records—but the radio—I mean, the surprise—

THE POLICEMAN: Just keep walking in the circular manner prescribed by the law—

THE GIRL (*makes one full circle, then*): This is some demonstration . . .

Makes one full circle.

You gonna beat up on us?

THE POLICEMAN (*running out of patience*): Look, girlie. Girl Communist.

THE GIRL: I mean, it's not like we're strangers.

THE POLICEMAN: Move on!

THE GIRL (*coming down behind him*): We met in Washington Square Park last spring. You beat up on me. You broke my girl friend's head? Remember? I spit on your nose. You remember? And I stepped over my girl friend's head to pull my sign back from you, but I stopped because my spit looked like a tear in your eye. Like you were crying because you had to do your duty. That was me.

THE POLICEMAN: Yeah? Well, that wasn't me. I don't do things like that.

THE GIRL: If we could just talk? Could you arrest me, so we can talk?

THE POLICEMAN (*very nervous*): Do me a favor? Please get back on line.

> She falls to the ground. He looks around. He's trying to be very cool.

Look, girlie, I did not become a officer—you stand up—become no officer of the—look—to get brainwashed by any Commie dope dupes like you. We was forewarned how you Commie dope dupes like to get the ear of unsuspecting patrolmen and pour in your own particular brand of poison and wash our brains till we're all like you. Well, I don't like brainwashing, so kindly arise to your feet and—and walk in the aforementioned manner.

THE GIRL (*looking up at him*): Officer, I'm not brainwashing, if that's what is holding up our relation—

THE POLICEMAN: Look—I became a cop to catch bank robbers. These dreams of breaking up Counterfeiter Rings. God! Delivering babies in taxis. Cats off roofs. Jeez, traffic. I even had dreams of towing all these cars away—far away. But if we wasn't here, mam, you see that American Legion Post across the street there, those old men frothing at the mouth with anger, they'd beat the Commie crap out of you.

THE GIRL (*getting up*): I'm no Commie dope dupe.

THE POLICEMAN: You think. You think. They got you so brainwashed and sanforized. I don't see no Made In USA on any those signs you carrying. Jeez, you're looking at the world through rose-colored rosies.

THE GIRL: No! The world is, could be lovely and tender
and wonderful if only . . .

THE POLICEMAN: Rosy ain't the color of your specs. No
sir. Pinko. That's the color they got you seeing. Boy,
would I like to straighten you out on the political
realities of our time. Boy, would you be in for a shock.

> She takes her sign and makes a full circle. She
> stops by him.

THE GIRL: Look, if beating up on me that time, if that's
what's holding up our relationship, I mean, I forgive
you. You have your job to do and I have mine and
there's no reason why we can't be friends.

THE POLICEMAN (*nervously*): Come on, huh?

> She kneels by him and pulls at her shoe.

THE GIRL: I'm tying my shoe. It's no electric chair to tie
your shoe.

> Pause.

I mean, it'd be all very West Side Story, you and me.

THE POLICEMAN: Boy, would I like to open your eyes.

THE GIRL (*standing up*): I'd be the PR's and you could
be the Polacks. Are you a Polack? I didn't mean anything personal. It's great to be anything, you know,
if you like it.

THE POLICEMAN: A cop. That's what I am. Oh boy, could
I straighten you out. I got some pamphlets that could
show you what enemies are trying to do to this country . . . they're in the back seat of the patrol car
. . . You ever see the back seat of a patrol car? Boy,
could I open your eyes . . .

THE GIRL (*a long pause*): You could put tears in my
eyes and you wouldn't even have to spit.

> They look at each other. She touches his billy
> club very gently. The strobe light in the screen
> behind them starts to flash. The sultry voice
> starts to sing:

Whodunit, my love
Youdunit, my love
With a love so completely new . . .

Blackout. The music turns into "Manhattan Sere-
nade," that early morning, day-like-any-other-day
B-movie music. ARROW appears behind the screen
in silhouette. Rumpled shirt, the fedora, the
double holsters. Hooked permanently onto his
shoulder is his jacket hanging there. He comes
downstage. He carries the piece of paper with the
names written in blood. The light comes up.

ARROW: I'm going to try this Larue first. One Million
Park Avenue. Classy address. I wonder if Mr. Big lives
here.

He pushes an elevator button and steps in.

Eighty-ninth floor, please.

And he steps out immediately. LARUE appears.
She is gorgeous, sultry. She wears a zowie green
caftan with a hood studded in diamonds. She
sits in one of those super chi-chi transparent
blow-up chairs. She wears large studious glasses
that she occasionally takes off and licks when
she's lost deep in thought. Papers are scattered all
over the floor. ARROW and LARUE meet. Their eyes
touch across the stage. Music begins: Lush. Sexy.
Ruby. Laura. All of them. He begins that des-
tined-since-the-beginning-of-time cross to her.

LARUE (*coooooool*): Don't step on my thesis.

He advances towards her, never taking his eyes
from her. However, he does avoid every page.

The pages are carefully filed all over the floor.

He steps gingerly.

That's it—oops—watch—yes—yes—no—yes!

And he stands by her. Very tough. Very cool. She
sizes him up.

I'm doing my thesis on metaphysical poetry.

Pause. She runs her tongue over her lips.

You like metaphysical poetry?

ARROW (*flashing his badge*): Look, lady, I'm here for a
    job—
LARUE: It's a lot like you and me, metaphysical poetry
    You yoke together two opposites and come up with
    something brand new, join together two ideas that
    never went together before and give birth to a—
ARROW (*cutting her off*): Lady, my brains are in my fist
    and my IQ is in my holster, so kindly dispense with
    the poetry shit. I am here to investigate a death. You
    get that. A murder. I'll advise you of your Constitu-
    tional rights—
LARUE (*dances seductively around him*): You don't want
    to improve yourself?
ARROW (*taking out notebook and pencil stub; tough*): I
    happen to be a student at the John Jay College of
    Police Science on East Twentieth Street in Manhattan,
    majoring at nights in Accounting, Sales Psychology
    and Leathercrafts—
LARUE (*touching him*): Name me a poet?
ARROW (*lighting a cigarette*): Look, lady—I'm here to
    find a murderer.
LARUE: Larue's the name—
ARROW: You're under suspicion of that murder—
LARUE: You don't know any poets!

    Singsong:

    The cop doesn't know any poets!
ARROW: I'm here to find a murderer, not get no degree.
    The laugh's on you, Sweetheart Miss Big, because I
    am formally charging you with the death, the brutal
    murder of Stockton and I'd like to see you buy your
    way out of this, you Arto Faggo.
LARUE: Stockton?
ARROW (*dragging deep on the smoke*): You said it and
    you did it.
LARUE: Arrow, the only Stockton I know is—

    She laughs nervously, unbelieving.

ARROW: Yes?
LARUE: My aunt's cat.

    She covers her mouth because she's laughing at
    him so hard.

ARROW: Your aunt's cat.

> The air is filled with the sound of hundreds of cats meowing and voices laughing at ARROW.

ARROW: Nobody laughs at Arrow.

> He strikes her hard a number of times. She falls back shocked, really hurt, then she leaps at him. She beats him. He gets her in a half-nelson.

LARUE (*violent*): I want your badge number, Arrow. I'll see you get busted to the engine room of the Staten Island Ferry—Let me go—
ARROW: What do you mean? A cat—

> She glares at him. He sticks his cigarette, holds it into her neck.

LARUE: A cat! A cat! Please stop! O God, my skin. Is that smell my skin?

> He pushes her away.

My neck, Arrow, is BLEEDING!

> Terrified:

You burned through the *skin*—what is your badge number? I want to know your badge number.

> She lunges at him, digging at his clothes.

Don't you wear numbers anymore?

> While she strikes his chest, he takes a long slow threatening drag on his cigarette. She backs away.

I'll tell. I'll tell. I'll—please, no more, Arrow. I'm calm now. See, the blood is pouring out and it's cooling the pain. All cool. Cool. The cat. Yes. You want to know about the cat. Every morning, Aunt Gertie sent out to Chicken Delight for five enormous chickens for Stockton's breakfast. And while Stockton ate, she'd pet him and coo him and rub his incredible stomach that drooped on the ground like an upside-down hump and she'd knead it like dough to aid his digestion and she'd sing and coo Oh Stockton Oh Stockton All My

Money Goes To You. To You. And he'd reach up and dig his claws into her sagging cheeks and she'd wag her yellow fingers Naughty Stockton with these tears of blood oozing down her cheeks like it's coming out of my neck and he would lick the blood off Aunt Gertie's cheeks to aid his indigestion and he'd leave the house, stopping only to pee on her gardenias. No, Stockton was not one of your Pink Pussycats.

ARROW (*quiet; after a beat, sympathetic*): Did you do it? Kill Stockton?

LARUE (*shaking her head no*): Gib.

ARROW (*finger snap*): Wait, hold it, I'm on to something. Gib is Big spelled backwards. Are you accusing your cousin?

LARUE: Arrow, I think I love you.

ARROW: Where's he hiding out?

LARUE: Check the papers. He's a playwright. His play is opening tonight. Did you hear me, Arrow?

ARROW: I'll nail him. So Mr. Big's a writer? Oh, I'll kill him. Arto Faggos, I'll get you all.

Starts to go.

LARUE (*blocking his way so he can't leave*): You show me a law against killing cats. Arrow, I love you.

ARROW (*firm, strong*): Larue, all I know is, an old lady came to me for help and that's all I know.

He pushes her aside. She runs after him, holding onto him.

LARUE: Arrow, I may deal in poetry, but all I dream about is violence. Violate me in the violets in the vilest way you know. I love you, Arrow. Violently.

She digs herself into his body. She sinks clutching him until she is hanging on passionately to his ankle.

I want to become you. I want to change into you.

ARROW (*pushing a button*): Don't play sweet with me, smartheart.

He steps into the elevator, dragging her with him.

Lobby, please.

LARUE: You really hurt me, Arrow.

> Elevator opens. He steps out, dragging her with him.

Arrow? Don't leave? Stay? At least till the blister forms on my wound. *Our* wound. Let me see just a little more of that police brutality?

> He grinds his foot into her hand. The Billie Holiday voice that opened the play begins singing and LARUE lip-synchs to it as he grinds his foot in her hand. He exits.

LARUE (*sings to her battered hand lovingly; lip-synch*):

If you beat me to death with your gun
I wouldn't blame you
And at your trial, would I name you
No
No
No

> She is on her back, her hand in the spotlight and the spot gets smaller and smaller and the strobe light behind the screen begins to flash and flash. Blackout. The sounds of a demonstration take over. A police barricade is down left. The POLICE-MAN stands at the stage center end of it, beating his stick against his palm. He seems quiet, nervous. The GIRL appears at the rear of the stage carrying her sign. She pushes and nudges and excuses herself through the crowd till she is at the barricade. She nudges him. He starts. Then sees it's her. He looks out front again, beating his club, but he's very pleased and happy. She sings very quietly and not quite on key:

THE GIRL:

I love a Cop
I love a Cop
What a situation
Ain't it awful
Life is really grim
I can only say that it's unlawful
What I feel for him

He's embarrassed and so pleased and looks around to make sure no one is watching them. She leans over the barricade, her picket sign by her side. They speak quietly and both look out front. From a distance, you wouldn't know they were together.

THE GIRL: That song is from the life story of Fiorello La Guardia—

THE POLICEMAN (*blushing*): They named the airport after?

THE GIRL: My roommate in college—

THE POLICEMAN: You're so smart—really—

THE GIRL: No social conscience at all this girl, but, boy, she loved show tunes and that song's from "Fiorello" and it won a Pulitzer Prize. I hate show tunes. But I love that song. I Love A Cop!

He shushes her.

THE POLICEMAN (*blushing*): Come on, I'm on duty.

THE GIRL (*whispers it*): I love a cop I love a cop. I'll whisper it from the cellars. We've known each other four months now and it's like all my life I waited for you. Maybe when I was little, you saved my life, a cop did, or maybe held me up at Coney Island when I got lost in the Easter Parade. A million different reasons, but whatever they are, I always knew I'd love a cop. And you got me the abortion so easy. They treated me like a queen. You know everybody.

He shushes her.

My own parents should've treated me as nice as that abortionist—you and the abortionist—that's the two times I been treated best in my whole life. The first nice time I ever had was our making love so tender in the patrol car on all the pamphlets that day we met four months ago and you turned on the siren and the flashing red light when I—when we *happened*—you were so tender and cars sped by the speed trap and you kissed me for every blipblipblip on the radar . . . you were so tender . . . and then the other man. He cut out the child so tender, as easy as you'd put it in. I don't like the word they have for that operation. I would like to think of it as a, yes, a premature Caesarean. We had our premature Caesar while he was still pure . . .

She is at his side.

THE POLICEMAN (*very quiet . . .*): You're so beautiful . . .

Duty calls. He beats the barricade suddenly with his club and she jumps back.

Look, behind the barricade!!!!!

To her:

Make believe we don't know each other.

THE GIRL (*back behind the barricade*): Hi, Stranger!

THE POLICEMAN: Listen to me—I'm up for a promotion.

THE GIRL: Oh, that's wonder—

THE POLICEMAN: Don't look happy. People can see us. Don't look like I'm talking.

THE GIRL (*dour face*): Oh, that's wonderful.

THE POLICEMAN: But, you see, they know I'm hanging around you. They are very suspicious down at the station house. I mean, you don't arrest anybody as many times as I've arrested you and then never book them. I mean, they're suspicious. You are a known demonstrator. Jeez, it'd be better for my career, better for me to hang around with murderers or gypsy cab drivers than consorting with known demonstrators.

THE GIRL (*clutching her sign*): You want me to stop picketing? I can't do that.

And she gives her sign a good shake upward.

THE POLICEMAN (*looking at the sign*): Well . . . then . . . there's no other choice. To show my faith in the Force before they promote me, I will have to have—a little op operation.

THE GIRL: Operation! Are you sick?

THE POLICEMAN: Don't look at me. It's a very simple op oper—I got a pamphlet on it right here. Most cops has it—

He takes the pamphlet from his coat, hangs it over his billy club, and passes it to her behind his back.

—like after, most cops *have* it like after two or three kids, you see, and it's really painless. It's like a club, a fraternity, and all the serious cops—well, ninety-five percent of the Los Angeles Police Force has them. Have them. I mean, you see the statistics right there.

THE GIRL: What kind of operation . . .

THE POLICEMAN: It's really simple. They just—you see this chart—they just snip the tube that leads to the pros prostate that fer fer tilizes the se se se. Well, it's not like you're Nothing. No. It makes you even more virile because there's no knockup fear like I knocked you up. It's just a little snip and ninety-five percent like I said of the LA Police—and that's the best in the country—the Best Force in the— Everybody knows that—and I knew I'd have the operation someday cos all Serious Cops has it. Have it. But I didn't think it'd be this soon. Vasec—Vasectomy. A pretty word, huh? I mean, I wish you hadn't had that abor abor—I mean, we woulda had one kid you know and I really want to be a cop and they're suspicious of me hanging around with you and it's just to show faith and I feel I thrown my life away because I love you and you're *still* carrying signs and can I ever trust you and I don't know what to do do do do.

He is trying not to cry.

THE GIRL (*dazed; touches his sleeve. Sings*):

What a situation
Ain't it awful
Life is really grim

THE POLICEMAN: I mean, ninety-five percent—LA—says it right here—very simple—just a snip—

Voices of a demonstration rise up. They are both very quiet and very lost. The lights fade on them. The screen appears with the flashing strobe light. Weird color lights and Indian music plays. ARROW appears behind the screen in silhouette. He strides out cocky, tough.

ARROW: Green Witch Village.
Blaaagh. Gib's Theatre is along here somewhere.
Look at them panhandlers.

Comes down to us. A closeup.

I'd like to take a few minutes here to tell any young
sports out there between the ages of eighteen and
twenty-nine, standing at least five foot two with
twenty-twenty eyeballs and a hatred of evil and no
previous bad stuff, I couldn't advise you about choosing this

Flashes his badge.

as a more better way of life.

He watches someone go by.

Out of the way, beads. Get a haircut.

To us:

With all the protesting going on today, I want to know
why you don't hear nobody squawking against this
country's name. America—get this—named after
Amerigo Vespucci. Dago Woppo. Amerigo Vespucci,
my ass. Shows you how the Mafia sunk its teeth into
America right from the Fourteen Ninety-Two.

And one of those legless panhandlers who wheel
around on dollies pushes himself up behind
ARROW. The PANHANDLER wears a heavy over-
coat and an old hat and scarves around his neck.
We can see a little mustache and dark glasses.

ARROW (*trying to ignore this new arrival. To us*): Mr.
Big, are you hiding down here in Green Witch Village?
THE PANHANDLER: Psssst.
ARROW: Hiding here under all this dirt?
THE PANHANDLER: Hey, Meester—
ARROW: Get out of here, Wheels, or I'll push you in on
a 902—

WHEELS looks around, then hands ARROW a large
red rose with a message hanging off it.

WHEELS (*Spanish Peter Lorre accent*): Meester, buy a
flower?

ARROW: There's only one old lady this gumshoe buys
  blossoms from—
WHEELS (*whisper*): Read dee message—
ARROW: "Call me Arrow . . . Larue." Larue????????
WHEELS: Call her.
ARROW: You got a dime?

> WHEELS whips out a walkie-talkie. An antenna
> shoots up.

WHEELS (*into walkie-talkie*): Miss Larue?

> Taps machine.

  Eins Zwei. Roger. Over.
LARUE'S VOICE: Arrow?
WHEELS: Eet's for you.
ARROW (*taking walkie-talkie*): For me?
LARUE'S VOICE: Oh, Arrow—
ARROW: Watch what you say in front of Wheels here—
LARUE'S VOICE: He can be trusted.
ARROW: Can you be trusted?
WHEELS (*offended*): I can be trusted.
ARROW: He can be trusted.
LARUE'S VOICE: Arrow, I hate to bother you on the street,
  but get in that play.
ARROW: I'm on my way to the play.
WHEELS: She means Get In The Play.
ARROW: Get In Gib's play??????
LARUE'S VOICE: Arrow, if you don't, Gib will never leave
  that theater alive.
ARROW: Is this a trap?
WHEELS: Save Meester Geeb. Save heem.
LARUE'S VOICE: Believe me.
WHEELS: Belbeeb her.
LARUE'S VOICE: You see, Arrow, I know who killed
  Stockton.
ARROW: Who, Larue?
WHEELS: Who, Mees Larue?
LARUE'S VOICE: It's—It's—It's—Oh No. No. No.
ARROW: Yes?
WHEELS (*takes walkie-talkie*): . . . The machine is
  dead . . .
ARROW: If Miss Larue is the same, you won't have a leg
  to stand on. Get me to that theater. Quick.

WHEELS: Quick????
ARROW: Pronto, Spicko.
WHEELS: Ohhh, Kweeek.
ARROW: Brett Arrow's got some acting to do.
WHEELS: Thees way!!!!

> Thrilling chase music plays. ARROW hops on the
> back of Wheels' dolly. Darkness. Voices: "You
> can't come in here. The play is on." Sounds of
> slugs and hits and people falling. Then patriotic
> music plays. Tootling fifes and drums. A little
> stage wheels on, big enough for the two actors.
> Curtains part. MARILYN MONROE and GEORGE
> WASHINGTON are in bed.

MARILYN MONROE: I don't want you doing that anymore
to me, George. You hear?

GEORGE WASHINGTON (*his head under the covers*): Yum
Yum Yum Yum Yum Yum Yum Yum.

MARILYN MONROE: You've got wooden false teeth,
George. And I've got splinters everywhere. Either you
take those wooden false teeth out and give them to
the termites or you leave me alone. I'm just a young
girl, a very young girl, and don't take, Mr. W., you
shouldn't take advantage of my youth. Oooo. Ouch.
George.

GEORGE WASHINGTON (*his head pops out of the covers*):
Look, I found you at Valley Forge and I can drop you
back at Valley Forge—

> ARROW plays all the presidents like Groucho Marx
> and W. C. Fields.

MARILYN MONROE (*looking strangely at this new performer. Beat. Then*): Oh George, Mr. W., I know I
should be really grateful that you're going to make me
the symbol of the country—

GEORGE WASHINGTON (*pouting*): Some girls would love
to be the symbol of a new country. I wrote you a song
today!

MARILYN MONROE: A song? For me?

GEORGE WASHINGTON (*sings vaudeville-style*):

> DaDaDaDa Dot Dot
> Your Cunt

Tree Tis of Me
Sweet Land O'

MARILYN MONROE: Where did you learn all these things?
GEORGE WASHINGTON: Martha was married before.

> He ducks under the covers. A clock begins ticking
> throughout the rest of the scene.

MARILYN MONROE: What did Millard Fillmore always
say? Time goes by so quickly. Here it is: Four Score
and Seven Years Ago Already.

> ARROW appears from under the covers as ABRA-
> HAM LINCOLN.

MARILYN MONROE: Couldn't you at least take off your
shawl?
ABRAHAM LINCOLN (*again as Groucho*): I need it to keep
warm, Marilyn.
MARILYN MONROE: It makes me feel old. And those
warts. I have to put up with your warts. You leave indentations in my skin. I don't want indentations in my
fresh white skin.
ABRAHAM LINCOLN: Think of them as dimples, Norma
Jean. Dimples that fell out. Babies have dimples.
Dimples are young. I leave dimples in you.

> Vanishes under the covers.

I need you.

> Sings:

My Country Tis of you
Sweet Land of Libertoo
Yum Yum Yum Yum Yum Yum Yum Yum Yum Yum
Yum Yum Yum

MARILYN MONROE: You're so wise. Oh yes. I like that.
Yum Yum.

> ARROW leaps up as TEDDY ROOSEVELT.

THEODORE ROOSEVELT: Speak softly and carry a big
shtick!

> He's back under the covers.

MARILYN MONROE: Oh Teddy, shoot me a bear and keep me warm!

ARROW (*under the covers keeps repeating over and over*):

My dear little pussy
My sweet little pussy
Dearest darling little pussy
Puss Puss Puss Puss

> She gradually mounts in ecstasy.

MARILYN MONROE: Oh Woodrow, I feel so old. Oh Calvin, say something. Harder Harder Harder Harding. To think one day Herbert Hoover would be mine. Oh FDR, your braces are cold against my legs. You don't tell me, Harry, you learned that from Bess. Oh yes, Ike, you put me to sleep. Hold me, Daddy Ike. Oh, Jack. We're young. You and I are young.

> Becoming an old lady.

Bobby, answer the phone?

> She gasps for breath. Desperate. Then bright and MARILYN again.

Hey Hey L B J, where'd you learn to kiss that way.

> Then as old lady.

Bobby? Answer the phone . . .

> Then MARILYN:

OoooooooOO, Mr. Nixon. Just cos I'm dead doesn't mean you can treat me like that. OooooOO.

> Old lady.

Bobby? Answer the phone? Say . . . we're both . . . young . . . both still . . . the dream . . . Bobby . . .

> She dies. Then brightly appears as MARILYN.

My last wish was to have my ashes scattered among you, among my fans.

> To ARROW, below her:

Hurry. Hurry.

> ARROW appears with an Uncle Sam hat on. He carries an ash tray full of ashes and a little battery-operated fan. He blows the ashes into the audience.

I'm now a part. A part of you all. Breathe. Breathe so very deep.

> The curtain falls on the little theater.
> Boos and applause. ARROW and MARILYN appear through the curtain for bows. She blows kisses.

ARROW: Porno Smutto . . . If one mind has got bended out of shape by this . . .

> They finish bowing. Move back behind the curtain. The theater rolls away. They are now backstage.

MARILYN MONROE: Who are you? You're Mondo Perfecto.
ARROW: I'll kill him. Out of my way, lady. I'm here to save Gib.
MARILYN MONROE (*blocking his way*): And who, Mondo Studdo, do you think you're talking to?
ARROW (*pulls back; looks at script*): The Role of America Growing Old will be played by—
MARILYN MONROE: Hi Ho, Mondo Mondo.
ARROW: Gib!!!!!!!!

> And a shot rings out. GIB leaps into Arrow's arms. ARROW draws his gun. Footsteps echo through the theater.

MARILYN/GIB (*terrified*): Save us?
ARROW: Get in this trunk.

> Which GIB steps into. An old theatrical trunk.

Gib, your cousin Larue asked me to save you. Which I have done.

> Stirring music plays underneath.

But I can't guarantee what will happen when you and this Porno Smutto arrive in Washington D. C. and J. Edgar and his boys get a hold of you.

GIB (*à la Judy Garland*):

Anyone can be born in a Trunk
But how many get to die there.

>   He slams the trunk down on GIB. The footsteps
>   resume. He sneezes.

ARROW: This American beauty is giving me the— Wait
—this isn't an American Beauty—this is a bloodstained—Oh no. Because the only other blood is the
blood on the—

>   He takes out the list.

Then that would mean that this was a bloodstained—

>   And GARDENIA GERTIE appears with a gun drawn.

Gardenia Gertie.

GARDENIA GERTIE: I pay you to be a flower sniffer?

ARROW: Gertie, we're on the honor system here. Go down
to the precinct and turn yourself in.

>   He advances toward her. She cocks the gun.

GARDENIA GERTIE: Dance, Arrow.

ARROW (*dancing*): Why'd you do it, Gertie. Why?

GARDENIA GERTIE: You think I liked being old so the only
thing could love me is a cat? I fed it and it scratched
me. I petted it and it bit me. I treated it good. It should
love me. But when you're no longer young, Power is
your only weapon. So I killed him. I done it and I'd
done it again.

ARROW: But, Gertie, what's Mr. Big's connection in all
this?

GARDENIA GERTIE: He gives me Power, and the Power
makes me feel young and I'm goink to travel the
whole woild—Europe Asia Effrica Everyplace—show-
ink I'm powerful and beautiful and still the dream.
Say I'm young.

>   She waves the gun.

ARROW: You're young. You're young!

GARDENIA GERTIE (*laughs insanely*): You'll never catch
me. Never.

> She backs out the door. There is a deafening scream of hundreds of meowing cats. ARROW dashes out. Then returns, clutching his stomach.

ARROW (*to us*): Stockton's revenge. Devoured by an alleyful of insane felines. All that's left are her crutches and the cats are using those for toothpicks.

> LARUE crawls on, dying.

A goddam messy case.

LARUE: I'm dying, Arrow. I've been working for a foreign power. Don't ask me any more. Not yet. But they had seen you coming to One Million Park. They heard me warning you. They got me. Right here. I did some surgery and got the bullet out—but it went through the heart—Oo Oo Oo—

ARROW: Steady, girl. Steady.

LARUE: I'm all right now. And I crawled out of my apartment, down those eighty-nine flights, wanting to get to you, needing to get to you, crawling all the way here.

ARROW: Crawled?

LARUE: Oh, Arrow, rats on Park Avenue. Mice on Madison. A Fifth Avenue Bus ran over me, but I'm here.

ARROW: You got the messy end of this case.

LARUE (*snuggling painfully in his arms*): Yes. But I met you.

> Sings:

Whodunit, my love
You done it, my love

ARROW (*holding her*): Don't die, Larue!

LARUE: Keep America young for me. You have to keep us young. At any cost. Keep it young for La—Oo Oo Oo. Rue.

> She dies.

ARROW: Who are you? CIA? FBI?

LARUE (*eyes opening, sings*): If you beat me to death with your gun . . . Oh, Arrow. D.O.A.

> She dies in his arms.

ARROW (*clutching her*): No!

> He tries not to cry.

I'll get you

> And his eyes search the theater.

for trying to kill off America. I know you're out there, Mr. Big. I'll get you all you Commie Jewo Niggo Dago Woppo Mafio Faggo Russki—I'll get you I'll Get You I'll Get You I'll Get YOU I'LL GET YOU I'LL GET—

> And the strobe light begins flashing on the screen behind. ARROW keeps yelling his threat over and over again. The sound of vroom vroom vroom of cars starting and stopping fills the theater. The lights are up and the stage is bare. The POLICE-MAN is taking tolls in a tunnel. In a deep anger.

Five exits down. Dim your lights. Ten exits down. Read the signs.

> The GIRL waits her turn behind a car. She comes to him. He reaches his hand out to take the toll, then sees it's her.

THE GIRL: I walked through the tunnel.
THE POLICEMAN (*angry; not looking at her*): Only cars are allowed here. No pedestrians in the Lincoln Tunnel.

> To a car:

Three exits down. Turnoff after the bridge, dope.

> To her:

Get out of here? You deaf?

> To a car:

Where'd you learn to drive?

> He pushes her behind him.

THE GIRL: You had the operation, didn't you?
THE POLICEMAN (*pause. Then, to a car*): You don't got nothing smaller? Four exits down.
THE GIRL: Is that why you don't want to see me?
THE POLICEMAN (*looks at her; fumbles; then, to a car*): Look at your map . . .

> Pause. To her:

and before the novocaine had wore off, they shipped me here as additional punishment for consorting with a known demonstrator.

THE GIRL: I—I would've come visit you . . .

THE POLICEMAN: You stay away. I got to earn my way back into the Force. Boy, did you dupe me. You Commie, carrying signs. You with your thinking. If you people would only stop to think where your thinking leads you—Boy, I had a chance in that hospital to do a lot of thinking and, boy, did you knit sweaters over these eyes. Well, now my eyes are clear and, boy, do I see.

THE GIRL (*not comprehending*): But—you and—we were going *steady*.

THE POLICEMAN (*tough; to a car*): Six exits down. Turn off by the fork.

To her:

It all comes back to me now. You trying to put thoughts in my head. Youda been happy if I wasn't *even* a cop. Well, I am a cop and I inhale every car that goes by, so the fumes will make me madder and tougher and, every tenth car, I steal fifty cents and put it in the PAL Fund.

To a car:

Fifty miles ahead, asshole.

To her:

So we'll have more cops. Younger cops. Teach kids to be cops right at birth and give them vasectomies and drill them—five-year-old, six-year-old police— that's what we need—And every kid in this country will wear Navy Blue and at high noon, the universe will be blinded by the sun fingering the gold on our brass buttons. LeasePo LeasePo the world will sing because the screws are turning, baby. You got the blackies all riled up and you'll probably start working on the Chinko riots and get the Indians all on war-paths again. Well, your days are numbered. Because there is going to be a White, the Whitest of White on White Revolutions you ever saw and all the people who want this country to be what it can be, well, wo are going to win. It's War, you Commie Dope Dupe. I had a lot of time to think in that hospital . . . Oh boy, my eyes are clear.

THE GIRL: Here's fifty cents. Treat me like any other car.

She starts to go.

THE POLICEMAN: Right into the PAL Kitty. This is gonna be the fattest Kitty on the block. Oh, I love my opera-ation. I feel I finally belong. I am finally something.

He becomes aware that she is looking at him. He fumbles.

I—I—I—

She picks up a sign and begins picketing de-fiantly in a circle around him.

I have my cophood. I have my promotion.

She stops by him. He fumbles.

I have my stick. I have my uniform.

She stops by him. He fumbles, but stops looking at her and begins beating his club against his palm: thonk thonk thonk thonk: trying to pull himself together. She moves faster and faster. He becomes tougher and tougher.

I have my *teeth*. I have my *fists*. I have my *spine*.

She stops by him. He is no longer self-conscious. He is beaming ferociously.

I have my *cock*. I have my *GUN*. LEASE-PO. LEASE-PO. LEASEPO. LEASEPO. You stop picketing. You stop running. You stop it. You stop.

She is running in a full circle, desperately.

I'm warning you. You stop.

She throws down her sign and leaps off stage. She runs up the aisle.
He shoots her. A deafening blast. Blackout. Thonk thonk thonk thonk. One spot overhead down on him, his cap pulled down to the bridge of his nose. He beats his stick as at the very

beginning. Ten counts. Blackout. He exits. Then house lights up. The actress lies in the middle aisle till the audience goes home. Then she gets up and leaves.

INJUN: A HAPPENING

by Claes Oldenburg

Introduction by Jonathan Price

Pull back the string—make signs vibrate. Make the familiar more: enlarge it by ten, transform it into vinyl, or lucite, take canvas for metal, and watch the draperies of light, showing. Bring neon into the museums. Blast apart the old ideas of what is appropriate in form, texture, light quality, and display: capitalize on it like a Ray Gunner, zapping the darting figures before the store.

An artist is a careful maker and understands the kinship with artisans of all sorts, magic makers all. Skill serves, when mastered, to express whatever the individual wants, whether in a cabinet or in a new work of art. In periods of taste we have one labeled *Modern*. Its effects are still with us. After that came a period which I call *the new*. We are in the news now. Skilled self-expression, whether in a hamburger or in a soup can, deserves recognition, and heightening, as one artist looks out at his people and at the dramas they perform each day, in pink neon.

I am for Kool-art, 7 Up Art, Pepsi Art, Sunshine Art, 39 cents art, 15 cents art, Vatronol art, Dro-bomb art, Vam art, Menthol art, L&M art, Ex Lax art, Venida art,

Heaven Hill art, Pamryl art, San-o-Med art, Rx art, 9.99 art, Now art, New art, How art, Fire Sale art, Last Chance art, Meat-o-Rama art.   *Store Days* (1961)

Articulation seems almost magic to the outsider, but that is just the natural energy of a human being showing there; you realize, enjoying the tricks of Oldenburg's gigantic bathroom, or of his lipstick first stuck at Yale, that his imagination is released, that his spirit is free to make red fireplugs look the way we sense them, like cut-off stumps, like sirens, like a crotch upside down, and to enjoy the sheer enamel of the red paint he is using as well. Oldenburg is one of the new artists: he is one of America's best writers, as is John Cage, and he works in plastic, cement, steel, aluminum, canvas, oil paint, acrylic, glue, hay, and people. Oh yes, he uses people in some of his productions, but he apologizes, saying the happenings were just studies in light and in transformation. True: and more, they were synaesthetic and led the audience through a makeshift number of rooms in the Dallas County Art Museum. Each of his gestures is practically simple and studied with care: but each seems a condensation of a thousand and one feelings about America, here, about the mysteries of our multiple pasts, about perception. Oldenburg himself dressed in a cloth bag and led the audience through, waving his brownish green mosquito netting, which had large rocklike shapes hanging down all over it. Michael Kirby says, "At a short distance, the man inside (Oldenburg) was practically invisible as he stooped under the folds of cloth, and in the darkness of the museum grounds only his general shape could be seen as he ran, suddenly stood still, crouched and hid." It is costumed much like Zen.

Roll the die to pick a view: discover therein more than was anticipated. The artist does not always know how well or how thoroughly he has created: a painter can usually not put it into words. But if the artist pays attention to the self, and to the people, intensely enough, an exchange and a growing take place: imagination at play at last in the fields of culture. These new artists, heavens to betsy, mehitabel or archy, are making a new culture of America.

Abstract expressionism guaranteed that art did not have

to be a photograph: huzzah; but one could still play with the reminders of the real—and the more the merrier. The new artists discovered that if everything was fair game, they could take culture itself as a subject and go on from there. The modern age, that period of steel-and-glass skyscrapers, is now receding into the backwaters of our civilization, just as today the 1920s have finally ebbed loose of Maine.

Books going into massive editions on an American scale —that, too, is a result of our development during the thirty years since World War II began, that rough period constituting the modern. And mass reproduction of art is now familiar. Print people used to isolate themselves from art, considering that but one subject. Now even print must attain the level of art.

Art processes information faster; that is all: it is a term of endearment, not a particular thing. There are no standards in art: the point is how much it expresses for you of what you want expressed. That is, its value to you depends in some profound way on how much the artist cared about you to lead you on to deeper perception. This all seems reasonable to us because of such books as *Moby-Dick*. Classics stick in our minds like harpoons. Oldenburg's plots are as old as Ahab or the frontier.

Free yourself. Play with your culture: transform it as you will.

Oldenburg's happenings, like his book, *Proposals for Monuments and Buildings, 1965–1969,* offer a number of prods to the imagination. His events are a series of shocks and jerks to the system, administered with mystery and with some real joy. What does it all mean? The point is not solely what it means. Meaning grows naturally enough out of actually imagining your way through such a house of horrors of our past and present, a mimicking of realities as dark and attractive as this.

Imagine having an entire house at your disposal. You are "the artist." You can lead one group of two hundred people through it. You have any loose material lying around the Dallas County Art Museum, and a lot of free actors, and they will all decorate the place any way you want. What's the subject? Oh, well, it's way out west. Let's call it something American, like "The Birth of a Nation" or "The American Flag" or "Injun."

How does it end? Raggedly. People walking all over, exploring, calling to each other to come look as a woman in white repeats some ritualistic gesture again, next to the bricks and the bathtub. Open.

That is a sign.

We wander through the house and shed of Oldenburg's personality here, and through his quarrel with the rules of America. It is a strange set of tableaux vivants, and the language is muffled, but the miracle is dramatic. One is opened in such play, and one receives irregular bursts of information below the purely verbal level. Articulation is not the task set for the audience: there is no task: the door is open, and the key was lost at least a year ago.

Transformations, imaginings, activities of magic: and all with the most familiar objects of our culture, flinging our own beings up into the artwork, as part of the exchange. Feedback enters art. Fans write to artists, now, by playing with their works. Why not? After all, play leads us on.

"Call me Ishmael" is the way one American era ended. History can now be told in drama: striking like an arrow at night, thudding the real, in all six senses.

A STATEMENT

Claes Oldenburg

What I do as a "happening" is part of my general concern at this time, to use more or less altered "real" material. This had to do with *objects*, such as typewriters, ping-pong tables, articles of clothing, ice-cream cones, hamburgers, cakes, etc., etc.—whatever I happen to come into contact with. The "happening" is one or another method of using *objects in motion*, and this I take to include people, both in themselves and as agents of object motion.

To present this material, I have worked out some structures and techniques which parallel those of the presentation of the static object. The static object is shown by me as one of a number of related objects, in a particular "real" place—itself an object. For example, *The Store* (1961, New York), containing 120 items approximately, within a real store (107 E. Second St., New York). Or, *The Home*, which I am now developing, with items of furniture and appliances, etc. (*Bedroom Ensemble*, 1964, a room at the Sidney Janis Gallery, New York), though a real house or apartment has not yet been set up. I present in a "happening" anywhere from thirty to seventy-five events, or happenings (and many more objects), over a period of time from one-half to one and a half hours, in simple spatial relationships—juxtaposed, superimposed—like those of *The Store*. The event is made simple and clear and is set up either to repeat itself or to proceed very slowly so that the tendency is always to a static object.

In some pieces I tried setting up events into a pattern, a pseudoplot, more associational than logical (*Ray Gun Theater*, those after *Store Days II* especially. March–May, 1962, New York). In the first "happening" I did, *Snapshots from the City* (March, 1960, New York), the events were fragments of action, immobilized by instantaneous illuminations. Otherwise, the "happenings" have been one pattern or another of discrete events: in *Blackouts* (December, 1960, New York), the events were illuminated at different stations across a long stage. In *Fotodeath* (February, 1961, New York), the events repeated themselves in superimposed lines of movement. In *Gayety* (February, 1963, Chicago), the events occurred at stations within and around the spectators. In *Stars* (April, 1963, Washington, D.C.) events moved in and out of sight along a right-angle stage. In *Autobodys* (December, 1963, Los Angeles), the audience (in cars) surrounded a rectangle on which widely spaced events occurred.

An individual event may be "realistic," and this may be quite direct, evolving on the spot with a player and certain materials and objects, or a reconstruction (of something I might have observed the day before or read about or dreamed, or of which someone else may have brought the account) or it may be, at an opposite extreme, an enigmatic, fantastic event, with altered objects and altered (costumed) persons. I mix realistic and fantastic events, as the imagination does, and I consider the imaginary event as real as the "real" one.

In the process of altering an object or event, I use various methods, some of which are purely whimsical, others having a rationalization, such as the alteration of real (tangible) furniture into its appearance (visual perspective).

The effect of my "happenings" will be missed if my specific intention and technique are not understood. Spectators will look for development where none is intended, or be bored by the repetition. Or the term "happening" by its vagueness will raise an expectation unlike the effect encountered; for example, spontaneous effect or an improvisation or a spectacle of some sort.

My aim is the perfection of the details of the events rather than any composition (except in the later *Ray Gun Theater*, with its "poetic" arrangement of incidents), and the composition is merely a practical structure (usually "real" f.ex. "snapshots" "blackouts" "circus"—a structure which is an object in itself).

The audience is considered an object and its behavior as events, along with the rest. The audience is taken to differ from the players in that its possibilities are not explored as far as that of the players' (whose possibilities are not explored as far as my own). The place of the audience in the structure is determined by seating and by certain simple provocations.

The place in which the piece occurs, this large object, is, as I have indicated, part of the effect, and usually the first and most important factor determining the events (materials at hand being the second and players the third). "Place" may have any extent, a room or a nation, and may have any character whatsoever: old, new, clean, dirty, water or land, whatever is decided.

There is no limit to what objects or what methods may be used to arrive at events. An account of the "rehearsals" or making of particular pieces will show the strategies employed to achieve results.

INJUN / *the script*

by Claes Oldenburg

Note: During the preparation of Injun, Oldenburg wrote the following description for himself.

The spectators experience the house from the outside, perhaps they walk around it first. Then the house from the inside.

They meet in the lobby of the museum with some doubt as to where the thing will take place. It is generally known something will come and get them. Which then happens: the tornado and possibly another form, with a hundred feet of rope comes to the door. The lights dim and the rope is stretched the length of the lobby people hold on to it, it has knots and a procession starts out the front door down the drive up the bank and into the yards of the houses. As the people go, the lights are turned out in and around the museum so that the area is very dark. There will be streetlights and streetsounds of course and the flying of the planes above.

There occur stations of activity along the way like night patrol or Coney Island fun house. Inexplicable pastoral scenes: boxes tumble off the roof of the garage. A spotlight plays down in the garden on some people moving around in bags? Someone is talking on the porch of the children's house. Perhaps a hanged man. Something is being done inside the garage which cannot quite be seen, perhaps a murder or a foal delivered. Legs protrude from the ceiling of the barn. People lie in the grass.

On the back porch there is going on an argument of some sort, a shadow play, one can barely make out.

Things are being thrown. The Tornado leads the people around the house. They see up and inside through the windows the activity there. Things are thrown out the window. Inside music plays. Curiosity developed, fragments. Cry of a baby, flushing toilet. House sounds, coughing crying singing dancing, eating. Feathers fall, shots, screams etc. sentimental sings. A windup phono Loudspeaker talk. Record wiretap?

On the street side and behind in the yard shapes are moving back where the spectators walked something is still going on in the garage. There is all around them considerable suggested activity. Then the lights in the house go out. The spectators are led to the rear of the house and slowly into the house through a ramp at the backporch. Slowly as if all one investigating the strange house. The tornado which led them out has now disappeared and there is another leader and perhaps a prompter. They are led counterclockwise through the kitchen the dining room the front room and back through the front bedroom, the hall past the second bedroom and the toilet and onto the porch looking as they go into and through the rooms. This first turn there is no activity in the house and it is quite dark.

The second time around. The light goes on in the far front room like a stage. There is moaning from parts of the house and a clear song from somewhere. The Injun is in the front hacking at something. Doors close in the hall rooms and there is knocking from behind them. In the front bedroom a man sits up in bed which is full of bricks. The spectators return out again.

The piece is divided into these trips through, let us say five to be made.

Thus five trips, six rooms, of cumulative intensity, until finally the whole house is alive with activity. It is then the front door is opened and the walkers diverted outside on the front porch and down, to dissolve and wonder if it's over. Then a black Cadillac drives up.

Shooting some bodies are dumped, a lot of running. This too quite inexplicable like things is.

Then the general sense of it being over. The actors in the house drift out the back of the house and return to the museum.

The path is this:

From the lobby through the gate to the yard of the CH [carriage house] then on and between the two houses (all very slowly). Little action in these areas at this point. In the driveway a car with dim lights filled with newspaper. Intimations. Calls from window etc. All quite slow. . . . Perhaps use CH windows too. Then up front porch and thru front door. Rooms in use will be front room, kitchen, bedrooms 1 and two and bathroom. The corridor and second front room for spectators who may mill about as they desire until instructed to leave when the back door will be opened not the front. All along there has been scurrying action in the porch glimpsed through the doors, but now the doors open and the action increases in the back yard, the garage and finally the garden. The spectators are pressed to walk in the direction of the museum. The apotheosis a body thrown into the garden and the confused motion of the Tornado from Yard MH [main house] thru to Garden . . . then subsidence and audience led back. The signal it is over is when the lights go on in the Museum again (someone sent ahead). . . .

The first bedroom is the man's bedroom. The second is the woman's. The Front room is for eaters and livers. The kitchen is for argument and the bath for murder. The entrances can be made in and out of windows . . . Need ladders . . .

INJUN / the production

by Michael Kirby

The Dallas Museum for Contemporary Arts no longer exists, but in 1962 it was located on Cedar Springs Road not far from the center of Dallas. When the museum organized a "1961" exhibit which was to include many of the major artists who had shown work in New York during the year, they also invited Claes Oldenburg to present a Happening. He accepted. A large room on the second floor of the building occupied by the museum was set aside for the production. Publicity was begun.

When Oldenburg arrived in Dallas a week and a half before the scheduled dates for the presentation, he had only very general ideas of what he would do. Somehow the Happening would be related to the place itself, what "the West" meant to him. For several days he sat in the space he had been given, but he could not crystallize a concept that satisfied him. Time was running out, and the pressure was intensified by the fact that several items of plaster food which were to be exhibited on the first floor in a re-creation of his New York store had been damaged in shipment. Day after day he worked many hours repairing them.

One day Oldenburg wandered out of the museum and across the long driveway that connected it to the road. Walking up a shallow hill, he discovered three buildings that he had not known were on the museum grounds: two single-story frame houses and a garage-like shed. He investigated. One of the houses was used on Saturdays for young people's art classes. The other was empty and apparently unused. Walking through the empty house, he remembered a scene from a Wallace Beery movie that he had seen years before. Beery, playing the part of a Civil War veteran who had just returned to his farmhouse where an axe murderer had slaughtered his whole family, had gone from one room to another picking up parts of the dismembered people. The concept for the Happening began to clarify itself.

Oldenburg asked the museum authorities if he could use the house. "Yes," they said, "but it's occupied by Mexican squatters."

"No, it's not. I went in."

"They must have gone. I suppose they left it in a terrible mess. They probably took all the light bulbs with them."

"No," he answered, "it's very clean. It's in perfect shape."

Most of the remaining time was spent in finding props and costumes and in transforming the house. There were no steps to the back porch of the house; the museum built some. The Frank Lloyd Wright Theatre offered Oldenburg lights, costumes, and performers, but he declined. As was his usual practice, found materials were used. The discovery of large rolls of heavy paper in the shipping room of the museum spurred the work. A member of the cast brought materials from her attic. Cheap "farm" dresses were found in an old store. Within a few days, the physical aspects of the Happening were created.

The performances themselves took shape at the last minute. The Happening was to be given on the 6th and 7th of April, 1962—Friday and Saturday evenings. Most of the details were worked out at a rehearsal on Thursday night. (On Saturday, after the first performance, a film was made to record the piece, and this served as further rehearsal, allowing certain points to be clarified.)

On the designated evenings, spectators gathered in the corridor of the museum. In one corner some of the visitors noticed a long rope tied at intervals with pieces of cloth. Single-page programs were distributed. "INJUN," the title read, and below it, in clarification, "Country piece for a house, a yard, a shed and a lean-to." The designation "Happening" was not used on the program. Twenty-three performers were listed: eleven women in one column, twelve men in the other. The spectators were asked to wait in the corridor of the museum until they were "picked up," and an outline of the presentation was given:

PART I
1. A Walk to the House (5 min.)
2. A Walk Through the House (30 min.)

PART II
Yard—Shed—Lean-to (20 min.)
Injun in Movement (20 min.)

A terse note at the bottom of the sheet read: "Please follow and obey masked leaders." Although it indicated that the "country piece" would not take place in the museum, the program did little to clarify the spectators' expectations. The audience waited.

Outside the brightly lit corridor it was dark. Spectators near the glass doors or waiting on the steps outside watched three strangely dressed men engaged in some sort of silent game. Two of them wore ordinary work clothes, had cloth bags over their heads, and carried long sticks of wood. The other was entirely covered with brownish-green mosquito netting. Large, irregular, rock-shaped lumps (actually cotton wrapped with tape) were twisted into the netting on all sides of the figure. Thin white streamers of torn cloth hung down and fluttered when he moved. At a short distance, the man inside (Oldenburg) was practically invisible as he stooped under the folds of cloth, and in the darkness of the museum grounds only his general shape could be seen as he ran, suddenly stood still, crouched and hid. After several minutes, the three figures entered the corridor where the people waited.

The spectators were requested to grasp the rope wherever there was a knot of cloth and to follow the masked men: they were the "leaders" to whom the program referred. (Two hundred reservations had been made. The rope was two hundred feet long, and the muslin knots were spaced a foot apart. Originally it had been planned to put the name of each spectator on a knot, but this proved impractical.) All the lights on the grounds had been turned out. Following the hunched, brownish-green figure, the line of spectators moved slowly out of the museum into the darkness.

Very gradually the procession made its way across the driveway and up the slight rise toward the houses. There

was little cooperation among the two hundred people:
while some attempted to step ahead, others would be
pausing, and the rope would not move. The masked men
prodded the line with their sticks, urging it on. Spring
rain had softened the ground, making more difficulty for
the spectators. High heels sank into the wet dirt. The
hunched figure covered with netting swayed and darted
around the column, disappearing and reappearing suddenly.

The file of people passed through an opening in an old
wire fence. To their right, a girl wearing a simple print
dress had been tied to a post. She did not move. Ahead of
them to the right was an unpainted frame shed with a
peaked roof. A flat-roofed extension jutted from the
side wall and on this extension, outlined against the
night sky, sat the hunched, motionless figure of another
girl, her hair teased out in a huge mass. To the left were
two houses, and from the screened back porch of the
nearer one came the deep, steady thump of a washtub
bass.

The spectators moved past the bound girl and turned
left between the houses. The house that was now on
their right appeared to be occupied. In the lighted rectangles of the windows, the passing column could catch
glimpses of various people as they moved about inside.
A large jet plane suddenly roared low over the dark
yards. (The museum was close to Love Field, one of the
busiest airports in the country. At unexpected intervals
throughout the evening, jets, either landing or taking off
from the field, would add their sound to the performance.) The spectators were noisy: they made jokes,
called loudly to each other, laughed nervously, and com-
plained. Gradually, the awkward, struggling column
moved around to the front of the house. There the
people were directed up the front steps, where they
let go of the rope (the original plan to have them retain
their holds as they passed through the house was not
practical) and stepped into the house. When all the
people were inside, the doors were locked.

The front room extended to the right of the entering
spectator. No windows were visible. The walls were
solidly covered with sheets of newspaper, and the floor
was hidden by a tangle of newspapers and refuse. Pieces

of broken furniture protruded from the rubble. Partially covered by a patterned piece of cloth, a small man with a mustache lay in the center of the room, his head propped against a bale of hay. He was wearing pajamas, and he played a violin that had only two strings. Occasionally, he appeared to sleep. (Oldenburg had been thinking of the recluses' rooms that he had seen as a reporter in Chicago. One rich old lady who had been one of the first female lawyers in Chicago had filled a mansion with torn newspapers and law books. Her possessions and furnishings were hidden under five feet of torn paper. After she died in a small rented room around the corner from the mansion, Oldenburg had seen the bed in which she had slept crosswise—she had been a small woman—the sides of the hollow that her body had made encrusted with food.)

In addition to the man with the violin, there was another figure in the room. The legs of a man wearing long underwear could be seen beneath a huge, ragged cardboard construction. Crumpled kraft paper formed a cowl around his head and body, hiding him almost completely as he moved slowly about the room in a stooped position picking up things. Sometimes he went to a corner and stood still.

The two hooded men carrying sticks directed the spectators into a corridor that connected the front room with the rest of the house. As they passed along the corridor, the people could look through a doorway to their right into another room. The walls of the room were covered with old, flower-patterned wallpaper. The board floor was bare except for two sets of white long underwear stuffed with newspaper, and two large white balls of cotton covered with tape. A dark-haired girl with stark white makeup lay on the dummies. (The performer was determined to wear the makeup—she claimed to have studied with Marcel Marceau—and Oldenburg did nothing about it.) She wore long white underwear under a dark sleeveless dress, slacks, high-heeled shoes, heavy bracelets and a large neckpiece. From time to time she crawled and slid along the floor, pushing the lumpy white shapes and rolling the balls about. Or she would stand suddenly and throw the dummies against the walls. A girl in colorful striped pajamas and high-heeled shoes sat on the windowsill, looking wistfully out at the night, oblivious of the other girl. Occasionally she got up, gently kicked a little bell around the room, disappeared into the closet for a while, and then returned to the window.

On their left, the spectators passed a doorway that was covered with a semitransparent plastic sheet dotted with scattered black spots. A man's voice, a radio, and sounds of movement could be heard from the other room. Now and then the swaying shadow of a dancing girl appeared on the plastic.

Farther down the corridor, another doorway opened on the right. This was the bathroom. Looking into it, the spectators could see the bathtub filled with soft mud. A man wearing long underwear threw handfuls of mud against the wall and ceiling and decorated the small room with long streamers of toilet paper.

At the end of the corridor, the path laid out for the audience passed through the door to the back porch, along the outside walls of the screened enclosure, and back into the house itself through the same door. (This was a last-minute innovation, devised to relieve crowding in the house.) It was dark on the porch. Torn pieces of heavy kraft paper hung from the ceiling, making a shifting maze through which the people pushed their way. In the center of the porch, inside a fencelike structure, was the man in the brownish-green net who had come for the audience at the beginning of the performance. Almost invisible under the layers of cloth, he thrashed about and grabbed at the legs of passing spectators. He improvised a stream-of-consciousness monologue, pouring out disjointed, irrational statements. Sometimes he sat quietly. Sometimes he scrambled around his enclosure like a monkey.

Looking out through the porch screens, some of the spectators noticed that there was activity in the shed behind the house. The shed was divided like a two-car garage, and in the left section three girls in simple print dresses moved aimlessly or lay on the hay that was piled against the rear wall. In the right section, a man slowly rolled a solid six-foot wheel from side to side. The people on the porch moved around the costumed figure in the center and back into the house.

Rather than passing back down the corridor, they turned to their right and entered the kitchen. Paint-splattered kraft paper had been stapled loosely to the walls (and over a window and door), softening the regular outlines of the room. A sink poked through the paper on the right. Near the far wall, a table had been constructed from two sawhorses and a plywood panel and covered with a layer of cotton batting. A girl, almost hidden under a disordered pile of old clothes, lay on the table. Jutting up from behind the table were two long rusty metal bars, their ends encased in ragged masses of concrete. At one side stood a small cupboard with a circular mirror and a broken, paint-splashed rectangular mirror on it. A bucket filled with water was nearby. A wide board was propped against the wall, and from it hung a baseball catcher's mitt, a doll, and a woven Mexican hat. The floor was scattered with torn bits of white foam rubber which looked like popcorn.

The girl stirred, shook off the heap of cloth. She rose into a crouching position on the table, her knees drawn up to her chin, and began to move along very slowly, pushing the cotton batting onto the floor. When the panel was clean, she got down and walked to the mirrors. Her black-and-white blouse left her midriff bare, and she wore a bouffant petticoat over white tights. Picking up a wide roll of masking tape from the stand, she tore off strips and fastened them across her mouth until the whole lower part of her face was covered. After a moment, she slowly removed the tape. Then she lifted the decorated board and, standing behind it, danced slowly around the room with it. Using an oil can with a long spout, she squirted more black paint on the paper walls or washed her feet with a scrubbing brush in the bucket of water.

The walls of the next room were also covered with heavy paper, but here smaller sheets had been used, overlapping each other. The walls, the semitransparent plastic which covered two windows on the right, and the plastic stretched across a doorway on the left were all spotted with large black dots of paint. A bunch of spotted balloons hung on the wall. There was a dresser with a mirror and a table covered with a white cloth. On the table were a radio, an electric fan, and a bowl filled

with small pieces of white foam rubber. As they moved
into the room, the spectators found that there was action
on both sides. To their left, seated next to the table, a thin
man in a baggy suit and a wide-brimmed hat was speaking into a megaphone. He improvised a long rambling
account of his life. After a long while, he slumped forward over the megaphone and remained motionless. A
brunette girl in a cellophane hula skirt danced nearby.
When she moved into the plastic-covered doorway, her
shadow was cast on the plastic. The fan blew her skirt
when she passed. From time to time the girl would
search through the pockets of a pair of men's trousers
that hung near the doorway, twist the dials on the radio
to change the station and volume erratically, or, moving
to the dresser, use a pressurized can to spray her hair.

To the right of the spectators was another performer,
only her head visible above a huge, crumpled, boxlike
costume of brown kraft paper. As she moved about the
space, the heavy paper brushed against the spectators
and rustled as it rubbed along the paper-covered walls
of the room. Behind her, light shone in through the
plastic which covered the windows, and loud noises were
heard. (Cars had been maneuvered so as to throw the
beams of their headlights on the house, and several men
with sticks were banging at the window frames. At the
first performance, they became too enthusiastic and
smashed a window. Neighbors called the police, report-
ing a riot at "the Mexican house.")

Then the spectators passed into the other front room
of the house. It was very dark. The walls were entirely
covered with black paper, and in the center of the room
a huge chicken-wire-and-paper construction that hung
from the ceiling and reached to within a few feet of the
floor filled much of the space. Four big men in work
clothes lounged against the dark walls. In the rear, frequently obscured by the hanging construction, a girl
walked back and forth. A few large sheets of crumpled
aluminum foil had been attached to the close-fitting
white jersey and tights that she wore. Occasionally she
would sit against the wall or, picking up a hammer,
noisily smash glass that filled a tub in the corner. From
time to time, the four men would plunge suddenly toward

the center of the room and wrestle violently on the floor under the construction.

The cycle had been completed, and the spectator was now back in the room that he had first entered with its newspaper-covered walls and littered floor.

Plans had been for the people to pass through the house several times at a set rate. Each time they went around, they would see another segment of the repeated pattern. During rehearsal the night before the first performance, stand-ins simulating an audience carried out the procedure smoothly, but when two hundred people entered the building, movement was far from fluid. If something were particularly interesting, the spectators would bunch up, watching it. Or a group would stop and wait for one of the activities to be repeated. The two masked attendants attempted to keep the crowd moving, pushing them with their sticks, but the spectators showed little cooperation. It was very noisy. Sounds of the performances—violin, radio, voices —could be heard throughout the house. People yelled at each other, joked and milled around. A photographer pushed through the crowd with his assistant, who was dressed in a black cloak and carried a mirror globe which, it was hoped, would allow them to shoot photographs in the limited space. When the shadow of the hula dancer appeared on the plastic in the doorway, men would grab at it. On the back porch, spectators analyzed what the caged figure covered with netting was saying, and he, in return, would mimic and twist their comments. The doors were locked. It grew very warm. The house throbbed with activity.

When half an hour had passed, the girl who had been alternately washing her feet, putting tape over her mouth, dancing with the decorated board, and squirting paint from an oil can onto the wall coverings in the rear room took off her petticoat—she was wearing tights —and lay down on the floor.

The door of the back porch was unlocked, and the audience was directed down the newly constructed steps into the open space behind the house. Several men wearing rough costumes made of burlap hung with streamers of torn white cloth and carrying long sticks to which newspaper had been attached wandered about the open space between the house and the shed. White shapes began to drift down over the heads of the spectators in the yard. Performers were throwing balloons covered with newspaper off the roof of the house. Visible in the darkness, they bounced softly and drifted about the space. When they broke, the costumed men would pick them up and put them on their sticks.

(At this point during the first performance, police with flashlights climbed over a fence to the left of the audience. Investigating the "riot" call, they began to question the performers in the burlap costumes. A police car pulled up at the side of the house behind the standing spectators, but the action did not stop. The police soon realized that they were part of a performance and gradually moved around to join the audience. The radio of the police car was heard throughout the remainder of the Happening.)

The man in the brownish-green net costume reached through a hole and pulled the girl who had been lying in the kitchen onto the porch. Spectators still inside the house watched her disappear suddenly. Carrying the motionless white figure in his arms, he climbed off the porch through an opening in the screening, put the girl down on a sheet of plastic to the left of the spectators, and pulled her to a spot near the shed. Then he left her and entered the left section of the shed through a hole in the wooden wall.

Illuminated by dim blinking lights, the three girls in simple print dresses were moving about the hay-strewn space when the stooped brownish-green form entered. He reached up and connected a bright, hanging bulb which also blinked on and off erratically. The spectators watched through the open side of the shed as the man and the girls started to fight, the net and cloth costume of the man swinging wildly as he flailed his arms, the girls darting about striking at him and throwing hay. Balloons wrapped in red-painted paper flew through the air. Buckets of red paint and plastic bags filled with red paint had been placed around the shed and were now used in the struggle. Red liquid splashed the crudely whitewashed walls and splattered the four frantic figures. Suddenly the girls fell into the hay and lay motionless.

The hunched figure hung with irregular taped balls and long ragged streamers of white cloth moved slowly back to the girl he had left lying on the plastic sheet and dragged her across to the center of the shed.

Inside the right section, a man dressed in white, his back to the audience, began to roll the huge circle of plywood from side to side. Sheets of metal had been fastened to the walls at either side, and the thick plywood struck with a loud metallic crash. Back and forth it went, shaking the small building. After a few moments, the net-covered figure stalked into the shed again and thrashed wildly at the operator who collapsed. The large wheel fell slowly against the rear wall.

Again the costumed man pulled the motionless girl along on the plastic sheet, stopping near the low addition attached to the right wall of the shed. A spotlight illuminated the roof of the smaller shed. To the right, held vertical by a wire running to the addition, was a tall canvas construction. Randomly painted green and brown, it bulged at the top, resembling a tree or a giant ice-cream cone. (This was a "tornado" that, in the original plans, was to have come for the spectators at the beginning of the performance. When it was stuffed, it became too heavy to move.) To the right of the audience, a record playing the music of a Mexican mariachi band was heard from the screened porch where the washtub bass had played earlier.

Lifting the girl in his arms, the green figure carried her up a ladder onto the almost-flat roof and laid her down. Water began to flow from a hose that hung against the tall peaked wall of the large shed. It ran across the low roof and poured in a waterfall off the right side near the canvas construction. Four suits of white long underwear, stuffed and daubed with red paint, were dangling from the overhanging eaves of the taller shed. The man snatched them down and threw the damp, headless, handless and footless bodies at the spectators. Then he crouched at the rear corner of the roof, dropped to the ground, and disappeared.

The girl who had been motionless for so long stood up and took down a costume hanging from the eaves. Putting it on, she began to dance vigorously, hopping up and down. Long hanging sections of the costume (made from old window shades) flapped wildly as she moved. Then she picked up a pair of shears and, kneeling, cut the wire that attached the large construction to the shed. It fell, landing with a heavy thud, and the spotlight went out.

Thinking that the Happening was over, some of the spectators began to wander away, but others watched silent activities in an overgrown sunken garden just to the right of the shed. Several performers, including the man in brownish-green netting, were running with long streamers of kraft paper. For a few minutes they wove about in the darkness, then lay motionless on the wet ground.

The spectators began to find their way back to the museum. The house was again without a tenant. And it was much dirtier than it had been when the Mexican family left.

MYSTERIES AND SMALLER PIECES

Collective Creation of
The Living Theatre
written down by

Judith Malina and Julian Beck

Introduction by John Lahr

> We are going so far out that they
> will never be able to catch us. . . .
>
> Julian Beck
> *The Life of the Theatre*

Nobody wants to accept The Living Theatre; but nobody can forget them. As radical innovators, Judith Malina and Julian Beck—the founders of the company—stand alone in the American avant-garde: isolated by their political rage, courageous in their tenacity, absurd in their idealism. They have made the theater dangerous again and turned it into a spectacle of rogue emotions. Jailed, raped, vilified, worshiped—The Living Theatre has sought to create situations that transform theater-going into an event, not an escape devoid of historical consequences. They want a Life Show; and, more brazen than other groups, they have found ways of making both audience and actors display feelings that reveal hidden fears and longings and hatreds to each other. The company discovers with its audience. As a consequence, the Living Theatre can be infuriating, outrageous, ugly, dumb, and brilliant. But the purity of its spiritual quest is as indubitable as its perilousness.

The Living Theatre is revolutionary in the most literal sense: it wants a *re-evolution* of consciousness, craft, and society. Whether the Becks and their theater are cheerleaders of change or are catalysts is a matter of opinion, but the Becks themselves are symbols of radical rebellion who sum up the sixties' obsession with trying to mutate to some higher form of consciousness. Julian Beck: "Discard the structure, metamorphose, leave the cocoon, pull yourself out of it." Change or die. Some members of The Living Theatre are now dead. Their work, and they themselves, embody the nostalgia for an erotic Eden and the yearning for immortality (*Paradise Now*), the belief in protean transformation (*Frankenstein*), the groping for spiritual alternatives to the bind of reason (*Mysteries*). Like all revolutionary performances, The Living Theatre exhibits an appetite for apocalypse. Their events have a schizoid quality: exaggerated by despair and exhilarated by revolutionary hope. They gamble with their lives. And their faces—the faces of all the troupe—combine a ferocious willfulness with a sense of brutalized fatigue. Changing is hard, sometimes deadly work. They have come so far, and the road is lonely. There is still so far to go. Julian Beck: "Actor's note: The essential preparation is finding the courage. Courage will then carry to the creation of plays and will make it possible to play them."

The Becks have paid their dues to the literary theater— a fact for which many theater critics will never forgive them. In their first incarnation (1951–1963) they did arcane works by Gertrude Stein, William Carlos Williams, W. H. Auden, Kenneth Rexroth, Jean Cocteau, Paul Goodman, as well as plays by Brecht, Strindberg, and Racine. They also provided the "new wave" of American theater in the early sixties with two of its most audacious plays: Jack Gelber's *The Connection* and Ken Brown's *The Brig*. While these plays depended heavily on improvisation, they could still be categorized and comprehended within a "literary" framework. Left-wing critics like Robert Brustein and Eric Bentley were dazzled: ideology did not offend aesthetics, craft and commitment had found an unusual marriage. The same critics would disown The Living Theatre in their second incarnation (1968) after five years of self-imposed exile in Europe. In the interim, the Becks had extended the idea of Improvisation and combined it with their desire to create communally toward specific anarchist ends and for mass audiences. Their revolutionary message demanded a transformation of style. To be present at one of their evenings was extraordinary: they raged, they screamed, they tortured themselves. They were expressing an urgency and an anger of tragic proportions.

> I rage: flailing my arms: metaphysical semaphore: I am performing: tantrum, flipout, flashout, agony, wail, insult, tirade, old techniques borrowed from Seneca and Racine, I am out of my mind, at last I am glowing, coal like, heat emanates: I will burn my way into you: this is my act . . .

> Julian Beck
> *The Life of the Theatre*

The limitation of this tactic is obvious: it wants mass communication, but it won't listen. The hectoring is crude and unfair; but also, like any public scene, it is unforgettable. I was present when the Becks and some of their troupe turned a $10-a-ticket "intellectual" debate into an anarchist happening. The topic of this Theatre of Ideas evening was "Theatre or Therapy." Robert Brustein read from a piece he'd written in the *New York Review of Books*. Paul Goodman (who later left the auditorium) waffled about reform; and then the Becks turned the decorum and sham of the occasion on its head. The audience went wild. Many of the intellectuals rushed out to get a scotch and hors d'oeuvres in an adjacent room and then scurried back into the auditorium to yell "Fascist!" at the Becks. The event had its moments of humor and insight. Everyone was forced to react and to define their position.

At one point, standing on a pew two feet from Julian Beck, I saw him toe to toe with a lady whose blue fox stole and butterfly eyeglasses pegged her as a New

Rochelle matron. Beck was livid. As he described it: "I made it tough for them to justify what I was doing. I tore hat, coat, glasses off the woman, shrieking: "The weight of your furs makes it impossible for the needs of the people to touch!" I threw things all over the room, to put human relationship in crisis. I despair of the intellectual ever really taking part in the real revolution when it comes to it. We walk around its edges. I despair of myself."

His account is accurate, except for one thing. He does not relate what the woman said. She kept repeating: "I don't see the poetry in you, Mr. Beck. . . . Where's the poetry?" This is more than a funny story: it poses the central aesthetic objection to The Living Theatre. Stage "poetry" in conventional verbal or scenic senses is abandoned. The beauty of the anarchist event is the *action* itself. In this case, the event capsulized the timidity of the intellectual debate as well as the paltriness of radical action. Communally, the audience and The Living Theatre were experiencing and evoking one of the deepest sources of America's violence: the sense of social impotence. People had paid to hear words: and they came away with a visceral experience much deeper and more complex than language. A set piece was turned into an improvisation.

Beck, who began his career as a painter, links The Living Theatre's improvisations to experiments in the visual as well as performing arts.

Improvisation: some precursors:
1912: Duchamps: Objets trouvés
1916: Arp: Collage: *Pieces of Paper arranged according to Laws of Chance*
1924: Breton: 1st Surrealist Manifesto: the principle of automatic composition
1942: New York School of Action Painting
1952: John Cage: *Music of Changes*
1962: Allan Kaprow's: Happenings . . .

In creating plays that emphasize the act as the art, the theatrical improvisation of The Living Theatre and Action Painting become analogous: both want to banish "schools of art" in their rebellion against the past, both mythologize the Self and the act of the imagination to reconstruct a new world, both stress the revelation of the tension in the act with its spectators. Beck has written: "We are living the myth of ourselves: we have to create reality." Translated, this means the avant-garde sweeps away the oppressive fictions of the past for the hopeful fictions of the future. They put themselves "in a new light," they become, as revolutionaries must, their own heroes. What Harold Rosenberg in *The Tradition of the New* claims for the drama of Action Painting can also be argued for a Living Theatre event.

A painting that is an act is inseparable from the biography of the artist. The painting itself is a "moment" in the adulterated mixture of his life—whether "moment" means the actual minutes taken up with spotting the canvas or the entire duration of a lucid drama conducted in sign language. The act-painting is of the same metaphysical substance as the artist's existence. The new painting has broken down every distinction between art and life.

It follows that everything is relevant to it. Anything that has to do with action—philosophy, psychology, history, mythology, hero worship. Anything but art criticism . . .

Art merges with life and improvisation brings the actor's private history into the public arena. The stage directions to *Mysteries* (1964)—The Living Theatre's first radical departure from conventional stage form—emphasizes this intention.

Performers circulate among audience. Everyday clothes.

Performers become part of the audience.

Contacts.

Beck explained: "If we acted in costumes rather than in our street clothes, we wouldn't be ourselves. By wearing our own clothes, we are signifying that we are all inside society, like anybody else, and not privileged, not the critics from outside. We are saying that we are part of society."

Theatrical experiment is always a few decades behind the art world. The Living Theatre's discoveries for the stage are aesthetic battles fought in painting decades ago. But to understand *Mysteries* and The Living Theatre's later productions, it is important to understand its original impulse. Julian Beck recounts the movement toward new theatrical action in his book *The Life of the Theatre:*

> The actors in *The Brig* reported that something special was happening out there, on stage in the "cage," something which didn't happen in other plays. All the years that performers had been talking about re-inventing each moment (the whole stack of evidence and exercises compiled by Stanislavski and his school), we had been fooling ourselves. Make it real: the real trip, physical, invented from moment to moment, reality, reality which is always changing and creating itself, the need for reality (life) in this period of alienation; improvisation as the breath that made reality live on the stage. It would never again be possible for us not to improvise. We would have to construct plays with forms loose enough so that we could continue to find out how to create life rather than merely repeat it.
>
> Inch by inch, step by step, thru the labyrinth towards reality. The Mysteries, 1964: (1) improvisation within fixed limits (as in *The Brig*). (2) exercises in freeing the body and the voice (the organization of expression) from the limitations of ideas contained by language.

Mysteries is a variety show of radical technique, a scenario for the more complete "action painting" of *Paradise Now*. There are no sets, no costumes, no text. The actors shout: "Change the world! Find a way!" And their political statement is reinforced by the improvisational accomplishment of having made the world of the stage "new." The impulse is similar to Piet Mondrian's: "The creation of a sort of Eden is not impossible if there is but a will." *Mysteries* has the strong, formal rhythm of Mondrian's *Broadway Boogie Woogie*. The play contains sharp, sculptured groupings: The Dollar Poem, The

Tableaux, The Plague. Other episodes—The Raga, The Breathing, Sound and Movement Called Lee's Piece—epitomize the movement toward mysticism and also the personal mythologizing of vanguard art. As Rosenberg observes: "The tension of the private myth is the content of every painting of this vanguard. . . . Some formulate their myth verbally and connect individual works with its episodes. With others, usually deeper, the painting itself is the exclusive formulation, a Sign." *Mysteries,* as its title implies, is a sign, a revelation that awaits those who, like the performers, improvise in the void and keep open to new possibility. The dramatic action stresses body and spirit. The actors aspire to the metaphysical condition of symbol. As Beck maintained after the opening of *Mysteries,* the stage must be returned to its essential spiritual dimension: "a congregation led by priests, a choral ecstasy of reading and response, dance, seeking transcendence, a way out and up, the vertical thrust." *Mysteries* brings The Living Theatre to an impasse with "art." As revolutionary theater it must be antiart; and yet it seeks to establish itself as the purest form of theatrical art. The contradiction is insoluble. In *Mysteries,* the concept of art and sincerity are at loggerheads. Art implies illusion, artifice, alienation from Being. The actor, in a revolutionary "priestly" role, must be sincere and whole. Honesty becomes the primary quality for this performance. Julian Beck: "Actors don't have to speak better than people. Nothing is better than people. We have to get rid of the idea that elocution constitutes good speech. I think elocution and the throaty way even our best actors often speak is related to some kind of respect for money. . . . I want actors to stop posing. I am talking to Method actors, too, to stop trying to create effects and to break through into the representation of honest life. . . ." Changing the categories of stage performance, searching for a future and denying the past, The Living Theatre—like all revolutionary art—puts criticism of it in a strange position. The radical experience demands to be accepted on its own terms. To link the work to a theatrical past, to compare or criticize language or stagecraft immediately puts the events in the tradition of conventional art. And what bearing does such categorization have on life?

And so the argument goes. The air is still fogged with rhetoric from both camps, each denying the right of the other to exist. But without The Living Theatre's bold attempts to change theater and society, there would be no debate. And American theater would be the less for it.

Mysteries is The Living Theatre's first communal creation. The section entitled The Chord celebrates the harmony and psychic bond of the anarchist community. This is an actor's exercise elevated to public statement. As in Action Painting, the dramatic process has become the product. The idea of communal creation carries many important implications to the Becks' radical departure from the conventional theater: (1) chance, (2) the importance of the performer to be himself and to contribute himself, (3) life themes become performance themes, (4) the denial of ownership (authorship), (5) survival through the group, not individual accomplishment. While the process has philosophical pertinence, it has its practical drawbacks: boredom, inefficiency. But the attempt itself makes a statement and tries to resolve many of the psychic complications in conventional playmaking in which everyone is a functionary for the playwright's words and themes. And where freedom to explore ideas is limited to the impersonation imposed by the script. Beck has described this first attempt at communal creation which happened, he stresses, naturally and without effort:

A group comes together. There is no author to rest on who wrests the creative impulse from you. Destruction of the superstructure of the mind. Then reality comes. We sit around for months talking, absorbing, discarding making an atmosphere in which we not only inspire each other but in which each one feels free to say whatever she or he wants to say. Big swamp jungle, a landscape of concepts, souls, sounds, movements, theories, fronds of poetry, wildness, wilderness, wandering. Then you gather and arrange. In the process a form will present itself. The person who talks least may be the one who inspires the one who talks the most. At the end no one knows who was really responsible for what, the individual ego drifts into darkness, everyone has satisfaction, everyone has greater personal satisfaction than the satisfaction of the lonely

"I." Once you feel this—the process of artistic creation in collectivity—return to the old order seems like retrogression.

Collective creation is an example of Anarcho-Communist Autogestive Process which is of more value to the people than a play. Collective creation as secret weapon of the people.

In collective you create both thru yourself and thru others: inter-inspiration. Superflash. . . .

The communal idea is both radical and nostalgic of a tribal life lost to the industrial state. Judith Malina is quoted as saying: "Nostalgia is reactionary. The derrière-guard is always looking to the past and praising it. 'The good old days.'" In all the spectacle and carnival excitement of The Living Theatre productions, the nostalgia implicit in the anarchist ideal is never acknowledged. But the combination of activist tenacity and the yearning for Eden is one of their most unwitting, but pertinent, accomplishments in *Paradise Now* (1968), which is at the other end of the arc that begins with *Mysteries*. In *Mysteries*, there are echoes of this longing. *Paradise Now*, which literally spells out anarchy, is a much fuller scenario, a four-hour depiction of man's search for regeneration and psychic unity. As Leo Marx points out in *The Machine in the Garden*, Eden denies "calculated human effort, the trained intellect, and the idea of civilization itself." The Living Theatre surrounds the audience, urging its audience to change and join them, seducing them with Dionysiac indifference to decorum. And what they want is a return, a simplification, an eternity of beginning and no decline.

> we will
> stop using
> money
>
> we will do
> only
> useful work
>
> we will

plan ways ahead of time
to bring apples to the city

and you will go to the public storehouse
and take
what you need

no money
no barter
no more bullshit

and if you dont want to work
you dont
have to

Where *Mysteries* is formal and restrained, *Paradise Now* is brazen and excessive. The actors act out a return of the mind to the body. The senses must live again, regenerated by a return to Eden: "We want to feed and to fuck everyone." The troupe talks about it, moving down the aisle mumbling "Holy land, holy eye, holy hair." They touch the audience. This is the Marxian "humanized nature" in which the "senses capable of human gratifications, senses confirming themselves as essential powers to man . . . brought into being." The Living Theatre tries to show this primordial state, creating love-zaps which soothe hostility with embrace, a group-grope in which performers and disciples spin together in a bond of touch and finally collapse in a flesh pile. At another time, they chant a chorus from R. D. Laing's *Politics of Experience:*

If I could turn you on
If I could drive you out of your wretched mind
If I could tell you I would let you know . . .

These are the mysteries that constitute the myth of Dionysiac pleasure the Becks expound. Their productions must fall because they can never produce the revolution. But they speak to the protean, spiritual, and political reality of the moment in all its chaotic and eclectic urgency. On a less dramatic emotional scale, they may provide and sustain revolutionary hope: the longing for transformation and the boldness to undertake it. Julian Beck writes:

> The youth of our time—the electric generation—is not acting in a play that takes place in three acts on a proscenium stage. They aren't writing their lives that way, they are writing their lives not as characters with little plots, their drama is electric media, planetary in its dimension, in turn with cycles and megacycles, the content is new, the form is free from literature, they have within them the knowledge of the Egyptian papyri, the Greek Anthology, without being emotionally attached, for them literature has no demagogues, they do not worship authors the way the Maids in Genet's play worship Madame—to their own undoing; and they are composing a different kind of play, electric, free; and written law will not bind them down. Hope exists in their imagination . . . if it can be freed. . . .

The Living Theatre attempts the unimaginable and turns stage spectacle into an exploration of uncharted emotional territory. This is their lasting importance to American theater. They make an audience look again at life and life choices. They long for new sources of energy. Their search for resilience is reminiscent of C. P. Cavafy's poem: "Strengthening the Spirit."

> He who longs to strengthen his spirit
> must go beyond obedience and respect.
> He will continue to honor some laws
> be he will mostly violate
> both laws and custom, and life beyond
> the established and deficient norm.
> Pleasure will have much to teach him.

Since The Living Theatre violates dramatic custom and challenges emotional taboos, the hostility toward their work must be great. Sometimes, it is justified. But like any ecstatic performance, theirs is both thrilling and horrible. They can't be dismissed. And what if they are right?

The original collective creation of *Mysteries and Smaller Pieces* in Paris, November 1964, was the work of:

Jim Anderson	Steven Ben Israel
Julian Beck	Tom Lillard
Carl Einhorn	Roberta Longhi
Reggie Gay	Judith Malina
Gene Gordon	Michele Mareck
John Harriman	Paul Prensky
Roy Harris	William Shari
Jenny Hecht	Steve Thompson
Leroy House	Jim Tiroff
Henry Howard	Luke Theodore
Nona Howard	Lee Worley

The premiere of *Mysteries and Smaller Pieces* took place on October 26, 1964, at the American Students and Artists Center, Boulevard Raspail, Paris.

The text was written down during August–September 1969 in Essaouira, Morocco.

Audience is coming in. Audience space. Stage space.

No curtain.

Performers circulate among audience. Everyday clothes.

Performers become part of audience.

Contacts.

BLACKOUT.

Pause.

Bright white spotlight.

Down center.

Performer stands rigid in spotlight (revealed).

Military posture.

Motionless. Silent.

Silence.

Unnoticed: other performers are standing behind the audience.

These performers are all male, indicating dominance of males in contemporary militaristic society.

They are at attention. Motionless. Silent.

Audience reacts.

The performer standing at attention remains indifferent to the audience reaction.

The performers hear the audience's reactions.

At least six minutes pass.

Choosing the moment, a performer (behind the audience) begins to mark time. Brig jog.

Several seconds.

Houselights.

From behind the audience, the performer marking time begins to move.

He moves down the aisle.

Brig jog.

He moves into the stage space.

He stops before an imaginary white line.

Additional lights on the stage space.

He crosses the space.

He stops at the white line in front of the imaginary storeroom.

He opens the door of the imaginary storeroom.

He crosses into the imaginary storeroom.

He does a military about-face.

He closes the door of the imaginary storeroom.

He puts on the light in the imaginary store-room.

Additional light on the stage space.

He stands at attention.

As soon as he has put on the light in the imaginary storeroom, the male performers who have been standing at attention behind the audience begin to jog down the aisle and into the stage space.

They move in a line down the aisle.

Brig jog. Military precision.

Sound of feet.

Each stops at the imaginary white line.

Each crosses the imaginary white line and the space.

Each stops at the imaginary white line in front of the imaginary storeroom.

The STOREROOM hands to each of them an imaginary cleaning utensil.

Military precision.

Each makes an about-face when leaving the imaginary white line in front of the imaginary storeroom.

Military jog never stops. Except when the performer is standing at attention.

Holding their imaginary cleaning utensils, the performers line up at military attention behind the man who never stops standing rigid.

Two performers leave the stage space and make imaginary beds in the audience space.

One performer leaves the stage space and jogs down the aisle into the lobby.

He returns with an imaginary bucket of water.

He throws the imaginary water at the feet of the men standing in line at attention with their imaginary cleaning utensils.

They spring into action.

Cleaning the brig.

Scrubbing. Mopping. Squeegeeing. Polishing. Jogging. Stage space. Audience space. Water. Formation. Bed making. Water carrying. Stomach punches. Standing at attention. Permission to cross the white line, sir.

Tempo very fast.

As the first bucket of water is thrown:

DOLLAR POEM.

Text taken from U. S. Dollar Bill S58414558A * by John Harriman.

> Text is spoken in loud clear bored voice by six to twelve performers from various parts of the audience and stage space.**

1ST SPEAKER: One
2ND SPEAKER: One
1ST SPEAKER: One
2ND SPEAKER: One
1ST SPEAKER: One
4TH SPEAKER: One
2ND SPEAKER: One
1ST SPEAKER: One
3RD SPEAKER: One
2ND SPEAKER: One
4TH SPEAKER: One
6TH SPEAKER: One dollar
5TH SPEAKER: One dollar
1ST SPEAKER: This certifies that there is
5TH SPEAKER: on deposit in the Treasury of
4TH SPEAKER: of the United States
5TH AND 6TH SPEAKERS: United States of America
3RD SPEAKER: One dollar

* Brought from New York City to Paris in the summer of 1964. This dollar bill was put back into circulation in Stockholm in December 1965.
** In 1969, after years of reading the Dollar Poem, the performers began to improvise it, always using only the words and groups of words which John Harriman had selected for the poem.

2ND SPEAKER: A2
3RD SPEAKER: S584
4TH SPEAKER: 1.4
1ST SPEAKER: 558-A
5TH SPEAKER: One dollar
2ND SPEAKER: One
1ST SPEAKER: of the   2ND AND 3RD SPEAKERS:
                                    the United States of
                                    America

2ND SPEAKER: of the
1ST SPEAKER: One
4TH SPEAKER: One
1ST SPEAKER: One
3RD SPEAKER: One   5TH AND 6TH SPEAKERS:
                                    United States of America
1ST SPEAKER: S584   3RD SPEAKER: One
2ND SPEAKER: 1.4
3RD SPEAKER: 4TH SPEAKER: 5TH SPEAKER: A
   558   One
6TH SPEAKER: A2
1ST AND 3RD SPEAKERS: One
2ND AND 4TH SPEAKERS: One
2ND AND 3RD SPEAKERS: One
4TH SPEAKER: One   5TH AND 6TH SPEAKERS:
                                    The United States
ALL SPEAKERS: The United States of America
5TH SPEAKER: One
6TH SPEAKER: One
1ST SPEAKER: This certifiies that there is
2ND SPEAKER: Washington
4TH SPEAKER: Washington D.C.
1ST SPEAKER: on deposit   3RD SPEAKER: One dollar
5TH SPEAKER: in the
1ST SPEAKER: Treasury   6TH SPEAKER: An Eagle
2ND SPEAKER: An eagle
1ST SPEAKER: on deposit
2ND SPEAKER: in the Treasury
3RD AND 4TH SPEAKERS: An eagle
5TH AND 6TH SPEAKERS: The United States of America
1ST SPEAKER: One
2ND AND 3RD SPEAKERS: One
4TH AND 6TH SPEAKERS: One
2ND SPEAKER: One

1ST AND 3RD SPEAKERS: One
5TH SPEAKER: One
2ND SPEAKER: Washington
3RD AND 4TH SPEAKERS: Washington D.C.
5TH SPEAKER: An eagle
1ST SPEAKER: Series 1957 B
2ND AND 3RD SPEAKERS: An eagle
4TH SPEAKER: A2   6TH SPEAKER: S
5TH SPEAKER: 584
1ST AND 3RD SPEAKERS: 1.4
2ND AND 4TH SPEAKERS: 558
1ST AND 2ND SPEAKERS: One dollar
3RD AND 4TH SPEAKERS: One dollar
5TH AND 6TH SPEAKERS: One dollar
2ND AND 4TH SPEAKERS: One dollar
5TH SPEAKER: On deposit   6TH SPEAKER: An eagle
1ST SPEAKER: Thesaur
2ND SPEAKER: Amer
3RD SPEAKER: Septant
4TH SPEAKER: Sigil
5TH AND 6TH SPEAKERS: E Pluribus Unum
1ST AND 2ND SPEAKERS: An eagle
3RD SPEAKER: One   6TH SPEAKER: Katherine
                                    O'Hay
2ND SPEAKER: One   6TH SPEAKER: Granihan
4TH SPEAKER: One   5TH SPEAKER: Treasurer
1ST AND 2ND SPEAKERS: of the United States
3RD SPEAKER: C
5TH SPEAKER: Douglas   6TH SPEAKER: Dillon
1ST SPEAKER: An eagle   3RD SPEAKER: Secretary
4TH SPEAKER: of the   6TH SPEAKER: One
    Treasury
1ST AND 2ND SPEAKERS: of the United States
3RD SPEAKER: In God We Trust
5TH AND 6TH SPEAKERS: In God We Trust
1ST SPEAKER: C. Douglas Dillon
2ND SPEAKER: One
4TH SPEAKER: Katherine O'Hay Granihan
3RD SPEAKER: An eagle
2ND SPEAKER: One   5TH SPEAKER: One
1ST SPEAKER: Washington
3RD AND 4TH SPEAKERS: Washington D.C.
6TH SPEAKER: E Pluribus Unum

1ST SPEAKER: Series 1957 B
5TH SPEAKER: Annuit Coeptis
2ND AND 3RD SPEAKERS: In God We Trust
2ND AND 4TH SPEAKERS: The United States
1ST AND 3RD SPEAKERS: One dollar
6TH SPEAKER: An eagle
1ST SPEAKER: Novus   4TH SPEAKER: One
2ND SPEAKER: Ordo
3RD SPEAKER: Seclorum
6TH SPEAKER: 1776
2ND AND 4TH SPEAKERS: 1776
5TH SPEAKER: Washington
1ST SPEAKER: Washington D.C.
2ND AND 4TH SPEAKERS: One
1ST SPEAKER: One
1ST SPEAKER: One   3RD SPEAKER: One dollar
2ND SPEAKER: in the   4TH SPEAKER: on deposit
    Treasury
6TH SPEAKER: An eagle
1ST SPEAKER: 1776   2ND SPEAKER: One
3RD SPEAKER: One
5TH SPEAKER: One
1ST, 2ND AND 3RD SPEAKERS: One
4TH SPEAKER: One
4TH SPEAKER: One dollar
1ST SPEAKER: Katherine O'Hay Granihan
3RD SPEAKER: on deposit
4TH SPEAKER: One
2ND AND 5TH SPEAKERS: One
4TH SPEAKER: One dollar
1ST SPEAKER: Washington
3RD AND 4TH SPEAKERS: 5TH SPEAKER: One
    C. Douglas Dillon
2ND SPEAKER: E Pluribus Unum
3RD SPEAKER: Novus
1ST SPEAKER: One   4TH SPEAKER: Ordo
1ST SPEAKER: Seclorum
4TH SPEAKER: on deposit
5TH AND 6TH SPEAKERS: In God We Trust
2ND SPEAKER: One dollar
3RD AND 4TH SPEAKERS: An eagle
1ST SPEAKER: A2
3RD SPEAKER: S584

4TH SPEAKER: An eagle
1ST AND 6TH SPEAKERS: 1776
2ND SPEAKER: on deposit
4TH SPEAKER: of the United States
ALL SPEAKERS: The United States of America
4TH SPEAKER: One dollar
1ST SPEAKER: One dollar
6TH SPEAKER: One

Brig cleaning. Dollar poem. Rigid performer at attention. STOREROOM at attention.
BUCKET CARRIER and BED MAKER start marching in stage space.
BUCKET CARRIER calls the orders.

One by one the other performers as they finish their tasks return their imaginary cleaning utensils to the storeroom and feed in to the marching.
Marching.
The rigid precision marching of the U. S. Marine Corps.
They call out their numbers loud and strong.
Cadence count.
The Dollar Poem stops.
Marching continues.

Double to the left flank, double to the right flank, double
　　to the rear, march!
　　Squadron halt!
　　One two.

Silence.
The STOREROOM turns out the imaginary storeroom light.
He opens the imaginary storeroom door. He crosses the imaginary white line. He executes a military about-face.
He closes the imaginary storeroom door.
About-face.
He makes a loud unintelligible sound.

THE MARCHERS, *standing at attention reply:* Yes, Sir!

The rigid man does not move. No one moves.

BLACKOUT.

THE RAGA.

In the darkness.
    Woman's voice.
    Guitar.
    The sound comes from the audience space.
    Indian raga.
    Ten minutes.
    The raga ends.

THE ODIFERIE.

Dots of light in the stage space.
    Incense sticks in the dark. (Each performer with several in his or her hand.)
    Moving very slowly.
    Procession.
    Darkness.
    Dots of light fill rear of stage space.
    Slowly, noiselessly, solemnly, performers move forward.
    White light comes up very slowly, revealing the performers.
    Slowly, noiselessly, solemnly, performers move forward.
    Procession.
    Slowly spilling into the audience space.
    Eye to eye.
    Procession. Up the aisles.
    Eye contact with audience.
    No language, no grimace. Silent communication. The performers establish love relationship with the audience.
    One performer does not leave the stage space.
    Sits in the center.
    Lights down. One spotlight. Stage center.
    The performers extinguish the incense.
    They become part of the audience.

STREET SONGS.

The performer in the stage space speaks.

TEXT:
Street Songs
by
Jackson MacLow

Pause.

Stop the war.

Pause.

Stop the war.

Pause.

Stop the war.

Pause.

Stop the war.

Pause.

Freedom now.

Pause.

Freedom now.

Pause.

Stop the war.

Pause.

Stop the war.

Pause.

Freedom now.

Pause.

Stop the war.

Pause.

Freedom now.

Pause.

Freedom now.

    Pause.

Freedom now.

    Pause.

Ban the bombs.

    Pause.

Ban the bombs.

    Pause.

Open the doors.

    Pause.

Open the doors.

    Pause.

Freedom now.

    Pause.

Freedom now.

    Pause.

Stop the wars.

    Pause.

Freedom now.

    Pause.

Open the doors.

    Pause.

Of all the jails.

    Pause.

The pattern of the rhythm is clear:
Between each song there is a pause only just long enough for the audience to respond.

The length of the pause is the length of an imaginary echo.

The performer speaks both in English and the

language of the country in which the play is being performed.

No fixed order. Text is decided by the performer at each performance.

The audience responds.

The performers support the response of the audience.

They encourage response.

The audience echoes the songs chanted by the speaker.

The performers echo the songs with the audience.

The speaker echoes the songs chanted by the audience.

The basic text used by the performer in the stage space consists of those songs which are in the air when the play is being performed.

SPEAKER: Stop the war.
AUDIENCE/PERFORMERS: Stop the war.
Freedom now.
Freedom now.
Free the blacks.
Freedom now.
Freedom now.
Freedom now.
Free all people.
Free all people.
Change the world.
Change the world.
Change the world.
Change the world.
Feed the poor.
Feed the poor.
Stop the wars.
Stop the wars.
Stop the war.
In Vietnam.
Stop the war.
Stop the war.
In the Middle East.
In the Middle East.

Free the blacks.
Free the blacks.
　　In America.
In America.
　　Free the blacks.
Free all people.
　　In Africa.
Change the world.
　　Change the world.
Change the world.
　　Abolish the state.
Abolish the state.
　　Abolish the state.
Change the world.
　　Stop the draft.
Stop the draft.
　　Abolish police.
Abolish police.
　　Change the world.
Stop the draft.
　　Abolish the state.
Abolish the state.

One by one the performers come on stage.
　　Audience too.
　　They walk in a circle.
　　The performer in the center joins them.
　　Moving chanting circle.

Abolish frontiers.
Abolish frontiers.
　　Abolish money.
Abolish money.
　　Ban the banks.
Ban the banks.
　　Fuck for peace.
Fuck for peace.
　　Viva Anarchy.
Viva Anarchy.
　　Change the world.
Change the world.
　　Find a way.
Find a way.

Make it work.
Make it work.

> Arms link. Standing side by side, clasping waists and shoulders, circle comes together. The community assembles. Circle of people standing still. Pool of light.
>
> > Silence.
> > Silence.
> > Breathing.

THE CHORD.

Out of the breathing, a small sound.

> Everyone listens.
> The small sound is a low hum.
> Hum increases.
> Louder.

Each one in the circle hears the sound made by the person on either side.

> Each one responds to these two sounds.

Out of this humming and listening comes an open-throated sound.

> It grows.
> It rises.

The sound gets high and carries everyone up with it.

> Unification of the community.
> It varies and continues.
> It continues as long as the joy sustains it.
> The sound diminishes.
> Moves out as slowly as it moved in.
> Returns to a hum.
> Slowly.
> Breathing.
> Silence.
> Pause.
> The circle holds. Eyes meet. The circle dissolves.

Audience and performers drift into audience space.

Several performers sit in a straight line across the front of the stage space.

THE BREATHING.

Derived from Yoga breathing exercises.

The performers sit cross-legged.

A performer distributes paper tissue (usually toilet paper) to all the performers.

They clear their noses. Thoroughly.

They meditate. They find a pleasant place.

They breathe deeply through the nose.

A pronounced inhalation filling the lungs.

Complete exhalation.

The mouth remains closed.

The breathing becomes more and more rapid.

At least forty inhalations and exhalations.

The lungs become very full.

They hold their breath.

They are very high.

They meditate.

The breath is slowly released.

Silence. Meditation.

MAKING THE LION.

The performers change position.

They kneel, sitting on their heels.

They throw the head and torso back, stretching.

They swing their bodies forward, resting their foreheads on the ground.

They wait. They find a pleasant place.

They begin to breathe.

Very slowly they raise their heads.

Very slowly the torso arches backwards.

They inhale. They do not exhale. They inhale in short pronounced breaths. They inhale alternately through the mouth and through the nose. Filling the lungs.

The back is fully arched.

Exhalation. The performers thrust their bodies forward, extending the tongue as far as possible, pushing the eyeballs forward, and, slamming the wrists on the knees, pushing their energy outward, extending the fingers to the limit.

Emptying of the lungs.

The performer is clear.

Is the lion.

Normal breathing returns.

Bows forehead to the ground.

Slowly lifts head and torso.

Sits back on heels.

Is high. Is in a very clear place.

Silence. Meditation.

THE ZH-ZH-ZH.

The performer kneeling in the center rises.

Free choice.

Example:

The performer makes a small repeated sound.

His or her body is moved by the sound.

Moves forward. The sound grows. The gesture grows. Intensity grows. Arms, head, torso, legs shake with the sound. It overwhelms the performer.

The performer stops and gives it to the audience.

The performers slowly rise and drift into the audience and backstage.

INTERMISSION.

THE TABLEAUX VIVANTS.

During the intermission the boxes are placed.

The boxes: 4 rectangular boxes set side by side, height 2 meters, width 1 meter, depth 20 centimeters. They are unpainted wood. They stand facing the audience.

Blackout.

Lights on. Flash. 2 seconds:

There are four performers, one in each box. They are motionless.

Blackout. 4 seconds.

Lights on. Flash. 2 seconds:

The four performers have changed positions.

Blackout. 4 seconds.

Lights on. Flash. 2 seconds:

The four performers have changed positions.

After 12 changes, longer blackout.

Lights on. Flash. 2 seconds:

Four other performers.

Blackout. 4 seconds.

Lights on. Flash. 2 seconds:

The performers have changed positions.

After 12 changes, longer blackout, four other performers.

72 Tableaux Vivants, 6 groups of 4 performers each.

The performers move in the blackout.

The positions are inspired in the blackout.

Free improvisation. Performers may remain in boxes, move in and out of boxes. Touch each other. Make formations. The performers do not see each other in the dark. Chance relationships are revealed to the audience.

After the seventy-second tableau there is no blackout.

The performers in the boxes hold their positions until they are joined by the rest of the company.

They walk in a circle.

The boxes are removed.
Circle.
One by one the performers leave.
Only seven remain.

SOUND AND MOVEMENT, CALLED LEE'S PIECE.

It is always dedicated to Joseph Chaikin who invented the piece. It can also be dedicated to someone else or something else. So can any of the pieces. This piece is called Lee's Piece because Lee Worley of Joseph Chaikin's Open Theater taught it to The Living Theatre Company.

The performers form two lines facing each other.

Any performer makes a small silent movement.
Sends it to someone on the other side.
A performer receives it.
Repeats it.
Changes it.
Sends it. To someone on the other side.
The one to whom it has been sent receives it.
Receives. Repeats. Changes. Sends.
The movements grow from small movements to larger movements.

Sooner or later small sound is added to the change.

The performer makes a movement and a sound simultaneously.

Sounds and movements change simultaneously.

Now the performer is making a sound and movement which is passed to a performer on the other side.

This performer takes this sound and movement, repeats it, and seeks an automatic change.

Free association as source of inspiration.

The movements and sounds grow.

A movement and sound will eventually cause a performer to move toward the center of the stage space.

The sound and movement is repeated and changed.

A movement and sound will eventually cause a performer to cross from one side of the stage space to the other.

In the center of the stage space the performer changes the sound and movement into something new and moves to the other side.

Gives the sound and movement to a performer on the other side.

A performer takes the sound and movement, repeats it and moves toward the other side.

In the center of the stage space the performer changes.

Then crosses.

Then passes the sound and movement to another performer.

A performer receives it, repeats it, crosses to the center with it, changes it, crosses to the other side with the change, and passes it on.

The sounds and movements are improvised.

The repetitions aim at precision.

Sometimes the piece is very long. Sometimes it is shorter.

Sooner or later a sound and movement move everybody.

All the performers take up this sound and movement together.

Sometimes they change it.

The piece is about communication. It unifies the community.

BLACKOUT.

THE PLAGUE.

After the conception of Artaud.

"Beneath such a scourge all social forms disintegrate." Artaud.

Dim light.

All the performers are in the stage space.

They are the city.

Their breathing is sick.

They are the plague victims.

Very slowly the plague, the symptoms of the plague, their awareness of the plague, the sufferings of the plague, the ravages of the plague, grow.

The light increases.

Artaudian action.

Fever. Fatigue. Nausea. Blisters. Vomit. Gangrene. Congestion. Boils. Pus. Around the anus. In the armpits. The skin cracks. Gall bladder. Softened and pitted lungs. Chips of some unknown black substance. Aberrations. Frenzy. Murder. Erotic paroxysms. Piles of corpses. Putrefaction. Stench. Disorder. Thick viscous liquids gush from the corpses. Flight. Hideous visions. Howling through the streets. The brain melts, shrinks, granulates to a sort of coal-black dust. Death everywhere.

Each performer chooses his/her role and acts it out.

Crawling, creeping, rolling, groaning, staggering, falling, they struggle fleeing the stage space, the geographical source of the epidemic, and spill into the audience space. The plague comes with them.

"The theatre is like the plague." Artaud.

The theater is filled with corpses. Contorted positions of violent death.

Silence.

Pause.

Very slowly the doctors rise.

There are six of them.

They take off their shoes. Very slowly.

They place their shoes in a line at the front of the stage space.

They move from corpse to corpse. Solemnly, they remove the shoes of each corpse.

The bodies of the corpses are rigid.

They place the shoes in the line at the front of the stage space.

The dead bury the dead.

The doctors work in pairs.

Two doctors slowly and solemnly unbend the rigid contorted body of a corpse.

Straighten limbs. Close mouth and eyes. Adjust clothes. Straighten fingers. Smooth hair. Wipe sputum.

The corpse is stiff. Straight as a board.

They lift the body.

They raise it, holding it by neck and ankles.

The body suspended is rigid.

They carry it slowly toward the stage space.

The dead are burying the dead.

They place it on the stage space.

Two doctors lift the body and place it in the center of the stage space.

The second corpse is placed alongside it. And the third. And the fourth. And the fifth.

A line of five corpses shoulder to shoulder, ankle to ankle.

The sixth corpse. It is placed on top of the line of five corpses. Its head rests on ankles, its feet rest on the shoulders of the corpses underneath.

A pyramid of corpses.

In the first line there are five corpses, in the second four, in the third three, in the fourth two, in the fifth one.

Pyramid of corpses, neatly stacked.

Pool of light.

The doctors disappear into the darkness.

Silence. Corpses.

The light slowly fades.

BLACKOUT.

AC/DC

by Heathcote Williams

Sadie: . . . Maurice is satirizing attitudes which haven't yet arisen.

AC/

Sadie: . . . I don't mind having a few of those cats inside my head when I'm eating, if that's where they want to be, or even when I'm fucking, but to have that Grade-B tinseltown shit batting round in my head when I'm fixin to Die . . . No man, no, no, no . . .

/DC

Introduction by John Lahr

There are plays which are visionary. They give shape to consciousness by making visible a culture's hidden anxieties and sickness. Theatrical prophesy speaks in its own language and in its own way. The visionary image takes us by surprise and often infuriates us: it becomes a source of energy, not a syphon. We must accept the mystery of its new vocabulary in order to touch a truth which holds us strangely spellbound. Heathcote Williams' *AC/DC* is such a play. What is it? A brilliant schizoid melodrama of the technological society's sensory overload. A brain buzz. A by-pass circuit for media rash. A word salad that juices language with the poetry of scientific terminology and the jazz of street talk. It is a virtuoso performance of intellect, where energy clears tracks in the audience's brain.

Williams is talking about energy (how it is gained and how it is lost) and imagery (how we destroy our minds and how they can be reclaimed). The schizoid stalemate of Williams' characters is induced by environments which flood them with imagery. They are receptors sopping up the media's electronic impulses. They embody the Faustian paradox, traveling everywhere in their minds while the circumference of their actions shrink, speeding so fast that they lose any sense of identity. *AC/DC* dramatizes this overstimulated isolation. We live our lives in other people's dreams: our emotional baggage is cluttered with mildewed images. We find our energy not by tapping our own sources but by lifting it from others. Perowne, a terminal schizophrenic in *AC/DC,* a man who has broken so many inner boundaries that he has become a protean paralytic, says: "I don't know. I don't know if it's not too late. The sensory assault is too great. It's really a stress situation." The problem is how to clear the mind's congestion and renew authentic energy. The drama of *AC/DC* is in watching an allegory of this metaphysical struggle to leap to a higher semantic-emotional-cognitive stratum.

Visually, Williams sets his play against the backdrop of two vivid, abrasive energy fields. The first is Playland, where the protean quality of these technological mutants is visible in their "spaced" dialogue, the talk of "mind-swaps" and "changes." The wild, frantic discharges of a penny arcade, with its blinking pinball neon lights, TV cameras flashing the technicolor stage image back to the audience in multiangled black and white, epitomize a world at once energized and disoriented. The current which makes it sizzle is matched by the characters yearning from some spiritual breakthrough, a transcendent consciousness to match the intensity and fusion of the media mosaic. People are trying to cross-circuit each other, to get into each other's "trips." Maurice, the arcade attendant, is the focus of energy in this environment. He protects his lover from electronic radiation and media fall-out.

The purity of his energy ("plugged me into their so-called amnesiac shockers. But I broke the box, and fused every light in the area for thirty miles") attracts Sadie. In his frenetic psychosexual fantasy Maurice talks the language of neural absorption and illustrates how our libidinal energy has been rerouted. He lives at such a distance from life that mental masturbation is the real thing!

Perowne filled my teeth in a certain way, you see, certain alloys in certain combinations, so that I was picking up TV programs in my head like a Jew's Harp, and he shoved David Niven-Richard Harris-Hemmings-Photo down my arteries and dialing my head very hard, and switching my body clock on, off, on, off, and every time I kissed Perowne I was forced to desalivate because of course Perowne didn't want David Niven's style of kissing.

The second environment is Perowne's room: a space where red and yellow wires climb around the walls like ganglia, where television sets are banked around the room flashing new imagery each second to compete with the glossy photographs of The Famous plastered against the flat surfaces of the walls. Williams' image is overpowering: the arid, monumental clutter of the room is a replica of Perowne's cranium. The violent, silent battle of imagery is matched by the room's narcotic, amnesiac quality. In this inner space there is no possibility of living at first hand. Surfaces are cast against surfaces. Discovery, and therefore growth, become impossible because the viewer must be passive to "receive" this stimulation. It acts on him; he cannot act on it. There is no possibility of selection. Images of good and evil, right and wrong, purity and debasement have the same visual weight and impact.

Sadie enters and tries to clear Perowne's static. She sees the room and realizes that images must be stripped away. She is direct current, and she describes the room, correctly, as a cybernetic model: all input, no output. She goes into a riff about psychic capitalists: people who take an idea and merchandize the original concept until it is a formula. Repetition is the key to profit; and it is precisely this phenomenon which confounds, dilutes, and paralyzes those who are exposed to it. Her long scene with Perowne is a breathtaking literary and theatrical tour de force. In its scope—the verbal power matching the pain and humor of the gesture—Williams creates one of the most stunning moments on the English stage in the last decade. An important idea is incarnated. Sadie proceeds to lead Perowne through his psychic imagery: a ritual of renewal.

Perowne: . . . Let's see who you've . . . let's see who you've got in Input Section. Marilyn Monroe.
Sadie: Yeah, she's Input. She's Basic Basic.
Perowne (*pointing along to the right, tracing a line*): But

then the Rot sets in. A kind of inverse Doppler effect.
The original imprint is defaced, and you get about
Forty randomized functions trying to restimulate a
need that's already been exhausted by Marilyn Monroe . . .

Sadie: THAT'S RIGHT!
   Pointing to the wall.
Carroll Baker, Sandra Milo, Anita Ekberg, Virna
Lisi, Sharon Tate, Edie Adams, Barbara Loden,
Kathy Kirby, Diana Dors, Jayne Mansfield . . . [. . .]
KYBERNETIC RUNAWAY! [. . .]

Perowne: You get the . . . the same thing here, I suppose—Input Section, you get . . .
   Pointing to a photo.
Wittgenstein . . . [. . .] then the breakdown of the
original imprint [. . .]

Sadie: Wittgenstein.
   Snapping her fingers.
He was a big philosophical connection, right? Wrote
the Tractatus, right. I remember. Proposition 43: "The
word 'fuck' is a picture of fucking." Right? [. . .] You
got Wittgenstein in Input. Pure. But then these little
cats, this Ayer, this Quine.
   Pointing at photos.
This Ryle, this Chomsky, this Strawson . . . these
little, little cats, they SOLD Wittgenstein's Tractatus
to the Daily News. They dismantled Wittgenstein's
little thoughtkit, which he packed so tight, and it got
syphoned off into the receptors of thirteen stagnant
behaviorist clerks. [. . .]

Perowne: YES. A lot of the circuitry's overloaded, and
I find it . . .
   Twisting.
I find it . . .

Sadie: Solid! there's gotta be some economy. Look at it.
   Closer to the wall.
Tom Jones . . . see? Cooked-down version of Sam
Cook and Otis Redding.
  Tears down the photo of Tom Jones.
Byo byo Thomas.
   Studying wall.
[. . .] How many times does Dylan go into Woodie
Guthrie?

Tears down photo.
Bye bye Dylan. [. . .] Elvis Presley, sanforized version
of Arthur "Big Boy" Crudup.
Tears down photo.

Sadie replaces Maurice as Perowne's psychic guardian.
She leads him into a new sphere of consciousness. Tre-
panning his brain, she symbolically relieves the pressure.
He is finally happy, and free. As with many visionary
images, it is the analysis of man's condition in *AC/DC*,
and not his new history, which seems most convincing.

It is rare to be in the theater and to have language
become a visceral event. But this is what happens in
AC/DC. The play is talking about new language and new
methods of understanding. Williams claims that it is "an
ESP play." Certainly we have no images in our brain for
many of the words he uses, and we do not comprehend
them on a rational level. But this is a play of vibrations:
and we cannot escape the authentic message whose moral
passion forces its way through the scientific and mystical
code words. Williams' images of psychic struggle are
horrifying and painful and funny.
AC/DC is Basic Basic.

AC/DC was first performed in The Theatre Upstairs at The Royal Court Theatre, London, on May 14th, 1970, with the following cast:

GARY	Robert Lloyd
MELODY	Patricia Quinn
SADIE	Pat Hartley
MAURICE	Henry Woolf
PEROWNE	Ian Hogg

The play was directed by Nicholas Wright.

AC/DC was subsequently presented at The Chelsea Theatre Centre, Brooklyn, New York, by Robert Kalfin and Michael David on February 16th, 1971, with the following cast:

GARY	James Cromwell
MELODY	Jillian Lundig
SADIE	Susan Batson
MAURICE	Ed Zang
PEROWNE	Stefan Gierasch

The play was directed by John Hirsch.

The text of AC/DC is convertible at all points to the frequencies of the actors and the director.

ALTERNATING CURRENT

It is 5 A.M., in an Amusement Arcade. Three people are playing the machines: MOONSHOT, MAGIC CITY, WAYWARD SKULL, TEACHER'S PET, TV BASEBALL, BUCKAROO, and BEAT TIME. Ultraviolet lights flashing. The ball bearings churn and wheep through the bumpers, and the neon gates in an electron spin.
Black. Three Americans are inside the PHOTOMATON half dressed, with the curtain drawn. The flashlight inside the machine is exploding. From the PHOTOMATON come sounds of heavy breathing, then a symphony of panting, laughing, sucking, billing, and cooing. The rest of the Arcade is in darkness. Flashlights explode in the PHOTOMATON, lighting it up from the inside.

GARY: MONGOLIAN CLUSTER FUCK!
MELODY: YEAAAAH! KICKED OUT ALL THE PHYS-ICAL JAMS!
GARY: GLUED US ALL TOGETHER!
SADIE: THREE IN ONE AND ONE IN THREE!

> Laughing and panting, they collapse to the floor of the PHOTOMATON, bare legs, and clothes sticking out from under the curtain.

SADIE: I wanta go solo.
GARY: Whaaat?
SADIE: I wanta go solo.
GARY: We just Blew ourselves together didn't we? We just melted ourselves altogether in a giant gentle atom bomb of sperm and cunt juice, an now she says she wants to go solo . . .
MELODY: Chinese Portraits. Come on. That'll zip us up. That'll get us together. That'll give us a real deep interbrain buzz. Ok Sadie?
SADIE: Ok.
MELODY: Come on now, I'm holding someone really tight in my head. I'm right into someone now!
GARY: OK . . . OK. What kinda . . .

> Sound of snapping fingers.

What kinda restaurant he or she remind you of?

MELODY: Hot dog kennel.

GARY: Ha!

SADIE: What kinda wallpaper . . . he or she remind you of?

MELODY: Oriental grass.

GARY: Shit, I'm gonna burn if it's me.

MELODY: YEAH, We'll wash your ego right out!

GARY: What kinda color?

MELODY: We had that before, last time we played.

GARY: Who for?

MELODY: Dunno. But whoever it was, they gotta high evaporation rate!

GARY: Ha.

SADIE: What kinda flavor?

MELODY: All snarled up. Like anchovies . . .

GARY: It's Sadie! It's Sadie.

MELODY: Yeah! Right!

Flashbulb explodes.

Cooled you out, Sadie!

SADIE: Yeah. Ha.

GARY: O.K. O.K. Come on now, I'm holding someone really tight now.

MELODY: O.K., er . . . What kinda . . . What kinda musical instrument?

GARY: Mouthorgan.

MELODY: It's himself. He's chosen himself!

GARY: No. No it's not.

SADIE: What kinda dirty habit?

GARY: Leaving the toilet unflushed.

MELODY: I wouldn't leave the toilet unflushed for fear of your robbing it.

SADIE: What kinda food?

GARY: A long white crisp cos lettuce.

SADIE: What kinda scent?

GARY: Testosterone.

SADIE: It's Melody!

GARY: Right.

MELODY: Me? What's testosterone got to do with me? You're switching everyone round.

GARY: That's right! It's a good way to stay fresh.

MELODY: Ha! Yeah!

SADIE: Kicked out all the flesh jams! Kicked out all the psychic jams.

GARY: Glued us all together.

MELODY: The Synergetic Conspiracy!

SADIE: Stereochemical Egodectomy!

> GARY and MELODY draw aside the curtain, and file out of the PHOTOMATON, pulling their clothes back on. Full lights.

GARY: Wow!

> Stretching.

Everybody's crash landed right into the middle of everyone else's fuckin buzz, right?

MELODY: Up into the air, Junior Birdmen! Hey, where are you man?

> GARY holds his hand about two foot above his head.

MELODY: Right! Healed all the crimps. Hey, we really laid some changes on each other, no? I feel completely Burst, completely Deconditioned. Just like I been doing some astral projections and I just slipped back into my body this second and it's a Perfect Fit.

GARY: Yeah! I knew a man once who didn't get back in time and his body didn't fit.

> He makes a series of paralyzed movements.

MELODY: Ha!

> Touching him.

Wow! Triple Interbrain BUZZZZZZ.

> Drawing her breath through her teeth.

Flushed all our aliases down that iron lung.

> She points to the PHOTOMATON and then goes back to it and takes out the photostrips from the delivery bay of the machine.

GARY: Transferred everyone's evil ego vibes, yeah! Transferred them into the photos. Free floating.

> Flapping his arms.

MELODY: Yeah!

> She folds up the photostrips and tears them up, and then slides them up and down against each other, so that all their features are mixed up.

GARY: Wow!

> Looking closely over MELODY's shoulder.

Wow!

MELODY: Hey, look at this. Your nose, see, my eyes. Your tits, my eyes, Sadie's cunt. Ha! Triple Interbrain Buzzzzzz!

GARY: Hey, SADIE! Come on out and dig this!

SADIE (*from inside the PHOTOMATON*): There's another little buzz I wanta get out of this machine and then we can get really spaced.

GARY: Ha.

MELODY: Oh come on, I'm spaced out already.

> To herself, staring at the photos.

So many days left unstoned.

SADIE (*from inside, flashing the flashbulbs*): Turn on satellite control, start ampex recorder. Computer to run condition. Computer print-out reading all zeros. Activate sun gun and direct light beam at Sun sensor. Sun pulse indication appearing on computer print-out . . . Check raster scan . . .

GARY: Come on out, Sadie.

MELODY: Yeah, you're givin us the space dumps.

GARY (*pointing to the PHOTOMATON*): It's not a space capsule, it's an iron lung!

> MELODY giggles.

SADIE: Deactivate Sun Gun. Main battery deep discharge. Chamber bleed up. Pre shipment Comprehensive. Main battery deep discharge. PRE-SHIPMENT BUTTON UP! VROOOOOM! WE HAVE LIFT OFF!

MELODY (*sticking her neck out, and shouting at SADIE in the machine*): They don't allow women to work in the Space Program, didn't you know? The acidity of their skin, once a month, it interferes with the delicate components.

GARY: You'll have to stick to Inner Space, baby.

SADIE (*from inside the machine*): Inner Space is over-populated.

MELODY (*turning away, and looking at the photostrips. To* GARY): Hey, you know I should have my photograph taken every five minutes all my life, then I could flick through the photographs and watch myself grow older. Hey, look at that one! I was doing that one twenty different ways in my head, and look how it's come out.

GARY: Yeah. Marlon Brando was in the paper the other day, you know, and he was complaining to a Finnish photographer that photographers were always photographing him with a transitional expression on his face.

MELODY: Yeah?

SADIE (*quietly*): Media freaks.

> MAURICE, dressed in a white coat, has been bent over the machine WEST CLUB, repairing it. The backboard of the machine has been stripped off, baring thick skeins of wires and valves. He moves across to GARY and MELODY, standing behind them as they examine their photos.

MAURICE: I used to work as a sound engineer on Henry Hall's Guest Night before I came here. I was responsible for blowing up all people like that to double their size so that they couldn't invite me. They were just started off as a pilot signal, only Perowne made me turn the volume up, so they're coming through now as a permanent fuckin echo. He's stuffed Marlon Brando in me kartso,

> Pointing to his crotch.

he's stuffed Jayne Mansfield in me cunt, and Lee Marvin in me liver finger, and pushing Mia Farrow's babies through me nipples; and he's got the rods and cones in my eyes as Radio receivers and Transmitters to a very first-hand frequency so that the way that that fuckin outfit exploits my photoconductivity can't never stop . . .

MELODY: Wow!

GARY: HEY, SADIE! DIG THIS!

MELODY: YEAH, HE'S REALLY SPACED! See if you can hit HIS Buzz with your space-craft.

> SADIE emerges from the PHOTOMATON. She stares at MAURICE, then turns to MELODY.

SADIE: Oh come on, stop laying all that second-hand head talk on everyone you meet.

MAURICE (*to* GARY): I don't mind Lee Marvin getting a charge off me, but when I get it back from him, it's the wrong fuckin amperage.

GARY: That's right. Huh, that's Right!

MELODY (*to* GARY): Hey, stay loose, stay loose.

MAURICE (*moving in on* GARY): Perowne filled my teeth in a certain way, you see, certain alloys in certain combinations, so that I was picking up TV programs in my head like a Jew's Harp, and he shoved David Niven-Richard-Harris-Hemmings-Photo down my arteries and dialing my head very hard, and switching my body clock on, off, on, off, and every time I kissed Perowne I was forced to desalivate because of course Perowne didn't want David Niven's style of kissing, and After I'd kissed Perowne I had to Defecate, i.e. make myself not Feke any more, and if I didn't Defecate after, they'd file down the David-Niven-Pat-Boone-fuckin-Hemming-Head to a Sharp Point and when it'd made its transmissions from my fuckin eye, it'd whip round and down to my optic nerve and SLASH IT TO BITS . . .

GARY: Hey! All the People he's into!

MELODY (*nudging him*): Yeah . . . Hey! Remember Sadie on that trip?

GARY: What? Oh Wow, all those telegrams.

> To MAURICE.

Yeah, She was on a trip like that. She was sending telegrams to all those people. Who was it? David Niven?

SADIE: No.

> Laughs.

It was J. Paul Getty.

GARY: Oh, yeah, J. Paul Getty. Ha. Yeah.

> To MAURICE.

Sadie picks up on him sitting in his black leather swivel chair, combing his hair with his checkstubs, right? and he wires Sadie. "Thank you Sadie for wasting this groovy idea about me combing my hair with checkstubs, but I am not rich, I cannot sign a check for five cents. I'll tell you my secret. I am meagerly paid by a Syndicate of the rich to be the Public Rich Man and the Easy Target Decoy. I am doing you a favor telling you this. Tell no one. Love Paul."

MELODY (*to* MAURICE): It's an E.S.P. telegram. Sent collect. You dig? So Sadie gets out her scratch-pad: "Dear Paul, thanks for the memo anent your position. I sympathize with your position, because I am paid by a Syndicate of the FAMOUS to be the Public Famous Person, as a decoy, to preserve their Anonymity. Love to your bald head, Signed Sadie."

GARY: Ha! that was groovy.

SADIE (*to* MAURICE *distantly*): Who's Perowne?

MAURICE: Who's Perowne? Perowne has me washing my hands every hour, the other day, because he said they weren't any good any more as exTENsores you see, and I should try and wear them away. Friend of mine, Colney Hatch, said there was a whole mob at that already and if I wanted to get that through, I'd have to top it up a bit, i.e. cut them off at the joints.

> Laying his finger across his wrist.
> SADIE laughs. GARY and MELODY move closer to MAURICE, pointing at him.

MELODY: Scatter language!

GARY: Yeah, and Metonymic Distortion.

MELODY: Synaesthetic Conglomerates!

GARY: Interpenetration of Themes. Neologisms!

MELODY: Twelve tone dirty jokes.

GARY: Delaminated word salad!

MELODY: The Asyndetic Putsch!

GARY: When are they going ta release the flip side of your speech center? We could do some great sleeve notes.

MELODY (*slowly, staring at* MAURICE): Do you know what a schizoid metonym is, Maurice? When the first man said: The Kettle is Boiling, it was noted down as a schizoid metonym by those present, because, as everyone knows, it's not the kettle but the water that boils. But, as the first man to say this phrase, quietly struggled in his straitjacket, his chroniclers, his gazeteers, and his warders, who were taking tea at the time, conversed amiably: "The Kettle is Boiling, the Kettle is Boiling, the kettle is boiling . . ." congratulating themselves on the economy of their language. So, keep on with it, some of it'll get through the customs.

GARY (*to* MELODY): Except there may be EVEN MORE economic linguistic structures around . . . than the one he's using.

MELODY: Yeah? You're puttin me on.

GARY: No, there's a language called Mescalero in which none of the verbs are tensed.

MELODY: So?

GARY: Well, none of the verbs in that language have any TIME sense. You dig?

Closing up to MELODY, cuddling her.

Maybe we ought to learn that language. People who speak that language probably LIVE longer.

MELODY: Ha!

SADIE (*staring*): Have you just gone into Public Relations?

GARY: No, why? Do you wanna join in my private life?

SADIE: What are you trying to whittle away at his trip for?

MAURICE (*waving at* SADIE): That's all right, that's all right.

To GARY and MELODY.

LOOOOOK, I got triple realities going on in slip language the whole fuckin time, but I can get my Influencing Machine talking Cool Straight Police Car Language from the Clapham Toilet Bureau, any day of the week, when there's someone who can ONLY BE NAILED like that.

Speaking in an American accent, and gesticulating in ham, servile gestures.

NOW, EXCUSE ME MADAM, WHERE CAN I CLOSET FOR YOU YOUR COAT? Get it? I'm not joining your private life because I've been told to keep out of my own. And as to what you said earlier: fuckin schizoid metonym. I'll go into that very deeply.

> Tugging at MELODY, dragging her down to the ground.

Loook, what have I got here? Look, this is my sock. Do you know what I've got in my sock?

> Sitting on the ground, he feels a swelling in his sock, and pulls it down.

I've got chocolate tinfoil, with tenebrations five point eight, I've got crucified orange peel, with tenebrations six point ten, I've got butterfly excrement with tenebrations eight point nine, and my whole sock's painted with British Museum Leather Dressing Solution. AND WHAT DO YOU THINK I KEEP ALL THIS SHIT IN THERE FOR? TO WARD OFF FUCKIN SCHIZOPHRENICS!

SADIE (*roaring with laughter*): Right on! Right on!

GARY (*to* SADIE): You wanta pick up on That?

SADIE: Yeah, that cat's a real high energy dude!

MELODY (*getting up*): He's really thick with being a schizo.

MAURICE: RIGHT!

> Pulling at his scalp.

And this is where three phrenologists lost their fingernails. In me riah. In me fuckin barnet. And five years ago, they shaved it all off, pasted wires on, and plugged me into their so-called amnesiac shockers. But I broke the box, and fused every light in the area for thirty miles.

SADIE: *RIGHT ON!*

> SADIE laughs, grabs hold of MAURICE, they growl at each other, and then roll over each other on the floor, grappling and laughing.

GARY (*pointing at them*): Hey, that was a quick seduction. You pinched her sloshy boobs. You chewed her bee stung lips . . .

MELODY (*standing over them, shouting*): You scarfed her box out, then you let her go down on you, and give you head, in spite of her awful ortho-creme mouthwash, then you shoved your raunchy little dick up her butt, sawed her to bits, with your toad testicles screech-ing to a halt, and she had an abortion . . .

GARY (*shouting*): An you drilled her again. Ya got married. Ya separated . . .

MELODY: An she got custody of the kids.

> At MAURICE.

Hey Schizo! you really moved it.

GARY: Yeah! Advertise your fantasies widely enough an you're bound to get Someone to populate them.

MELODY: Acid Positive!

> MAURICE and SADIE collapse breathless underneath the PHOTOMATON. GARY and MELODY move across to one of the pinmachines, BEAT TIME. SADIE looks up and watches a man standing beside the machine that is being repaired: WEST CLUB. Its glass cover is off. He is picking the ball bearings out of the sump and rolling them with his hands against the inside edges of the pin-table.

SADIE: Is that Perowne?

MAURICE: Yes. He's been trying to go bald a lot, but there's always one hair holds the others up.

> PEROWNE breaks off momentarily and stands clasping his hands together, cracking the joints, then holding them tightly together.

SADIE: Why's he holding his hands like that?

MAURICE: So that only one of his hands need do the sweating. He's getting a displacement current going, because there's a Dead Field Structure moving round those

> Pointing at GARY and MELODY.

and I've been building up his resistance to that Dead Field. I've got him up to 25 megohms already.

> PEROWNE leans over the slotmachine, staring at it.

PEROWNE: A ball is cued from a corner on an N times M foot table, at an angle of forty five degrees (N and

M are integers). How many sides will the ball strike before it again goes into the corner?

Drawing a pencil across the glass.

You tesselate the first quadrant with M time N rectangles. By reflection each boundary intersected by the line X equals Y, corresponds to a side struck by a ball cued from the origin at a forty five degree angle. The line X equals Y first intersects a vertex at (L,L), where L is the lowest common multiple of M, N and en route intersects $L/N-1$ vertical and $L/M-1$ horizontal boundaries. Accordingly, the ball strikes $L/N-1 + L/M-2 = (M+N) L/MN-2$ sides. The result may also be stated $(M+N) (M,N) - 2$, where $(,)$ indicates the greatest common divisor.

Looking up—moving away from the machine.

Five and a half hours ago, I was in Imperial College Library, and I discovered that the problem had already been set in the Pi Mu Epsilon Journal of Mathematics in 1959, and solved by the following people: J.G. Abad, J.P. Celenz, Yu Chang, R.B. Eggleston, Michael Goldberg, R.S. Kaluzniacki, R.L. Kammerer, Liselotte Miller, Edward Moylan, Robert Patenande, Stanton Philip, J.M. Quoniam, Steven Ruse, J.J. Segedy, K.N. Sigmon, T.R. Smith, Laurence Somer, Steven Tice, P.S. Vitta, Allan Wache, John Wessner, Oswald Wyler, and J.W. Zerger.

SADIE (*standing up*): Yeah. Well, no emotion's worth having twice.

PEROWNE: You know what your lifetime's storage capacity is? Ten to the power of seven bits. That's all. I've wasted four, five, maybe Ten bits on that.

Pointing at the pin table.

WHY DON'T THEY KEEP THE IMPRINTS CLEAN? The thing was shopsoiled from the Start. Centralized Data Storage. That's all it needs. The simplest thing. Centralized Data Storage.

PEROWNE moves toward MAURICE and SADIE, holding his hands together. Cracking the fingers. He seems armored. Totally encased.

MAURICE (*getting up*): You've been overamping.

PEROWNE (*stares at him. Smiles quietly at him, then recognizes him*): Hello.

Clasps him, looking at SADIE.

Hello.

MAURICE: What else you been doing?

PEROWNE stares at him, clasps his hands again, and twists his head tensely.

SADIE (*loudly*): What made you have the emotion in the first place?

PEROWNE: Do you mean mathematics? I don't know. It's a sentimental metaphor: mathematics. I used to work for IBM as a researcher. They were a lot of superstitious mafiosos.

Twisting his head.

I'm trying to get through to something on my own.

SADIE: Einstein was psychotic.

PEROWNE: I just watched a program about Einstein. Einstein apparently said that to explain soup was probably not the same as tasting it. If he was so uneasy about it, why did he choose such a boring example?

There might be a thought somewhere about Einstein starting to SCREAM at the taste of soup.

PEROWNE starts twisting again and looks at MAURICE.

I've been watching a lot of television.

MAURICE: You've got fuckin radiated, haven't you? You've got fuckin media rash haven't you?

PEROWNE (*moving closer to him*): I feel a little overloaded.

Smiles weakly at him.

MAURICE: What else you been going?

PEROWNE: Well, I watched the news. The television. You see. I watched the news.

Twitching.

Then I went into the street. Whole place is a noisy

ashtray. Then . . . Then I met a boy from the . . .
London Street Commune. I listened to every word he
said . . . I even suggested they take over a whole
street. Knock the connecting walls of the houses together, build a refectory table on the ground floor,
and a refectory bed on the top floor running the whole
length of the street. I enjoyed talking to him. But it
was too . . . he gave me a . . . I . . . I had to
Drink Him Off . . . I got . . . double-exPOSED. I
. . . Some kind of sensory Bottleneck . . . I feel a
bit . . . double exposed. He Bared His Teeth A Lot
. . . it was . . .

MAURICE (*holding him*): You got overloaded, haven't
you.

PEROWNE: YES.

Moving his shoulder inside his clothes.

YES.

MAURICE (*springing away*): RIGHT! I can clear all those
tracks. The Boy with the Heady Views . . . The
Mathematics . . . The Drink Track . . . The TV
News program. I can flash all those tracks clean as
a whistle for you again.

PEROWNE (*staring at him, smiles*): You can?

MAURICE (*Placing his hands on* PEROWNE's *head, grip-
ping tufts of hair, moving* PEROWNE's *scalp across his
skull. Closing his eyes*): Can I? I'm pitching into the
boy you met with the heady views right now. I've got
to get the exact Anti-Dotal Wave Form you see. To
rub off that track for you. I've Got It! I've Got it! Closing his eyes, rocking his head. I'm getting an engram
of Exact Weight to discharge you. I've got it! I've got
it! What's this?

Screwing up his face, eyes closed.

I'm going to the airport to meet them? From Barcelona: Oswald Mosley, and William Joyce with their
twisted tuning fork (drawing a swastika in the air)
and from Glasgow: Palme Dutt and Harry Pollitt with
their tin opener (draws a hammer and sickle in the
air). What's happening? What's happening? They
won't let them through the customs. They're making
them take a urine test. They're looking for the pink

spot in the urine that's going round now as fashionable. One of them said he had had it, but he'd wasted it. Another one started chucking all papers into the air. He said somebody'd bought it off him before he could go into it. Only one of them refused to take it: I'm leakin nothing, he said. A slip of the lip costs a ship. Huh. None of them are getting it. They've got to take the first plane back. They're letting them keep their samples though. The glass pipettes.

> PEROWNE laughs. MAURICE bends down over PEROWNE and touches heads.

A Clean Break? I hit it?
PEROWNE (*smiling*): Pretty much.

> He begins to move in a less armored way.

MAURICE: I switched you fit of that track, right?
PEROWNE: Yes.
SADIE: Why do you have to put it into words?
MAURICE: I KNOW. I KNOW. Every word that I utter is the radioactive waste of eighteen million telepathons. Every word that's pumped through me is eighteen million telepathons down the drain. I don't Want to use words.
SADIE: Why doncha use karate sound blows on him, to clear all his hangups?

> To PEROWNE.

You know about that? Practitioners place a rat at a hundred yards distant from their mouth, then pitch into the rat's frequency, sound off, and the rat drops dead. Sonic laser beams.
PEROWNE: What does it sound like?
SADIE: KIIIIIIIIIYAAAAAAAAAAAAAAAAAAAAAA!
PEROWNE: KIIIIIIIIIIIIIIIYYYYYYYAAAAAAAAAAAAAA AAAAAAAAAAAAAHH!!

> GARY and MELODY emerge from the other part of the Arcade.

GARY: What's going on now?
MAURICE: What's going on between Perowne and me is peak to peak amplitude.

GARY: Yeah? Well you wave your length, and I'll wave mine.

MELODY laughs.

SADIE: Oh shutup, they're behind some heavy shit.
MELODY: Yeah?

Looking at PEROWNE.

Hey, he looks wired up.
GARY: He's gone solo years back.
MELODY: He was twitching all the time.
GARY: He was really chewin out some inner riff.
MELODY (*to* PEROWNE): Why were you twitching?
PEROWNE: I've been watching television. Television always makes me twitch.
MELODY: We'll cool you out. See that Photomaton? We just turned that into an orgone chamber. We had a Mongolian Cluster Fuck in there just now. Get in there and pick up the vibes we left in there. That'll cool you right out.
MAURICE: Leave him alone.

Holding PEROWNE.

I'm the only one that can get into his head and clear the tracks. I'm picking up his brain waves and picking up his alpha rhythms . . . I know exactly which tracks got blocked.
PEROWNE (*staring at him, smiling*): Yes.
MAURICE: Right. Ha. I'll take the . . .

Flipping his fingers, pointing at the bottle.

I'll take the drink as a starter. 1961. 1961 being pumped through now Perowne. Ha.

Leaning forward.

I'm in a clinic in the Dordogne, France. I find out the S.P. They're short on alcoholics. So, two days later, to extend my visa, I have them find me scammered in a ditch with eight bottles of Pernod. They bring me back, fill me up with Brands Essence and a raw egg, lay me flat. Now this place is run by a shrink and his lady who wrote some very famous books in the thirties about her previous life as the Queen of Egypt.

PEROWNE: I've heard of her.

MAURICE: And their method of cure, Perowne, is Regressive Hypnotism. They start the cure. She's on call all the time to see that I don't turn out to have been anyone more famous than her, in a previous reincarnation. How old are you, Maurice? 23. Right, he says, lie down on the bed, take off your shoes, and stare at that stud in ceiling. Like all hypnotists, he's got ophthalmic goiter, and he keeps the stud in the ceiling as a . . .

PEROWNE: An understudy.

MAURICE: Relax your right leg. Move your right leg. You can't move your right leg? Right, we're off. Now, Maurice, I'm going to count from 23 to 1, and when I get to one you will lose touch with my physical voice. He counts me back down my ages . . . 23, 22, 21 . . . and every number he calls out, I'm to remember things . . . 13, 12, 11 . . . little things coming out every number. Then his voice gets fainter; we get to 2, then 1. I still remember things: nappy rash, gripe water, cock like a snail just been given a prussic acid dip. Then, Zero. Nothing. Minus One. Nothing. I remember nothing. Minus 2. I can't come up with a thing. His voice is fainter and fainter. Minus Three. Nothing. Then, very low: Minus Four, Maurice . . . And then I'M SHOUTING, PEROWNE, AND I'M FLAILING ABOUT ON THE BED, AND I'M JERKING ABOUT AND I'M ALL OVER THE PLACE AND I'M SHOUTING: THEY'RE CUTTING MY TONGUE, STOP THEM, STOP THEM, THEY'RE CUTTING MY TONGUE OUT . . . I know he's bringing the Queen of Egypt in from the next room. I can see her face. It's white. They try to count me back up again, but I'm stuck at minus four, my age of minus four: THEY'RE CUTTING MY TONGUE OUT, THEY'RE CUTTING MY TONGUE OUT . . . and he's going minus 4, minus 3, minus 2, minus 1, nothing, 1,2,3,4, . . . 21,22,23. Up and down, up and down SEVEN times to fetch me back, and eventually they do. But I can't speak. I'm just going . . .

Mouthing.

So they counted me back down again, to minus four, to fetch my tongue off the people, then back to 23. I stood up. Drank three jugs of water straight off, and I said to her: Your face is very white. I am going to do a level-shift, she says, and she covers her eyes. I can see a dark cell, she says, covered with a straw, somewhere outside Barcelona. You're a spy. In the Spanish Civil War. You're refusing to pass information. They're cutting your tongue out as a last ditch stand. That is all. Then she comes out of her level-shift, swings her external camera onto me, and says: They cut your tongue out, in that incarnation, and this left a bleeding scar on your supraphysical self and your etheric body, which you have had to assuage by excessive drinking. The Lunar Stagnancy is finished. The waters are no longer violent.

> MAURICE takes the bottle off PEROWNE, takes a shot from it, and puts it into his pocket.

A clean Break?

PEROWNE: A clean break.

MAURICE: They said they'd never had such results. So, I free loaded there for a couple of weeks, until the word got around they were suddenly going to be short of pernicious catatonics, and I didn't feel like filling that one up for them: ripping off bigger and bigger scabs and eating myself . . . die in ten days; so, I left. I went to Paris. But I was extremely grateful to her for having allowed me to have fought the Spanish Civil War, in a previous incarnation.

PEROWNE: Yes. Where did you stay?

MAURICE: I stayed in Hotel d'Alsace. Where Oscar Wilde died. But anyway in the Next Room of this hotel was staying a man called Wittgenstein or Frere, I can't remember which. He was a historian. Struck up conversation with him, and you know what he told me? Only the RIGHT side cut people's tongues out in the Spanish Civil War, so that I must have been on the WRONG SIDE.

PEROWNE: She'd swindled you.

> PEROWNE stares at MAURICE, then reaches for

the bottle in MAURICE's pocket. MAURICE moves away.

MAURICE: No.

Staring at PEROWNE, rubbing the bottle in his pocket.

Still a faint flicker? isn't there? Still a faint flicker from that drunk track. Right. I'm gonna swab you down completely now. Little microwave welding to switch you fit of that aspect completely.

Chanting.

Brendan Behan, Dielan Thomas, Churchill-hill, which one do you want?

Closes his eyes.

It's all right now, I'm picking him up.
Huh. I had to dress up in jodhpurs and show him the skid marks on my knickers.

Holding PEROWNE's hair.

I caught him creaming his pants once when the local lending library caught fire. He was a lesbian . . .

PEROWNE: It's Dylan Thomas?

MAURICE (rocking his head, trancelike): I'm catching Dieland Thomas leaving electro-magnetic patterns of himself outside the Black Horse and Cafe Ann. Anyone standing there now has cranial drunk patterns and changes into him. Their bowels get corrupted to his frequency. I have to get there first to save Perowne from his emissions and depolarize him on that score.

SADIE: Ha.

MAURICE (to PEROWNE, holding PEROWNE's head in his hands): Flashing Him Through to De-Imprint you, right?

PEROWNE nods.

MELODY: How the fuck can you do imprint anyone?

SADIE: FOLD UP YA FUNKY DISHRAG, that's how.

MAURICE (ignoring them, closing his eyes, and changing his voice: three syllables for the price of one, he speaks in Dylan Thomas's voice,

MELODY: Ah, CRANK UP YA TONGUE AN KEEP IT INSIDE YA HEAD.

GARY: THINKS HER STINKIN NASTY'S LINED WITH MINK.

SADIE: LOOK, SHITHEEL, GET OUTTA MY TRIP, OR I'LL BUST YA PROGRAMMED LITTLE NUTS!

MELODY: Anyone feel de-imprinted?

SADIE: Yeah! I'm beginning to!

GARY (*pointing at* MAURICE *indicating* SADIE): Tie her to your tail, she's just the right voltage for all that vintage schizoid shit.

and pours away the bottle of drink at the same time): Dieland Thomas being pumped thro me now to clear up Perowne's drunk tracks. I am no Boily Solitary Lover, Tuning Up his Unnotched nerve, and Crying OH MAN! BE MY SIMILE. I am the Ghost that Goes for Any thing in Sheets! But I shall sell the blind worm in my Thighs down the Old Kent Road.

Going back into his own voice.

I'm the heir to Shakespeare, he said to me; I said you're the anal heir, no one else's. Get off my back, you fuckin Druid tart.

PEROWNE gets up, smiles, and moves around the Slotpalace as if something has been taken off his shoulders, his movements now flowing where they were just now constricted. SADIE looks from MAURICE to PEROWNE, intrigued.

SADIE: I saw Dylan on the subway the other day. He had a green nosebag filled with laughing gas. One more breath and the whole history . . . the whole history of . . .

Almost psyched by the energy flowing between PEROWNE and MAURICE.

the whole history of something would have been different.

GARY: Oh man.

To PEROWNE.

Do you know why women can never deliver good

epigrams? It's because of the nature of the orgasm. A man's orgasm is INtensive, right, and a woman's orgasm is EXtensive.

MELODY: Sure is. Ha! Hey, she's talking about Bob Dylan an they're talking about Dylan Thomas. Everyone's Gettin Spread Around! We're getting right back into that Beatiful ego loss that we had going just now in the Photomaton.

GARY: Yeah!

Pointing at MAURICE and PEROWNE.

Hey, Let's get Five in One and One in Five!

PEROWNE disappears into the Photomaton. SADIE wanders off into another part of the Arcade.

MELODY (*pointing at* MAURICE): Yeah, let's spread EVERYONE around.

GARY: Get out your scratch pad Melody. Telegram. Museum of Modern Art New York. My name is . . . What's your name troll?

MAURICE: My sister slated it up to hollow me out. She stuck Maurice Chevalier, Maurice Kaufman and Maurice O'Dwyer on her pay roll before she did it.

GARY (*taking the bottle off* MAURICE): My name is Maurice, and I read of your forthcoming kinetic art exhibit. I will stand in front of wall C.2. (I have seen your map cum guide in the hallway), and I will drink myself to death in three days. Please give my forthcoming visit full coverage. When the public have seen your exhibit, me, and my kinetic death, they will leave your museum and go out into the street and look at people differently, which is your current squalid gambit. Please give my forthcoming visit full coverage . . .

MAURICE: Looooook! I can get drunk on the smell of lamp-post wine.

MELODY: Know what Joan of Arc said, Maurice? She said, I find if I drink heavily and then blow a loud whistle very hard, the voices go away.

Taking the bottle off GARY and handing it to MAURICE.

Here, this is what you want, isn't it? Go on, it's not every day that someone picks you up so good.

MAURICE: For me to say "it is," that's a prepared game. So, fuck off.

> Going closer.

Look, these personality techniques you're trying on me, any beatnik would scoff out of court. In fact, that beatnik would go back to his personality of 1946, and say I Don't Like The Cut of Your Jib, My Man, in order to finish you off . . . So, shove.

MELODY (*to* GARY): What kinda . . . What kinda . . . destination . . . he or she remind you of?

GARY: Destination?

MELODY: Yeah, like religious destination. Like Sheol, like Hades, yeah? Like Atlantis, Elysium, Valhalla, Gehinnom . . . Kismet.

GARY (*staring at* MAURICE): A bar, permanently open, like a running sore.

MAURICE (*shouting*): The drinks got nothing to do with me, you silly cunt. I was demagnetizing Perowne.

MELODY: Demagnetizing? Whatcha mean, demagnetizing?

MAURICE: All right. I'll put it very simply for you. I was being Perowne's Jesuit Confessor just then if you like. He said to me: The Divinity behaved hysterically at three points in HUMAN time: his birth, the marriage feast, and his death. I put my hand through the grill, I warmed up his balls, and I said: Never mind, father, the upper classes still call their dogs by working-class names.

MELODY: I don't understand.

GARY: Insane.

> To MELODY.

Who's PEROWNE anyway?

MELODY: YEAH! I mean, there's so much fuckin static in here you don't know Who's Who, do you?

> PEROWNE puts his head through the curtain of the PHOTOMATON.

PEROWNE: I can see what you're trying to do. Spreading

everyone around. It's entirely unnecessary. Spreading Maurice around anyway.

Coming out.

Maurice was in court the other day, and they asked him to give his name, and he said his name was Dead Wood pronounced East Light. There were several people present who could see that he was going to be asked Why, and prepared the appropriate expressions on their faces. Maurice said: Because my stomach thinks your throat is cut.

SADIE emerges laughing from the back of the Arcade.

MELODY (*pointing at her*): And I wouldn't suck you with HER mouth.
GARY: Aaaaah ha ha . . .

Moving toward PEROWNE.

We can spread YOU around though, can't we?
MELODY: Right.
GARY (*studying* PEROWNE): What kinda . . . sex, he or she remind you of??
MELODY: A wink-off. Takes two years.
GARY: Ha. And?
MELODY: Mmmm . . . Goosing people with records of Winston Churchill wartime speeches.
GARY: And?
MELODY: Fellatio. In the mouth of an alcoholic.
GARY: The Wrong Substance for the Wrong Appetite!
MELODY (*twitching, in imitation of* PEROWNE): It's not Ergonomic!
GARY: Perowne?
MELODY: Perowne.
PEROWNE: What are you doing here?
GARY: WE'RE COSMIC SHIT AND HER SPASM BAND!

They move around PEROWNE, snapping their fingers

PEROWNE: Do you play Music?
GARY: MUSIC? You know where Music is on the electro-magnetic spectrum? It's down there, by your feet. No,

man, we just get up on the stage an send out vibrations. Silent Vibrations.

MELODY: We send out silent mantras and mudras that
Kill people. We pick up on the audience. We steal all
THEIR vibrations, then we mess them all together and
we give them back to them Minus their egos.

PEROWNE: Where do you play?

GARY: Where? We gotta coupla gigs.

SADIE: We don't play anywhere. If we're sending out
vibrations, people will pick them up wherever they are.
We don't need any Stage for them to pick up on it.
We don't need any of that Media shit.

> PEROWNE smiles.

MELODY: We need a stage.

SADIE: Uhuh? well, drop down an get on it.

MAURICE (*to* GARY *and* MELODY): Perowne is a very
complicated person. You can't catch up with him.
With your tatty Chinese Portraits. He's So secretive
that one of these days he's going to disappear up his
own arsehole. He's a psycholinguist. He can kill off
hundreds of years of your lives with one joke, and so
can I. I'm his agent.

MELODY (*to* PEROWNE): What's you psychic color?

MAURICE: Whatever you say his psychic color is, he's
having it dyed.

> PEROWNE sits down, takes hold of SADIE's suit-
> case, and puts it on his lap. Then he goes through
> it, fondling a pink shirt inside it. He gradually
> pulls it out of the case and slowly furls it around
> his head, pulling it tighter and tighter.

GARY (*pointing at* PEROWNE): Hey, look at the soles of
his shoes. Wow. Look at them. Not a scratch, see. Not
a scratch on them.

MELODY: Yeah. He must lead a soft life.

GARY: Maybe his feet never touch the ground.

SADIE: Oh, what are you pokin up all these negative
vibes for?

MELODY: So that we can all take off again.

> GARY notices PEROWNE twisting the shirt tighter
> and tighter around his head.

GARY (*to* MAURICE): You sure you demagnetized him, huh? Because I'm still picking up a bit of karmic congestion there.

MAURICE: You are. And that's because of the TV program he was listening to. I've got to burn off that track right now.

> *To* SADIE.

Fuckin Newsreader leaving his live cigarette ends in Perowne's stomach 9.30.

> *To* PEROWNE.

What was one of the programs about?

PEROWNE (*turning, then twisting the shirt tighter and tighter, and pulling at his head*): Nepal . . . something . . . NEPAL.

> MAURICE darts around the Slotpalace, touching and pointing to the Slotmachines.

MAURICE: Autocue . . . Master Switch . . . Soundboom . . . Videophones . . . Flick flick . . . hello, this one's leaking sixty cycles a second to help us out.

> He stands behind the machine WEST CLUB, behind the raised glass of the broken machine, as if on TV.

Flick flick.

> He splays his hands, and waves them horizontally in front of his face. SADIE goes over and stands in front of the screen and near PEROWNE's chair. She meshes her fingers in front of MAURICE's face and vibrates them. She splays her hands and moves them quickly against each other, creating an optical illusion of flicker.

SADIE: STROBE STROBE FROM THE MONITOR SCREEN! LINE BEAT THE LINE BEATER!

> Moving her hands faster.

PSYCHIC TEEVEE STUDIOS!

MAURICE: I want it up to the critical flicker frequency.

> Pointing at SADIE's hands, MAURICE speaks

through the glass, only the top half of his body
visible. Mechanical chant.

ITV Newsroom 9.30 Caught you hollowing out Perowne's Travel Instincts and Striped Muscle Responses
in a Cheap Fuckin Way. Bio-Photo-Metric reduction
of Perowne 70 grams. Reduction of Perowne's capacitance, 17 microfarads.

To SADIE.

FASTER FASTER. These are the details omitted . . .

SADIE: These are THE DETAILS OMITTED, NEWS-
BUG!

GARY: Hey hey hey.

MELODY (*laughing*): He's really groovin on Sadie's head
now. Remember the time Sadie was so tripped out on
Marshall McLuhan she sprayed the TV with com-
munion wine an licked her way through the screen?

MAURICE (*shouting in a high chant, vibrating his hands,
creating flicker effect*): FASTER! FASTER! These are
the details omitted: In Nepal, CUNT, they believe in
Sympathetic Magic, and when a woman is late in
giving birth or a Cow in Calving, they rub their bellies
with RAILWAY tickets, as Railway Engines are the
fastest things they know. SO, NEWSREADER CUNT,
has my request for a Grip Bag filled with Concorde
Jet Plane tickets been televised? So that I can deliver
Perowne from all your pranky tenebrations at Top
Speed? NO. I know who is dealing with this, and I
also laughed at it, until I realized that it was child-
ishly seducing. In any case, the electrical "e" was
taken out of my name to Run the Concorde so you'd
have only been doubling up . . .

SADIE: We're Squashing you, Newsbug!

MELODY (*to* GARY): Hey, Sadie's gettin really leechy.
Tear her off.

GARY: SADIE! You're really beginning to warp the
beautiful buzz we had in that photomaton, right?

SADIE: That buzz gave me about as much charge as a
peanut butter sandwich.

MELODY: Oh, rip her off, it's spooky.

GARY (*to* MAURICE): Look, troll, what is it? Some boob
tube show that bugged you? Why don't you just com-
plain to the duty officer in charge of the station?

SADIE: Oh, jus listen to Eleanor Roosevelt.

MAURICE (*to* GARY): Not Only the Duty Officer, but also Program Reception Researchers, Personality Receptionists, and TV Relations Officers, ALL have the same legally endorsed speech patterns which are pitched at a certain decorative voltage so that they Cannot Ever release the Electrostatic Charge they've built up in you the night before.

He resumes.

It's got to be done like this.

GARY: Seems a bit like praying.

MAURICE: Not at all. TZZZZZZZAAAAAAHHHH! I'm getting my head out as an electromagnet to deflect the cathode rays. I'm setting up a smoothing cycle to damp down their energy fields. I'm sending out highly concentrated protein flux via various psychic rheostats to block them off, so shutup because I don't want you to abort any of my discharge mechanisms.

Flicking his hands faster.

TZAAAAAAH! TZAAAAAH! These are the details omitted. Bio-photogalvanic reduction of Perowne 200 amperes.

SADIE (*vibrating her hands in time with* MAURICE's): THESE ARE THE DETAILS OMITTED!

MAURICE (*mechanical chant, high speed*): FUCKIN MOB IN NEPAL, now working on a Version of the Absolute Mind, i.e. En-Soph of the Cabbala, Transfinite Sabbath of the Eternity, Interlocking Dharmadhati World Soul, and the Unfrequented Frequency, but YOU, Newscaster Cunt, and eye-contact-pattern-sludge, you DISMANTLED THAT, and parts of Perowne went out with it too . . .

MELODY: Whooops! the Cosmic Consciousness Freak Strikes Again.

GARY (*pointing at* SADIE): Yeah, I thought they'd given you JABS for Asian flu.

SADIE: LET HIM DO HIS SHOT!

MELODY: Of what? Groovin on your smashed up mind? Maybe we want some validation too.

SADIE: Let him do his shot. He's into HIS head,

Pointing at PEROWNE.

not mine. But if he IS pickin up on my head, I wanta
Complete Exegesis. I don't wanta be gouged out of
it. I don't want you to gyp me of any of my characteristics.

MELODY: Dig that, she's buckin fa promotion.

GARY (*pointing at* MAURICE): He's gonna gyp you of
your characteristics before you got to them yourself
baby.

SADIE: YEAH! He's Stereo Chemical Energy!

Flicking her fingers strobing her hands.

Right On, Maurice.

MAURICE (*vibrating his hands, and spitting at the mock
up TV screen. Rolling his head and eyes*): I'm sending out psychic laser beams so that they can never
come up with their version of Nepal before they did,
or psychometabolize Perowne's vibrations or Impound
His Energy on that score, and set up Negative Ion
EXCESS EVEREVER EVER EVER!

And if you don't believe me, turn the television on,
while I'm doing this, and you won't be able to understand what's going on.

MELODY (*shouting*): Who cares about television? It's
all Ted Serios. He can develop pictures on unexposed
film, just by thinking. He can develop thoughto-
graphic videotapes by remote control. Every program
is Ted Serios. All you gotta do is kill him. I bet you
never heard of him? He got there before you. He's
way ahead of you.

MAURICE's hand movements slow down; they
become more and more jerky. He twitches, and

contorts his hands and his head.

MAURICE: I can't Operate!

He points at MELODY.

I can't operate . . . She's hollowing me out. She's
trying to soak up all the fuckin electricity in here.

Shouting at MELODY.

I KNOW TED SERIOS. Last year with Ted Serios I went to the Wigmore Street Electrolysis Depilation Unwanted Hair Removal Clinic, and I got Twiggy's unwanted eyebrows, and Terence Stamp's armpits, and Bobby Kennedy's nasal clippings, and Elizabeth Taylor's crutch fud, all Put In Here,

> Pointing to his head.

so that PEROWNE could have an Economy Sized TV for easier to deal with. Just cut it off. CUT IT OFF.

> He turns back to the screen, and shouts at SADIE.

FASTER! FASTER!

> SADIE stares at him, then lowers her hands from in front of the screen and moves away.

FASTER! FASTER!

> GARY and MELODY laugh at him.

SADIE (*moving away*): Nah, I might get travel sick.

> SADIE goes over to the pinmachine BEAT TIME, and starts playing it. MAURICE follows her.

MAURICE: You're using mental traces of Their limb movements to go like that.

> MAURICE imitates one of SADIE's gestures, and points at GARY and MELODY. SADIE freezes slightly. MAURICE turns round and looks at PE-ROWNE, who is slowly emerging from under-neath the pink shirt. He untwists it and takes it off his head, smiling.

MAURICE: A Clean Break? Cleared that TV track?

PEROWNE (*smiling and stretching*): I feel good! I liked that!

> Standing up and clutching MAURICE.

I'll tell you something odd. The English Commercial channel I.T.V. was started at exactly the same time as they withdrew X-Ray machines from shoe shops.

> He moves around.

MELODY (*pointing at* SADIE): But howdja get so next to

HER, Maurice, like, you know, you never met her before, an she freaks on all those things you mentioned. TV and that . . . Howdja get so into her?

MAURICE: I masturbated in your favor last Tuesday.

GARY (*to* MELODY): Looks like we didn't lose that three-way buzz after all

MELODY (*stares at him and points at* SADIE): Yeah? we lost it.

> MAURICE goes over to MELODY, pulls her cheek away from his jaw, and makes cunt-slurping noises.

MAURICE: Charver, charver?

> MELODY ignores him. Pointing to her crutch.

Picks her nose and doesn't hand it round. Charver, charver?

> Pulling his cheek in and out, then stopping.

I don't want you to earth any of my currents anyway, unless you can earth them all.

> Looking up at PEROWNE.

Just trying to set up a little sex noise in her head, for you to listen to in case there was any plasma on that score left over by the boy with the heady views.

PEROWNE: Thank you.

MAURICE (*going over to* PEROWNE): I've cleared that sex track for you anyway, in another way.

PEROWNE: Yes?

MAURICE: Yes, Last Week, Inner London Sessions. Mrs. Gellot's bastard five-year-old pointed to me and said, "That man grabbed my privates." The judge said to him, "If I'd been him, you sex-mad little gossoon, I'd have cut them off and pickled them in aspic like St. Paul. So, Shove."

> TO PEROWNE.

A Clean Break?

PEROWNE: A clean break.

> He smiles.

GARY (*moving toward* PEROWNE): Don't you ever get like . . . Stump hallucinations? When Maurice has amputated all these areas of your personality, right? Do you ever get stump hallucinations?

PEROWNE: Slight tingling at the nerve endings, nothing more.

MAURICE: Ha!

Then he points at GARY and looking at MELODY.

You go with him? he'd rob his own granny and then scratch her fanny on the way out for a bit of skin.

GARY: Hey! I've hit it now! I've just picked up on his True lick. He's Hurtin Fa Pussy, Melody. Whatcha gonna do about it? Sex Terrorist!

MELODY: Look Maurice, lemme trim your head on one thing. If I ever get an itchy snatch, right, he does a bit of Vacuum talking, and he raises my skin to the same level as the itch, and he cures me of it for ever. Dig?

MAURICE: I don't Need that, you see. I was sold fifteen thousand sticky second-hand comes, Wandsworth Registry Office, 1959, and I had to keep her stench on my rod for five years after she died in order to combat Hugh Hefner and all the other sex revolution Stalinists.

Watching PEROWNE moving free, and grabbing him.

Look at him! Quite a few more people than me like him too, because he's trained his mouth to go up at the corners instead of down, which cost him seven amps, but he's making up for it by spreading himself very thin.

PEROWNE smiles.

GARY (*to* PEROWNE): Do you like Americans?

PEROWNE: Five years ago you would still impress them by showing them a reproduction of Van Gogh. Two years ago you had to show them the real thing. Now you have to give them his ear.

MAURICE: See! See! I switched him fit!

He disappears.

GARY (*moving toward* PEROWNE, *baring his teeth as he speaks*): Know what the G.I's do now? they take a lot of acid, and acid gives them a very perfect sense of timing, see. Soon as they kill a Cong, they rip off his pants, and plunge their pricks into his ass, and they know just the right moment to catch his death throes in order to get their rocks off.

MELODY: Yeah. Everyone's speedy on death. There's a cat laying down this trip now that Cancer's some kind of Pearl being cultivated by Human Oysters.

PEROWNE: What for?

MELODY: I don't know.

GARY (*to* PEROWNE): They assassinated the man who invented the nylon stocking which wouldn't run, they assassinated the man who invented the match which you could strike twice, they assassinated the man who invented the permanent light bulb.

SADIE: If they'd forcefed everyone with a bit of Kennedy's corpse, maybe they'd have cooled out on the others.

MELODY: America's just a broken-down old vending machine, and the only thing to do is to kick it and kick it and kick it again.

GARY (*to* PEROWNE): Shall I tell you the Great American Secret? It's written into the American Constitution in Invisible Ink. Put a hot iron on it, and you can bring it up. Item: Fellow Americans, always remember that killing fires more of your brain cells than fucking.

SADIE: Everyone's fixin ta die. They been told Death Is Pure Sensation!

PEROWNE: So how many people are there left?

GARY: About three. And they're South African. Two men and a woman. They're flashing them through to me right now. On 42nd Street. Two men and a woman. They're so ashamed of what they're doing to the woman, they're killing her.

     Closing his eyes.

     They've killed her. Now they're so ashamed of what they're doing to each other, they're digging her up.

SADIE: An what are you doing about it?

MELODY: What are You doing about it?

     Pointing at MAURICE.

Just Splitting an scoring yourself a Freak!

SADIE: YEAH! Who else is gonna keep me so spaced
out that I can forget about that shitpile and about
the two mementoes of that shitpile I was dumb enough
to bring with me? A FREAK! A FREAK!

MELODY: Sadie's really pullin all the vibes out of synch
now.

GARY: Yeah.

Going over to PEROWNE.

Hey, tell me something. Has Maurice Really straight-
ened out your head? You don't really get a pump out
of him, do you?

SADIE: Sure he does. Maurice is satirizing attitudes
which haven't yet arisen.

GARY: Yeah, an if the bomb goes off, make sure you get
higher than the bomb. We know.

MELODY (moving over to PEROWNE): No, what's he
really do for you? Because I get the feeling you're
gonna put him down very soon. Just the way your
face changes, when he comes on . . . Little muscles
moving, then you cancel it out very quickly with a
little smile . . .

GARY: That's called "Intermittent Reinforcement," that's
the strongest schedule for keepin behavior going. Any
behavior you want.

MELODY: Hey! You're a Control Freak! Come here, Control Freak!

They grab hold of each other.

PEROWNE (to SADIE): Why did you leave?

SADIE: They've just discovered that dead black flesh is
very rich in uranium isotopes. That's why.

PEROWNE (stares at her): Americans. I don't know
about Americans. They talk about meaningful relationships all the time, when you know that the most
meaningful relationship they can conceive of is the
relationship between the murderer and his victim . . .

SADIE: Mmmmm.

GARY and MELODY are clustered together, MAU-
RICE reappears and goes over to them.

MAURICE: I was completely dehydrated once, and my body was so dry that I doubled the capacitance of my plasma membranes and excitory fibers. I built up a huge surface charge of static electricity. I could lay my hands on Perowne's head, and wads of hair would come out by simple electrostatic action.

GARY: Ha!

MELODY: Hey, remember little Frankie?

GARY: Oh yeah, tell him about little Frankie.

MELODY: He pissed on an electric fence once, an his voice never broke.

MAURICE: Come here, come here. You were thinking about the police ten seconds ago, right? Now, my electricity's been PROVED, you see. It's down to the collagen in the bone, and under shearing stress, the cross linkages in the chain molecules of the collagen will result in a displacement of electric charge. NOW, if you're HOLDING, you know?

MELODY: Like, like dope?

MAURICE: Anything like that. And the Police is coming toward you along the street, you put your hands like this

> He holds his hands together away from his body, in a ring.

and they won't Dare accost you. Because it's alchemy. It forms a Circuit. An insulated circuit. Skin wavelengths of five to twenty mu. And they won't Dare accost you, because you're not giving them any Base Terminal to convert your currents to their frequency . . .

MELODY: What about your Head, that's a Base Terminal, isn't it?

GARY: No cop that I ever met went on a head trip.

MELODY: Ha.

MAURICE: They won't dare accost you

> Separating his hands.

unless you break the circuit, and then you get your collar felt.

MELODY: Hey, that's Beautiful!

GARY: A Fairy Ring to Fuck the Fuzz!

MAURICE goes over to PEROWNE and holds his hand. GARY puts his hands round MELODY's waist and forms a circuit. He squeezes her, kisses her. SADIE stares at them.

SADIE: Try it out in Chicago, sagnuts. Look at it.

Pointing at them.

That's the Seed Shit. That's the Start of the Whole Poison. Just that. That little gesture. Oooo oOOOOO- ooH she's MINE.

GARY: You wanna get laid again Sadie?

MELODY (to GARY): You're so stoned you couldn't find your way to her cockpit. Could you?

GARY: Ha. You wanna get laid Sadie?

SADIE: No thanks. I never do it properly with less than twenty people. I like to spread the load. I like to spread the charge . . .

GARY: What about Maurice? He's twenty people.

MELODY: He's THIRTY people. Don't hand us that shit, Sadie.

SADIE: I wouldn't. My shit travels badly.

GARY and MELODY rub up against each other ostentatiously.

SADIE (moving round them): That's where it was at the whole time. That's the only fuckin flash you been after. Whyntcha go an bury yourselves in a cave for five years an SEW yourselves together?

GARY: That'd be groovy.

GARY rubs up and down against MELODY, jerking his pelvis and then looking provocatively at SADIE.

SADIE (advancing on them, and pointing to GARY's crotch): You really think I need that, don't you? Prick. PRICK!

MELODY: I think she's after some binary fission.

SADIE: Yes. I am. But I'm not getting it from there.

Pointing at GARY's crotch.

That's a three-billion-year-old con. My vaginal walls were built in Berlin. There's no sensation there. There's no such thing as a vaginal orgasm, dig? That's a three-billion-year-old male supremacist con.

GARY: Oh, come on, Sadie. What about that time you were telling us where you put some mercury up your cunt, then get on a hammock, roll around from side to side until you bring yourself off?

SADIE: Mercury's got a very high boiling point. Pricks got a very low one.

> Pointing at MELODY, who's touching GARY's crotch, moving her finger down his thigh, and over his fly.

Look at her, tripping out on that gruesome bit of snail flesh.

> To GARY.

You really think that when the chips are down, that that's the thing that's gonna finally cool me out. Dontcha? Prick. Prick skyscraper. Prick argument. Prick gun. Prick robbery. Prick fuckin bullets. Prick-a-dickadildo dontosaurus. Well, dig this, my clitoris is a transistorized prick. Everything's tending towards greater and great miniaturization, right? And my clitoris is a security leak from the future.

> Pointing at GARY's crotch.

So, how much of yours did they trim, kid?

MELODY: He's still got a pretty little lace frill.

SADIE: Yeah?

> To GARY.

Well, GET INTO IT, an cut the rest off. Bring yourself up to date. Then treat yourself to a sandwich or shove it round the corner up your dirt track where it belongs. I don't need it. MY WHOLE BODY IS A COCK!

MELODY: She's speeding on pussy power again.

GARY: Yeah. Always a nice dry little fuck in that number.

MELODY: You didn't pick up on that, didja Maurice, when you were groovin on her head back there . . .

GARY: No, so now you got it double strength.

SADIE: Ah, stop trying ta whale the tar outta me.

> Horning in on MELODY.

All right, so you got a sharp little come-on, you're for integrated toilets or some shit . . . and you're into a little pot ego-loss for decoration, but at Gut level, you're into the same territory-sex-adrenalin bullshit as the stone men who run the insurance companies. Shoot, you're just a bag of meat aintcha, waitin for some john to buy you the right gold doorstep to clean. PAIR BINDING PROPERTY PIGS!

MELODY: I think Sadie's getting a bit paranoid.

GARY: Right, and you know the only thing to do with paranoia? You Ride right into it, just like you'd ride into a skid.

MELODY: Ha.

SADIE: I dig a bit of paranoia sometimes. It keeps your antennae bright. Where's that oh so groovy little communal buzz you were laying on me, huh? "Up into the air, junior birdmen?" Huh? You were just using me as an in-off for your tacky little sex trips. Fuckheads.

GARY: Oh, stop comin on like some amphetamine mutant.

SADIE: You're agents from the abattoir, same as everybody else. You're just Mr. and Mrs. Jones.

MELODY (to MAURICE): Sadie can only experience people through aggression. I hope you're prepared for that.

MAURICE (separating from PEROWNE, who he's been holding hands with all the time, and going over to SADIE): I don't like those two people any more. I thought I liked her, but then she started combing her hair, and I picked up on her comb crackling. She was trying to short circuit some of my transmissions against the TV . . .

SADIE: Too right she was. They're two TV sets! THEY'RE MEDIA TURDS! Look at this she carries next to her heart.

> Ripping a necklace with a plastic picture from MELODY's neck.

Who's this? Now who's this?

MELODY (separating from GARY): Give it back.

SADIE (waving the necklace, catching it and looking at the picture inside): It's Mick Jagger.

MELODY: Give it back!

SADIE: It's Mick Jagger. Now the cat that gets him, he's really gonna get it off.

To MELODY.

MEDIA TURD.

Dig this, Maurice, this cat's had sixteen million teeny bopper orgasms laid on him, so the cat that gets him, an it won't be long now after Altamont, he's really gonna get it off. He's really gonna pick a heavy duty flash . . . He's really gonna get loaded behind THAT charge when he rips it off.

MELODY: You're Evil Sadie. You're really Evil.

SADIE: Better than being a TV set.

GARY: Can I have that photograph?

SADIE: What for? to track him down? You'll find him.

Silence.

MELODY: Shutup. That's how things start.

GARY: You're casting spells, Sadie.

MELODY: That's how things get set up.

Silence.

SADIE: Brought yourselves down with you negative shit, an now you're lookin for fall guys.

MELODY: Oh come on Sadie. You got the little buzz you came for.

SADIE (*staring at her*): What? WHAT?

Prowling round them, touching MAURICE.

You leucotomized even the fuckin taste of it before I could get into it. MAURICE? You wanta know the Real reason I left America? Take this: the Bird Man of Alcatraz spent twenty years storing up electricity, and then some jive Hollywood film unit comes along and they throw the switches, and they spend it all in five minutes. They burn him down. They BURN that fucker down. I know who it was. And they're his fuckin agents. Look at him.

Pointing to GARY.

He's using perforated back scatter left over from the Rosenberg case to operate a facial tic that he's got, to give himself an air of intelligence, but he doesn't acknowledge it, of course he doesn't. He likes to think of himself as an unfrequented frequency. And if he was here now, I'd gut him. Only he isn't, because he knows I wouldn't like to do the Rosenbergs any damage . . .

MELODY: HANG ON TO YOUR PLUMAGE MAURICE, SHE'S GONNA STEAL IT ALL!

GARY: Yeah! MINDSWAP! Clickety Clit.

> Pointing his fingers, and switching one hand across the other.

MINDSWAP!

MELODY: Yeah! Some Real Grid Leakage now!

GARY: She's eating out your head Maurice.

MELODY (*cupping her ears*): Can you hear a faint hum? Wow. ALTERNATING FIELD VORTICES, AND MINDSWAP!

> SADIE stares at them.

SADIE: KIYYYYYYYYYYYYYYYYYYYYAAAAAAAAAAAAAA AAAAAAAAAAAAHHHHHHHHHHHHHH!

GARY: Well. Well, I guess that raises me out.

MELODY: Yeah, me too.

> GARY and MELODY move toward the exit.

MELODY (*holding GARY*): Hey, I bring you down?

GARY: I don't know . . . I'm no great judge of distance.

> They leave. SADIE flings the necklace across the floor. She turns to MAURICE.

SADIE: You got me out of a whole bag, Maurice.

MAURICE: Yes, but I've only got to rub a few heads and I can get that bag back for you.

SADIE: I don't want it back. You cleared all my tracks. I finally left Amerikaka. You cleared all my tracks. Yeaaah! I'm goin solo.

MAURICE: You are hollowing me out. I was clearing Perowne's tracks.

> Looking inside the PHOTOMATON.

Where's Perowne?

SADIE (*moving toward him*): You didn't mind me borrowing some of your freak juice to finally flip them with, did you? Dig what I was doing. I was gathering up All their fuckin vibes into one big greaseball and pitchin them into the No-Osphere, there to be purified and never to descend, You dig that? You like that? Ha.

> MAURICE is standing inside the PHOTOMATON. He clutches the curtain hanging down in front of the PHOTOMATON, and twists it round his neck.

MAURICE: They're flashing Hitler through to me now. "What's that in the corner of your mouth," I said. "Quicklime," he says. "It's quicklime." "No, NO, be-FORE that," I said. "I don't know the technical word for it," he said.

DIRECT CURRENT

PEROWNE's room. PEROWNE and MAURICE are sitting at a table with some cards in front of them.

Three walls are covered with pictures of personalities, arranged in lines. Like sheets of stamps. About two thousand.

A bank of video-screens.

PEROWNE (*pinching a tacky card several times with his finger and thumb*): Do you call these cards? They're more like Farley's rusks.

MAURICE: I shuffled them.

PEROWNE: You'd need a cement mixer.

PEROWNE picks up a newspaper. He stares at it, twitching slightly. MAURICE watches him.

MAURICE: Elizabeth Taylor came round Playland last Tuesday. She asked me to take her round the back. I had to chew her clitoris for seven hours.

Twitching slightly.

I got media rash all over my body.

PEROWNE looks up at him, smiles.

MAURICE: Gave me an insight into all the media victims all over the world, that did.

PEROWNE: Mmmn.

MAURICE (*almost to himself*): Tried to think of her face afterward. Couldn't get it. I tried to think of her face afterward to give me a hard-on to fuck someone else with. No good. Couldn't get it. Gone to dust . . .

PEROWNE smiles.

MAURICE: Just media rash, all over my body.

Silence.

MAURICE: Perowne, I got eighteen different speech tracks, haven't I? I mean I have to have, because of the environmental bombardment. I have to have eighteen different speech tracks . . . enough to soak up all the vibration excrement, and acting as psychic rheostat to spare them hitting you all the time.

PEROWNE: Yes.

MAURICE: But I . . . I wanted to . . .

PEROWNE: Mmmn?

MAURICE: I wanted to . . . THERE'S SO MUCH PRINT THROUGH ON THE TRACKS YOU SEE? I wanted to . . . I wanted to take the edge off it, just a bit. I thought, Maurice, you're getting into too many shapes. Like . . . here.

> Pointing to his head.

I went to see someone.

PEROWNE: Who?

MAURICE: It was getting into too many shapes.

PEROWNE (*leaning forward*): That's all right. Nothing wrong in that.

MAURICE: I went to see someone.

PEROWNE: Who?

MAURICE: Someone.

PEROWNE: WHO?

MAURICE: He gets an erection from the vibrations from mental hospitals. He has smoked glass on his car. He likes to have people clocking him twenty-four hours a day. He gets a buzz off their eyes, but he's very ashamed of this unprofessional weakness, so, he has smoked glass on his car.

> Pause.

I smashed my fist through his car window once. Got lampblack all over my sleeve.

PEROWNE: Huh.

> Goes back to the paper.

MAURICE: Don't go back into that, Perowne. I want to see him. I thought: If I can hollow Him out, I can scotch the whole mechanism, for you, for good. Smash up the whole psychophagic powerhouse. You are who you eat, right? It's going on all the time, all right; but THIS man's got an Omnivorous fuckin appetite. He's a fuckin cannibal. I rang him up.

PEROWNE: Who does he answer the phone to?
MAURICE: Oh, only the most decorative schizos. Only the most picaresque.

> Pause.

Scots accent.

> He points to the wall of photos.

PEROWNE (*glancing at the wall*): Oh, I know who you mean. He used to work as an underpaid leucotomist in Glasgow.
MAURICE: Right. Scots accent. I said: "How many patients you steal that Scots accent off? Pay them all back." "Your voices are shortening your life," he said. "So's yours," I said, "and there's more people propping up your voice, poor sods, so your voice is shortening my life at double strength."
PEROWNE: Ha. Then what?
MAURICE (*Scots accent*): "Come round anyway, we'll have a pilot lunch." Couple of dog rolls and a raw wimpy. "We'll lop off some of your extensions." Now I could have used a certain combination of words to buzz-saw his medulla then, an leucotomize him completely. But at that point it would have been too early, and it'd have left a few scraps over for his doubles to live off. I had to hollow him out completely.
PEROWNE: So you went around?
MAURICE (*nods*): "Well what started it off," he said. Well, doctor, I said. It doesn't feel like me talking. It's not me interested in talking, you know, so to an extent it's not me talking. And I've got to get rid of it, haven't I?

> Winking at PEROWNE.

It's a pony tail haircut inside me talking.
PEROWNE: That must have touched him where he liked it.
MAURICE: YEAH! he almost CAME. "It's NOT," he said, "you are talking In response to my version of you."
I've got beyond that years back, I said.
"You're not," he said. "Look.

> MAURICE stands up.

What you are is based on my totalization of you. My totalization of you, fed back into you, is what you are."

"Look at it now," he said, "there's an escalation of totalizations.

> MAURICE raises his left hand.

Your totalization of Me

> MAURICE raises his right hand.

My totalization of You

> Raising his left hand higher.

Your totalization of Me

> Raising his right hand higher.

My totalization of Your META Self

> Raising his left hand higher.

Your totalization of My META Self."

> Raising his right hand higher, bringing his left hand level with it, and slapping his hand violently together.

Exactly, I said, and I'm beyond that. Stop trying to verb me up, because what you say doesn't last any longer than the length which you take to say it. Whereas what I say, I'm converting into protein molecules, tied to the backs of neutrinos, going Straight through you and coming out the other side. I had your mind in 1935, and it was a messy little fuck then. Sod your totalizations. There are too many people in London with their trouser pockets all joined together, and you're just adding to the mess. GIVE ME THE JUICE.

"The concept of cure," he said, "is very outmoded."

CURE? I want the juice.

"We're trying to help you to hang on to what may be a very precious experience. Electric shock treatment, if that's what you're referring to, is only used by the Sergeant Majors of the industry. We're Officer Class . . ."

And all this time, Perowne, he's marching round

the inside of my head, grabbing every bit of electricity he can lay his hands on.

PEROWNE: Stealing his patients' best ideas to give his trips a little local color.

MAURICE: THAT'S YOUR MAN! He's the root virus. He's the terminal Adjustive psychologist. But he still doesn't acknowledge them . . . his bastard patients are put down as "D" or "F.M." or Occasionally "Arthur," whereas he has his Own name come up fifteen times in the credits.

"Oh, so you've read my books?" he said.

"I read your books at source."

"GIVE ME THE JUICE DOCTOR. I like it. I need it. NOW."

He started getting slippery. He wanted to talk to me about sublimation. I said, "How can you ride a bicycle and pull your pudding at the same time, or fight a war? If you could you should be in a fuckin circus. GIVE ME THE JUICE."

He said it was unfashionable: Electro-Convulsive Therapy.

The Last True Mental Fuck on Earth, and you get Puritanical?

He said I should keep listening to him talking. Total voltage of his talk: two volts. "YOU'RE STARVING ME, DOCTOR. I've been graduated. They've been running the Rolling Bones Eamonn Andrews Joe Pyne show off me for seventeen years, and now they're masturbating my electricity into a fuckin nightclub called Electric Circus, Electric Lotus, and a pop group called the Electric Grape even fetching my car battery sluggish, and Even a shitty little film, POOR COW, poncing off spurious distinctions of Working Class, when they KNOW that anyone who does any work at all is only trying to muscle in on my masturbation fantasy, which is all any work is . . . They're Stealing my electricity to describe THAT Crock of Shit as a Thousand VOLT SHOCKER . . . They're Stealing my electricity, all down the line! SO, Give me the Juice, you bitch."

PEROWNE smiles.

MAURICE: "You talk too much about electricity," he said.

"WHO STARTED ME OFF?" I said. "Who injected ideas about electricity into the fuckin mental trade? You did, with your fuckin shock machine."

"Not me," he said.

"LOOK, I don't want any pansified inter-departmental squabbles. I want the electronic tapeworms in my stomach INVESTIGATED. I want Warren Beatty tying his tampax strings to the short hairs of my cunt, I want him INVESTIGATED. I want the wires in my head INVESTIGATED. I want the people in the next room transmitting amnesiac blocks so that I can't tell which thought I'm going to have next, I want them INVESTIGATED. I don't want these landmarks of my flying fuckin sensorium ASSIMILATED by "How Colorfully Allegorical of the Human Condition." I want them INVESTIGATED. Go back to the slab. Get neurological. Hire A.J. Cronin as your scriptwriter. I'll pay. OR, GIVE ME THE FUCKIN JUICE!"

PEROWNE: Then what?

MAURICE: He was pacing up and down, pacing up and down. Then he stood over me. Implying that I could have some of the luster reflected from his white coat.

PEROWNE: In exchange for what?

MAURICE: ANYthing . . . anything. He's always on the fuckin sleeve. But I'd really started to gut him now. He was pacing up and down. I was saying things like: You see, doctor, I'm very grateful for the E.C.T. If it wasn't for the Electro-Shock Therapy, I'd never have had the technical qualifications for that job in Play-Land, would I? Ha. I was running him flat. He left the room.

PEROWNE: Did he come back in?

MAURICE: Yeah, but while he was out, I thought, well, why don't I give him something to help him go Straight? So I stood up and had a little pee in the sugar bowl. The pink spot, right? in the urine of every schizophrenic. DIMETHOXYPHENYLATHYLAMIDE. He comes back in. He's a bit edgy. "GIVE ME THE JUICE, DOCTOR."

"Well," he says, "we've got some . . . some Stuff."

"Stuff?"

"Yes, sometimes if I'm in a corner, I find that . . ." And he's holding it out to me on a little bit of blotting paper. "STUFF? You tried to give that to Tuffnell last week, didn't you? And you remember what he said to you? He said I've been sufficiently attentive to death's sublimations throughout my life not to need an early warning system. STUFF? That corner you mentioned is one shape at five o'clock and another shape entirely at five past. I don't need your stuff to make me realize that. And I know exactly how it would go down: standing behind me with your Tibetan machine gun saying GO ON, Be Introspective, Go on, Now's Your Total Cosmic Chance. STUFF???? I want the spriochaete, not the symptoms. GIVE ME THE JUICE."

PEROWNE: Mmn. You didn't take the stuff?

MAURICE: No, I wanted the juice. What else had he got? Fuckin verbing people up all his life. I'd run him flat almost. I'd put him right in the fuckin donniker.

PEROWNE: So he had a cup of tea?

MAURICE: He had a cup of tea full of my pee. With sugar. A cup of tea full of my pee, and then he went Right Up the fuckin pictures. All wrapped up in suede and smugness one minute, then suddenly he drops off the chair, kicks his sandals off, heels flying in the air: "I CAN SEE THE SUN—I'M IN THE SUN . . . I'M FRAGMENTING WITH THE SUN . . ." Come on, you can do better than that. "I'm in the sun." Tchah. You'll bankrupt yourself paying for the press cuttings.

"MY COCK IS CORUSCATING SOLAR AUREOLES —I'M SYPHONING OFF THE SUN'S RADIATION AND CORONAL CALORIES 1,000,000 A SECOND AND TYING IT UP TO MY WORLD INFLUENC-ING MACHINE . . . AAAAAAH HAAA HAAAAA HAAAAA . . . SO WHAT THE HELL DO I NEED YOUR TWENTY WATTS FOR?"

He stepped on his own prick there.

"I'M IN THE SUN—OUT OF MY BODY—ETHERIC DOULBES IN THE NEW AGE OF LEO! I'M IN THE SUN WITH THE BIRDS OF PARADISE." Bird of paradise? That's a raw wimpy stuck in front of your face. He hadn't eaten any of his pilot lunch. EAT IT UP. Wouldn't. Trying to get high on protein deficiency as well. Huh. MacGuinness has been contact high on Oxfam since 1912 . . .

"I'M IN THE SUNNNNNNNN! BINARY POLARI-ZATIONS AND EPICYCLICAL PRAXES! CATHEC-TIC PARADIGMS AND CHANGING WORLD FUNC-TION WITH UMBRELLA CONSENSUAL SCHEMES . . . I'VE GOT THE OVER VIEW OF THE META VIEW OF THE MEGA SYNTHESIS!

"You've got nothing. All you've got is a bit of polari picked up from a couple of half-chat existentialists and ex-wobblies.

"I'M IN THE SUNNN!!" Look Icarus, there's no need for that. There's a planetoid called Icarus with or-bital eccentricity of point eight three, and it's come ninety miles closer since you got on the floor. "I AM THAT PLANET!" Yeah? It's killed two thousand people already with its gravitational pull, earthquakes India China, freak snow storms Arizona, and tidal waves in the Aleutians. When it gets a bit closer, It'll suck the sea up 500 foot and drown you and your second-hand visions.

"I'M INNNN THE SUNNNNN." You been mixing with some low-lifers. I made the sun a dead letter years back . . .

Faintly.

"I'M IN THE SUNNNNN.

Looking down on to the floor.

"I'M

IN

THE

sunnnnnn . . ."

TCHACH. Give me the fuckin juice.

PEROWNE: Was he in a position to then?

MAURICE: I lopped off all his extensions. He's lying on the floor. He's rubbing his joystick. Trying to set fire to himself. I pulled all the muscles in his head. I stomped him into the carpet. He's not going to eat anyone else.

Pause.

PEROWNE: Don't you think it left you a bit shopsoiled,
seeing him?

MAURICE: No. After I seen him, there was so much electricity in my body, the whole telephone exchange
went dead.

PEROWNE: What's happened to him now?

MAURICE: Now? He's so fuckin paranoid he's had to
have his eyelids pierced.

Pause.

I hollowed him out for good, didn't I? I paralyzed that
people eater for good.

> MAURICE turns the television on. PEROWNE stares
> at MAURICE, smiles slightly, then bends down
> and stares at SADIE's suitcase. He takes her pink
> shirt out, fondles it, then drapes it over his body,
> and puts his hand underneath it. Pointing his
> finger, he simulates a nipple, moving under the
> surface of the material.

PEROWNE: I believe that in Electro Shock Therapy an
Alternating Current is less injurious to the brain than
a Direct One, unless . . . unless one frequently
changes the polarity.

> MAURICE stares at him. The television comes on.
> The bank of video screens start rolling. Volume
> wobble. Some heavy psychic static from the wall
> of photos.

PEROWNE: WHY DON'T YOU DO SOMETHING ABOUT
THAT! Instead of making philistine jokes about doctors being madder than their patients.

MAURICE: I DID MORE THAN THAT! PSYCHIATRY
PSYCHOLOGY of any Good is above LOVE, Getting
Close to People through LOVE, and anything that falls
short of that is no Good. And he was 17,000 protein
holograms short of LOVE. Fancy starting a love affair
with "Totalizations of your cathectic meta-selves."
The only psychiatrists of any good are the ones who
fuck with their patients. I went back there two days
later and taught him love. He was still on the floor
where I'd left him, so I ripped off his trousers and
rogered him. I put a sperm bung in his arsehole to

keep the pink spot from coming out. It was the least I could do.

> PEROWNE contorts his body. The Media Load gets heavier. The video screens start mounting a surge of news bulletins and programs. The Wall of Photos starts humming.

PEROWNE: I SAY, MAURICE! I SAY WHEN ARE YOU GOING TO DO SOMETHING ABOUT THAT! See that TV? That TV causes choromosome damage. See that TV? Listen to it. That miserable version of coherence trying to fire cells in my brain that I dismantled years back.

> Pointing to an image on the screen.

Why don't you infect THAT man with your schizophrenia, with all your subvocal speech patterns, so that he finds it completely impossible to TALK in that residual way? I mean, when are you going to mop up all these dead co-ordinate points? WHEN ARE YOU GOING TO MOVE, MAURICE? WHEN ARE YOU GOING TO NEUTRALIZE ALL THIS So That I Can REALLY take off?

> MAURICE stares at him, then goes over to the radio, takes the back off it, pulls out a valve, and crushes it with his foot.

MAURICE: Fuckin roach.

> Pointing at the radio.

Whenever I have an expression on my face, he AMENDS it with an expression on his. Worse than a sex maniac. But it never ENDS with him. It never comes to the crunch. He tried to do it then, didn't he? But his expression didn't interlock, HA, so he got no purchase on it . . .

PEROWNE (*pointing to the TV*): THEY'RE ALTERING MY NEURAL RHYTHMS. THEY'RE PULLING THEM INTO SYNCH WITH THEIR NEURAL RHYTHMS. THEY'RE CODING ALL MY CELLS. WHAT ARE YOU DOING ABOUT IT? THE WHOLE ATMOSPHERE NEEDS CLONING. WHAT ARE YOU DOING ABOUT IT???

MAURICE: I've gone down in history before, but I've always come up for a shit and a shave . . . I'll de-magnetize it for you, Perowne . . . I'll rub it all off . . .

> Skidding round the room, staring and pointing at the screen, splaying his hands toward them. Pointing at one screen.

I had to suck Richard Nixon's cock once. In a home movie called "Parental Advice." He had galloping knob rot as well, but I scraped it off and fed it to the mice. After that he put us all on double bubble, so I thanked him for it and set about his wife. A clean break?

PEROWNE: I can't feel ANYTHING. When are you going to move?

> Pointing at another image on the screens.

Look at HER!

MAURICE: Tchach. That oscillating dumb show and de-mobilized skin pageantry has been on my back since 1951, trying to pull the carpet from under my feet. Know what she's really saying, Perowne? "I'm not working for the International Stench Factory. I'm not pulling the carpet from underneath your feet every-where you tread." NO, because she's fuckin wearing it out. Oh, "Nobody understands me," she says . . .

> Pointing at the screen. Still image of Virna Lisi.

But she still carries on with disseminating what they're told by law to call their filthy unapproachability . . .

> Turning to PEROWNE.

Ha. That rub her off for you? THAT RUB HER OFF?

> PEROWNE makes no response. MAURICE turns off all the TVs and video screens.

I'm wearing out all her electrical movements now Perowne. I'm wearing out all her facial movements. Watch inside my head. I'm fuckin slamming her. I'm spreading out her fuckin resonance. I'm fuckin cauter-izing her bio-electrically.

PEROWNE stands up, twitching still, picking up on the media. Twitching, then looking at MAURICE. SADIE comes into the room. She moves toward her suitcase. PEROWNE smiles at her. Cools out immediately.

PEROWNE (*to* MAURICE): Why don't you turn your mind into a neutrino trap? Neutrinol's carry no electric charge.

MAURICE (*scowling*): A lead wall twenty lightyears thick has only got a fifty-fifty chance of trapping a neutrino, so that is handy.

Pointing to the wall of photos, now silent, and the bank of screens.

Everytime I slash their tentacles, You flash through some More people to me, and I have to scrape the mess off.

PEROWNE stares at him, then shrugs his shoulders.

Hitler had to eat his own shit, to stop rival black magicians getting hold of it, and all his nail parings and all his hair cuttings. Why can't you be that tidy?

PEROWNE: What are you talking about?

MAURICE (*pointing to the wall of photos, the TVs and the radio*): ALL THAT, AND ALL THAT, AND ALL THAT!

PEROWNE: I don't know. I never look at them. It's a kind of miscegenation.

MAURICE: Yeah, an part of your phone number's unlisted. Never look at them.

To SADIE.

HE'S FUCKIN PARALYZED BY THEM. Perowne's trying to rat on me.

SADIE stares at him.

I've given you enough planks to walk on.

MAURICE moves toward the door.

PEROWNE (*to* SADIE): Maurice was talking about his mind. Maurice's mind is totally porous.

MAURICE: Poor as piss.

He starts at PEROWNE and then leaves the room. PEROWNE folds up the newspaper on the table and then goes over to the pile of newspapers in the corner, puts it on top of the pile, and replaces the large metal magnet that belongs on top of them.

SADIE: Why don't you just buy heavier newspapers?

SADIE looks at the shirt PEROWNE has been fondling and puts it back into the suitcase.

PEROWNE: I must say. I like your shirt.

SADIE twists a loose flap of the shirt she has on. Not knowing whether PEROWNE is referring to this or the one in the bag. She twists a loose flap of the shirt, almost edgily, furls and unfurls it round her finger. Tucks it back in. PEROWNE goes over to SADIE, pulls the flap of shirt out, smooths out the wrinkles, tucks it back in.

SADIE: I LIKE YOUR SHIRT? What's that? My feedback loops have gotten a little bit more selective than that. "I like your shirt?" Didn't you know: any personalization paralyzes the system for at least three seconds.

She counts a two-second pause.

I like my shirt.

Laughs.

PEROWNE (smiles, then looks toward the door and then back to SADIE): Prove your vibrations.
SADIE: What's that?
PEROWNE: Somebody said to Maurice the other day: Prove what you call your vibrations. Maurice said: Tell yourSELF a joke, and then watch everyone around you laughing.
SADIE: Ha. Maurice's mind can get into anything. Every fuckin word he says is like a joint. You live with him or something?

SADIE walks around the room, taking in the TVs and then the Wall of Photos.

Sheeeeit, LOOK AT THAT! Wow. That really taps the needle. It's a Mandala, right?

> PEROWNE makes no response, seeing MAURICE come back in with his fingers curled and ringing his eyes like spectacles. He crouches and stares at SADIE.

MAURICE: My staring at her is a unified field theory which will account for everything. She can't stare at me because she's not my eye doctor.

SADIE (*staring at him*): I got things going for me, right?

> She blows at him with her mouth.

PHEWT! PHEWT!

> MAURICE leaves. SADIE stares at PEROWNE. PEROWNE looks cowed. SADIE looks back at the wall of Photos.

SADIE: Hey, you know, I did this gig in Amsterdam last week, and like one afternoon, we went to this place: The Ann Frank Huis, 263 Prinsengracht. And we went upstairs to the little secret room she had, little achterhuis, when she was hiding from the Nazis, and she had a wall of photos just like that. It has photos of Ray Milland, Sonja Henie, Princess Margaret, Shirley Temple, and Clark Gable, and I thought . . . like that was what was wallpapering the inside of her skull when those groovy ole Nazis came to get her you know, and I was thinking, well I don't mind having a few of those cats inside my head when I'm eating, if that's where they want to be, or even when I'm fucking, but to have that Grade-B tinseltown shit batting round in my head when I'm fixin to DIE . . . No man, no, no, no . . .

PEROWNE (*smiles wanly*): Maybe she went to the death camp to kill off all the photos in her head.

SADIE: Whaaaat? Ha. You can't kill them off. With those cats death's just a weak dogma kept up for the sake of appearances.

> Staring at the wall more closely.

Hey, it's really coming through, Perowne. It's a Mandala . . . a Panoptic Mandala of the Zeitgeist Committee . . . Dig this.

> She stands on the table with her back to the wall, arms outstretched.

Radiant green light from there.

> She encloses a group of photos with her left hand.

Radiant red light from up there.

> She encloses a group of photos above her with her hands.

Radiant white light from there.

> Enclosing a group of photos on the right.

I'm in the center, right?

> Closing her eyes.

Coming through is Wheels, Wheels, OM, Vairocana, Dharmadhatu and the Lion . . . Right?

> PEROWNE stares at her. Nods.

SADIE (*waving her arms in circles*): Eastern Section of Mandala of the five Dhyani-Buddhas, and protophenomena from the photosphere . . . Tantric symbol of integration . . . Vehicle of Eastern Section: BIRD-MAN!

> Opening her eyes.

Now, let's see who you got in Eastern Section . . .

PEROWNE (*peering down at the wall*): Lindbergh. It's Charles Lindbergh!

SADIE: Lindbergh. Huh. Well, maybe it's not a mandala.

> Stepping down.

It's your current mindpool though, isn't it?

> PEROWNE almost nods.

SADIE: Best place for it. All these silly ass dumb fuckin heads talking about their heads. GET IT ON THE WALL.

> Walking around in front of the wall, staring at the photos.

What do you think it's really like, huh? Proliferating millions and millions of photos of yourself without giving a shit where they land? Maybe they're told that it's some kind of cure for cancer. Stops the Real cancer cells from proliferating. Works like sympathetic magic. Like giving jaundice to a yellow bird.

PEROWNE smiles.

SADIE (*stares at him*): Maybe it's a new version of the I Ching you've invented, huh? With photos instead of yarrow stalks. Throw the photos around every morning; tells you who you're gonna be today.

PEROWNE makes no response.

Maybe it's just Maurice's old socks which he threw against the wall, an they stuck.

Pointing to a photo.

There's a sweaty little charisma coming off that one.

Standing back from the wall.

HEY! SHEEEEEEEIT! SHEEEEEIT! It's really hypodermic. It's really comin through now, Perowne. It's beautiful. You know what it is? You know what it is? It's a Cybernetic Model. It's a Flow Chart, you dig? Look, look.

Pointing at the wall, section by section of photos.

Input, see, autocorrelation, anticipatory feedback, meromorphic functions there, anasmatozing channels there, wave filters, postural loops . . . A Cybernetic Time Series of Sign Stimuli releasing adaptive patterns of behavior . . .

Pointing to the right.

then . . . OUTPUT!

Pointing to Perowne.

and AFFECT!

PEROWNE: You could take it as a cybernetic model if you like.

SADIE: It's a bit big, though. You know you could have all

these circuits on a silicon chip an just carry it round with you in your pocket.

Looking back at the wall.

And you got a lot of schmocky parameters set up.

Tracing a line through about eight photos.

See this one? Look at the whiteness of their teeth. People's teeth getting whiter and whiter and whiter . . .

Reaching the end of the line.

and look at HIS teeth? We don't NEED teeth any more, you dig. Couple of years' time all the food'll be predigested and pre-shat, an people's teeth now are falling out in anticipation of that. So you shouldn't have a trajectory like this set up. It's anti-eugenic. Besides, you never been sucked off by a woman with no teeth, or a baby?

PEROWNE stares at her, then looks at the wall.

PEROWNE: I did . . . I did half think of it as a cybernetic model. Let's see who you've . . . let's see who you've got in Input Section. Marilyn Monroe.

SADIE: Yeah, she's Input. She's Basic Basic.

PEROWNE (*pointing along to the right, tracing a line*): But then the Rot sets in. A kind of inverse Doppler effect. The original imprint is defaced, and you get about Forty randomized functions trying to restimulate a need that's already been exhausted by Marilyn Monroe . . .

SADIE: THAT'S RIGHT!

Pointing to the wall.

Carroll Baker, Sandra Milo, Anita Ekberg, Virna Lisi, Sharon Tate, Edie Adams, Barbara Loden, Kathy Kirby, Diana Dors, Jayne Mansfield . . .

PEROWNE: Servo-mechanisms which tend to over-correct the whole mechanism (to conceal their origin) so that the Whole Mechanism no longer proceeds toward the target area, but performs a series of lateral zig zags, and eventually stops all forward progress altogether . . .

SADIE: KYBERNETIC RUNAWAY! Hey, I'm getting in on your trip, right?

> PEROWNE makes no response.

But dig this, Perowne. Maybe she farmed herself out to those bitches, DELIBERATELY, Marilyn Monroe. To SPREAD THE LOAD . . .

> PEROWNE smiles—then moves with SADIE toward another section.

PEROWNE: You get the . . . the same thing here, I suppose—Input section, you get . . .

> Pointing at a photo.

Wittgenstein . . . then

> Tracing a line with his finger through the photos.

then the breakdown of the original imprint into random functions . . . Random noise.

SADIE: Wittgenstein.

> Snapping her fingers.

He was a big philosophical connection, right? Wrote the Tractatus, right. I remember. Proposition 43: "The word 'fuck' is a picture of fucking." Right?

PEROWNE (*smiles*): But the man himself left it unsigned.

SADIE: Too bad. But getting back into your trip, you got Wittgenstein in Input. Pure. But then these little cats, this Ayer, this Quine.

> Pointing at photos.

This Ryle, this Chomsky, this Strawson . . . these little, little cats, they SOLD Wittgenstein's Tractatus to the Daily News. They dismantled Wittgenstein's little thoughtkit, which he packed so tight, and it got syphoned off into the receptors of thirteen stagnant behaviorist clerks. SHEEEEEIT. Look at it. Ha.

> She sways in front of the wall.

Ha. ALL THE PSYCHIC CAPITALISTS IN ONE GHETTO!

Turning round to PEROWNE.

There's gotta be some economy, no? Who's running the economy?

PEROWNE: YES. A lot of the circuitry's overloaded, and I find it . . .

Twisting.

I find it . . .

SADIE: Solid! there's gotta be some economy. Look at it.

Closer to the wall.

Tom Jones . . . see? Cooked-down version of Sam Cook and Otis Redding.

Tears down the photo of Tom Jones.

Bye bye Thomas.

Studying wall.

How many times does Donovan go into Bob Dylan? Bye bye Donovan.

Tears down photo.

How many times does Dylan go into Woody Guthrie?

Tears down photo.

Bye bye Dylan.

Studying wall.

The Beatles. You can't smoke the Beatles.

Tears down photo. Studying wall.

Huh. Mary Baker Eddy? Neutralized version of P.P. Quimby.

PEROWNE looks puzzled.

Quimby? You never heard of Quimby? He was some cat, Quimby. He said to a patient once: If I as a typical doctor tell you that you have congestion of the lungs, I impart my belief to you by a deposit of MATTER in the form of words . . . If you eat my belief, it goes to form the disease. The belief grows,

comes forth, and at last takes the form of pressure
across the chest.

PEROWNE: Huh.

SADIE: Bye Bye Mary Baker.

Tears down photo.

Shall I go on?

PEROWNE smiles, nods.

Elvis Presley, sanforized version of Arthur "Big Boy"
Crudup.

Tears down photo.

Marshall McLuhan, Readers Digest version of William
Burroughs. Bye bye Marshall.

Tears down photo. Moves along the wall.

Here's Fletcher Henderson, still being fraudulently
restimulated by Benny Goodman.

Tears down photo.

So long Bennie.

Pointing.

Emperor Roscoe. Stationary version of Murray the K.
Twiggy. Dehydrated re-run of Jean Shrimpton. R.D.
Laing. Haight-Ashbury Xerox of Harry Stack Sullivan.
Bye Bye R.D.

Turning to PEROWNE.

Doctor Harry Stack was on the same horrible trip,
dig, but at least he kept his exhibits in better condition.

Tears down photo.

PEROWNE (smiling): He may have had better exhibits.

SADIE: Yeah. You want me to go on?

PEROWNE: Mmmn.

SADIE: Dusty fuckin Springfield. How many times does
she go into Baby Washington. Too fuckin many.
Take a walk, Dusty. The Maharishi Mahesh Yoga.
Fuuuuuck. He Sold the same mantra word to me, as
he Gave to Ronald Fucking Reagan. Bye bye Bed Bug.

Tears down photo.

Wilhelm Reich, paranoid version of Count von Reich-
enbach an his Blue Odic Force. Bye bye Wilhelm.

Tears down photo.

Timothy Leary. Huh! Aleister Crowley was preachin
Hash Ecstasy and distributing Acid, under the name
of Anhalonium in New York in NINETEEN TWELVE,
and handing out DNA cuttings of Eliphas Levi, Roger
Bacon, and Paracelsus to anyone who wanted them.

Tears down photo.

Bye bye Timothy.

SADIE stares at the pile of photos on the table
and the floor.

Bye bye, random noise.

To PEROWNE.

Got you some breathing space, huh? Feel better?
PEROWNE: They're still there.
SADIE: REALITY AT WHITE HEAT IS HOLINESS!
Yeah. They're still there. So what else do you do with
them?
PEROWNE: You could make them non-computable. So
that they exceed the memory of the model.
SADIE: Hey! How?
PEROWNE: Change their names.
SADIE: Change their names? They done that already
most of them.

Pointing.

Cyd Charisse, real name Tula Finklea. Susan Shaw,
real name Patsy Sloots. Laurence Harvey, real name
Larushka Skikne . . .
PEROWNE: There's not that much difference.
SADIE: Right! They're not really changing them. I change
my fuckin name every time I cut my nails, every time
my metabolism runs through, every fuckin thing I say,
I change my name. They don't though. Still trying to
come on like some fuckin Continuum. CHANGE
THEIR NAMES! GOTTA REALLY CHANGE THEIR

NAMES! Individualism is wasted on individuals, right? Ha.

> PEROWNE stares at her, smiles. SADIE bends down and picks up a photo that she's plucked from the wall. Looks at it.

SADIE: Now, let's see who's gettin ready to have his Name changed, huh? Who's getting ready to have his Vibration rate changed?

> Looking at the photo. Voodoo chant.

Doctor R . . . D . . . Laing.
PEROWNE (*in time with* SADIE): R . . . D . . . Laing.
SADIE: Doctor WHO? Doctor Richard Dover Rover . . . change his name an set up a Blanking Signal, right?

> Moving her hands over the photo.

Richard Rover Dover . . . Who's that?

> Casting aside the photo.

I don't know. Must have gotten wiped out some place. WITHDRAWN FROM THE ZEITGEIST COMMITTEE. ORIGINAL IMPRINT OF DOCTOR HARRY STACK REINSTATED.
PEROWNE (*looking at the gaps in the wall of photos*): IT'S BECOMING A STRATEGIC WAR MAP!
SADIE (*scuffing through the pile of photos on the floor*): Come on now, more prescriptions! What else can you do to kill off all this random noise? All these psychic parasites?

> PEROWNE picks up a paper from the table.

PEROWNE: Withdraw their feeding grounds. Cut down their pulse length. Render them completely autistic. Kill them.

> PEROWNE picks up a photo in the paper and stares at it.

SADIE: Or FUCKING THEM! Celebrity fucking! that's a strategy to level out the circuitry.

> Going over to the wall.

Now let's see who I fucked.

Pointing.

I fucked her . . . and him, and him,

Pointing.

and him. Shit, I could suck his clitoris up one nostril and down the other . . . and Him.

Pointing.

I fucked him like a stone fox.

Pointing to the photo in the paper PEROWNE is picking at.

Is that someone you fucked?

PEROWNE: No, it's a newsreader . . . Reginald Bosanquet.

SADIE (*standing behind the table*): Hey, have you noticed how RANDY those newsreaders have been getting? They used to get to a disaster an put on a nervous little smile,

Cupping her hand, and moving it up and down between her thighs as if jacking off.

but now they go: PAN AM AIR CRASH . . . FIVE HUNDRED . . . DEAD!

PEROWNE (*pinning the photo of the newsreader to the TV set, and staring at it*): Maurice gutted him in Wigmore Street, BUT HE'S STILL THERE!

SADIE: Who's that?

PEROWNE: The newsreader.

SADIE: Hey, I helped you out with the newsreader before, remember?

PEROWNE (*staring at the photo*): I find that I need about one micro-kinesically described item of news a month. But This man is obsessively devaluing the currency. Talking about the same derelict master minds with their faces daubed in excrement by the newsroom make-up girl, shoved in front of my face for me to pull the same expressions of disapproval. I mean, Am I really meant to chew Ian Smith's clitoris every five seconds?

Pointing at TV.

Why do I have to repeat HIS mental processes?

What does he do, the Newsreader? He takes a collection of event-radiation modules, initially all separate, and then he merges them all together. Consequently all my receptors start merging and I get . . . I get . . .

SADIE (*taking the photo off the front of the TV*): Don't get carried away. I'll strip your gears for you.

PEROWNE: What? I've had my gears stripped on this issue already. Maurice gutted him in Wigmore Street.

SADIE: Hey, that was a bit showy, Perowne.

PEROWNE: Uhuh. They knew he was living here, so they came round. But Maurice is very fly. He wasn't in. But this man's wife started shouting at me, and they had to restrain her. Her name was Pixie . . .

> PEROWNE turns on the video screen and shows a picture of the room, the same as now, with a woman pacing up and down, round PEROWNE, and then raving.

PEROWNE: She came round. I said: I'm not sure that I really care about you, or your voguish little life.

VIDEO

WOMAN: You're a FASCIST.

PEROWNE: How can I be a fascist when I'm prepared to acquiesce in my own liquidation, at any given moment? That's why Maurice had to slip cancer buds into your husband's tea, or whatever he did.

WOMAN: HE SLASHED HIS FACE AND HIS NECK AND HIS CHEST AND HIS . . .

PEROWNE: I don't care if Maurice drowned your husband in cement, or hung him up to dry on a piece of nervous cheesewire . . .

WOMAN: You're mad.

PEROWNE: Madness is wasted on madmen. Besides, thanks to your husband, my mind's not worth leaving. Maurice—gave him every chance. Did you know that Maurice was tromping ten hours a day in the back yard to combat the psychic damage being done by your husband?

WOMAN: What the hell's tromping?

PEROWNE: It's a deep-breathing exercise practiced in the West Indies to get more blood into the brain and to flush it out. Your husband is very LOUD, you see, especially amplified over TV networks. And some noises actually inhibit physical growth. I should think your husband's noise, spread over the period of his employment as a newsreader, has accounted for about three hundred malformed legs, and seventeen cases of goiter. And then before the Tromping, Maurice used to send your husband parcels of poisoned phone calls, delivered by hand. Wouldn't trust the post office, they'd spill them and they'd leak all over the place. Did you ever get them?

WOMAN: YOU'VE GOT NO RESPECT FOR PRIVACY!

PEROWNE: Privacy? Your husband's altering the shape of my face. Privacy? what have we got to deprive you of?

Look, Pixie. Your husband is currently posing as my phantom limb and trying to flatter me by asking me whether he can work the seams in my head, which consist entirely of his own waste products.

Let me give you a humorous version of it, Pixie. You see, your husband's technique involves the theft of a facial expression that he used on the Middle East crisis, for announcing the cricket scores. And the Middle East never gets this facial expression back, because your husband is ashamed of being found out. So the cricket scores are then of exactly equal weight to the Middle East crisis.

You say Maurice cut up your husband. All right, he cut up your husband, the newsreader, but let's look at it, micro-kinesically. Your husband may have been using a tone of voice during his encounter with Maurice that he normally squanders on announcements from Vietnam. Every tone of voice should have its own currency, wouldn't you agree? If your husband, the newsreader, had used

the tone of voice, the phonemes, that vibrate in your
pelvic bones, when he giggles in a French accent
and sucks you off, then Maurice wouldn't have cut
him up. He'd have taken him around the alley, and
pulled his pudding for him. He was imprecise, your
husband.

WOMAN: MY HUSBAND IS CLEVERER THAN THAT.
HE'S GOT PARALLEL MENTAL TRACKS. HE HAS
TO IN HIS JOB.

PEROWNE: Well, Maurice has just knocked one of
them out of commission, hasn't he.

SADIE: Stopped them meeting at infinity. Right on!

PEROWNE: She starts using her voice very precisely
now . . .

WOMAN: I'LL GET MY HUSBAND TO ANNOUNCE
YOUR DEATH.

PEROWNE: I've never been able to understand a word
your husband's said. All he's ever said to me is: This
is the semantic stratum in which you shall live,
move and have your being, and if you move out
of it, what means have I got to report your death?

PEROWNE turns off the video screen.

SADIE: Sheeit. Did Maurice really cut him up? The
gouger gouged. What a slimefest. I mean, really that's
the same fuckin paranoid bag the newsreader's in.
Cutting him up. Did Maurice really cut him up?

PEROWNE: The news was given a different emphasis
when he was in hospital. It was some time ago.
Maurice has a friend called Tuffnell who makes videotapes. We can cut ourselves into the news now, instead
of cutting up the newsreader.

SADIE: What effect does that have?

PEROWNE: I don't know. We only did it once. I think it
made me impotent.

SADIE: Tchah. Newsreaders are only warlocks. They're
not the seed shit,

Pointing to the video screen.

and all that schtick don't clean up their poxy vibes.
I'll get you through to a Real Strategy. Pick any one
you want. Any one.

PEROWNE stares at her, then smiles. He goes
over to the wall and picks off a photo.

Now, the thing is with these cats is to set up a By
Pass Circuit.

She looks at the photo.

It's the Famous Film Star . . . Stanley Baker. A By
Pass Circuit. Right?

PEROWNE nods.

Now, the other day, I'm walking down the street with
Grogan.

Guttural.

"Do your own thing, man, do your own thing." "I'll do
YOUR little thing, Grogan." Ha. When . . . When
down the street, and moving toward us and acting as
an Inhibitory Gestalt, comes . . . Stanley Baker. Now
this cat's had TWELVE phantom limbs syphoned off
him: ZULU, ACCIDENT, EVE, THE GAMES, ROB-
BERY etcetera etcetera. TWELVE cut-price versions
of him are walking the streets, and as he comes
toward us, he doesn't know which areas of my personality are subject to which of his affects. So, to stop
him disintegrating when he meets us, and Definitely
to stop ourselves being confused as to which of his
leakages to react to: we decided to eliminate him altogether. We injected ourselves with puromycin which
lops off the polypeptide chains, and causes memory
synthesis to stop altogether. "Do your own thing,"
said Grogan as we passed him. Stanley Baker nodded,
AND WE FED HIS NOD RIGHT BACK INTO HIM.
Then we passed on; restored our memory with saline
solution. No affect.
PEROWNE: That's only possible in mice.
SADIE: WHO ELSE DID HE THINK WE WERE? So
many of him, so few of us . . . coming down the
street Twelve Handed. Fuckin primitive situation.
Primitive techniques and manipulations called for.
The Sea Cucumber's got ejectible intestines . . .
pheut! some trip that must be . . .
PEROWNE: But what did you do exactly?

SADIE: WE FED HIS NOD RIGHT BACK INTO HIM! We set up Anti-Conduction coils so that he couldn't graft his radiated aura onto us, or any of his characteristics, or steal any of ours. We shoved his video current right back up his ass: That's Your Trip Baby So You Stay With It. "And STAN," Grogan shouts after him, "STAN, you Gross Behavioral modulator . . . Take this from a fading psycho-cyto-cybernetician . . . IT'S ALL FEEDBACK, STAN, ALL OF IT. EVERYTHING IS FEDBACK So . . . don't START anything, Stan."

Holding up the photo.

Zapped him . . . Shall I tear him up?

PEROWNE: But why . . . Why Stanley Baker . . . exactly . . .

SADIE: Why Stanley Baker? You mean all these photos are stuck up for no reason? Why Stanley Baker?

Slipping her fingers.

He made a film based on the Great Train Robbery, right. Well, there was a chance to finally Crap on Money, dig? Call in Ezra Pound as technical adviser and really shit on Money as Energy Token from ten storeys. What happens? Same paralyzing con. Same bullshit riff. If you got all that bread, Stan, why not spend it on springing them out of jail? They were revolutionaries. Any menopausal housewife who boosts a frozen chicken liver from the supermarket's a revolutionary. PROPERTY EATS SHIT. You know the name of the bank in Berlin that's still handling all the Nazi hoards? It's called the Mercke Finke Bank. Straight. An that energy's still circulating.

Waving the photo.

So, shall I tear it up? Or shall we open a joint bank account with it?

PEROWNE smiles, nods. Stares at her. Smiles.

SADIE (*casting aside the photo*): I'm getting onto your trip, huh?

PEROWNE smiles. SADIE wanders round the room. Opens a bookcase. She finds a metal stake driven

through a pile of books. She takes it out and
holds it up.

HEY, WHAT THE FUCK'S THIS?

PEROWNE: Maurice felt that . . . that some of the
books in here were . . . that they were going . . .
going off . . . I hadn't read them. He felt that they
were giving off . . . that they were going Bad. He
drove that rod through them to let out the . . . vibrations.

SADIE: Yeah. But aren't you frightened of catching
schizophrenia?

PEROWNE: No. I'm frightened of him losing it.

PEROWNE sits and stares at the wall of photos.
They begin to hum and flash very slightly, then
stop. PEROWNE twitches a little, then stops.

SADIE (*moving closer to him*): You know, five years
time, there won't be any problem of this fuckin psychic
capitalism.

PEROWNE: No? why not?

SADIE: Cybersex. Set up directional electrodes, X-Ray
Thermal Videos, MeatHeat pickup guns . . . Set em
all up outside Bucking-ham Palace, the White House,
Apple, R.C.A., Ten Downing Street, wherever. Make a
5-D 8-track Flesh Reception Movie of them all Fucking. Then you turn it into a cassette, slot it into your
Cybersex module at home and you Can Have Them!
And then when any of these cats try to lay their
horrible little one-way trips on you, you can say:
Baby, I have had Your True Juice. All of it! What is
this surface shit you're handing me?

PEROWNE (*laughs slightly, then catches himself*): But
what do you do until then?

SADIE: Do what you want. Dig what you got there.

Pointing to the wall.

You got a Total Map of Personality Radiation. You
gotta Cosmic Metabolism there which you can adjust
to give you any fuckin flash you want. Too much
adrenalin comin through. ZAP IT OUT! Too much
sex energy coming through? ZAP IT OUT.

SADIE takes two photos off the wall and lays them on top of each other, face inward. She splays her fingers and rubs the photos together hard and fast.

Fucky! Fucky! Fuck! Fuck! SUCKY! FUCKY! SUCKY! FUCKY!

RUBBIN YOU DRY.

Quickly looking at the photos.

MIA FARROW—RUBBING YOU DRY AS A WITCHES TIT! JOHN WAYNE—NEVER GONNA BE ABLE TO LAY YOUR GRADE BE SEX ENERGY ON ME AGAIN. NEVER BE ABLE TO SYPHON ME OFF AGAIN WITH YOUR TEEVEE COCK AND YOUR TEEVEE CUNT.

Throws down the photos. Laughs. Sits down. PEROWNE stares at her, smiles. More intrigued.

PEROWNE: I like that. I worked briefly with a man called de la Warr, just before he died. He could diagnose illnesses from photographs. He claimed that if you had a varicose vein, the radiations from the varicose vein would be transferred to the photographic emulsion, and if he put your photograph into an electronic box that he had, a black box, he could detect the varicose veins, or the cancer cells or the gallstones, or whatever disease you had. Every condition has its own radiations. He had a chart of them all.

Getting up and looking at the wall.

I never mentioned it to him but I often wondered if it mightn't be possible to work it the other way round.

Forking his fingers and his hand landing on Richard Nixon.

SADIE: Hey, I really did hit your trip! And make all these cats sick, right? Just by treating their photos!

Going over to the wall and pointing.

Zap! you gotta period baby. Zap! you're white! Zap! you're black! Zap! you got hepatitis. Zap! you're never gonna come in my brain again.

PEROWNE smiles, then sits down again. Awkwardly.

PEROWNE: I suppose Maurice operates like a sort of
Black Box. His antennae are right out, you see, right
out there. He's at all the points of emission. He's
pitched himself into a totally noncognitive area. He's
not distracted by people's eye-contact patterns, how
their faces move, what they say. He picks up on their
total resonance, and then immediately can compute
the anti-dotal wave form and just finish them off, without their knowing if necessary.
SADIE: Maybe. But Maurice is gonna flip you out soon.

Pointing to the wall.

The thing to do is to colonize them before they colonize
you. Right? And that's Maurice's big mistake. They've
really eaten into Maurice. Maurice has short-circuited,
and that's just what they want. They WANT you to
short-circuit, so they can shove another wire up your
toes.

PEROWNE looks fazed. SADIE gets up, pulls a joint
from her pocket, lights it, takes up, and then
hands it to PEROWNE.

SADIE: Devon laid this on me before she left.
PEROWNE: What is it?
SADIE: Thunderfuck. One taste of this and you're the
star of every fuckin movie ever made.

PEROWNE takes a drag.

Can send you into psychic spaces where they treat
Einstein as the village idiot.

PEROWNE takes another drag. They are sitting
down opposite each other. Staring at each other.

PEROWNE: Have you ever tried astral projection?
SADIE: Uhuh. Cat I knew in place called Coconut Grove
got into that very heavy; an back to Coconut Grove.
Hard work, though. Big inner scene. Worth it, though.
Get that together an you can really go down on your-
self.
PEROWNE: I sometimes think that what those . . .
those people have . . .

Gesture toward the wall of photos.

is a sort of astral body on the cheap. Mmn? And perhaps that accounts for the sense of cosmic irritation that other people have.

SADIE: Irritation? Come on, they're bugging the shit out of you. Everyone's famous. Everyone's the star of their own movie in their own heads. That's the only fuckin star system that's worth breaking down.

PEROWNE: Maurice has done that. Maurice has videotapes of himself playing inside the heads of people he's never met, and vice versa.

SADIE: Yeah. Maurice can spit at the sun.

Silence.

PEROWNE: Maurice can spit at the sun and make it spark.

SADIE stares at him. PEROWNE gets off his chair and onto the table and crawls toward her, lying along the table.

PEROWNE: Your . . . facial movements.

SADIE: Yeah?

PEROWNE: At one point I was trying to . . . I don't know . . . trying to find, you see, some kind of Unified Field Theory of facial movements, eye contact patterns, speech intonations . . . so on . . . I mean, everything's interconnected, you know. If you drop a bottle of tomato ketchup in Tokyo, ultimately it affects the red gases on Jupiter.

SADIE: Hey, have you got into Ectohormones yet?

PEROWNE: No. What are they?

SADIE: There's this Biochemical Effluvia that's comin out of us the whole time. Pheromone trails. Hexanol transmitters and receptors. Ectohormonal BEAMS, and they may be the TRUE PLOT. There's an Ectohormonal Molecule, right, composed of all the ectohormones coming out of all the people on this street, right, and they're LINKED by that biochemical juice, and not by any exchanges of wordshit, or sexshit or whatever shit. So, dig this: Maybe the people in that room up there say, through that wall,

Pointing.

maybe they're cooking their dinner, and maybe the patterns of ectohormones that's coming out of them is making me sit down in this way. In exactly this way, in order that the biochemical balance of the whole ectohormonal street molecule is kept at the right temperature, or right balance, or right whatever it is that that molecule needs. That's what goes down with ectohormones.

PEROWNE: I like that. It's a bit like Maurice and his electricity though, it's a bit deterministic.

SADIE: Yeah, you could get strung out on it.

SADIE stares at the wall.

PEROWNE (*leaning across*): Will you shake my hand?

SADIE: Are you trying to make a meat scene with me?

PEROWNE: I just want you to shake my hand. Why so much aggression?

SADIE takes his hand and shakes it.

SADIE: Sloppy handshake.

PEROWNE: Yes. Five years ago I'd have shaken it like this.

He squeezes SADIE's hand and shakes it firmly.

SADIE: So? you're gettin old, that's all.

PEROWNE stands up on his chair and turns round.

PEROWNE: I'm swiveling round on this chair now.
Just swiveling round.
Quite instinctively.
But I'm setting up some molecular pattern.
I may be acting one out.
I met you.
The molecular pattern accumulates.

It might be that these molecular patterns are Sponsored by the magnetic core, by gravitational fields, by other fields, I don't know.

Maybe they're some sort of safety net, to prevent electromagnetic deflection. These instinctual patterns.

Because there's only 2033 years before the earth's magnetic field falls to zero and lets in solar radiation: the Second Ice Age, terrestrial inundations, mutations, monsters.

Whatever it is . . . I just feel that these things there,

> Standing on the chair, pointing at the photos.

these people, that they're somehow Weakening this safety net, because they're stealing one's instinctual patterns. THEY'RE STEALING THEM. THEY'RE FORGING THEM. THEY'RE SLOWING THEM UP. THEY'RE SPEEDING THEM UP. THEY'RE RE-PRODUCING THEM TWENTY TIMES A DAY. THEY'RE UNLOADING YOU. THEY'RE OVERLOAD-ING YOU . . .

You understand how we're upsetting the ecological balance? There's a bacteria in the North Sea which converts carbon dioxide back into oxygen. A fertilizer they're using now, kills it off. We might walk out of this room now, go out into the street, and drop down dead because there's no oxygen.

Now, These People . . . call them FAmous people if you like . . . FAm-e is just a measure of electro-magnetic waste . . . these Famous people they're up-setting the ecological balance in exactly the same way as the fertilizer.

It's no accident that film stars are called stars, you know. They use up the magnetic field to the same ex-tent as any asteroid. Every star that surfaces is using up the Behavioral Field of anything from forty to a hundred ordinary people.

Let's say I'm two gauss. You're two gauss. But BARBRA STREISAND is 75 gauss . . . and the BEATLES . . . THE BEATLES are probably a THOU-SAND gauss.

SADIE: Sheeeit, you really got the creeping meatball staked out.

PEROWNE: It's brain surgery, that's what it is. It's brain surgery, without anaesthetics. The only anaesthetics they offer is more brain surgery.

SADIE (*leaping up and facing the wall, shouting*): ELEC-TROMAGNETIC SHEISTERS! PREDATORY SEW-AGE! FUCKIN MOCK UPS! It takes a hundred and forty-eight muscles to frown, and only three to smile, so keep fit and Frown, and man am I Frowning at all you fat cats . . .

PEROWNE: I like that.

SADIE: Come on, shall I kill them all off? And finish off this TV Yoga to give you some breathing space?

PEROWNE: I don't know. I don't know if it's not too late. The sensory assault is too great. It's really a stress situation. It's somehow even too late even to take an attitude to it. Taking an attitude's a form of epilepsy anyway. They want you to take an attitude. They probably use the electricity from your epilepsy.

SADIE: I thought it was Maurice was the fuckin electrophiliac, not you. It's not too late. I killed Mick Jagger. I set it up. With a tantric spell.

PEROWNE: Why?

SADIE: He got some karmic debts to pay for, that's why. Poncing off a few back-dated revolutionary vibes to pay his Hilton Hotel Bill. Writes a song Street Fighting Man, but when it comes to the crunch you know he couldn't fight his way out of a bag of smack.

But don't get me wrong. I'm not going into the Rights and Wrongs, you dig, I'm going into the NEUROLOGY, and the Neurology is this. ALL these psychic capitalists are hustling Feedback all the time, more than anyone else, they're hustling Attention Molecules, and Validation Molecules, and Look at Me molecules, and after a bit those molecules and that feedback gets TOO much for them to process, because they ain't that big enough to accommodate them you dig and so those attention molecules build up inside them, and get Radioactive, start overheating the whole fuckin Network and so those fat cats gotta be DISCHARGED, you dig, they gotta be Detonated. Psychic jiu jitsu. ESP terrorism, or just knock them on the head like rabbits.

Sitting down.

Phew, I really hit the seed shit then.

PEROWNE: You came close.

SADIE: Does Maurice get closer than that?

PEROWNE: Maurice does it. He does it in the way he talks. Cholinergic. Adrenergic. Shamanistic. He closes down their transmissions. He generates such an amount of psychic static that they can't get through.

SADIE: Look, I changed my ground crew, when are you

gonna change yours? Huh? I'll tell you something. Even if Maurice Could demagnetize you of all your hang-ups, logically, you'd go blind. The magnetic phosphene effect. Human head experiencing changes in the electromagnetic field gets subjective light sensations. No more field, because Maurice has cleaned the slate,

Indicating the wall and the TVs.

no more light. Are you prepared for that? Whenever I see a lame man, I get a sympathetic limp, but whenever I see a blind man, I ignore him.

PEROWNE (*standing up*): Shall I give you some kind of policy statement? I'm trying to automate my mental activity. Trying to get my thoughts to announce their color, their weight, their valency, in advance of my having to think them. You see. It's much too serious to leave to chance electrical discharges. I'm trying to get some kind of feedforward. I can get close to it on an inner level. I can begin to see it. But I'm trying to steer the technique round to cover everything. All my sensory networks. All my sense perceptors. So that when they're confronted with newspapers, movies, TV and so on, so that they can quantify the charge in advance, before I have to suffer it, so I can arrange the kind of infusion more precisely . . .

SADIE: How?

PEROWNE: Synchronicity. The noncausal connection between events. It's all there with synchronicity. You can often pick up the charge before the event itself has occurred.

SADIE: On a time-reversed trip?

PEROWNE: Yes. Happens at particle level. Happens here.

Points to a photo.

Here's a publicity photograph of Virginia Rappe, 1920, with a large bottle. She's spilling a bit of it down her leg. In 1921, she was raped with a large bottle, by Fatty Arbuckle, and died of a ruptured bladder.

Billy Sol Estes, remember him?

SADIE: Big Con man.

PEROWNE: He chose as his theater of gypping operations a place called Pecos, West Texas. Pecos means

Crooked in the Indian language. William Herschel discovered Uranus in 1781. Uranus is 1781 million miles from the sun. Herschel lived until he was 84.01, exactly one Uranian year.

SADIE: So it was all there already. He needn't have bothered.

PEROWNE: You mentioned Aleister Crowley. He had a lover called Parsons. Parsons tried to resurrect Babylon, by making concoctions of sperm and menstrual fluid. He used to lean over the saucepan chanting: "I shall be blown away on the breath of the father, even as it is prophesied." He was blown away by a rocket explosion in his experimental laboratory in Pasadena in 1952. It's all there with synchronicity. It's a bit crude. But you can use synchronicity as a sort of geiger counter.

Pause.

A sort of early warning system.

SADIE: Yeah. Did you know this one? Roman Polanski was having dinner at the Playboy Club with a friend. Dig? And he and the friend were discussing the death of a mutual friend. Polanski said: Eeny meeny miney mo, who will be the next to go? A few seconds later the phone rang an he was told of the death of his wife.

PEROWNE: It's a little hard to explain, but somehow having Maurice around . . . it . . . We used to have a physical relationship: that gets things sparking the gap quicker I suppose . . . but somehow having Maurice around enables me to see into synchronicity more clearly. You see, he's moving in an entirely non-cognitive area. He blows all the fuses, so that I can build fuses of a different caliber. Somehow having Maurice . . .

SADIE: Uhuh. You know they made a film of that? Those Sharon Tate murders, they were set up as a film. When one of them escaped and ran down the drive, they shot him and shot him on camera. They followed the whole thing with portable arc-lights. They forced Jay Sebring to cut his cock off on camera, and shove it in his mouth, on camera . . .

PEROWNE: What for?

SADIE: For the porno-film circuit. It was set up as a film to fuck to. It was set up as a jack-off film. Frank Sinatra's paying about thirty thousand dollars a year to keep himself off the death-orgasm film circuit. There are a lot of West Coast Freaks who'd like to jack off with a film of him being shot up, blood squirting . . .

PEROWNE: Phew.

SADIE: Yeah. Phew. Well, Like you say, sooner or later people gonna get tired of humping your astral body, and they're gonna want to fuck you.

Standing up.

Your synchronicity couldn't tell you that. Your precious Maurice couldn't tell you that. What thought are you going to have three thoughts from now? Your Cybernetic Model's no good. It SUCKS. It's got no self-consciousness, like all machines. Can't tell you which NEW photos are going to come up next.

PEROWNE: If you had enough photos it could tell you.

SADIE: Don't give me that computer shit. Lot of fuckin symbolism. Give a kid a hammer and suddenly everything needs hammering.

Looking at wall.

They're clogging you up. They're really clogging you up. Aren't they? Aren't they?

PEROWNE nods.

You need a clean machine.

PEROWNE: A Clean Machine!

SADIE: A clean machine.

He smiles.
    SADIE moves around the wall of photos, splaying her hands, as if warming them on the photos, as if feeling their vibes, looking for the heaviest charge.

More Beatles. You can't smoke the Beatles.

Ripping the photo down.

Hey, I'm gonna jack you up, Beatles. I'm gonna rip your ass. Cotton candy bullshit. They were the

Tonettes for five years, on the biggest groveling fuckin ego trip ever seen, which everyone's chosen to forget, just because they dropped a couplea caps. Phew, all those main niggers all the way down the line lettin their wee wees get sucked: "Oh man, jes look how dose four nice ofay boys finally gettin our riffs through the customs fo us." Big brain damage repair strategy comin up now, Perowne. The biggest I've laid on you. Grab you?

PEROWNE smiles.

SADIE (*chanting*): "I am you and you are me and we are all together." Let them eat cake. How many people's nerve cells had to be killed off to put them up there?

Pointing to the wall.

I can still smell the phenol.
"COME AND DELEGATE YOUR TRUE HEAT TO US."
No, Kids, give it to Us. No, US, NO, US WE'RE the Sharpest Shitwagon in the Great Needery Node.
THINK of all that energy that went into the Beatle-machine.
THINK if you'd had a Cosmic Energy Transformer when they first surfaced in Hamburg 1960.
THINK what might have been created.
FUUUUCK! Man Powered Flight!,

Flapping her arms.

A Nation of Fuckin Harpies. If you can run up 150 foot in a minute, given the right harness. You can do it. You got the energy to fly. I been into it. Could really nail the pig with a machine like that.
But THINK Perowne, what fuckin circuits would have come up if you could have stolen the Beatle-machine's energy.
I mean: REAL BRAIN TO BRAIN CONTACT, instead of just exhausting the energy needed for that by selling the same Fake Chauvinistic Sex Bonds.

Chanting.

Ooo-ooOOOO OOH Love Me Do, I Love You . . . Love Me Do I Love You . . . Love ME do? When my fuckin revolution comes, people are gonna change into each other fifty times a day to switch themselves fit. Maybe it's already starting. Love Me Do. I Love You. I mean What IS that catatonic little buzz they're pushing out? When some cats are into a Real Erotic Footloose Fuck an Mass Balling in the Streets, to SMASH all those inter-personal hypes . . .

PEROWNE: What else? What else would have come up if you could have . . .

SADIE: Oh man, what else. You could have been your own father, with a post-dated check from the sperm bank. You could have had moving roads. Just get out your deck chair an sit there. No More Fuckin Toxic CARS. There's some real ecological alterations down to cars. Half of my right leg is made from sulphur-dioxide exhaust-waste. And like Traffic NOISE, man, that like sets up an Unresolved Chord in my head, dig? and something really Precise and Manic has to happen to clear that up.

PEROWNE: Such as what, an accident?

SADIE (*breathily*): A car accident. Phew! I get my rocks off every time.

PEROWNE (*closer*): And what else, what else would have come up if you could have stolen the Beatlemachine's . . .

SADIE: Anti-Gravity waves, Mass Levitation, Logical Language, Ocean Farming, Houses you could squirt out of aerosol cans, wherever you happened to be standing, Centralized Data Storage . . .

PEROWNE: Centralized Data Storage!

SADIE: Direct Brain to Computer Construction of anything you want with sub-atomic building blocks: THINK! SHAZAM!

    Splaying her hands.

BEATLES! THINK! SHAZAM! BOTTLES! THINK! SHAZAM! BOOSTERS!

    Crumpling the photo.

Oh Beatles. Ha, I'm comin on so strong they can feel their assholes puckering.

PEROWNE: Didn't you ever think they were rather . . . nice?

SADIE: They pissed me off from the get. I had holographic beatles that fitted my cunt exactly in 1939. Ok. I laid a few incandescent little currents on them. But, shit, I'd like those currents back, and at crippling interest rates. 5000 million bev energy went into that Beatle-machine, an what came out? One's a bum comic, one's a society poodle, one's a third-class astral ticket collector, an the other one's makin a little progress. At one time, they had all the fuckin Power Freak Juice, and they let it slip from under their ass. They coulda taken murder off the fuckin statute book. But they were still into Heroes, an Heroes just suck up everybody else's energy and then explode. All these people laying their One Way Unilateral trips on you. There are more sophisticated transactions available, dig? The trips I coulda been on. There's a MUTATIVE BLOCK now, down to all these . . . these Psychic Knots . . . these . . . If there wasn't that Block, anyone my age would have Anderson shelters growin out their shoulder blades; The Genes would be pickin up on it that quick. And Earlids that Blink. And . . . And . . . shit a whole lot more. The GENES are BLOCKED. Blocked by psychic capitalists heading off all the energy. When my fuckin revolution comes, Everybody in the World's gonna be on television ALL THE TIME. THEN there's gonna be an "Information explosion." No more names. No more signature artists. No more selective newsreader psychosis. No more selective Beatle psychosis. There's gonna be TOTAL ACCESS . . . TOTAL ACCESS.

ACCESS . . . TOTAL ACCESS.

She slings down the photo, and flops into the chair.

PEROWNE: What else? What else would have come up, if you'd been in Hamburg, 1960, and stolen the Beatle-machine?

SADIE: I don't know. I got the visionary cramps.

Looking up at him. Smiling.

Didn't think I could come across, did you? Didn't think I could deliver the goods, did you? Lay it all on me, I'll cool you out. I'll bite through all your biopathic armoury. And I can cook up that jive lick of Maurice's anytime you want, but I'm into something much heavier.

SADIE gets up and turns on the television.

Now, let's see what goes down here. You should be able to take anything now.

SILENCE. The Television comes on. PEROWNE stares at it.

PEROWNE: America should be put to sleep for a hundred years. America's a psychopath. But psychopaths can still deploy themselves. They can still make strategies, they can still make very careful plots. The thing to do is not to try and Check it, but to Continue the parameter. To combat irrationality with irrationality. To make it entirely schizophrenic. Properly schizophrenic.

Holding out his hand, as if holding a gun. American accent.

How am I expected to fire this gun, when it looks like a cabbage? HEY MACK, I CAN'T FIRE THIS GUN, THE TRIGGER'S STARTED MENSTRUATING.

SADIE: Oh shape up, shape up willya?

PEROWNE: What shape did you have in mind?

Pointing at the TV.

LOOK AT THAT. Posing as my blood brother. I'm not anaemic. Dovetailing his sly wink into my face . . .

SADIE: Come on, don't let the hash smoke you.

PEROWNE (*pointing to the TV*): Look at that. Can't you feel that? Mountains of media scar tissue clogging up my . . . There's got to be some kind of Media Ecology. There's this giant electronic exo-skeleton groping at the globe, like some hideous totentanz, and fucking it in all the wrong places. Plunging its cock into the globe to syphon it off every five micro-seconds. Plunging its cock into the globe and fucking it IN ALL THE WRONG PLACES. Can't you feel it? CAN'T YOU FEEL IT? MOUNTAINS OF MEDIA SCAR TISSUE TO BE SCRAPED OFF . . . MAURICE knows the anti-dotal wave form . . . Only Maurice knows the anti-dotal wave form. MAURICE! Maurice is no longer inductive. He can't pick up this any more. You know what he said to me the other day? He said that UFOs have an affinity with electrical installations, and that that was why he worked in the Amusement Arcade because they often flew over and paralyzed the machines and let him get off work early.

SADIE: Huh. Electricity's a fossil fuel.

PEROWNE (*pointing to the TV*): CAN'T YOU FEEL IT? CAN'T YOU FEEL IT?

He begins to writhe.

Maurice is no longer inductive. He says that extraterrestrial beings are using mental hospitals as launching pads. He's no longer inductive. He can't pick up this. CAN'T YOU FEEL IT?

SADIE: It's Maurice that's got into you, not the fuckin machine.

PEROWNE stares at the television, twisting his hands, twisting his body.

PEROWNE: They're firing the same cells in my brain there as they fired last Tuesday. All these sensory equations over and over again. They're injecting me. WHERE'S THE TOILET IN MY BRAIN? HOW DO I FLUSH IT? None of these dead sensory equations should be allowed to enter my brain unless they're disposal wrapped. LOOK AT THEM NOW! trying to dilute all my morphisms to a more polite level.

IF IT'S ME IN THERE . . .

IF IT'S ME IN THERE . . .

WHEN ARE YOU GOING TO GIVE ME VACANT POSSESSION?

Look at that expression there.

Pointing to the television.

He's using all the billing and cooing, nuzzling and sucking now that's gone on on my bed to run that SMILE. I mean fusion of nuclei's apt to pall, isn't it? FUSION OF NUCLEI'S APT TO PALL. Why don't YOU take the load?

SADIE moves back against the wall. PEROWNE turns back to the TV.

And now they're wiring up my bed radiation modules to their STOP AND THINK.

> Pointing to TV.

He's saying STOP AND THINK and using energy from MY BED to say it STOP AND THINK. WHICH OF THE STOPS BETWEEN THEIR SECOND HAND SILENCES ARE THEY TRYING TO STOP ME FROM THINKING ABOUT? Can't you feel it?

> The videos are rolling, the wall of photos humming, the sound from the teevees throbbing.

Look at it now. They're cutting all the lines of force in all the wrong places. They're putting the conductors in all the wrong places. IT'S A DRIED UP MAGNETIC STORM. WHERE'S THE DISPLACEMENT CURRENT?

> He starts rocking his head.

WHERE'S THE DISPLACEMENT CURRENT?

SADIE (*from the other side of the room*): Don't look at me.

> PEROWNE contorts his body, falling down in front of the TV, performing a series of myoclonic jerks and akinetic seizures. He has a severe torsional spasm.

PEROWNE: AAAAAAAAH AAAAAAAA AAAA AAAAAA

AAAAAAAAAH AAAAAAAAA.

> The sounds from the video screens and the wall fade. PEROWNE sits frozen with one hand locked in front of him, one hand locked behind his neck. SADIE stares at him, almost cowering against the wall. MAURICE comes into the room.

MAURICE (*toward* PEROWNE, *but not seeing him*): Your friend Tuffnell's got into my head. Last week he had one foot on the grave, and the other on a bit of orange peel, but now he's onto it. Yesterday, he was only on the bottom rung: People sending him their bad dreams for him to have, and the War Office putting nerve gas in his wallpaper. But Now, he's Right onto it: The

Gods using his brain as a telephone exchange and saying fucking fucking fucking all the time to tot it up to Gmm Cos Theta squared. WHO GAVE HIM THE FUCKIN VISA THEN? WHO TOLD HIM WHERE MY HEAD WAS? THE FUCKIN CUNT. HE'S HOLLOWING ME OUT!

To SADIE.

HE'S HOLLOWING ME OUT! TUFFNELL'S HOLLOWING ME OUT! CUNT! CUNT!

> MAURICE glances at PEROWNE, and notices his position for the first time, he stares at him, stares back at SADIE, and then walks over to PEROWNE, taking a photo off the wall en route.

MAURICE (*brandishing the photo in front of* PEROWNE's *face*): Gypsy Rose Lee Dead! From telling you whereabouts in your crutch you live. Dead.

> PEROWNE makes no reaction. MAURICE stares at him.

MAURICE (*to* SADIE): Did you jack him up like that? Did you? You been over-amping him. I thought you were going to demagnetize him.

> He takes a bone from his pocket, and forcibly opens PEROWNE's mouth and sticks it in across his jaw.

I thought you were going to discharge him. You been over-amping him.

> To PEROWNE.

Never mind. I can still demagnetize you. I've got a lot of schizophrenia left. Tuffnell didn't hollow me out completely. Ha.

> He goes over to the pile of newspapers, and takes the large magnet weight from the top of the pile and brings it back to PEROWNE. The TV set in front of PEROWNE is still on.

Ha. I'm gonna switch you fit. HA! I'M GONNA WEE WEE ALL OVER THE TEEVEE, AND DRIVE IT

CRAYZEE! SO THAT YOU NEVER HAVE TO MESH
WITH IT AGAIN, EVER EVER EVER!

> He pisses all over the television screen, then he
> takes one of the video mikes and plugs it in to
> the straight TV, superimposing his own com-
> mentary onto the sound coming from the straight
> TV. And he bends down, with the mike in one
> hand and the magnet in the other, drawing the
> magnet across the screen, distorting all the
> images, gathering them all up, making them
> swirl and merge with each other, in exploding
> anamorphic bubbles.

MAURICE (*high-speed—metallic*): She's—pointing—to—
me—and—strafing—my—tongue—with—her—
eyelashes—and—she's—saying—You're—Sitting—
Too—Close—To—Me—and—Why's—That?—
because—she's—Smashed—up—my—version—of—
my—body—1963—toring—off—scabs—like—wet—
kleenex—Saying—even—I—know—about—your—
Teeth—Mauricio—and—how—they—got—Persistent—
Pulp—and—if—you—watch—me—long—enough—
I'll—knock—one—out—of—kelter—and—it'll—
grow—into—your—head—HA—Glint—in—her—eye—
size—of—a—fuckin—cataract——I—said—that—
What—you're—saying—is—a—Trumped—up—
Deluge—and—Lacerating—Field—Flux—and—I—
was—let—Past—that—1959—with—the—aero—
crash—even—though—they—wheeled—it—on—as—
Porfirio—Rubirosa—Playboy—and—hydraulic—
lizard—to—say—in—a—car—crash—and—shouting—
Where's—My—Fuckin—Handbag—?—When—he—
regained—a—bit—of—conscience—about—operating—
on—me—decanted—from—the—crash—car—which—

was—impresarioed— as—a—Joke—But— then—I—kicked—him— up—a—space—and— he—was—told—to— go—back—into— into—a—Dead—Set— Piece—and—the—bolt—	SADIE stares at them, then moves toward them, shouting. SADIE: THEY'RE NOT RECEIVING YOU MAURICE ABSO-

he—shot—made—a—
tremendous—fuckin—
noise—and—stopped—
him—trying—to—
circumcise—my—skull—
so—that—all—the—
hard—cells—would—
form—up—and—
desensitize—and—
also—to—show—the—
strength—of—his—
operation—on—me—
all—this—time—with—
the—leather—on—his—
high—heels—being—
worn—down—to—the—
steel—peg—But—Even—
When—I'd—got—Past—
that—they're—coming—
up—again—with—his—
blisters—and—his—
breathing—on—them—
long—distance—and—
watching—his—breath—
condense—inside—
and—get—confident—
UNTIL—THEY—GOT—
IT—UP—AGAIN—TO—
THE—LYMPH—
RATION—LAID—
DOWN—BY—THE—
1969—AERO—
CRASH . . .

Why—don't—you—
just—find—the—end—
of—his—tether?—
They're—saying
saying—to—me—now—
I—said Somebody's—
cut—it—off—

MAURICE unplugs
the video mike,

LUTELY NONE OF
THEM! PORFIRIO
RUBIROSA'S NOT
RECEIVING YOU,
OTHERWISE THERE
WOULDN'T BE THAT
PLASTIC CUNT SHOP
IN PARK LANE . . .
DIELAN THOMAS
ISN'T RECEIVING
YOU, OTHERWISE
THERE WOULDN'T
BE CROWDS OF
SECOND HAND AUTO-
DESTRUCTIVE
DIONYSIAN DRUNKS
WITH VOICES LIKE
CIGARS TUNING UP
THAT I MET IN SOHO
AN FULHAM—
CHURCHILL HILL'S
NOT RECEIVING YOU,
OTHERWISE THERE
WOULDN'T BE SIX
HUNDRED CONSER-
VATIVE POLITICIANS
IN YOUR PARLIA-
MENT WITH THEIR
HAIR CUT SHORT
BECAUSE THEY'RE
SO PROUD OF THEIR
LOBOTOMY SCARS,
AN WATERING DOWN
CHURCHILL-HILL'S
SPEECH PATTERNS
IN ORDER TO DROWN
THE BLACKS AND
THE PAKISTANIS AND
EXTINGUISH THEIR
BEAUTIFULLY
ROLLED JOINTS.
JAYNE MANSFIELD
ISN'T RECEIVING

puts down the magnet, and stands behind PEROWNE, massaging his scalp.

A clean break?

PEROWNE nods. MAURICE massages his shoulders.

YOU EVEN THOUGH SHE WAS DECAPITATED AND THEREFORE DOUBLED THE AREA OF HER RECEPTIVE THRESHOLD. SHE'S NOT RECEIVING YOU, OTHERWISE THERE WOULDN'T BE SWARMS OF UNCLE TOM BITCHES CATAPULTING THEMSELVES INTO THE UPPER AIRS WITH YOUR COCK AND CLEANING THE SWEAT OFF THEIR MENTAL LIGAMENTS BY RUNNING THEM THROUGH YOUR ASS . . .
    THEY'RE NOT RECEIVING YOU ABSOLUTELY NONE OF THEM!

MAURICE (*taking his hands off* PEROWNE's *shoulders*): Who brought him off? WHO BROUGHT HIM OFF?

SADIE: I brought him off. I brought him off with some superior techniques to that crap. Well, I was just about to.

PEROWNE: You didn't.

MAURICE: WHO BROUGHT HIM OFF?

PEROWNE: It's not a live issue.

MAURICE: She's hollowing me out.

SADIE: No shit. You schiz are all the same. Signature artists. You want the same feedback as anyone else. Ok, you shat on your ego. You're all over the place. Solid. But it's only to give your super-ego more elbow room. You're still panhandling for validation.

MAURICE: She's hollowing me out.

SADIE: Sure I'm hollowing you out. If you wanna work

up any kind of communal buzz, how else is the game to be played?

MAURICE: She's hollowing me out.

SADIE: Yeah, I'm stealing your vibes in relays. Every hour, on the hour I'm stealing your vibes, so that he can factorize the neat little mess that's left.

MAURICE: Come here. I had a vision three micro-seconds back: I was told the only cure for schizophrenia is to make at least two other people schizophrenic. I've sent Tuffnell up the pictures, so that only leaves one to go. What's your feeling about that?

SADIE: Not Much. I think you got your work cut out with Perowne. He was pretty freaked out just then, when you weren't here.

MAURICE: Yeah? That was NOTHING. He's been Training the television set to Give him epileptic fits.

To PEROWNE.

You didn't know I knew that did you?

To SADIE.

Get him to tell you about it. That's HIS seal of good housekeeping.

SADIE: Yeah?

To PEROWNE.

That right?

PEROWNE shrugs his shoulders.

I tied 300 epileptics together once, timed to go off a minute apart. I got a real charge out of it. Set up an E.S.P. card guessing experiment at the same time, and when the last epileptic fired, I'd got 24 of the 25 cards right, it really vamped up the psychic static.

PEROWNE gets to his feet.

PEROWNE: They're masked fits. They're not grand mal motorized convulsions. I'm not a pack horse.

SADIE: Yeah? Junior epilepsy. Only knock down the things you wanta knock down.

PEROWNE: Nothing stylized.

MAURICE: Right. No fuckin froth with Perowne.

PEROWNE: It's custom built for me though. All the right
signals are swamped. A few carefully selected focal
discharges in the appropriate areas. It's like chess. It
leaves no mental traces.

> To SADIE.

Would you like to understand the mechanics of it?

> He goes over to the television and points at it
> briefly.

Newsreader Honeycombe sets the tempo of an audi-
tory and photic pulsed discharge through the centren-
cephalic temporal-lobe circuit at a frequency which
I can match exactly with the "K" complex of an epi-
leptiform seizure. There's one program for everybody,
of course. And then taking the television as the epileptic aura, I can float anything I want into it and
burn them into cancerous dust.

SADIE: Sheeeit! That's the Heat Death of the Universe.
You didn't tell me about that. That's the Total Buzz
of the Future, Perowne! That's Home-Made Genera-
tion, right? That's Pure electricity. That's your Private
By-Pass-Circuit . . . you could wipe anything off the
slate with that, no?

> To PEROWNE.

So what were you grooming me for, huh?

> To MAURICE.

An you weren't into him at all. "Who brought him off?"
He's getting right through without you now, Maurice.
He's self-discharging.

MAURICE: Not at all. Perowne has his epilepsy to keep
up with my electro-shocks. He has the fits and I have
the shocks, to level up our energy systems (i.e. to
equalize the phosphocreatine which is lowered in the
bloodstream by shocks, and also by fits), so, we're still
running at peak to peak amplitude; and in case anything goes wrong, I keep a souped-up version of
epilepsy in there

> Pointing to his crotch.

to level it up. COME ON, SADIE, WE CUT YOU A
LOT OF SLACK. WHAT YOU GOT TO MUSCLE IN
ON THAT? HUH? HUH?

SADIE: I got something to muscle in on that, but Look.
I thought you were gonna get me into a Totally New
Motivational Bag, dig, of ESP motivation, an you're
into the same territory-sex-adrenalin-bullshit, however
freaky you've made it look . . . Who brought who off
. . . who's hollowing who out, Etcetera. Who's stealing whose psychic zoot suits. Let me cool you out for
a start, Maurice. I'll tell you where it's at. You know
what he was doing when you weren't here just now?
He was trying to get ME into the same terminal bag
that he's had you in for years. Rappin all that seamless
shit. Trying to get me into that, so he'd have a
Double Field set up, and two schizoid toilets for his
psychic offal. Look at that fuckin wall, Maurice,
because he's made you so like them. Look at the way
you do your hair. You do your hair the same way as
that cat there.

Pointing to the photo.

Perowne's made you eat so many of them you've
picked up on their DNA. I'm not gonna Touch you.
You're the worst media sludge of them all.

Turning to PEROWNE.

And dig this, Perowne, you CAN'T factorize it. It's a
totally non-operational model; you know what the
band-width is? It's like that.

Holding her finger and thumb with a tiny gap
between them.

They're all pushing the SAME resonance field. J. Edgar
Hoover equals Abbie Hoffman equals Richard Nixon
equals Enoch Powell equals Neil Armstrong equals
Bob Dylan equals equals equals. Because they ALL
got an interest in keeping the SAME resonance field
going, otherwise they wouldn't be able to jack-off into
your head on a one-way trip. I'm not competing with
Maurice to see who can trip out on it most, because I
got a resonance field stashed in my head that they

can't get NO FUCKIN PURCHASE ON and I'll move
you into it to cool you out if you like.
MAURICE: Oh poodle off.
PEROWNE (*quietly, staring at* SADIE): I can always tell
when it's coming. The props to be defaced, erased. I
set them all out. Press my eyes.

> He gazes at SADIE, then presses his eyes.

When the little dots, the phosphenes, when they start
glowing . . .
SADIE: Oh Come On. STOP TRYIN TA FREAK ME! And
take me OUTTA THERE.

> Pointing at PEROWNE's head.

I KNOW! I KNOW! THOSE LITTLE DOTS GOT SUB-
TITLES WITH SADIE WRITTEN ON! YOU'RE NOT
BURNING ME INTO NO CANCEROUS DUST.
MAURICE: Hey, hey, hey. Who's a signature artist?
Who's frightened of getting lost in the shuffle? Ha.
SADIE: Sittin roun with a couplea cracker fags gossipin
about the brain. I had a sweet tight little high goin,
you muthafukkas. YOU BLEW IT, YOU MUTHA-
FUKKAS! YOU BLEW IT!
   I gotta realign myself
   I gotta get the current flowing right.

> Picking up some photos from the table and the
> wall, and rolling them into a tube.

Whole earth's got an exoskeletal nervous system.
Geodetic. You gotta keep in with that. Terrestrial currents. I gotta realign myself.

> She stands up on the table.

I'm gonna get rid of all your teevee heebie jeebies. I'm
gonna douse all your negative juice with the only
fuckin amnesiac weapon there is. All these freakpuke
radiations, making you like this. I'm gonna Douse
them.

> She rips open her fly and shoves the roll of photos
> up her cunt.

COME ON IN, NIXON JAGGER HOOVER AND ALL
YOU COSMIC MENTAL PATIENTS! COME INTO

MY DARK ROOM AN LET ME DEVELOP YOU! COME
IN AND RADIATE MY CUNT! YOU REALLY WANT
ME TO MERGE WITH THE CREEPING MEATBALL,
WELL I AM, WHY AREN'T YOU WATCHING?

Moving the tube of photos in and out.

I'M SOAKIN UP ALL THE MEDIA RASH THAT'S
GIVIN YOU BAD VIBES. I'M LOADING UP ON ALL
THEIR FACES, AND ALL THEIR VOICES, AND ALL
THEIR IMPRINTS. I'M GOIN RIGHT DOWN ON
THEM.

I'M GONNA MASTURBATE EVERYBODY'S RE-
VERBERATIONS INTO NEUTRAL. I'M STASHING
THEM ALL INTO MY COSMIC SQUELCH CHAM-
BER, AND THEN I'M GONNA FIRE MY SWEET
ORGONE GUN.

Rubbing the photos against her clitoris.

AND DOUSE THEM ALL WITH MY AMNESIAC
PEARL JUICE!

She turns round on the table, rubbing harder and
harder, then breathing and panting in heavy
gasps, gyrating her crotch. PEROWNE is kneeling
down beside the chair, staring up at her. MAURICE
watches him, and then moves quickly toward the
table, walking round it, looking up at SADIE.

MAURICE: Tchah. They had me masturbating twenty
times a day at the Maudsley Clinic to balance their
case history books.

Singing.

Oh rambling rose, the more you feel it the more it
grows. I thought it was my job. Servicing one-armed
bandits. Why don't you go over there, Perowne? Give
the girl the feeling that she fits-in? Do you want
rimming, girl? I can put you in touch with some very
complicated meat.

SADIE moves the photos in and out.

She's taking someone's temperature.
PEROWNE: Yes.
MAURICE (*shouting at* SADIE): Fancy a gay lick? Pe-

rowne's manky teeth have been at the scene of many an untimely accident. COME ON PEROWNE. She's waiting for your big kartzo in her split level cunt.

PEROWNE: SHUT UP.

MAURICE (*staring; quietly*): She's trying to decathect my prick. I can feel it growing back up inside me. IT'S COMING OUT. IT'S COMING OUT.

He sticks his tongue out at SADIE.

PEROWNE: STOP TRYING TO LEVEL OFF THE CHARGE!

MAURICE: WHAT YOU MEAN? SHE'S TRYING TO SCUTTLE ALL THE IMPREGNATIONS IN THIS ROOM! I had to depopulate all those Gadarene corpse photos, and hack fuckin talismen before she could be wheeled on. I staked all this out. She's a fuckin claim jumper.

SADIE: Nrrrraaaah . . . nrrrraaaaa . . . hrrrraaaaaahh!

MAURICE: It won't make any difference you know, what she's doing. I sprayed all those photographs with anti-static lamination.

SADIE: Nnnnnrrrrraa . . . nnnrrrraaaagggh . . . nrr rraaaaa . . .

MAURICE (*pointing at* SADIE): I'm not taking you any-where. You get travel sick.

SADIE: I'M SOAKING UP ALL THE MEDIA RASH IN ALL THE REVERERBATIONS AN I'M MERGING ALL THE PHOTOEMULSION EVER AND I'M SENDING IT ALL ON A HUGE COSMIC COME MISSION FROM WHICH THEY'LL NEVER RETURN. errraaaa HH . . . NRRRRAAAAAHH . . .

MAURICE: Tchah. I've got an electric waste basket which shreds things into unreadable strips of one eighth inch. That was part of my Influencing Machine admittedly, but some parts Perowne dismantled and other parts, he Brought Up to Date.

SADIE: NRRRRAAAA NNNNNRRAAAAAANNNRRAA AAAAAAA . . .

MAURICE (*shouting up at her*): LOOK HERE. I AM PEROWNE'S EXPERIMENT IN BEHAVIORAL SEN-SATIONALISM! SO STOP THAT. ANYWAY He's got hundreds and hundreds and hundreds, and they're better than a fuckin outboard motor.

SADIE (*shouting at* PEROWNE): I'm gonna demagnetize you at twice the speed of your epilepsy, an forty times the speed of Maurice . . . SO OPEN YOUR CUNT WIDE, PEROWNE, I'm really gonna treat you now.

> PEROWNE looks up and smiles at her. She pumps faster and faster, jamming the soggy roll in and out.

MAURICE (*going close to* PEROWNE): It's all right to be indirect, but not in the way she is. You're not going for that, are you? That's not doing anything. Maudsley Clinic first time in: they said to me: Why don't you pitch it a bit lower for us? Why don't you stick to clenching your jaw and rippling your cheek muscles every railing you pass in the street? We won't look. Promise. I said You think I'm going to try it out all right walking, and then get on a fast moving bus and get fuckin lockjaw. If that's all you can cater for, forget it. What's she catering for?

> Pointing.

WHAT'S SHE CATERING FOR?

SADIE: Nrrrrraaaah nnnrraaaaaaa nrrrnnnnnnneeeeeee aagh neeeeeaaaaagh rah rah!

MAURICE (to PEROWNE): I was going to chop off some of my fingers today, to intensify my other faculties for you.

> PEROWNE pays no attention to him.

MAURICE (*to* SADIE, *pointing at* PEROWNE): Did he talk you into this? HE wasn't talking to you. He was just putting a bit of scent on your jam rags to make you more tolerable. Doubles, doubles, doubles. I've got doubles everywhere being reconditioned.

SADIE (*pumping harder*): PULLING TOGETHER ALL THE SPECTRAL LINES. KICKIN OUT ALL THE JAMS!

MAURICE (*pointing at* SADIE): She's tearing off certain currents there, then I needed exactly microsecond then . . .

PEROWNE: Quite.

SADIE: Nrrrraaaa nrrrrraaaaa nrrrrraaaghgh . . .

MAURICE (*to* PEROWNE): You been shooting stuff through me without my knowing.

> To SADIE.

Perowne opens the newspaper with a scalpel and turns on the TV with rubber gloves because of ingrown mentalisms which he's got which are too good to be true and he doesn't want MUSSED UP.

> MAURICE rolls over on the bed, face down, screws up the pillows, his foot pounding slowly at the end of the bed.

I'm wearing out Perowne's bed patterns now, which you can't ever get into and demagnetize . . .

> Acting out a blowjob.

which YOU CAN'T EVER GET INTO.

PEROWNE: I'm glad she can't.

MAURICE (*twisting, to himself*): Thing going now where I squeeze my knee

> Holds his knee.

and I get a stinging pain here

> He points to his arm.

or on the shoulderblade, and a LOT of the souped up tensions I got to pick up's traceable to that mechanism, going on now, WHICH SHE'S PONCING OFF.

> He points at SADIE now breathing stertoriously, and still pumping.

Breath she caught then was trying to act as a triode valve to similitudinize my thoughts.

PEROWNE: About breath?

> MAURICE stares at him, scowls at him.

SADIE: LEAVE IT ALONE, MAURICE. YOU JUST STAY LOOSE. STAY LOOSE.

> Facing the bed.

BECAUSE I'M GONNA ALIGN MY ATOMS WITH YOURS, MAURICE, AND WHEN I GET THEM

RIGHT, AN IN THE RIGHT POLARIZING FIELD, I'M GONNA PASS STRAIGHT THROUGH YOU, LIKE A DOSE OF SALTS, AND THAT POLARIZING FIELD WILL LEAVE YOU VERY VERY VERY COOLED OUT.

MAURICE (*springing up off the bed*): COOL? COOL? We've had that necrophiliac nightmare of cool. WHO'S PUTTING THE SOUNDTRACK ONTO COOL, while you're being too beautiful and cool to listen?

To PEROWNE.

Look, I built up that hum hum hum in her head that's going on now, and All she's got to slash it to bits with is COOOOL.

SADIE (*long lithe strokes*): Cooling out all the objects in this room. Cooling out all the vibes. Down to the temperature of liquid helium. Coo-ool. Cool Kundalini serpent coiling through my spine colors! Om Sri Maintreya!

MAURICE (*cupping his ear*): She's making fashionable noises now with her middle ear muscles to try and opt me out. Perowne's not getting a buzz off you.

PEROWNE: I think she's becoming highly operational.

MAURICE: LOOOK. I KNOW that state of mind she's in. It's not worth a casual snapshot. Tuffnell was up there last Thursday. "I can hear trees talking to me," he said. "I'm in touch with the vibrations of vegetative life." "Don't let me interrupt a thing," I said. "You won't," he said, "You can't." "You're so right," I said. "Trees," I said, "Who's ever stopped them from working their passage. Trees? They're putting on a proper circus."

SADIE: NRRRRRRRAAAANNRRRAAAAA . . . Creepin up on all your vibes, Maurice . . . nrrrraaa . . . nrrrr aaaa . . .

MAURICE (*pointing up at* SADIE): Play the same note long enough, cunt says it begins to sound like a tune. WAIT A MINUTE. I know what it is. "Spine colors?" Wait a minute, I know what it is. Has she gone chemical for you as well?

To SADIE.

Have you gone chemical for him as well, to speed him up? She's gone chemical, that's what it is. I was chemical in the fuckin bucket. They used to give me six whites to calm me down, and six reds to make me jerky. I used to put all the reds down the toilet. In the end every lavatory in the building was flushing itself. Oh, look what you've scooped up, Perowne, some temporary bug-eyed chemical amateur. You been laying a lot of talk on her? Look at her, she's got the jollies. She's wired up, but she's not picking you up. She's been sitting round getting happily wasted.

PEROWNE: SHUTUP! SHUTUP!

> MAURICE scuttles round the table, picking up two photos dropped from SADIE's crotch.

MAURICE: Twenty-three menton photons still coming off that one, and some fuckin mush artistry still having to be worn out there.

> Pointing to the second photo, he moves his face in exorcism of it, then looks at PEROWNE. PEROWNE shrugs his shoulders.

PEROWNE: You lost a lot of power when you went to see that psychiatrist.

SADIE: I got my piezo-electric transducers really singggg-inngggg now! I'm reading mental masses you didn't know existed, Maurice.

MAURICE: She's as much use as a fart thrashing in a fuckin bottle.

SADIE (pumping harder and harder, swiveling all over the table, with the roll of photos): NRRRRRRAAAAA AAAAAAAAA!

MAURICE (hysterical): I DIDN'T ASK YOU TO PICKET ALL MY SCABS. How did she get that far into it? Because I started her off. I gave her one of my Julie John Reginald Halliday Crystal Sets made out of their victim's pubic hair. But she can't tune it. SHE CAN'T GET A FUCKIN SOUND OUT OF IT. She's nowhere.

> To PEROWNE.

SHALL I PULL HER OFF?

PEROWNE: No.

MAURICE (shouting at SADIE, clawing at the roll of photos, almost crying): GET YOUR POISONOUS

CHROMOSOMES OFF MY PICTURES. YOU'RE GONNA MUTATE THEM SO MUCH I'M NEVER GOING TO BE ABLE TO CATCH UP WITH THEM.

> SADIE laughs and whirls around the table, pumping the roll of photos in and out, shouting in frenzied little cries, jumping, shrieking and dripping in sweat.

SADIE: I'm CATCHING UP WITH YOU NOW, MAURICE. I'M CLOSING IN ON YOUR FIELD. CAN YOU FEEL ME PRICKLING? CAN YOU FEEL ME FRIZZING YOU UP? I'M ZAPPING RIGHT THROUGH YOUR HEAD NOW, MAURICE.

MAURICE (*standing against the wall of photos, holding his crotch, he grinds it like a small boy, starts trembling, and jumping up and down, copying* SADIE's *gyrations*): Look LLOOOOOK LOOOOK YOU DUMB BITCH, IT'S NOTHING TO ME, BECAUSE I'VE HAD IT SET DOWN WITH THE BEATLES GOVERNING SOLICITORS, I'M GOING TO BE BURIED WITH MY OWN COCK IN MY OWN FUCKIN MOUTH . . .

SADIE (*jumping and jiving with the roll*): Boddhisatva don't come till everyone come! SMASH KARMIC CONGESTION. LOSE IT ALL ITS POWER.

I'M FEEDING YOUR WHOLE SCHIZOID MEDIA RASH CRAP INTO MY CUNT, AN ALL YOUR BEHAVIORAL PARAMETERS . . . I'M CLIPPING IT OFF WITH MY BIG FAT CUNT PETALS, AND WHEN I TOUCH MY CLITORIS I'M GONNA FIRE IT INTO OUTER SPACE!

> SADIE triggers her clitoris with the roll of photos, and then flops down on the table, shouting FIRE FIRE FIRE FIRE. MAURICE watches her, jerking off, beating his meat, he comes in his pants, his orgasm synchronized with hers. He collapses onto the floor underneath the wall of photos. PEROWNE is sobbing.
>
> Silence.

MAURICE (*moving up slowly, his eyes wide open, he stands up, and stares at* SADIE *with a wide-angle smile*): She's hollowed me out. She's hollowed me right out. I feel good. She's . . . I feel very very good. I've got a lot of light in.

> MAURICE moves around the room, collecting his things, his white coat from behind the door. As he moves, his gestures seem released, the armory dismantled. He stares at PEROWNE. PEROWNE watches him edgily, waiting for him to go.

PEROWNE: Good.

MAURICE (*slowly*): Look at you. Psycho-photo-galvanized Me into a fuckin lush, in order to wear out YOUR drinking habits.

PEROWNE: That was a long time ago. I've pitched my diseases higher than that.

MAURICE: Yes, you had me turning into a schiz, in order to stave off your own gig in the googoo house. Well. I don't care. I'm out of it. It's all been knocked on the head. I feel good. I feel very light.

> PEROWNE looks away.

MAURICE: I can tell you now where my head's really been all this time, now I'm shot of you. You thought I was demagnetizing you of all your chronic little hang-ups. I wasn't demagnetizing you of one. Even when you dropped me for your fuckin epilepsy, I was there, but I was juggling the little dots in front of your eyes to get you onto THEIR frequency.

> Pointing at the photos on the wall.

See those? I'LL tell you now what those Really are. Those are all Homing Devices. They are Tektites and Space Grass, dropped down by solar winds, as agents for the Saucer People, because they know that those film stars and behavioral tarts can over-magnetize you to the Saucer People's frequency at twice the speed of anything else. Tell me Heisenberg's Uncertainty Principle: Everything's insoluble because whatever's measured is altered by the act of Measuring it. Right?

> PEROWNE stares at him.

MAURICE (*pointing at the photos*): That is why the

Saucer People only have the very best measuring instruments.

PEROWNE: Oh shutup.

MAURICE: Huh.

> Picking some photos off the floor and tearing some off the wall.

I WASN'T DEMAGNETIZING YOU, I WAS COMPLETELY FUCKIN RADIATING YOU!

> Pause.

They are very extreme and agile people, the Saucer People. They're breeding Dwarves on this earth now, and have been for thousands of years in preparation of us living on excess gravity of the outer planets. They've been sporing Autistic and Thalidomide children in preparation for when we've delegated all limbs and dead mentalisms to Mega-machines. They've been pumping through people born with webbed hands and feet, in preparation for when we have to circumnavigate the globodurenal ooze of Venus, and they're pumping through people with dermo-optical perception for when the sun gets too bright for our eyes to see. People who are so-called Vegetables from car accidents are being attuned by them to JUST ONE TWITCH OF THE LIFE FORCE, and are keeping it Warm, and rehatching it, and purifying it, and then passing it on to us completely purified.

> Standing behind PEROWNE.

They're pushing through more Siamese twins now because they know that Siamese twins is the most biologically economic unit. They're pushing through eleven per cent of all men being born with supernumerary nipples for suckling computers. They've been softening people's voices recently, in preparation for the changeover to telepathic communication. They're turning catatonics into Fakirs, preparing us for the limb movements of life on other planets. They're taking measures against over-population, by merging people, and getting out doubles, and then personality units composed of ten people, and Whole Personality

Fields Shared. Schizophrenia's just the tip of the iceberg. They're Beautiful people. But they're working in
negative time, and we're trying to shit on their time
reversed state of being. We're just using their negative
time to enable ambitious psycho-sluts to see themselves coming up on the way down. We're trying to
shit on that taste of the fourth dimension that they're
pumping through, by just using it to see if we can
turn an orange inside out without breaking the skin.
We've SHAT on their Faustian universe. WE'VE SHAT
ON IT, which is why None of the Super-Dwarves, and
the Super Autistic-Schizo-Thalidomides that they're
Spawning specially for us, in preparation . . . which
is why . . . WHICH IS WHY NONE OF THEM FIT
IN. They reward me sometimes by fetching me back
into the original squitting sex noise that hasn't been
in my bum since I was ten.

> MAURICE moves around the room slowly, holding
> his things in his hands. Clutching his white coat.
> Smiling. He stands at the door. Laughs. He wraps
> a rubber bandage from a box of his belongings
> round his head.

I don't have to have any more people's head electricity
from now on.

> Bending over SADIE.

I've got a proper buzz. I'm feeling Light.

> PEROWNE stares at him, wide-eyed, then almost
> jealous. MAURICE leaves. Closes the door. PE-
> ROWNE stares at the door, then slowly round the
> room. SADIE gets up from the table.

SADIE: Outta sight. Outta sight.

> Silence.

But he ran you flat, didn't he?
PEROWNE: Yes.
SADIE: That's a bummer.

> She gets up, goes over to her suitcase, and then
> hands PEROWNE the bottle.

SADIE: Why don't you take yourself back to where you were before Maurice got into you.

PEROWNE (*drinking*): Goes down like cream.

SADIE: Do you really get fits?

PEROWNE shrugs his shoulders.

I think it's quite common actually, if you stop drinking quite suddenly, to get some kind of arbitrary discharges.

They sit drinking.

SADIE (*indicating the bottle*): Flash him out for you, huh?

PEROWNE nods.

SADIE (*staring at him*): Still picking up a lot of random noise.

PEROWNE: Mmmn.

SADIE: Gotta cool you right out now. Wanna REal Launch, don't you?

PEROWNE nods. SADIE takes a scroll out of her case, unrolls it, and shows it to PEROWNE. PEROWNE peers at it, reading several phrases aloud to himself.

PEROWNE: "Homo Sapiens Correctus . . . Man's position is upright . . . cerebro-spinal fluid . . . brain blood volume . . . the third eye . . . restores the intra cranial pressure . . ." Looks like another Utopian heresy.

SADIE: You want me to lay a real taste on you, don't you?

PEROWNE: Yes. I liked you with the photographs just now.

SADIE: What was that. Maybe that was just a little heavy competition to cool Maurice out. I was just playing back his tracks so that he could see where he was at. A real Christ Complex, dig? Christ was too vain to do that. I was just sealing Maurice off. He wasn't into you any more.

PEROWNE: Some of his anti-dotal wave forms were getting a little toxic themselves.

SADIE: Right.

PEROWNE stares at the scroll, drinking.

PEROWNE: Seems . . . rather primitive.

SADIE (*rolling up the scroll*): Well, you're into a lot of these mechanisms already, so it might seem primitive. But this would change the vibration rate of every molecule in your head. It's pretty much virgin territory, Perowne. Give you a completely out-front life style that no one else'll be able to copy or devalue.

PEROWNE: The Delectable Mountains. What do you mean, "pretty much virgin territory"?

SADIE: Couplea Dutch guys got there before you. But only just recently.

PEROWNE: I've always liked the Dutch. I've never understood how they gave rise to the South African Dutch. On the other hand, I suppose, the only way to convince people of the error of their ways is by drawing close to them.

SADIE: Jesus. Where did that track come from? That track come from before you met Maurice? Listen, don't worry about South Africa; pretty soon we'll be switching from the gold standard to the vibration standard an we'll STARVE them out.

PEROWNE: Get ahead, get a hole. Have you done it?

SADIE: How do you think I stood that jive photo kick just now? All that blood with nowhere to go. Look, rats fed on a diet of ecstasy live longer. You had a good little scene going with Maurice one time, yeah? But you're due for something else.

PEROWNE (*taking the scroll out of the case, and looking at it again*): The Aztecs did it, didn't they? And I think they used to do it a lot in Cornwall, when tin ore fell on the miners' heads: to decompress them. What did you say about the Dutch people?

SADIE: It was done all over. Earliest operation known. The Dutch guys?

PEROWNE: Meningitis?

SADIE: NO MAN. One of them just got straight up and walked off down the street.

PEROWNE smiles.

They did it on a trip. They're spaced out all the time. They just sit round playing the Go Game. Chinese

Chess. Lot of counters on the board: Object of the game: Conquer territory. No army can be surrounded or its territory taken so long as it preserves a hole in the middle of the army, a hole covered by no counters. They like the symbolism of it. They see holes everywhere. But you know a lot of the mechanisms already, Perowne. You wouldn't waste the high.

PEROWNE: What do they use for counters in the Go Game? The little discs of bone? They're called RONDELLES, aren't they? those little discs of bone that come out of the . . .

SADIE: I told you: there's not enough of them around yet. It's still pretty much virgin territory.

PEROWNE (*staring at the trephine in the suitcase*): Where did you get it? I suppose blind people must have it naturally, I mean when their eyeballs atrophy, more gravitational pressure must act on the brain, through the sockets, and drive the blood into other areas not normally in commission, so that they can . . . so that they can . . .

> SADIE takes the trephine from her suitcase, wrapped in a silk scarf.

SADIE: Where did I get it? I went moppin last week. I levitated it from the Hunter Museum, Royal College of Surgeons, Lincolns Inn Fields.

> Unwrapping it.

Other areas? Sure. Undreamt-of areas. Blind people. You're right. They can hear lamp-posts coming, on quiet streets, they got their pineal stalk, the only unpaired gland in the body, traditional telepathic center in occult thought, filled with brain sand . . . and they got it responding to unknown light quanta, through having something like this.

> She unlocks the two parts of the trephine.

PEROWNE: Are you going to kill me with that thing?

SADIE: Death is PURE sensation, didn't you know? I told you, this is very slightly radiated already.

PEROWNE: By the Dutch people.

SADIE: And me. It's only for the top meat, Perowne.

Grade A Clears. Occupants of the 35th Bardo, and 7th Astral Plane. It's a Crux Ansata for hooking yourself out of samsara. Out of names and games. It's the biggest by-pass circuit of them all. Speed up your biological clock so that you can contract right out of time, and smash all those second-hand pacemakers.

> Pointing to the wall of photos.

Smash all those electric pricks.

> Pointing to the TV.

Clean up all your bad vibrations. Letting the spirits out of the hole, that was the Greek version of it. Thaumaturgic initiation into a higher caste.

PEROWNE (*taking the trephine, and turning it over in his hands*): Block the openings, shut the doors, and all your life you won't run dry. Unblock the openings, add to your troubles, and to the end of your days you'll be beyond salva-tion. Lao Tzu.

SADIE: Very nice, but there've been no trepanned skulls ever found in China, as far as I know. Some of them obviously had the Third Eye, but Lao Tzu can't ever have got into it. Lotta creatures have it naturally. The Sphenodon's got it. Ever had your hair punched or popped? To spread out the follicles, if you're going bald? Same scene with this. Scalp's got a very low pain threshold. Osseous integuments got none.

> SADIE sits PEROWNE down on the chair in front of the table. She sits behind him on the table, massaging his shoulders.

SADIE: Got any cotton wool?

> PEROWNE indicates a drawer. SADIE gets it and stuffs some into PEROWNE's ears.

So you can really get into it. Saw some pictures of the Loyalty Islanders doing it with bits of broken glass, and sharpened shells, and sharks' teeth. It went on for hours. You can really get into your head changes when it goes on that long. They got male and female trephines now, you know. Male one's got a spike in the middle to position it right. This one's AC/DC.

> Pitching her voice low and rhythmical.

Drive your influencing machine on a completely different fuel. Fire cells you haven't yet invested in. Wipe all your information channels clean. It's gonna return you to state zero an give you a double run.

> She splashes the bottle on PEROWNE's head.

Those adrenal circuits. Starve it to death. Auto-Rhythmical Mental Ice. Graft new circuit space onto the neo-cortex. It hasn't been there long, you gotta give it breathing room. Speed up your mitochondria. Increase your channel capacity. Speed up all your mutative patterns. You're gonna have a Real Fuckin Fuel Cell.

> She holds the trephine above the left parietal zone.

Are you prepared for this now? Good deeds can often be very shocking.

PEROWNE: I think so.

> SADIE clears his hair and presses the trephine onto the scalp.

SADIE: There really was a Lost Paradise, dig? When the Deva Eye, the eye of Shiva was open, in the days of the Cyclopean root race . . . and then man fell into matter, and the Third Eye atrophied, leaving just the pineal gland as witness. A Lost Paradise of Lost Brain Blood Volume. Lost again when your fissures and fontanelles closed up at three. Lost again when your cranial sutures ossified. Lost when you stood vertical. More and more horrible adrenalin, the more upright you stood.

> SADIE alternately pronates and supinates the trephine with her hand in neutral position.

Lost the brain as a valve. Lost the cerebral heart beat. Starved the neuronoo. Lost the cerebral pulsations. Starved the glia. Constricted the arterioles.

> Pressing the trephine down harder into PE-ROWNE's head.

So? Gotta correct the mechanism. Bring yourself back into the galactic metabolism. Let in some Light. Restore the Outside Pressure. Let in more Blood, and drive out the superfluous spoonful of cerebro-spinal fluid that's bringing you down . . . Can You Feel It?

Leaning over him.

Can you feel it? It's comin out now, like a little slug of scum. Little spurt. Speut! It's warm.

She lifts the trephine up, then replaces the trephine in the groove in PEROWNE'S scalp and continues revolving.

Kundalini flame vibrations moving up and down your spine, opening all the chakras, burning out all the dross. Waiting until your brain is prepared for it to enter . . .

PEROWNE: I can feel no pain.

SADIE: No, and soon that ego trip of YOU feeling pain, you thinking about you feeling pain, that'll disappear. It's a mind-body chakra to get the pineal gland pickin up on cosmic energy of the highest quality . . .

PEROWNE: Suppose it doesn't work?

SADIE: Suppose it doesn't? What were you doing with Maurice? Widening the irrational threshold, right? Publicizing the unofficial environment, right? Giving the shadows genitals. So that some bureaucrat like me could come along, clean up on that energy, get it together and get us off the fuckin planet.

Pointing at the trephine in PEROWNE'S head.

Well, this is the form you gotta fill in. We're gonna drop this planet like a hot potato.

PEROWNE: Maurice kept talking about hollowing out.

SADIE: Yeah. There's your synchronicity. He was pickin up paracognitive traces from the trephine in my suitcase.

PEROWNE: I can feel the pressure changing. It's built up. It's a strange density. It doesn't hurt.

SADIE removes the instrument, she pulls out the hair, scalp tissue and a small disc of bone from

the teeth of the trephine. She stares down at PE-
ROWNE.

SADIE: It's the Total ESP Fuck. Eight orifices in your
head now, Perowne. Get you responding to undis-
covered electro-magnetic fields. Your psi-plasma field's
now been uncoupled from gravitational contraction
and adrenalin constipation. Whole of the Aztec Space
People's civilization was a trepanned society, Perowne.
All had to have it done when they got here because
the gravity wasn't right. They all had to decompress
each other to keep in touch with the central morpho-
genetic psi-plasma field they'd left behind.

PEROWNE seems to be cutting off. SADIE scrutinizes PEROWNE. He sits quite still. SADIE swabs
his Third Eye.
    Silence.

I can feel you picking it up. There's a taste of the true
heat around. Shit awful field flux. But there's some
winner beams tryin to make it. Can you get a fix on
their pitch?

PEROWNE nods.

They're shifting all the spectral lines. They're shifting
my detectability threshold. Gotta metabolize their
radiations. It'll be like a couple of micro-cocaine flashes
all over your astral tastebuds . . . VIBIN YOUR
ASTRAL BODY, when they hit you. Stick out your
psionic telescope. FURTHER. FURTHER.

PEROWNE: Above the . . . above the . . .

SADIE: Yeah, like that. They'll get it. They'll get it.
They're probably using some of Maurice's ectohormonal beams to track us.

PEROWNE: Above the . . . above the . . .

SADIE: That's all right. That's all right. They always get
you into some bag like that when they first issue visas.
Don't worry about that.

PEROWNE makes a series of small, noncognitive
movements.

SADIE: FUUUUUUUUUUUUUUK! IT'S ON! Keep your
mind still. They'll zap it in. They'll zap it in. Keep

your mind still. FUUUUUCK! THEY'RE TWANGING
THE WHOLE FUCKIN ELECTROMAGNETIC SPEC-
TRUM. FUCKIN ANTI-MATTER TELEPATHONS
FRIZZIN ME UP! OPEN YOUR CUNT TO THE SUN,
PEROWNE, OPEN YOUR CUNT TO THE SUN!

> PEROWNE makes a series of minute movements.
> SADIE holds her ears, then moves her hands
> through her hair, then squeezes her head.

Fuuck, they're Really shifting the field. Fuckin fifty
seven thousand gauss. What is it? What is it? They're
gettin us through to some Total Aggregate of Mental
Fluid. CAN YOU FEEL THEM ENJOYING YOU?

> PEROWNE moves his limbs as if in low gravity.
> As SADIE speaks, the resonance of her voice is
> totally altered as if the balance of the gases in the
> air has been altered. All cognitive clues as to their
> behavior beginning to implode.

SADIE: YOU'RE SO CLEAN NOW, PEROWNE. THEY'RE
WHISTLING THROUGH YOU!

> Snapping her fingers.

I fucked it up calling you, Perowne. They don't use
those shop-soiled co-ordinate points. It's gettin attenu-
ated again. Don't filter them. Little automatic gain
control to boost it.

> She tightens up her body. Giant breaths.

Flashover the flashpoints of neuronic discharge to
fetch them back . . . RADIATIVE COLLISION!
FUCCK THEY'RE ONTO YOU! DON'T FILTER IT.
DON'T FILTER IT. Bit of . . . I gotta Blip then . . .
bit of magnetic torque . . . They're exploding psi-
plasma blanks in my head, to black me out . . . to
cut me out of the circuit to give you full power. No, no
they're not. DON'T FILTER THE PULSES, PEROWNE
. . . Full field. FULL FIELD. Shit, did you feel that
bit that went through then? That was shorthand for
a fuckin microcosm. That was a Joke! Did you feel it?

> PEROWNE nods; he stares at her and smiles.

SADIE: They gotta socket now, you dig. They gotta Free Connection Point.

She touches the hole in PEROWNE's head.

Don't flash out. Lay it all out now. LAY IT OUT. All the deepest coagulations.

PEROWNE makes a series of minimal facial expressions, corresponding to no known emotions.

SADIE: Lay it out now . . . It's good . . . It's good. It's . . .

She moves rapidly from side to side, emitting high-frequency clicking speech.

It's trying to get into . . . It's inter . . . kinetic . . . inter demalio . . . deliving . . . derrrthusp . . . derrthusp . . . derammm yeah . . . delidio . . . decram . . . decramm . . . Feeling good with it, yeah, it's . . . Pick it up again, Perowne. IT'S FADING, PEROWNE. THE FUCKIN BUZZ IS GOING OFF. PICK IT UP AGAIN, PEROWNE. STOP CHANGING THE RATES. STOP CHANGING THE RATES! They're preparing to do a real number on us. Play that fuckin E.S.P. riff you had going at the start off . . . Play that again.

PEROWNE: Above the . . . above the . . . Above the . . . (Metronomic.)
I Like It Very Much.

SADIE: Are you back into it? I can't feel it.

She moves her hands all over her body.

I can't feel it.

She moves off the table, and crouches over him.

Gotta amplify those fuckin vibes, man. Gotta draw ALL the vibes down here. I don't think they're scrambling them. Gotta get back through to it. There's a huge fuckin vibesurge there floating round. It's fading . . . gotta . . .

She puts her hand inside PEROWNE's fly.

Bit of ESP Protein. Sharpen the impulses with a bit

of sex static. Use it as an astral dowsing wand. Bio-lectric aerial to vampup the charge. They'll come back in now. Don't move the blood into your cock. Your brain's got an erection. That's why it's like that.

PEROWNE stares down.

Hold that sex static just like it is. That's a heavy duty field they can find. Don't blow it. ARE YOU GETTING INTO IT AGAIN?

PEROWNE nods. SADIE moves her hand inside his fly.

ARE YOU GETTING INTO IT AGAIN?

PEROWNE closes his eyes.

SADIE: OPEN YOUR EYES. Don't need any introspective freakshow to pick up these radiations. OPEN YOUR EYES. DON'T FLASH OUT ON ME. ARE YOU TRY-ING TO SCUTTLE THAT FUCKIN BUZZ?

She rubs his cock faster and faster.

PICK IT UP, PICK IT UP. YEEEEEEEEEEEEAAAAA AAAAAAAH! WHAT? WHAAAAAAAT? WHAAA Wow . . . wow . . .

SADIE tenses up, then discharges all her muscles. She flashes and creases, and stares. There is the sound of giant electronic breathing. The psychic static amplified. She claws at PEROWNE's body. Turning every cell of his body into a brain cell.

SADIE: FUCKIN PARA-PIERCING VIBESURGE . . .
THEY'RE FUCKIN YOU IN YOUR THIRD EYE NOW PEROWNE . . .
I MEAN THE STIFFEST E.S.P. RIFF EVER BLOWN!
DOUBLE EUPHORIA HEAD!
PLAY IT . . . PLAY IT . . . RELAY IT . . . RE-LAY IT!
GET INTO THEIR ASSEMBLY LANGUAGE. LAY IT OUT FOR ME! YOU GOT IT
YOU'RE HITTING IT . . . YOU'RE HITTING IT!
GET INTO THEIR ASSEMBLY LANGUAGE!
LAY IT OUT FOR ME.

PEROWNE opens his eyes slowly, raises his head, screams, and then turns and looks around, smiling.

PEROWNE:

ABOUT THE EDITORS

JOHN LAHR was graduated from Yale University and Worcester College, Oxford University. A regular theater columnist for the *Village Voice*, Mr. Lahr was recipient of the George Jean Nathan Award for Dramatic Criticism. He is the author of several works, including *The Autograph Hound*, and *Notes on a Cowardly Lion*. His edited works include *Astonish Me*, and *Up Against the Fourth Wall*. He has served as literary adviser to the Lincoln Center in New York City and the Tyrone Guthrie Theatre in Minneapolis. Mr. Lahr is currently preparing a biography of the British farceur Joe Orton, and is completing another novel.

JONATHAN PRICE is a graduate of Harvard College, and received a doctorate degree from the Yale School of Drama. He is a concrete poet, and his three-dimensional poems, including an ice cream poem, a balloon poem, and a word salad, have been exhibited on four continents. Mr. Price has taught modern drama and Shakespeare at New York University, and has written scholarly articles for such magazines as *Shakespeare Quarterly*, *Modern Drama*, and *Harper's*. He was editor of the book, *Critics on Robert Lowell*, and is currently working on a book on video.

DISCOVER
THE DRAMA OF LIFE
IN THE LIFE OF DRAMA

- [ ] FOUR GREAT PLAYS BY CHEKHOV Anton Chekhov 4140 • $ .75
- [ ] INDIANS Arthur Kopit 4421 • $1.65
- [ ] THE CRUCIBLE Arthur Miller 4498 • $ .95
- [ ] LOOK BACK IN ANGER John Osborne 4611 • $ .95
- [ ] THE GREAT WHITE HOPE Howard Sackler 4663 • $ .95
- [ ] NEW PLAYS FROM THE BLACK THEATRE Ed Bullins, ed. 4790 • $1.25
- [ ] THE LOVE-GIRL AND THE INNOCENT
     Alexander Solzhenitsyn 6600 • $ .95
- [ ] THREE PLAYS BY THORNTON WILDER Thornton Wilder 6677 • $ .95
- [ ] FOUR GREAT PLAYS BY IBSEN Henrik Ibsen 6985 • $ .95
- [ ] THE NIGHT THOREAU SPENT IN JAIL
     Jerome Lawrence and Robert E. Lee 7155 • $ .95
- [ ] CREATIVE FILM-MAKING Kirk Smallman 7213 • $1.65
- [ ] THE EFFECT OF GAMMA RAYS ON MAN-IN-THE-MOON
     MARIGOLDS Paul Zindel 7294 • $ .95
- [ ] THE CITIZEN KANE BOOK Pauline Kael,
     Herman J. Mankiewicz, and Orson Wells 7321 • $2.25
- [ ] SLEUTH Anthony Shaffer 7420 • $ .95
- [ ] THE GREAT AMERICAN LIFE SHOW:
     9 Plays from the Avant-Garde Theater
     John Lahr and Jonathan Price, eds. 7652 • $2.25
- [ ] TEN GREAT ONE ACT PLAYS Morris Sweetkind, ed. 7850 • $1.25

Buy them at your local bookstore or use this handy coupon for ordering:

Bantam Books, Inc., Dept. EDH, 414 East Golf Road, Des Plaines, Ill. 60016

Please send me the books I have checked above. I am enclosing $_____
(please add 25¢ to cover postage and handling). Send check or money order
—no cash or C.O.D.'s please.

Mr/Mrs/Miss_____

Address_____

City_____State/Zip_____

EDH—1/74

Please allow three weeks for delivery. This offer expires 1/75.

15-101